ATTACK ON TITAN 29

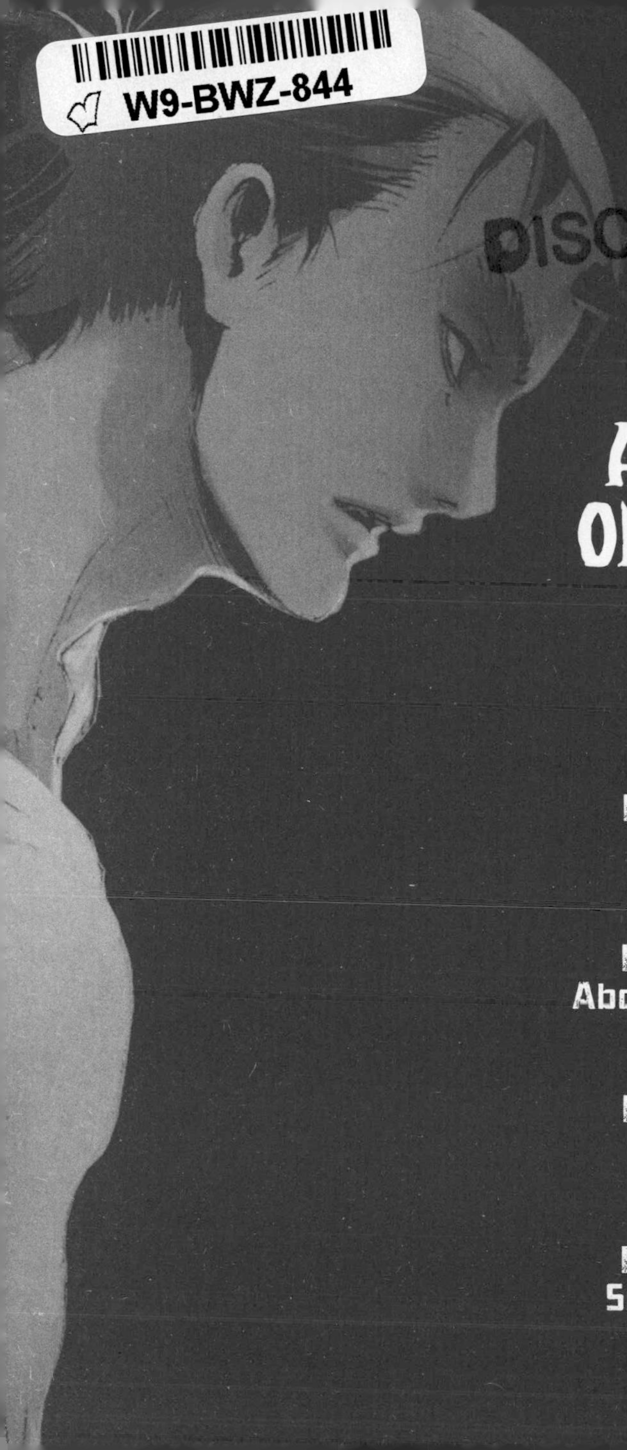

HAJIME ISAYAMA

Episode 115:
Support
5

Episode 116:
Above and Below
51

Episode 117:
Judgment
97

Episode 118:
Sneak Attack
143

THE CHARACTERS OF ATTACK ON TITAN

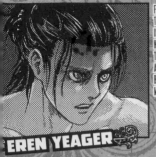

EREN YEAGER

FROM THE 104TH TRAINING CORPS; NOW IN THE SURVEY CORPS. HOLDS THE POWER OF THE ATTACK TITAN AND THE FOUNDING TITAN. BOLDLY INFILTRATED MARLEY ON HIS OWN.

MIKASA ACKERMAN

FROM THE 104TH TRAINING CORPS; NOW IN THE SURVEY CORPS. SHE HAS SHOWN INCREDIBLE COMBAT ABILITIES EVER SINCE SHE WAS A RECRUIT. SHE SEES PROTECTING EREN AS HER MISSION.

ARMIN ARLERT

FROM THE 104TH TRAINING CORPS; NOW IN THE SURVEY CORPS. HOLDS THE POWER OF THE COLOSSUS TITAN. HE HAS SAVED HIS COMRADES COUNTLESS TIMES WITH HIS SHARP INTELLECT AND BRAVERY.

HISTORIA REISS

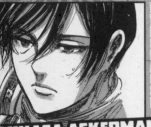

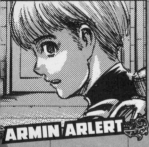

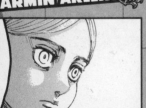

A DESCENDANT OF THE REISS FAMILY, THE TRUE ROYAL BLOODLINE, HISTORIA HAS ASCENDED TO THE THRONE AS QUEEN. SHE ONCE BELONGED TO THE SURVEY CORPS UNDER THE NAME KRISTA LENZ.

THE NATION OF ELDIA [THE ISLAND OF PARADIS]

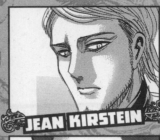

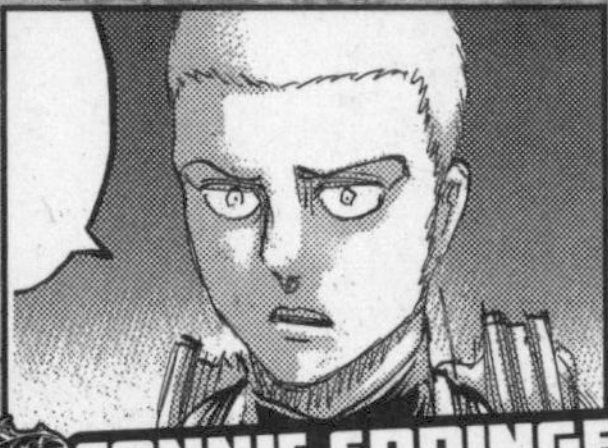

JEAN KIRSTEIN

FROM THE 104TH TRAINING CORPS; NOW IN THE SURVEY CORPS. ONCE KNOWN FOR HIS SARCASTIC PERSONALITY, HE HAS NOW GROWN INTO A LEADER.

CONNIE SPRINGER

FROM THE 104TH TRAINING CORPS; NOW IN THE SURVEY CORPS. HE IS CHEERFUL IN PERSONALITY, BUT FINDS HIMSELF LOSING EVERYONE IMPORTANT TO HIM... ORIGINALLY FROM RAGAKO VILLAGE.

FLOCH

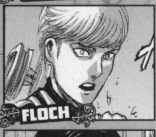

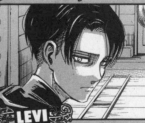

A MEMBER OF THE SURVEY CORPS. A SURVIVOR OF THE DECISIVE BATTLE FOR SHIGANSHINA DISTRICT, WHICH CLAIMED MANY LIVES, INCLUDING ERWIN'S.

LEVI

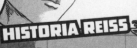

CAPTAIN OF THE SURVEY CORPS. KNOWN AS "HUMANITY'S STRONGEST SOLDIER." HE FIGHTS THROUGH HIS STRUGGLES IN ORDER TO CARRY ON HIS GOOD FRIEND ERWIN'S DYING WISHES.

HANGE ZOË

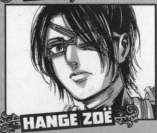

COMMANDER OF THE SURVEY CORPS. KEEN POWERS OF OBSERVATION LED ERWIN TO NAME HANGE HIS SUCCESSOR DESPITE OBVIOUS ECCENTRICITIES.

THE ELDIAN WARRIORS OF THE MARLEYAN ARMY

REINER BRAUN

HOLDS THE ARMORED TITAN WITHIN HIM. SINCE HE WAS THE ONLY ONE TO MAKE IT BACK FROM THE MISSION ON PARADIS, HE SUFFERS FROM A GUILTY CONSCIENCE.

ANNIE LEONHART

HOLDS THE FEMALE TITAN WITHIN HER. A MEMBER OF THE 104TH, SHE HAS BEEN SLEEPING WITHIN A HARDENED CRYSTAL EVER SINCE HER TRUE IDENTITY WAS DISCOVERED.

PIECK

HOLDS THE CART TITAN WITHIN HER, CARRYING THE PANZER UNIT ON THE BACK OF THE "CARTMAN" TO FIGHT. HIGHLY PERCEPTIVE.

PORCO GALLIARD

HOLDS THE JAW TITAN WITHIN HIM. THERE IS STRIFE BETWEEN HIM AND REINER OVER BOTH THE INHERITANCE OF THE ARMORED TITAN AND THE DEATH OF HIS OLDER BROTHER, MARCEL.

THEO MAGATH

LEADER OF THE WARRIOR UNIT, A MARLEYAN WHO LEADS A UNIT OF ELDIANS.

COLT GRICE

FALCO'S OLDER BROTHER. THE OLDEST OF THE WARRIOR CANDIDATES, AND, IN EFFECT, THEIR LEADER.

THE ANTI-MARLEYAN VOLUNTEERS

ZEKE YEAGER

HOLDS THE POWER OF THE BEAST TITAN. A LEADER OF THE WARRIORS, HE WAS ONCE KNOWN AS THE "WONDER CHILD." HIS MOTHER IS A DESCENDANT OF THE ROYAL BLOODLINE. HE IS ALSO EREN'S HALF-BROTHER.

YELENA

YELENA COMMANDS THE VOLUNTEERS AND FOLLOWS ZEKE. SHE DRESSED AS A MAN DURING THE EXPEDITION TO MARLEY IN ORDER TO WORK IN SECRET.

ONYANKOPON

AFTER TRAVELING TO PARADIS WITH YELENA, HE TELLS ITS INHABITANTS OF MARLEY'S ADVANCED CULTURE.

GABI BRAUN

BOLD DESPITE HER SMALL SIZE, GABI IS A DYNAMIC WARRIOR CANDIDATE. HER GOAL IS TO EVENTUALLY INHERIT THE ARMORED TITAN, REINER'S COUSIN.

FALCO GRICE

A WARRIOR CANDIDATE. HE HAS AFFECTION FOR GABI AND WANTS TO PROTECT HER. DURING EREN'S INFILTRATING MARLEY, FALCO CAME IN CONTACT WITH EREN WITHOUT REALIZING HIS TRUE IDENTITY.

ATTACK on TITAN

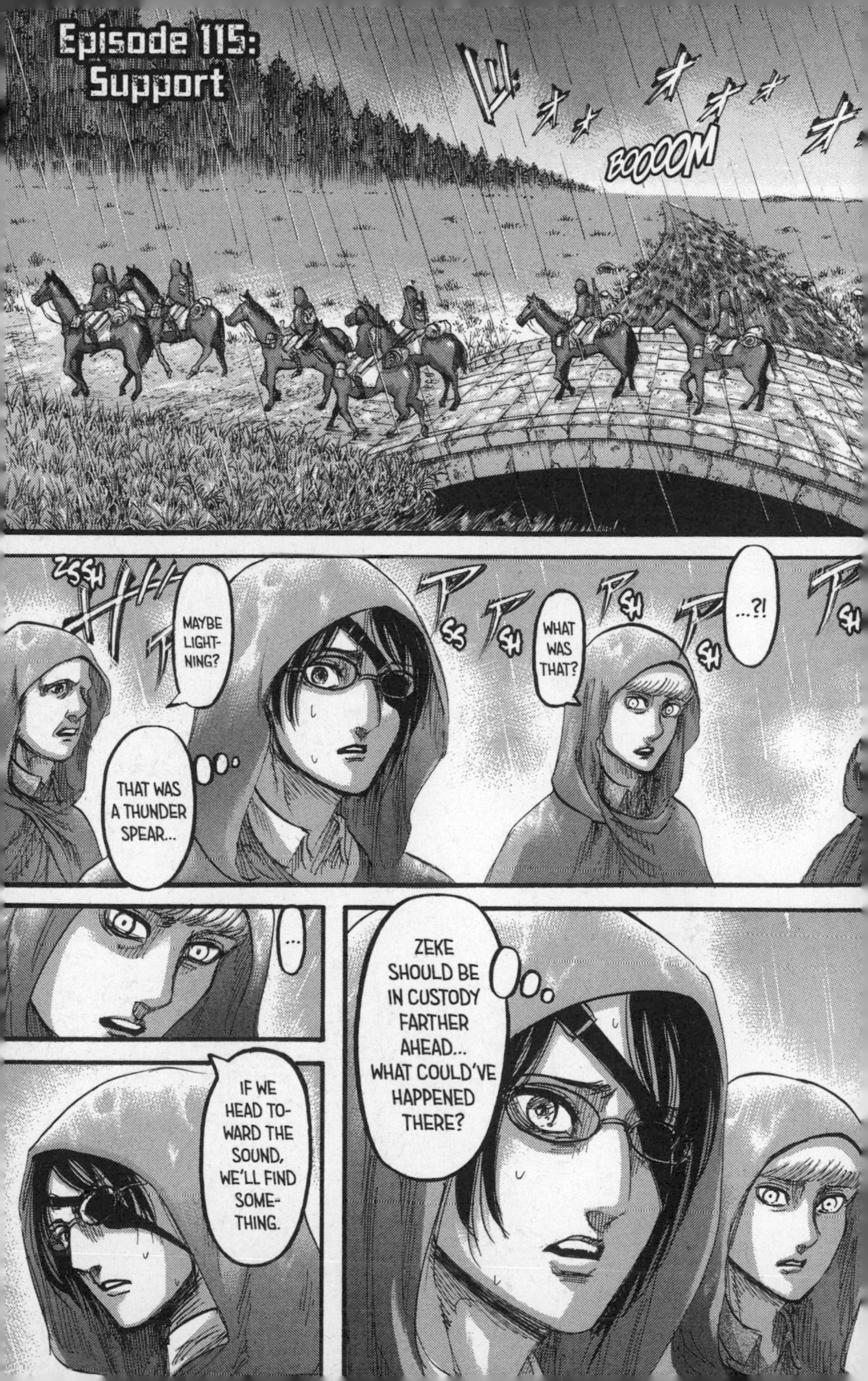
Episode 115: Support
BOOOOM
...?!
PSH
SH
PSH
SH
PSS
WHAT WAS THAT?
MAYBE LIGHT-NING?
ZSSH
THAT WAS A THUNDER SPEAR...
ZEKE SHOULD BE IN CUSTODY FARTHER AHEAD... WHAT COULD'VE HAPPENED THERE?
...
IF WE HEAD TO-WARD THE SOUND, WE'LL FIND SOME-THING.

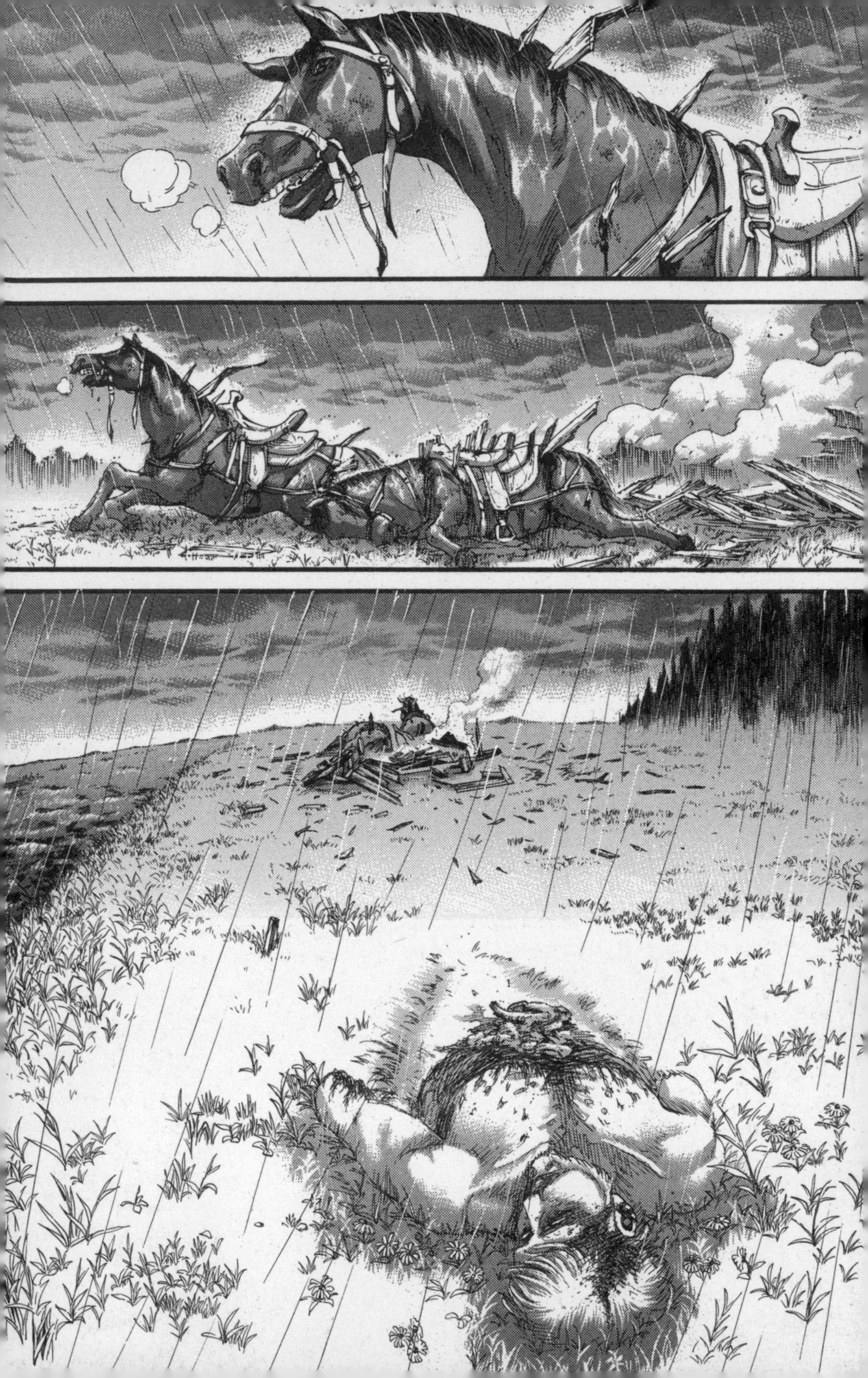

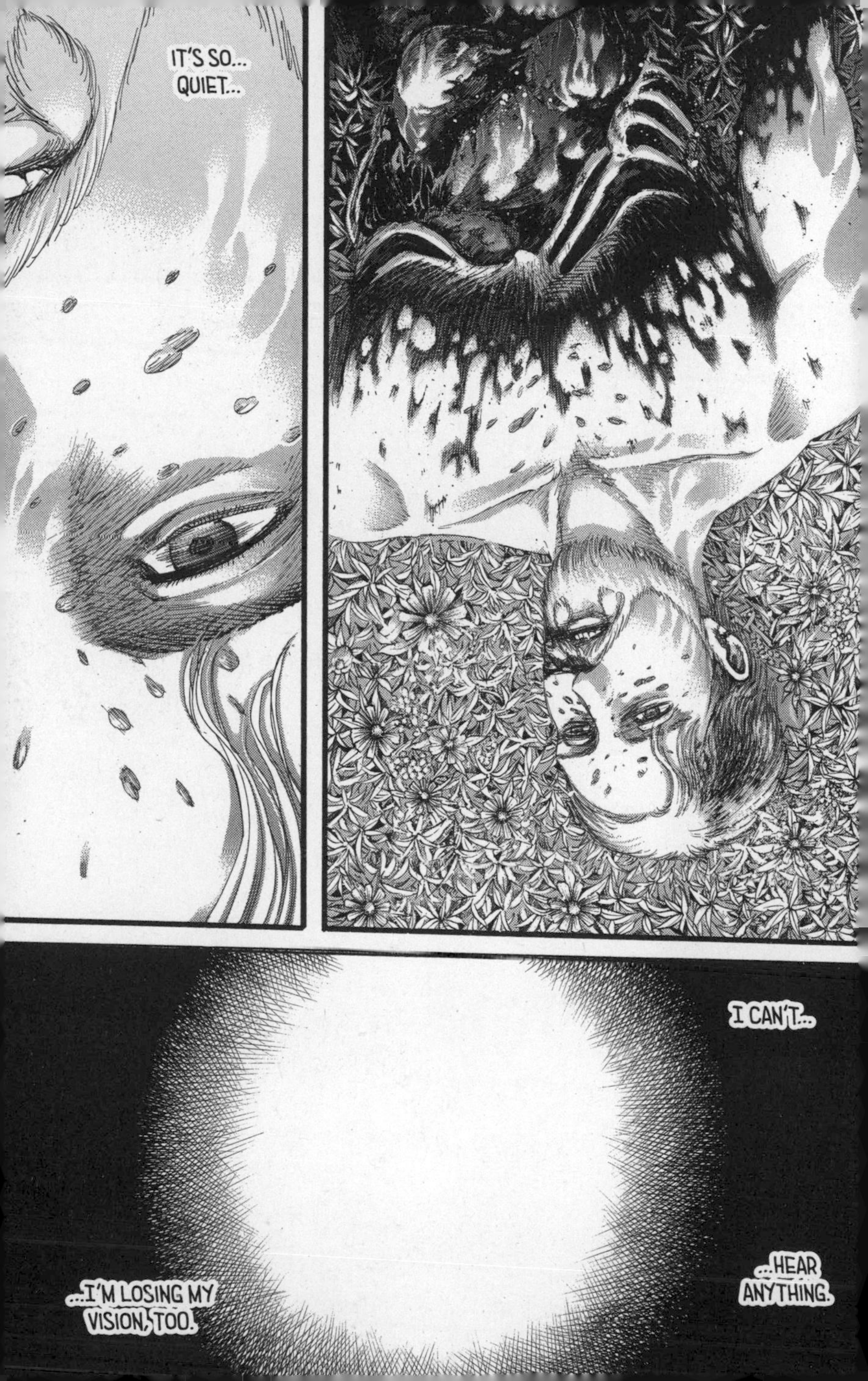
IT'S SO... QUIET...
I CAN'T...
...HEAR ANYTHING.
...I'M LOSING MY VISION, TOO.

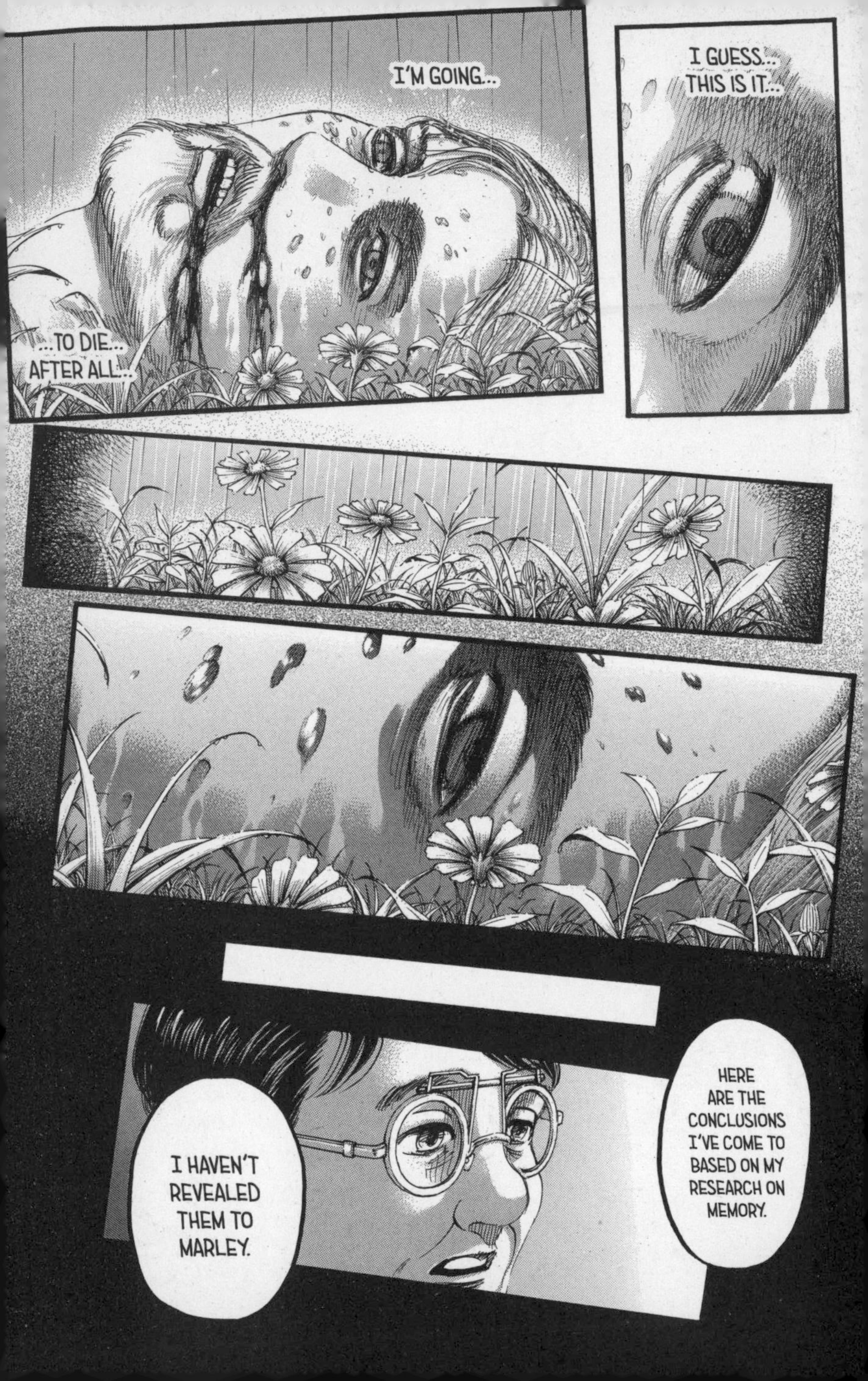
I GUESS... THIS IS IT...
I'M GOING...
...TO DIE... AFTER ALL...
HERE ARE THE CONCLUSIONS I'VE COME TO BASED ON MY RESEARCH ON MEMORY.
I HAVEN'T REVEALED THEM TO MARLEY.

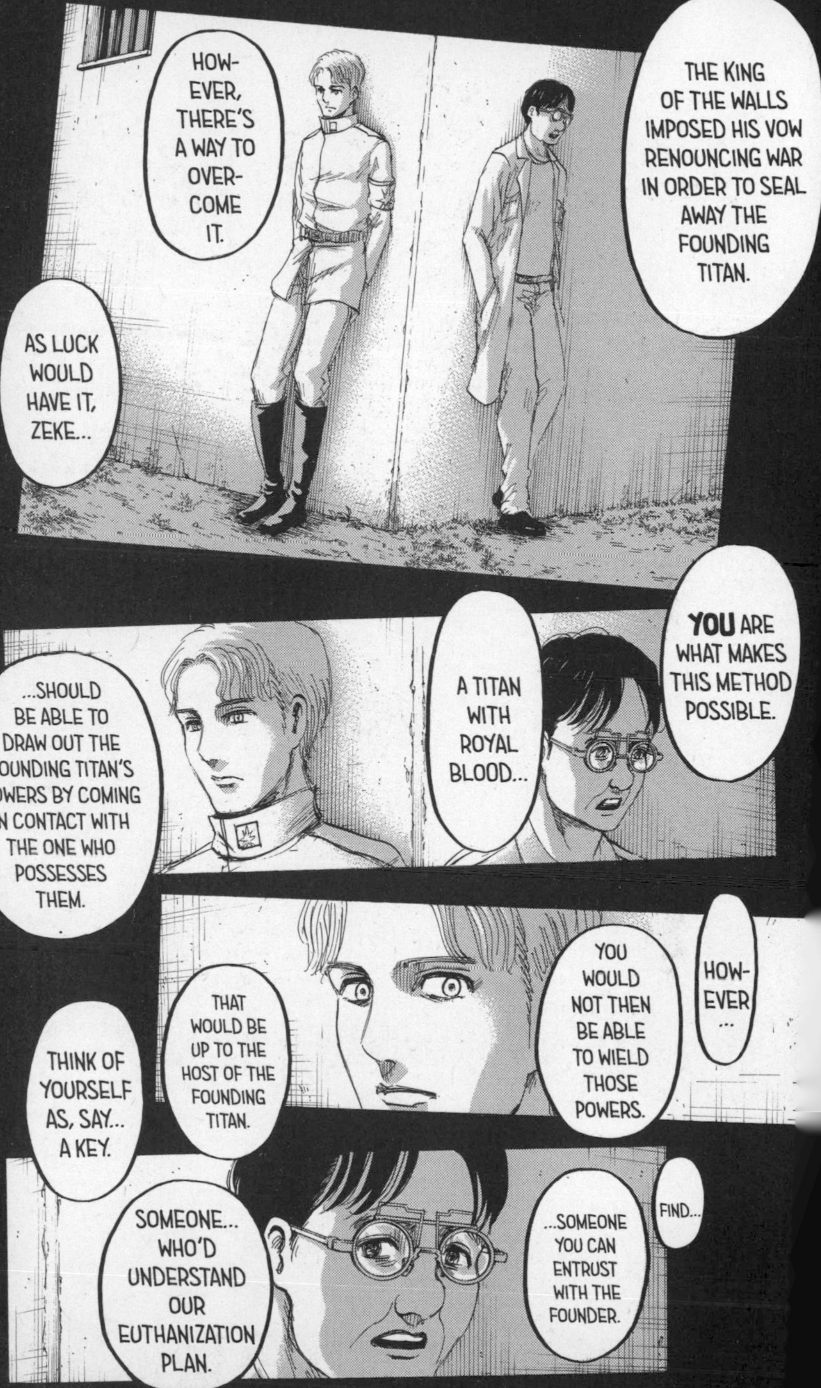
THE KING OF THE WALLS IMPOSED HIS VOW RENOUNCING WAR IN ORDER TO SEAL AWAY THE FOUNDING TITAN.
HOW-EVER, THERE'S A WAY TO OVER-COME IT.
AS LUCK WOULD HAVE IT, ZEKE...
YOU ARE WHAT MAKES THIS METHOD POSSIBLE.
A TITAN WITH ROYAL BLOOD...
...SHOULD BE ABLE TO DRAW OUT THE FOUNDING TITAN'S POWERS BY COMING IN CONTACT WITH THE ONE WHO POSSESSES THEM.
HOW-EVER...
YOU WOULD NOT THEN BE ABLE TO WIELD THOSE POWERS.
THAT WOULD BE UP TO THE HOST OF THE FOUNDING TITAN.
THINK OF YOURSELF AS, SAY... A KEY.
FIND...
...SOMEONE YOU CAN ENTRUST WITH THE FOUNDER.
SOMEONE... WHO'D UNDERSTAND OUR EUTHANIZATION PLAN.

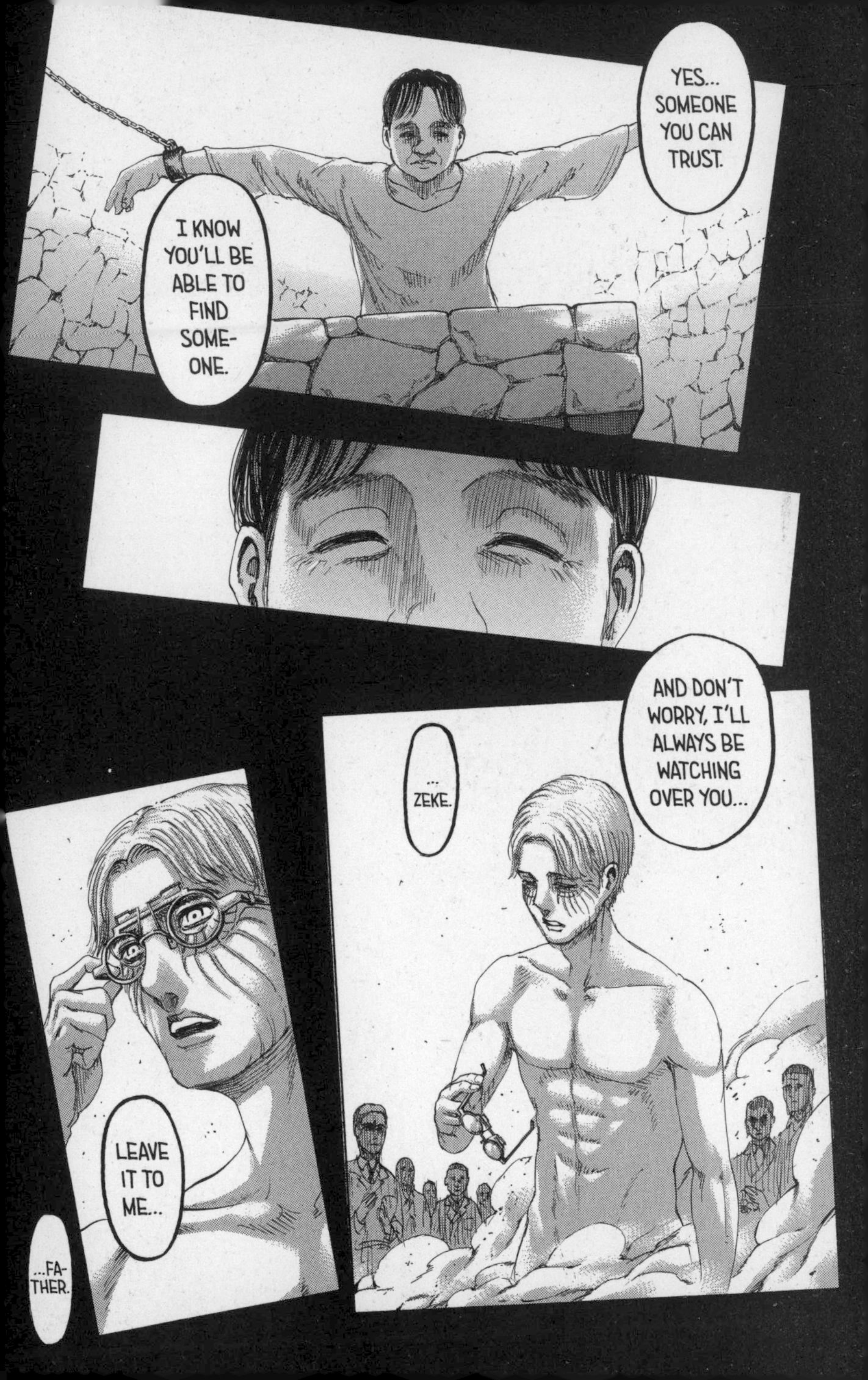
YES... SOMEONE YOU CAN TRUST.
I KNOW YOU'LL BE ABLE TO FIND SOME-ONE.
AND DON'T WORRY, I'LL ALWAYS BE WATCHING OVER YOU...
...ZEKE.
LEAVE IT TO ME...
...FA-THER.

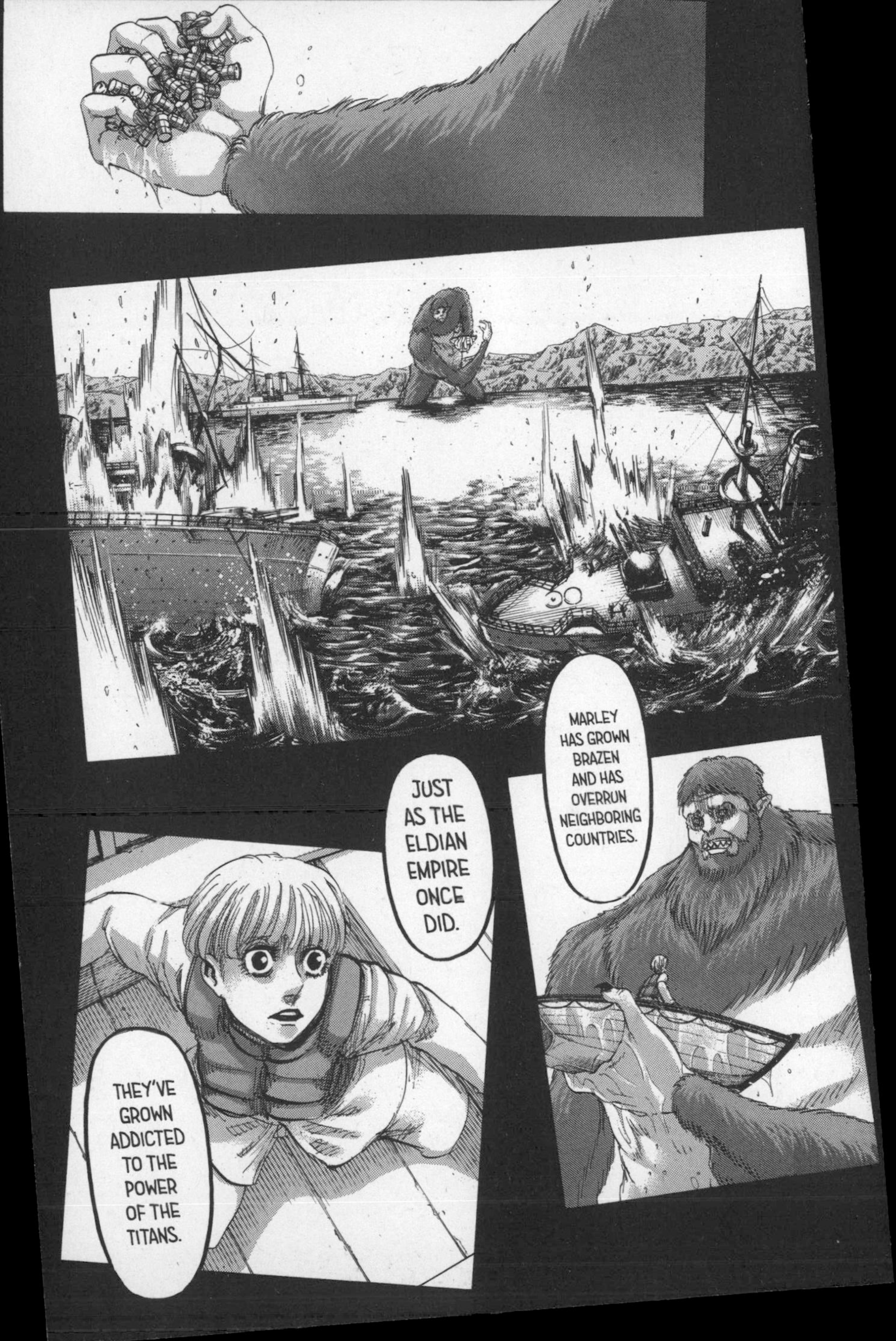
MARLEY HAS GROWN BRAZEN AND HAS OVERRUN NEIGHBORING COUNTRIES.
JUST AS THE ELDIAN EMPIRE ONCE DID.
THEY'VE GROWN ADDICTED TO THE POWER OF THE TITANS.

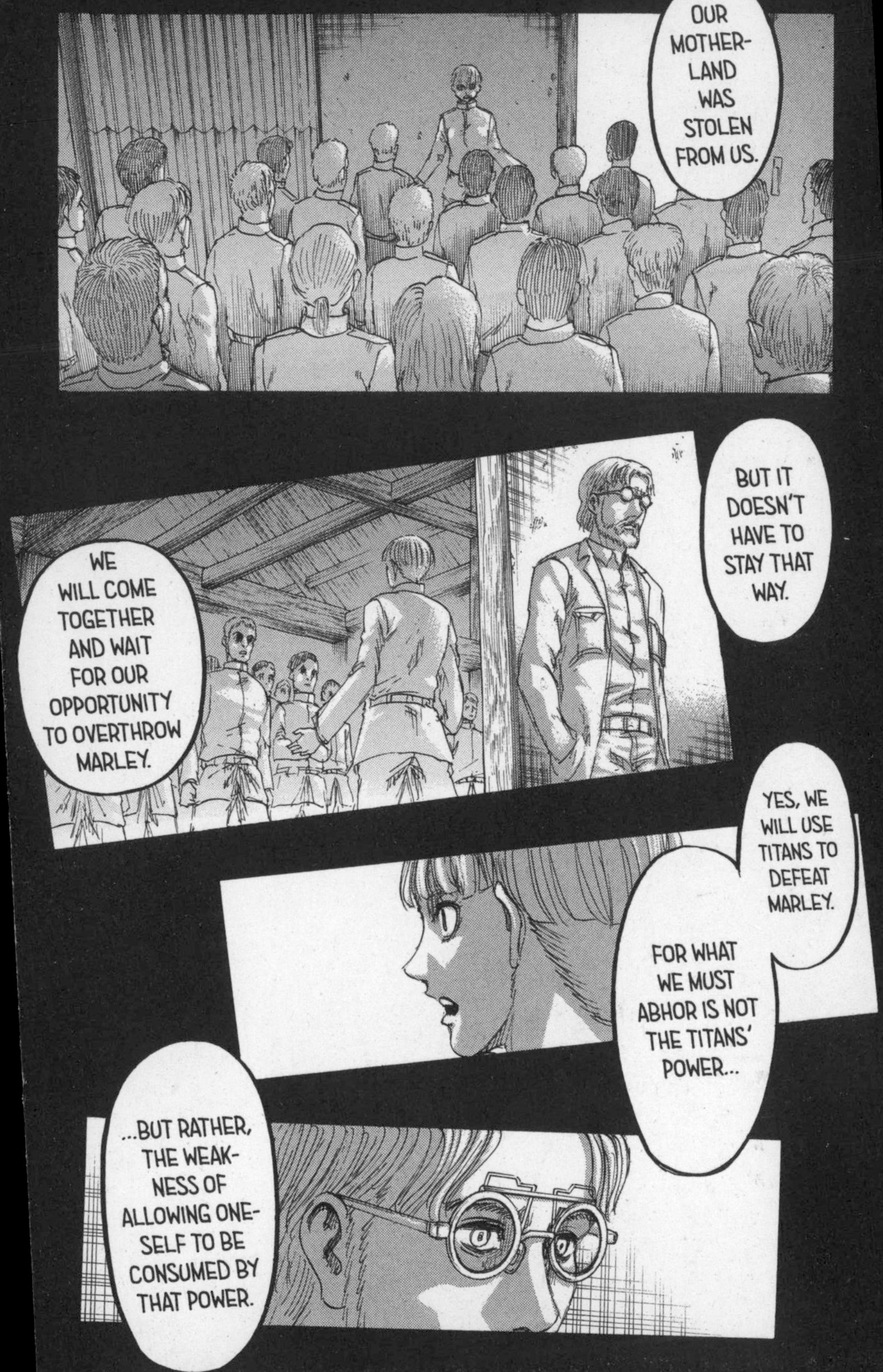
OUR MOTHER-LAND WAS STOLEN FROM US.
BUT IT DOESN'T HAVE TO STAY THAT WAY.
WE WILL COME TOGETHER AND WAIT FOR OUR OPPORTUNITY TO OVERTHROW MARLEY.
YES, WE WILL USE TITANS TO DEFEAT MARLEY.
FOR WHAT WE MUST ABHOR IS NOT THE TITANS' POWER...
...BUT RATHER, THE WEAK-NESS OF ALLOWING ONE-SELF TO BE CONSUMED BY THAT POWER.

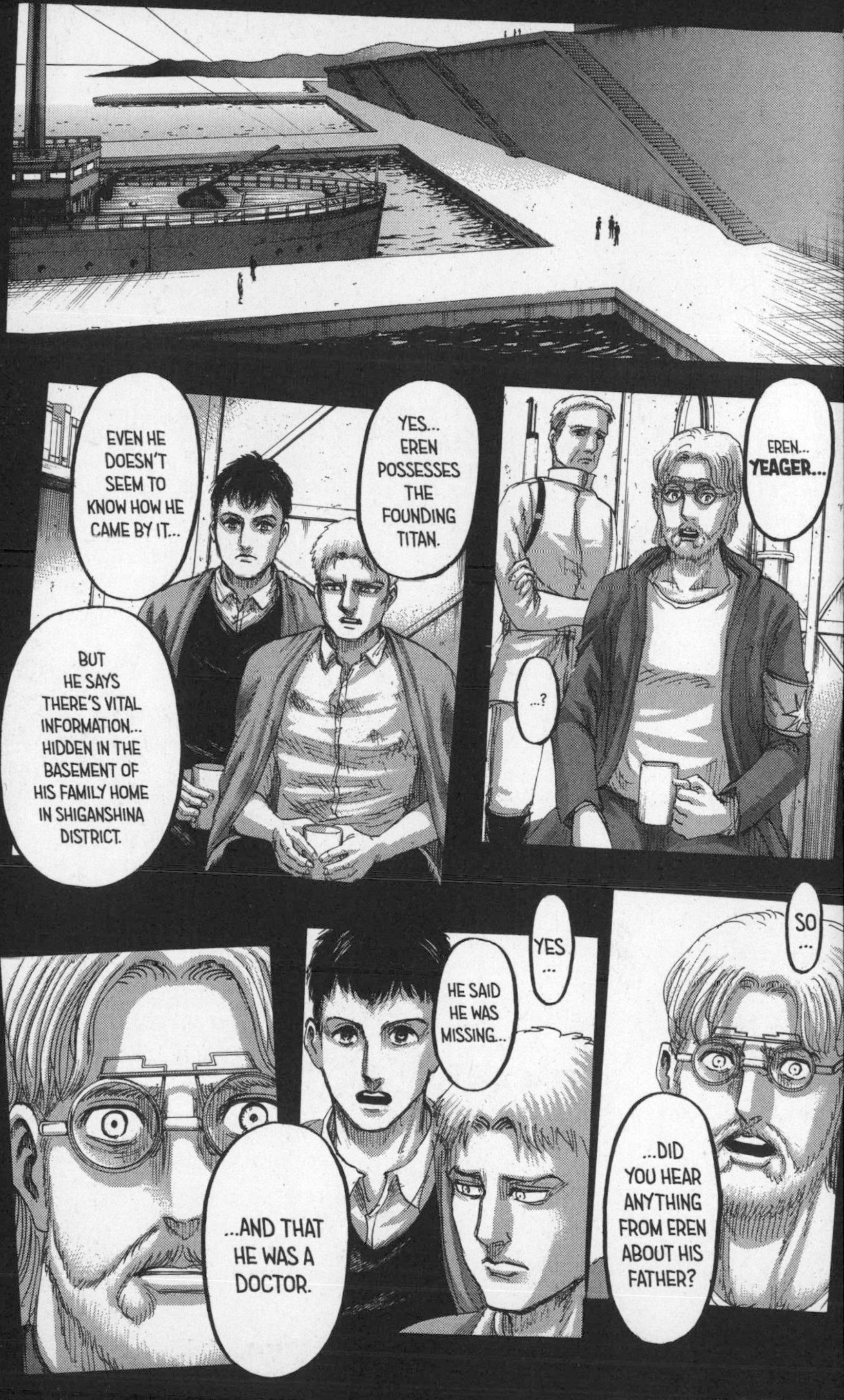
EREN... YEAGER...
...?
YES... EREN POSSESSES THE FOUNDING TITAN.
EVEN HE DOESN'T SEEM TO KNOW HOW HE CAME BY IT...
BUT HE SAYS THERE'S VITAL INFORMATION... HIDDEN IN THE BASEMENT OF HIS FAMILY HOME IN SHIGANSHINA DISTRICT.
SO...
...DID YOU HEAR ANYTHING FROM EREN ABOUT HIS FATHER?
YES...
HE SAID HE WAS MISSING...
...AND THAT HE WAS A DOCTOR.

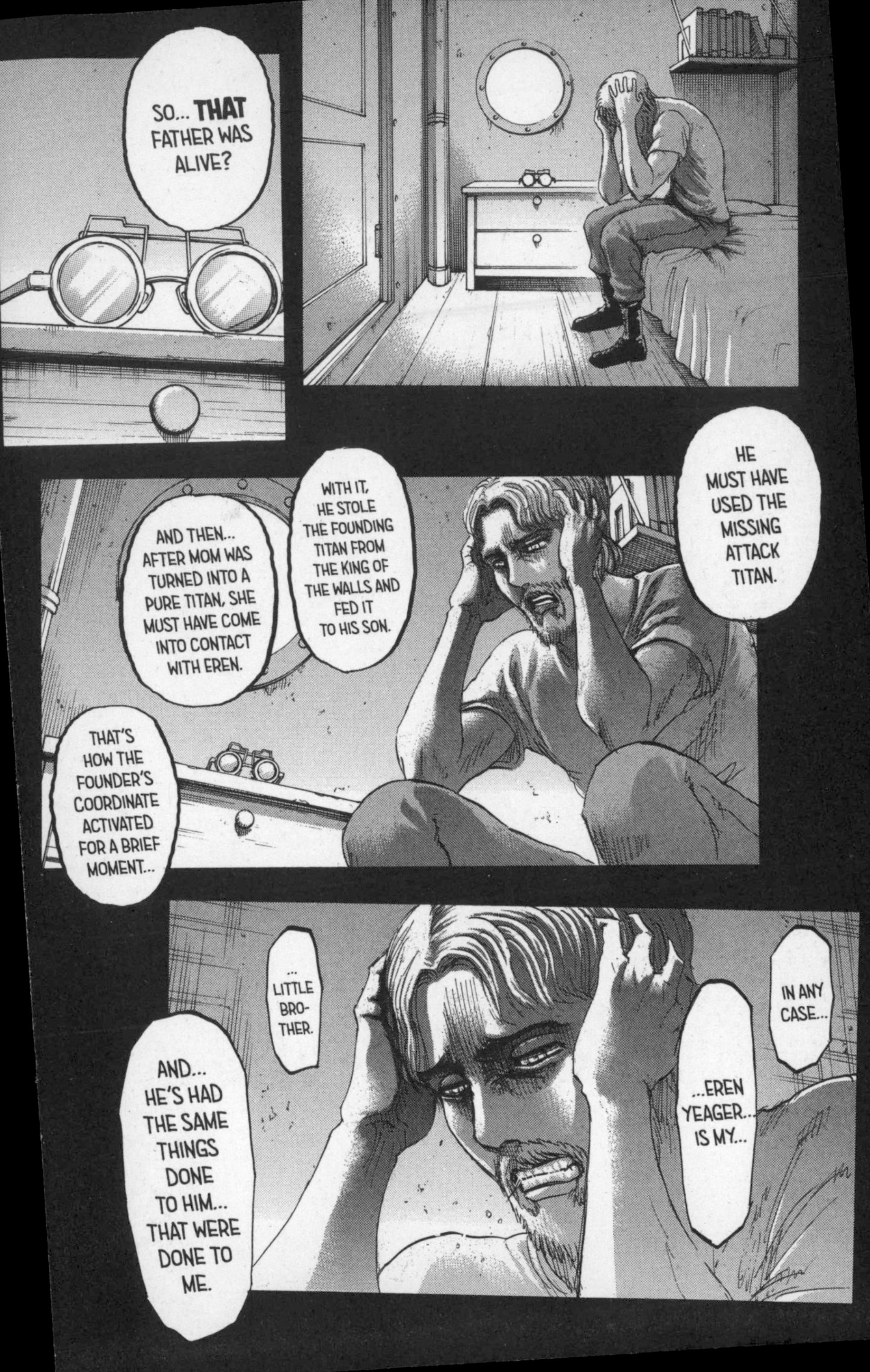
SO... **THAT** FATHER WAS ALIVE?
HE MUST HAVE USED THE MISSING ATTACK TITAN.
WITH IT, HE STOLE THE FOUNDING TITAN FROM THE KING OF THE WALLS AND FED IT TO HIS SON.
AND THEN... AFTER MOM WAS TURNED INTO A PURE TITAN, SHE MUST HAVE COME INTO CONTACT WITH EREN.
THAT'S HOW THE FOUNDER'S COORDINATE ACTIVATED FOR A BRIEF MOMENT...
IN ANY CASE...
...EREN YEAGER... IS MY...
... LITTLE BRO-THER.
AND... HE'S HAD THE SAME THINGS DONE TO HIM... THAT WERE DONE TO ME.

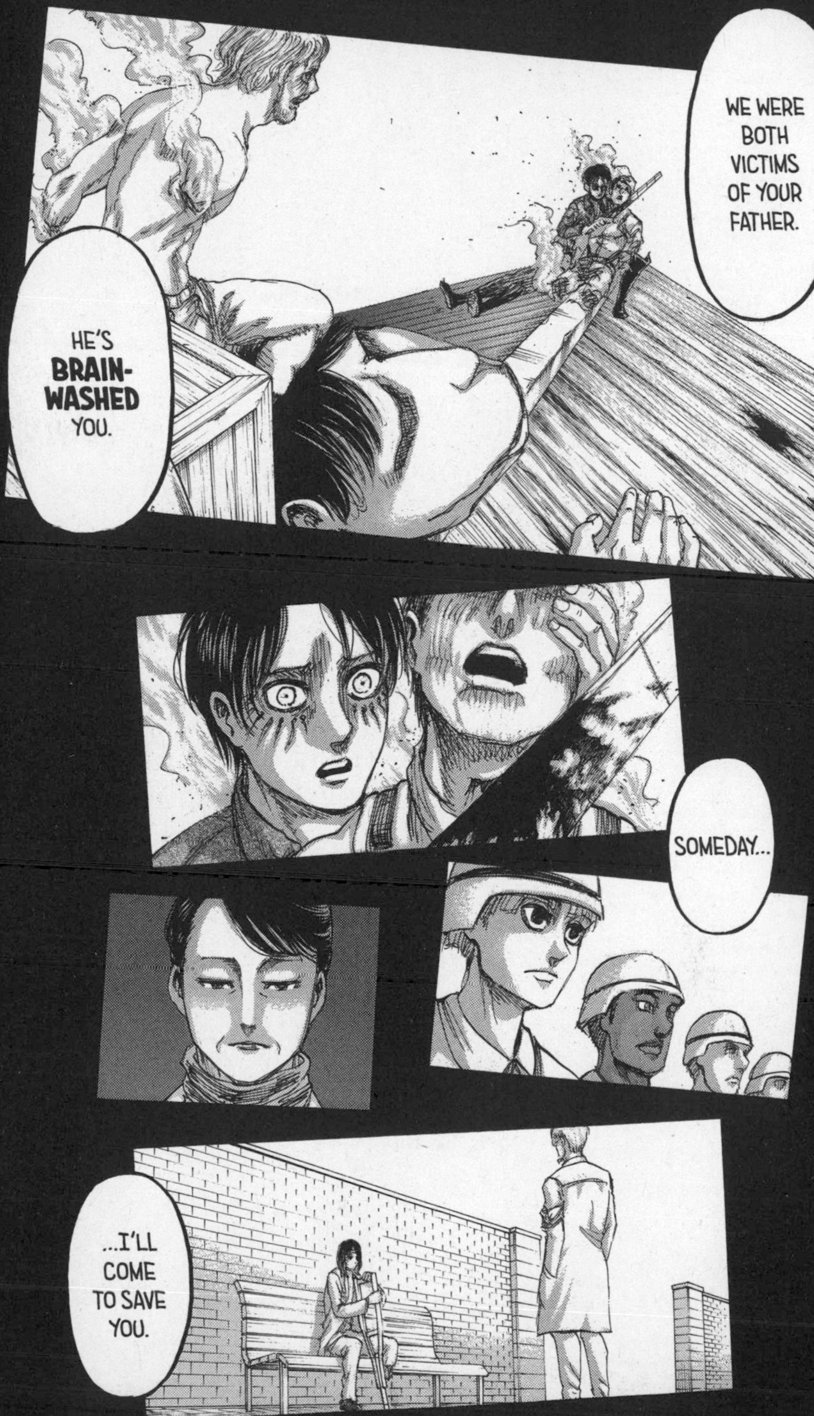
WE WERE BOTH VICTIMS OF YOUR FATHER.
HE'S **BRAIN-WASHED** YOU.
SOMEDAY...
...I'LL COME TO SAVE YOU.

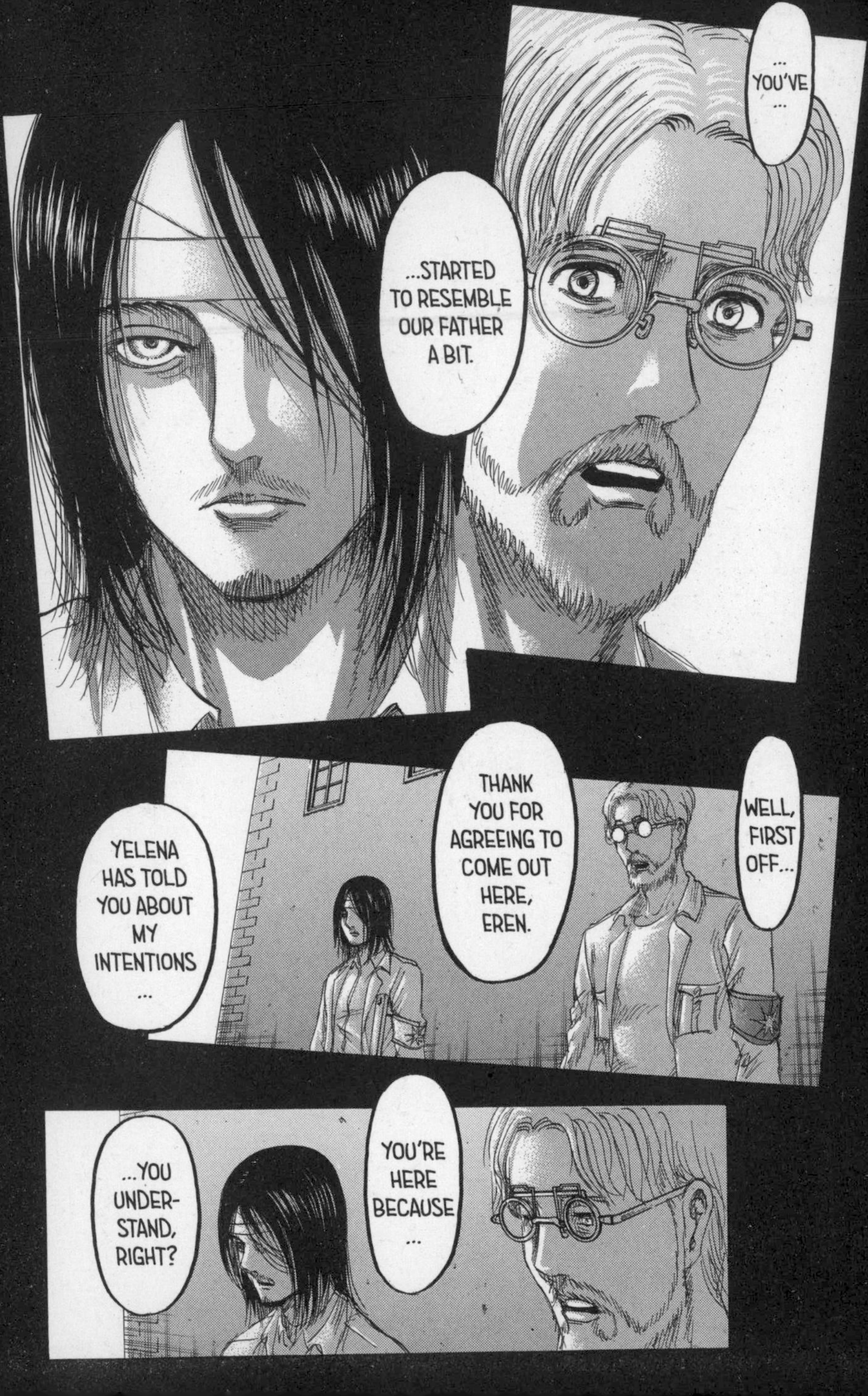
... YOU'VE ...
...STARTED TO RESEMBLE OUR FATHER A BIT.
WELL, FIRST OFF...
THANK YOU FOR AGREEING TO COME OUT HERE, EREN.
YELENA HAS TOLD YOU ABOUT MY INTENTIONS ...
YOU'RE HERE BECAUSE ...
...YOU UNDERSTAND, RIGHT?

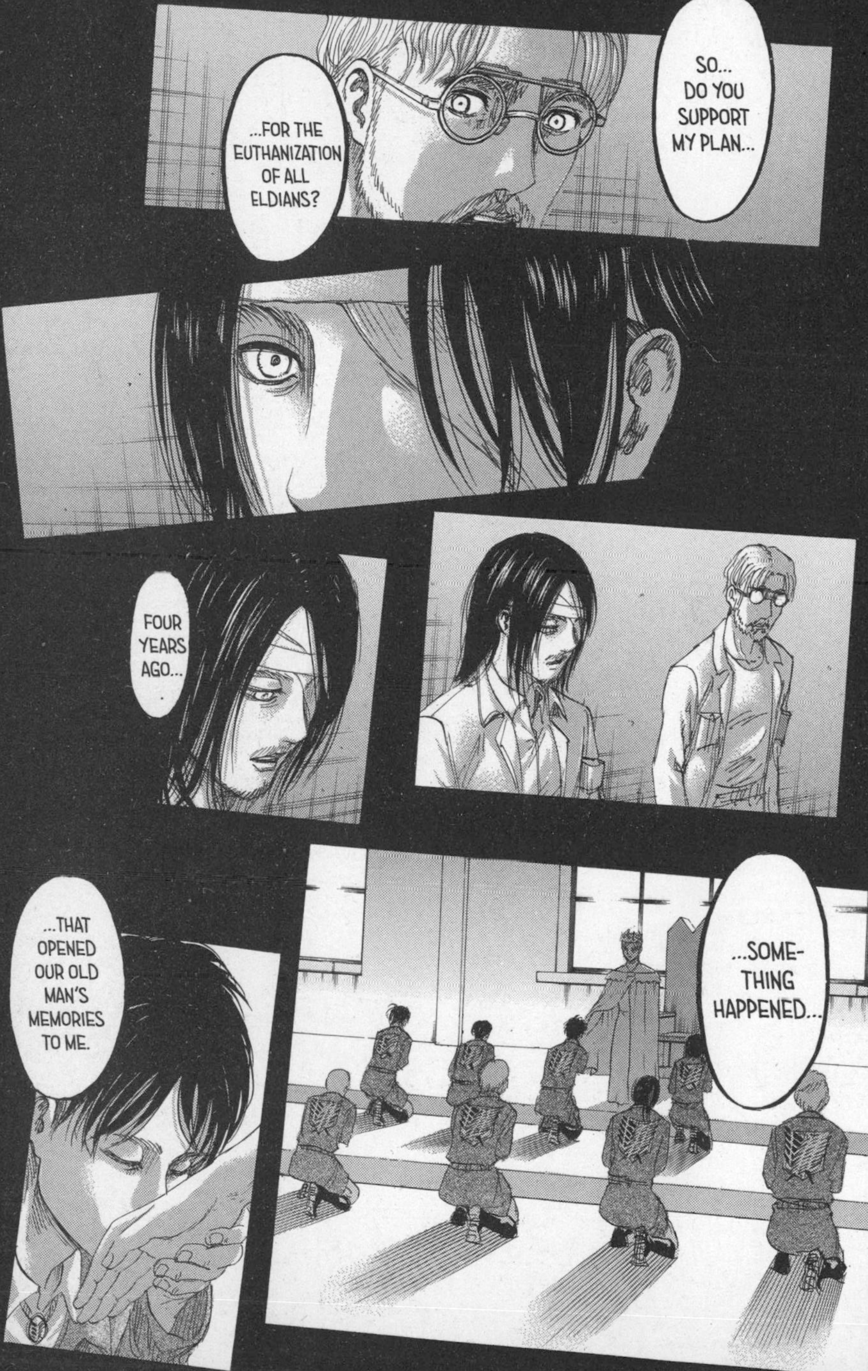
SO... DO YOU SUPPORT MY PLAN...
...FOR THE EUTHANIZATION OF ALL ELDIANS?
FOUR YEARS AGO...
...SOME-THING HAPPENED...
...THAT OPENED OUR OLD MAN'S MEMORIES TO ME.

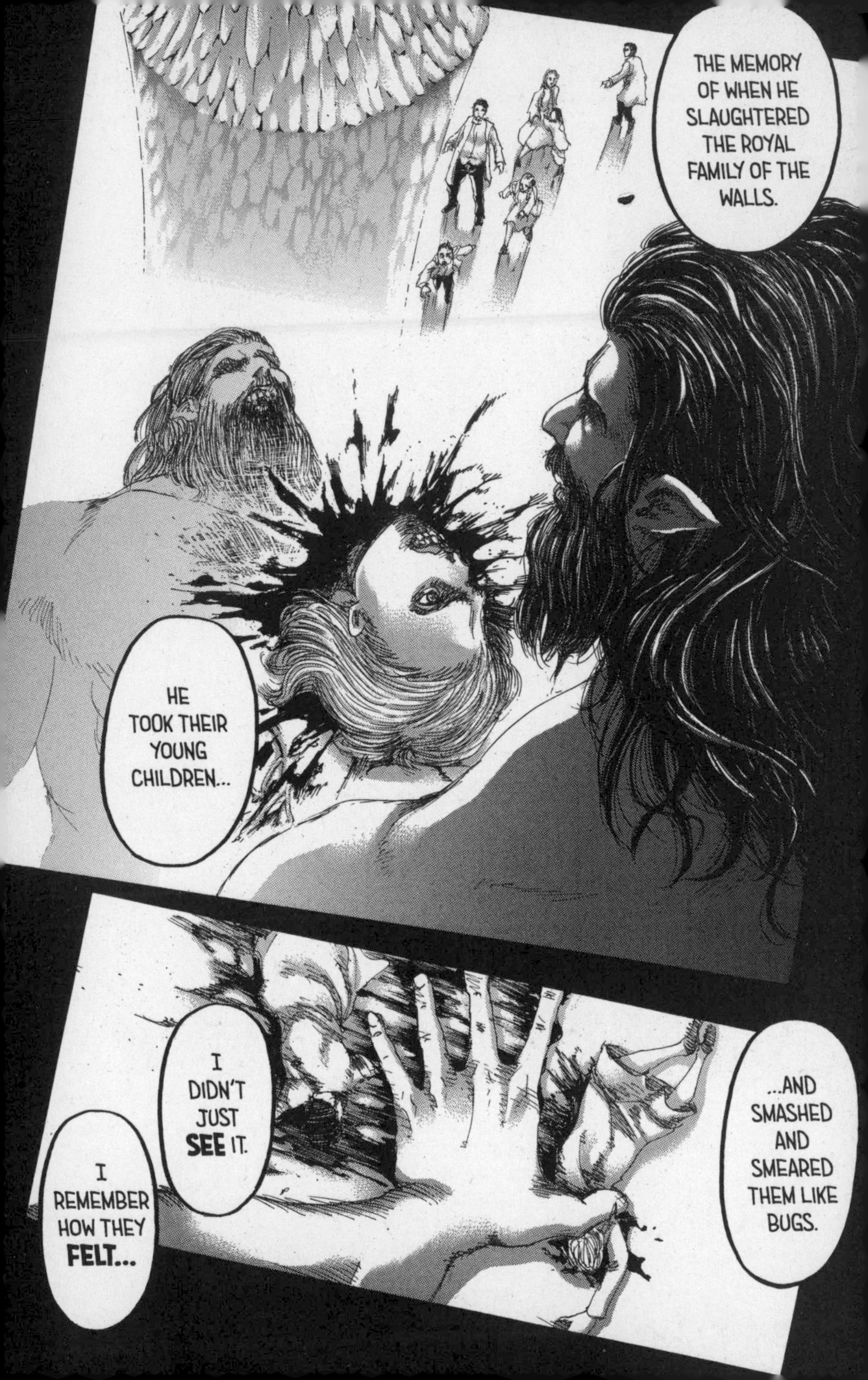
THE MEMORY OF WHEN HE SLAUGHTERED THE ROYAL FAMILY OF THE WALLS.
HE TOOK THEIR YOUNG CHILDREN...
...AND SMASHED AND SMEARED THEM LIKE BUGS.
I DIDN'T JUST **SEE** IT.
I REMEMBER HOW THEY **FELT...**

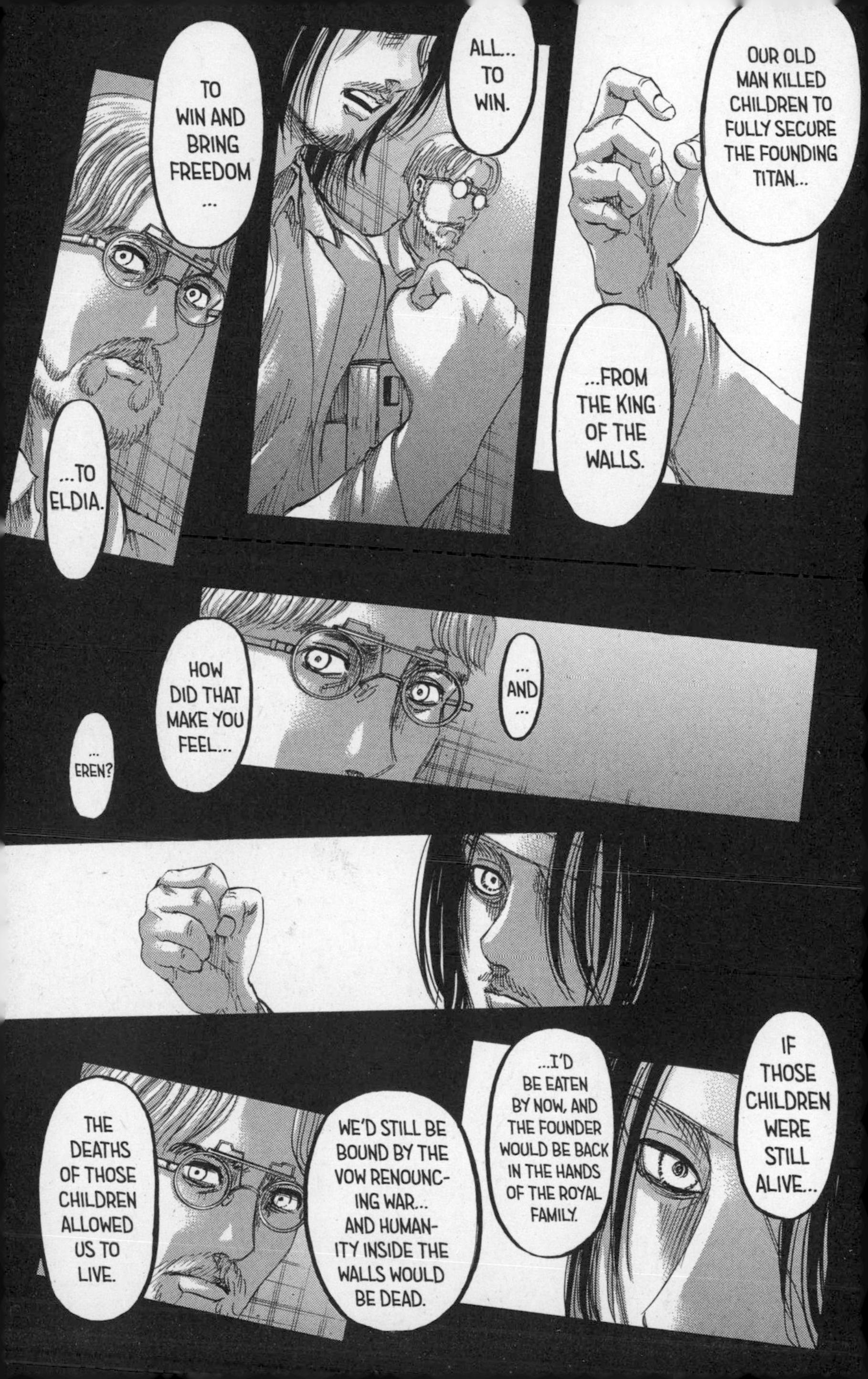
OUR OLD MAN KILLED CHILDREN TO FULLY SECURE THE FOUNDING TITAN...
...FROM THE KING OF THE WALLS.
ALL... TO WIN.
TO WIN AND BRING FREEDOM ...
...TO ELDIA.
... AND ...
HOW DID THAT MAKE YOU FEEL...
... EREN?
IF THOSE CHILDREN WERE STILL ALIVE...
...I'D BE EATEN BY NOW, AND THE FOUNDER WOULD BE BACK IN THE HANDS OF THE ROYAL FAMILY.
WE'D STILL BE BOUND BY THE VOW RENOUNCING WAR... AND HUMANITY INSIDE THE WALLS WOULD BE DEAD.
THE DEATHS OF THOSE CHILDREN ALLOWED US TO LIVE.

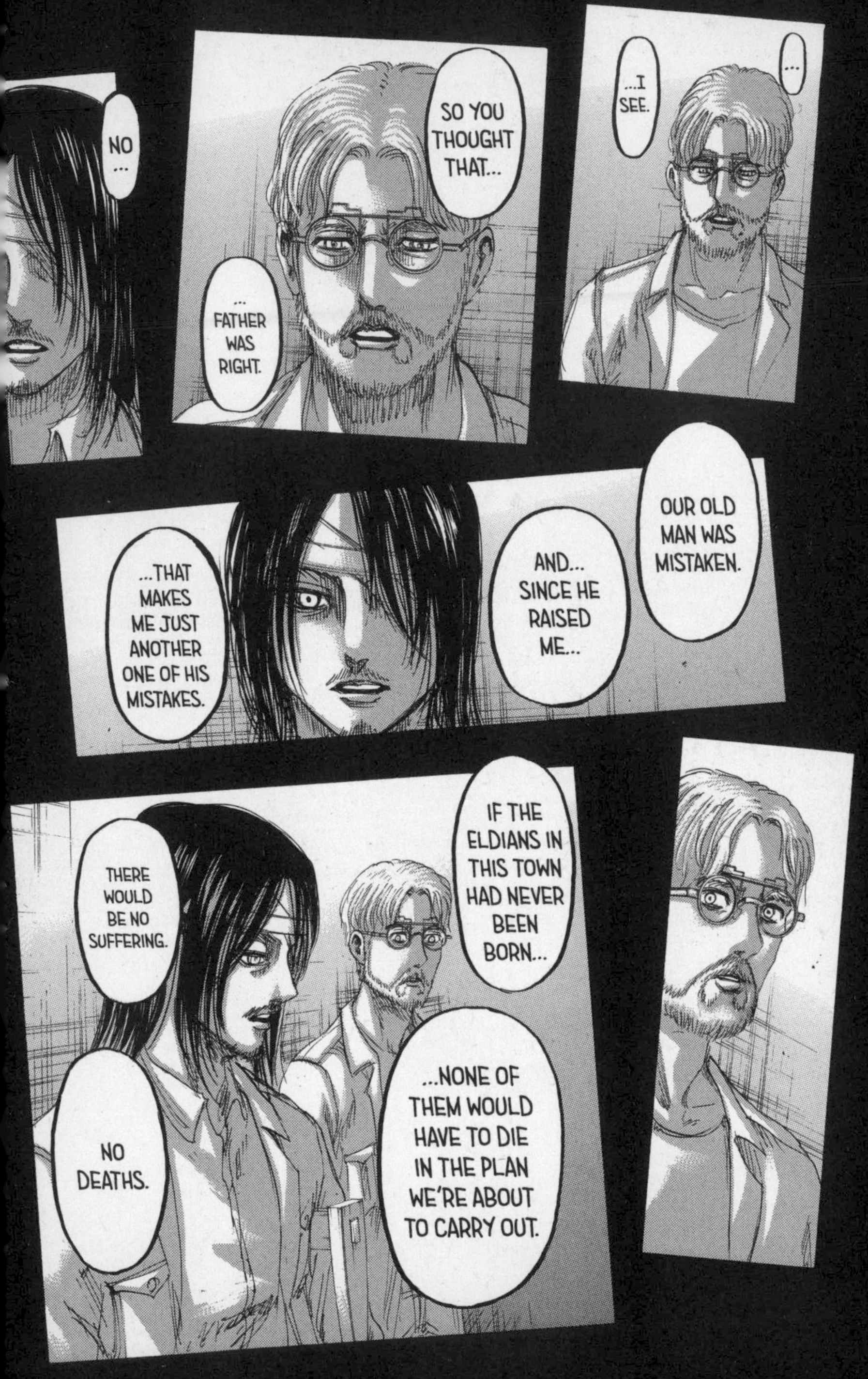
...
...I SEE.
SO YOU THOUGHT THAT...
... FATHER WAS RIGHT.
NO ...
OUR OLD MAN WAS MISTAKEN.
AND... SINCE HE RAISED ME...
...THAT MAKES ME JUST ANOTHER ONE OF HIS MISTAKES.
IF THE ELDIANS IN THIS TOWN HAD NEVER BEEN BORN...
...NONE OF THEM WOULD HAVE TO DIE IN THE PLAN WE'RE ABOUT TO CARRY OUT.
THERE WOULD BE NO SUFFERING.
NO DEATHS.

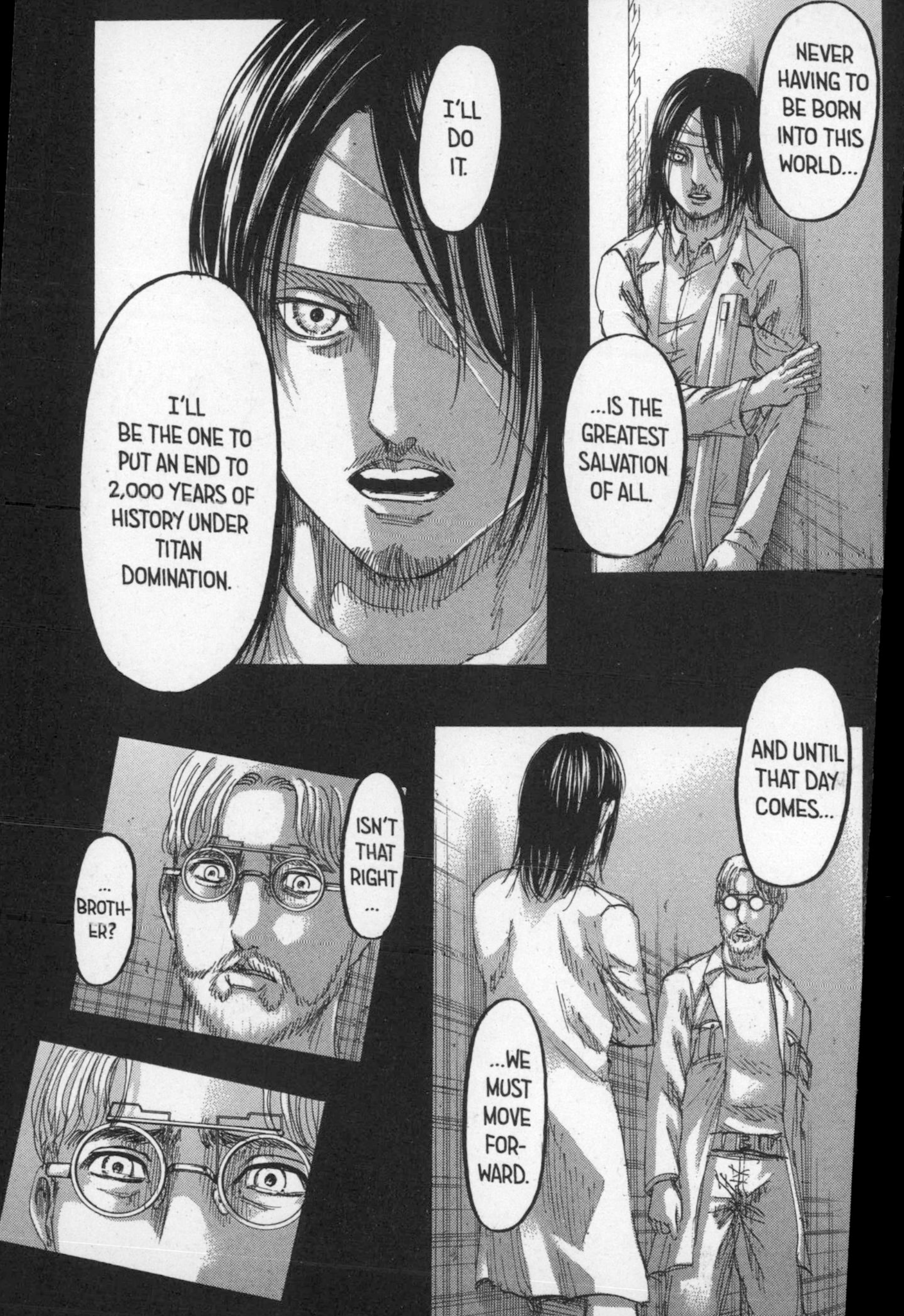
NEVER HAVING TO BE BORN INTO THIS WORLD...
...IS THE GREATEST SALVATION OF ALL.
I'LL DO IT.
I'LL BE THE ONE TO PUT AN END TO 2,000 YEARS OF HISTORY UNDER TITAN DOMINATION.
AND UNTIL THAT DAY COMES...
...WE MUST MOVE FOR-WARD.
ISN'T THAT RIGHT ...
... BROTH-ER?

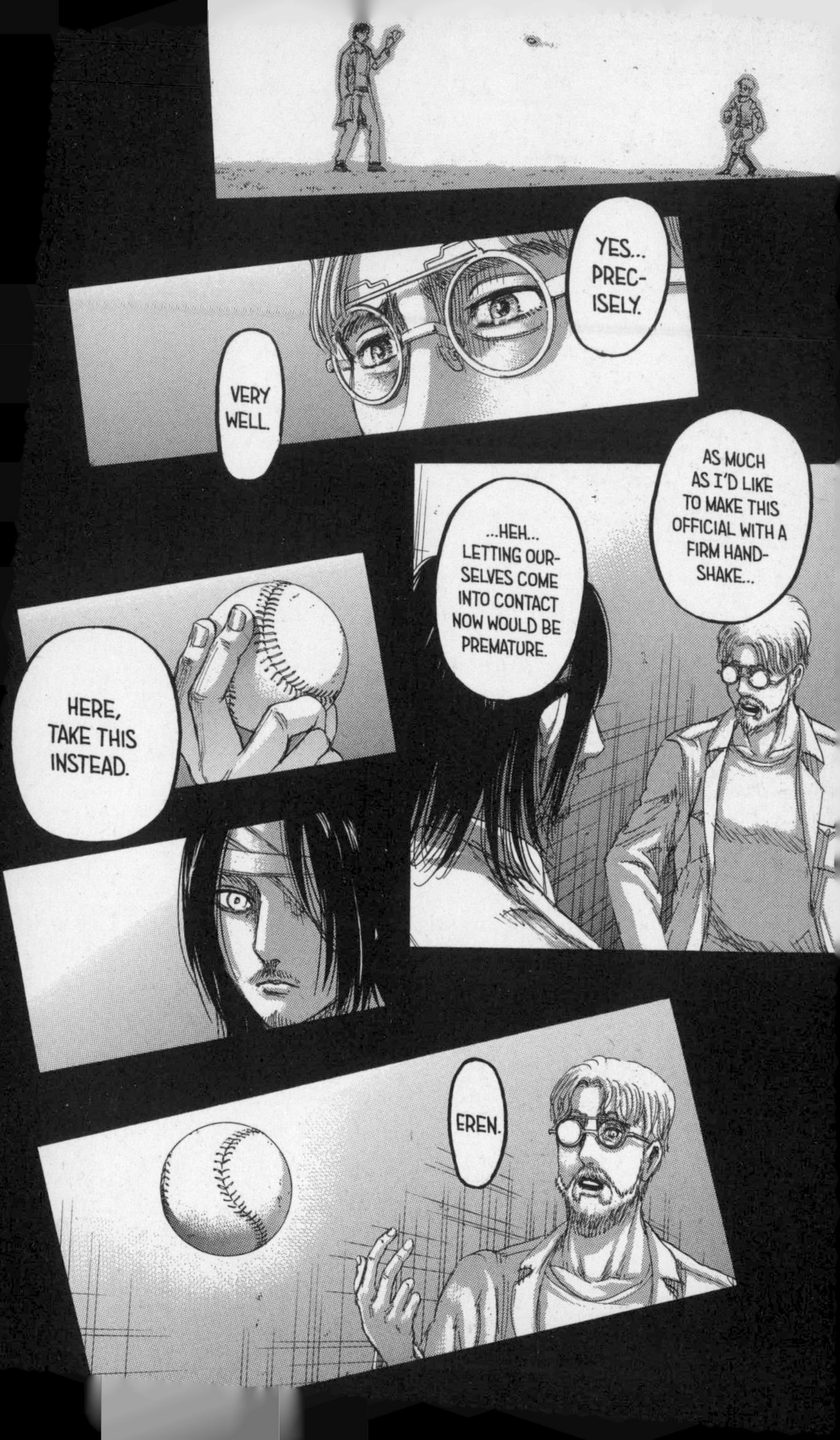
YES... PREC-ISELY.
VERY WELL.
AS MUCH AS I'D LIKE TO MAKE THIS OFFICIAL WITH A FIRM HAND-SHAKE...
...HEH... LETTING OUR-SELVES COME INTO CONTACT NOW WOULD BE PREMATURE.
HERE, TAKE THIS INSTEAD.
EREN.

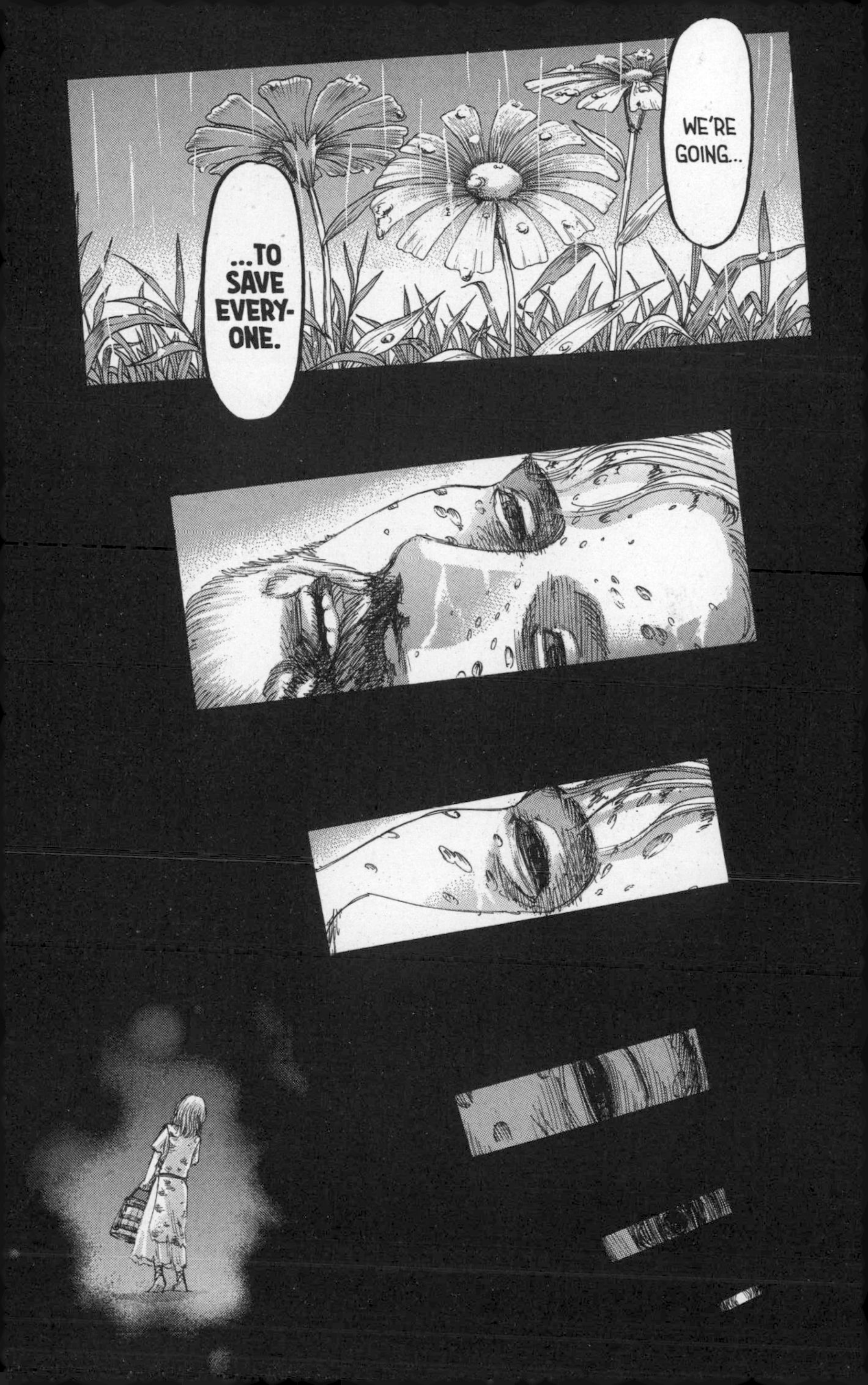
WE'RE GOING...
...TO SAVE EVERY-ONE.

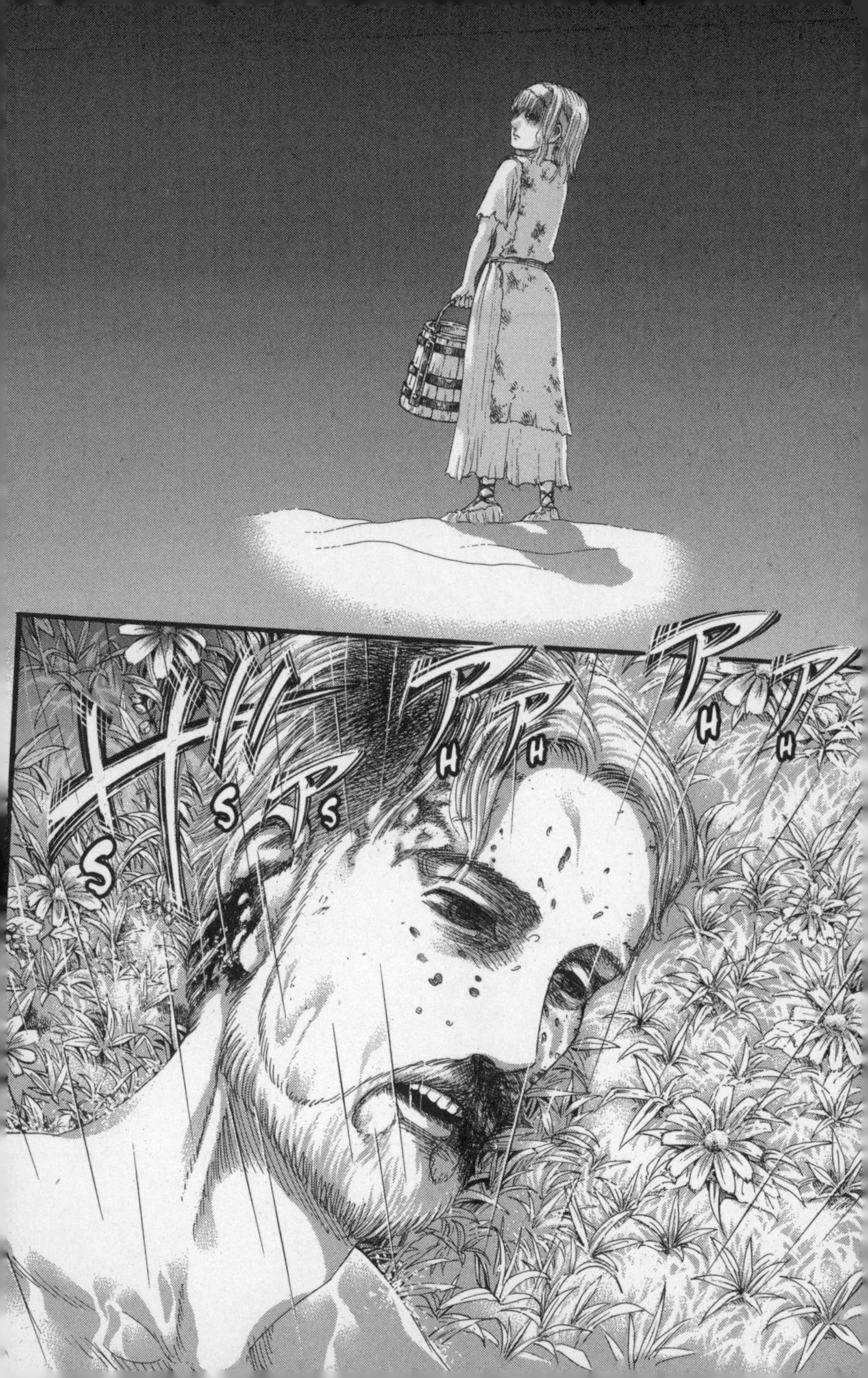
SSSHHH

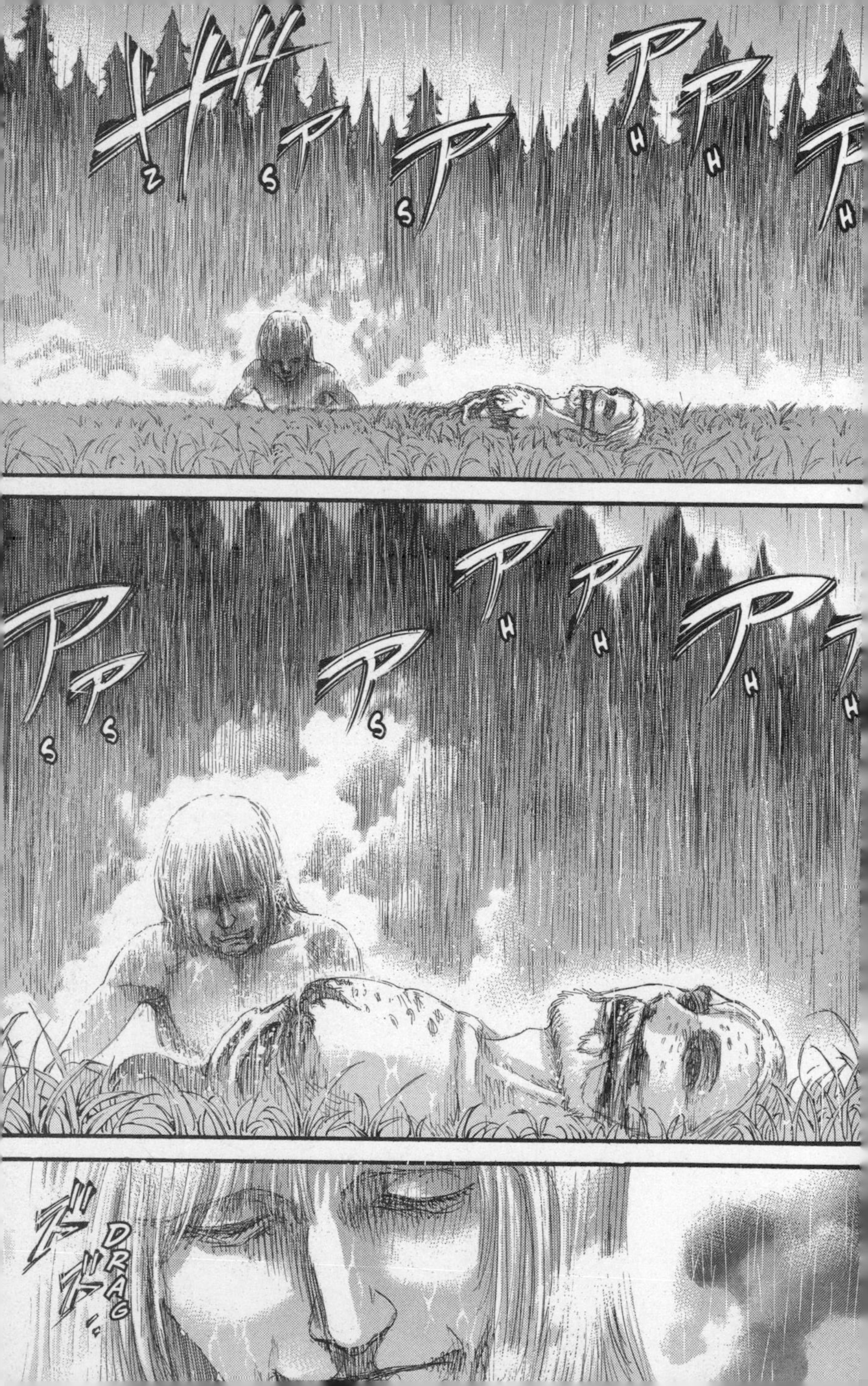
HHH
ZSS
HHH
SSS
DRAG

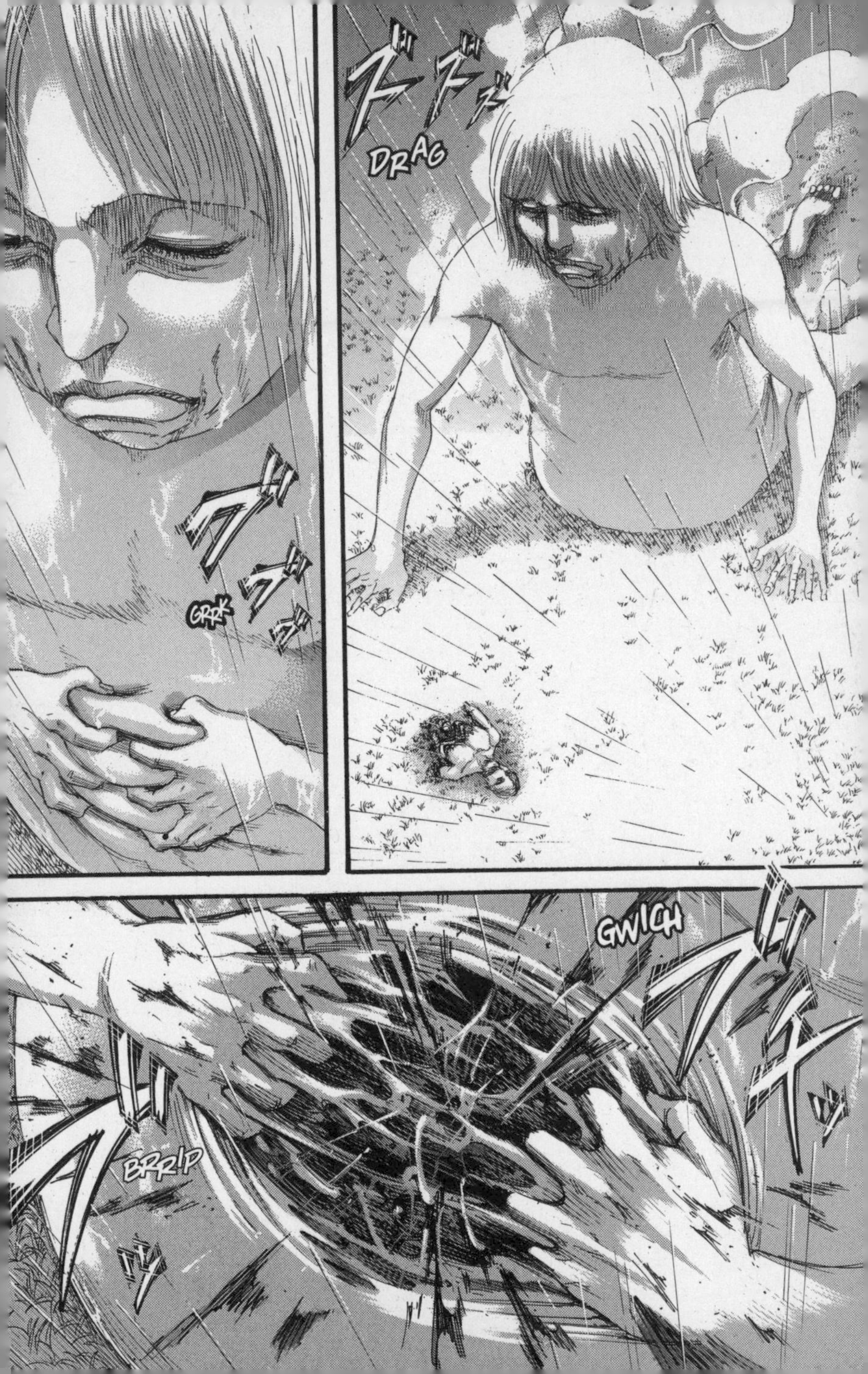
DRAG
GRRK
GWICH
BRRIP

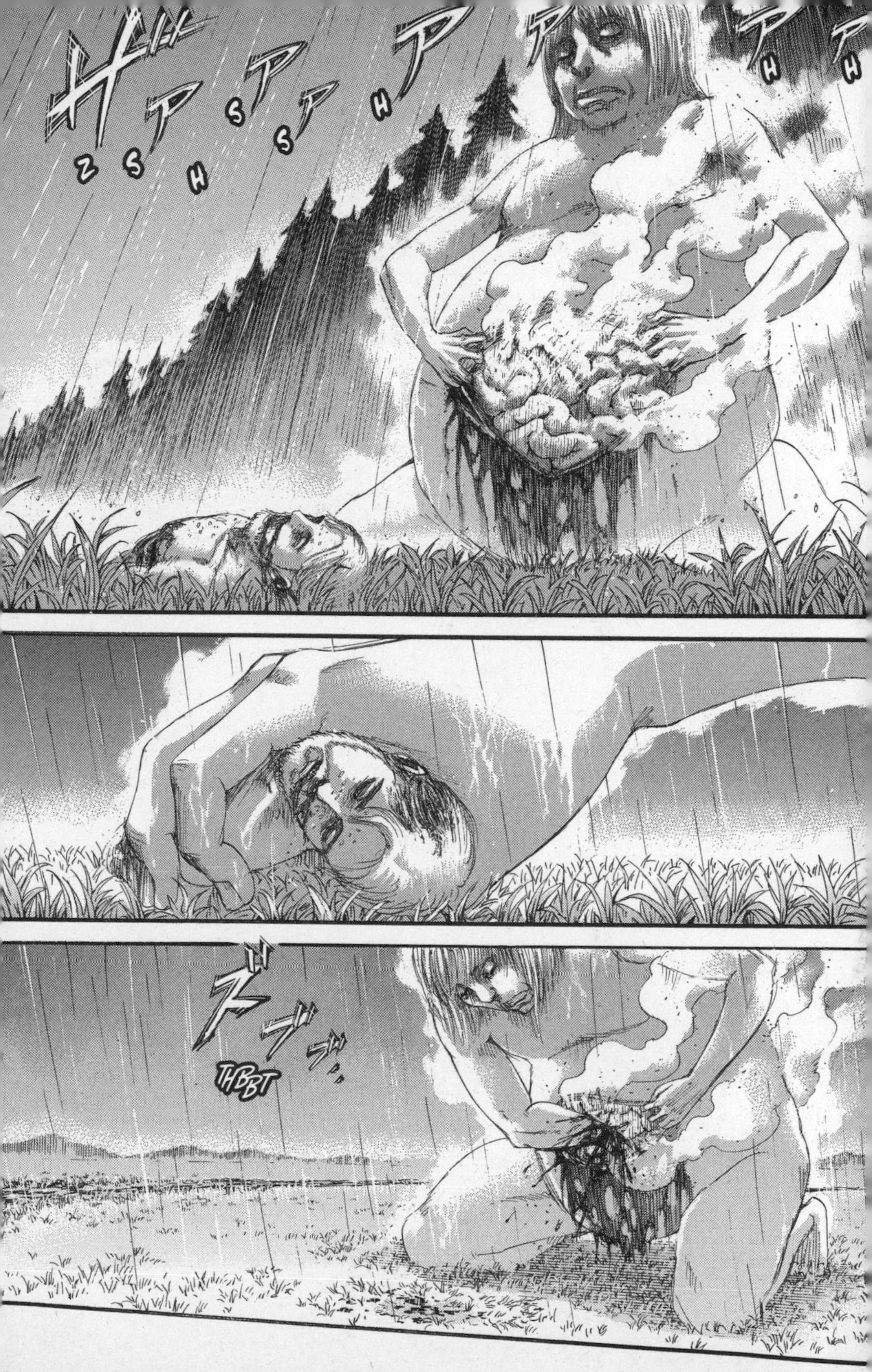
ZSHSSHHH
THBBT

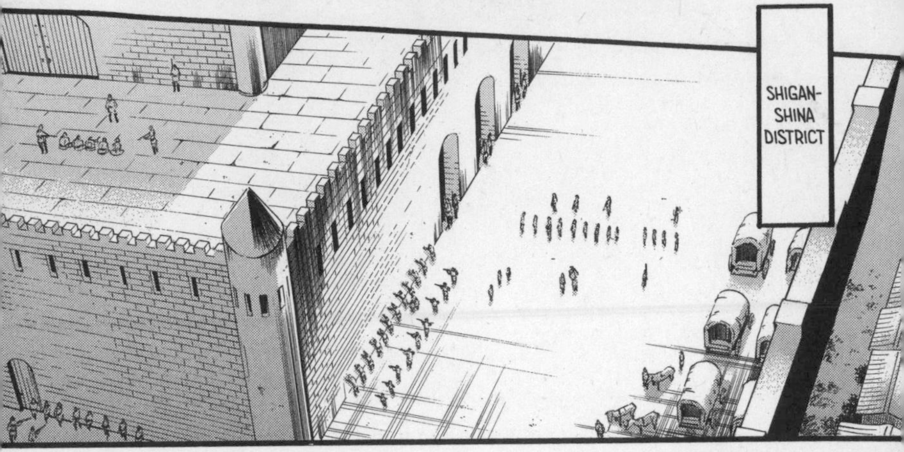
SHIGAN-
SHINA
DISTRICT
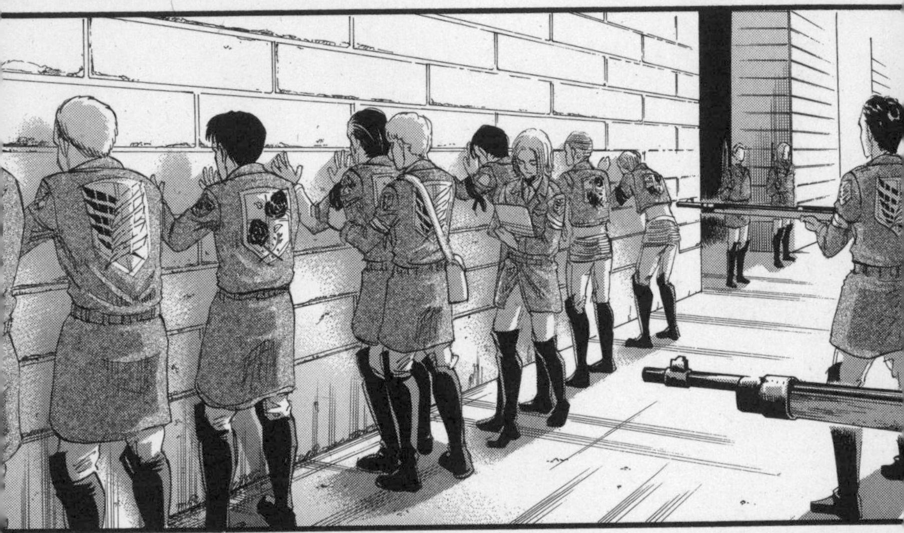
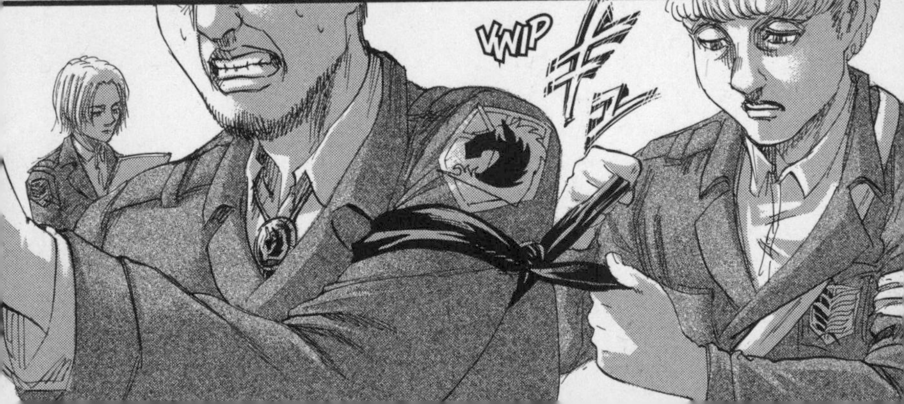
VWIP

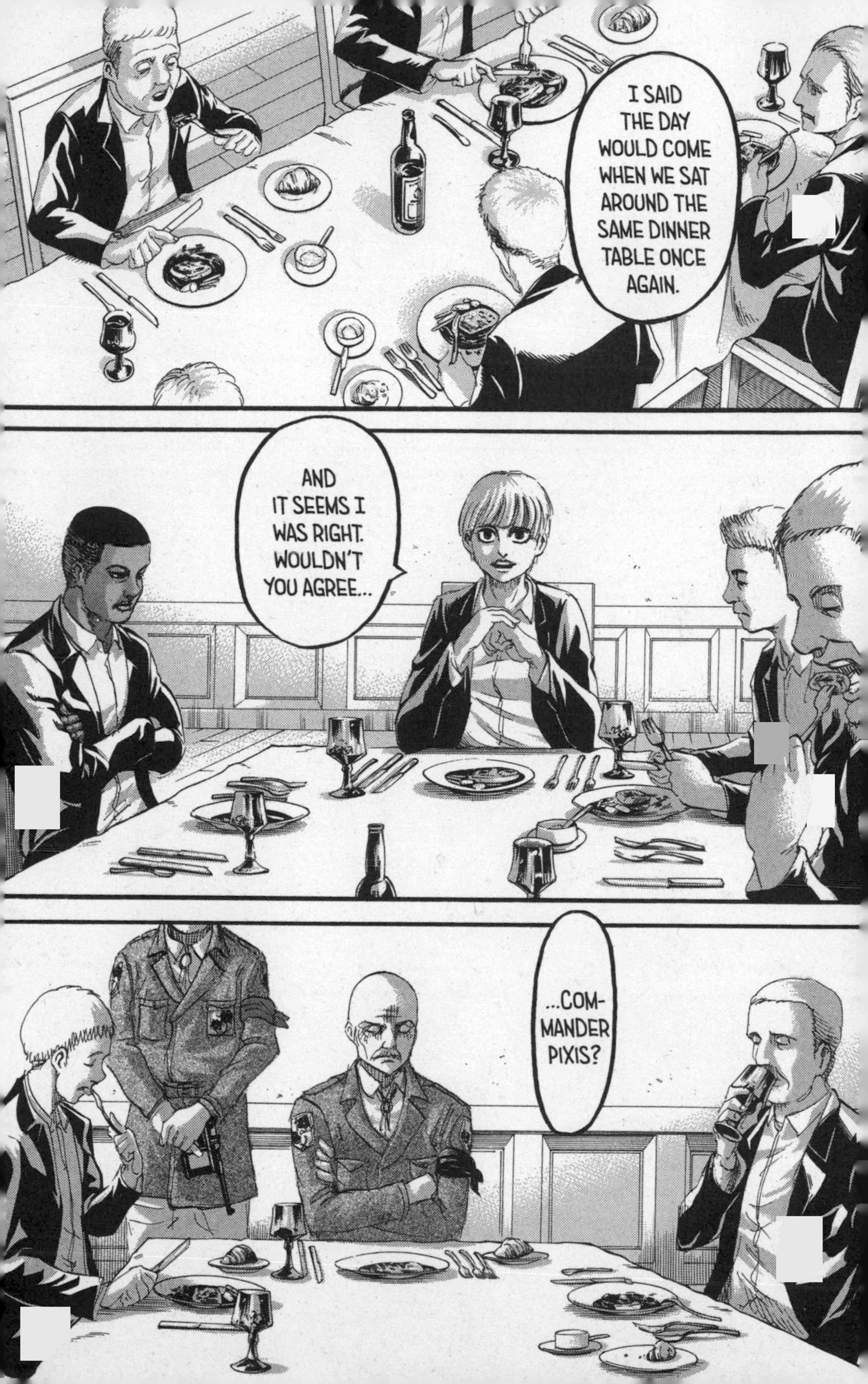
I SAID THE DAY WOULD COME WHEN WE SAT AROUND THE SAME DINNER TABLE ONCE AGAIN.
AND IT SEEMS I WAS RIGHT. WOULDN'T YOU AGREE...
...COM-MANDER PIXIS?

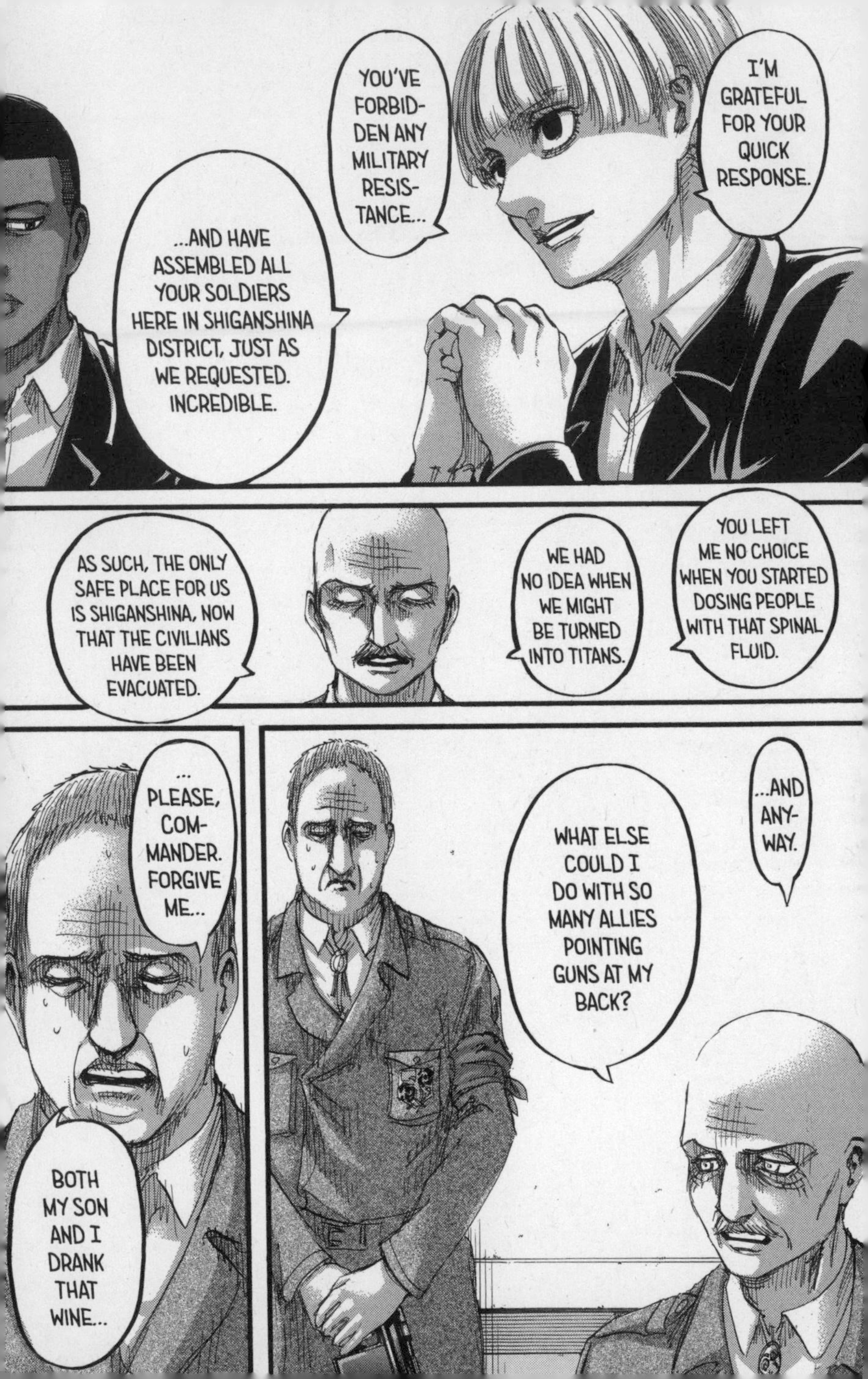
I'M GRATEFUL FOR YOUR QUICK RESPONSE.
YOU'VE FORBIDDEN ANY MILITARY RESISTANCE...
...AND HAVE ASSEMBLED ALL YOUR SOLDIERS HERE IN SHIGANSHINA DISTRICT, JUST AS WE REQUESTED. INCREDIBLE.
YOU LEFT ME NO CHOICE WHEN YOU STARTED DOSING PEOPLE WITH THAT SPINAL FLUID.
WE HAD NO IDEA WHEN WE MIGHT BE TURNED INTO TITANS.
AS SUCH, THE ONLY SAFE PLACE FOR US IS SHIGANSHINA, NOW THAT THE CIVILIANS HAVE BEEN EVACUATED.
...AND ANYWAY.
WHAT ELSE COULD I DO WITH SO MANY ALLIES POINTING GUNS AT MY BACK?
... PLEASE, COMMANDER. FORGIVE ME...
BOTH MY SON AND I DRANK THAT WINE...

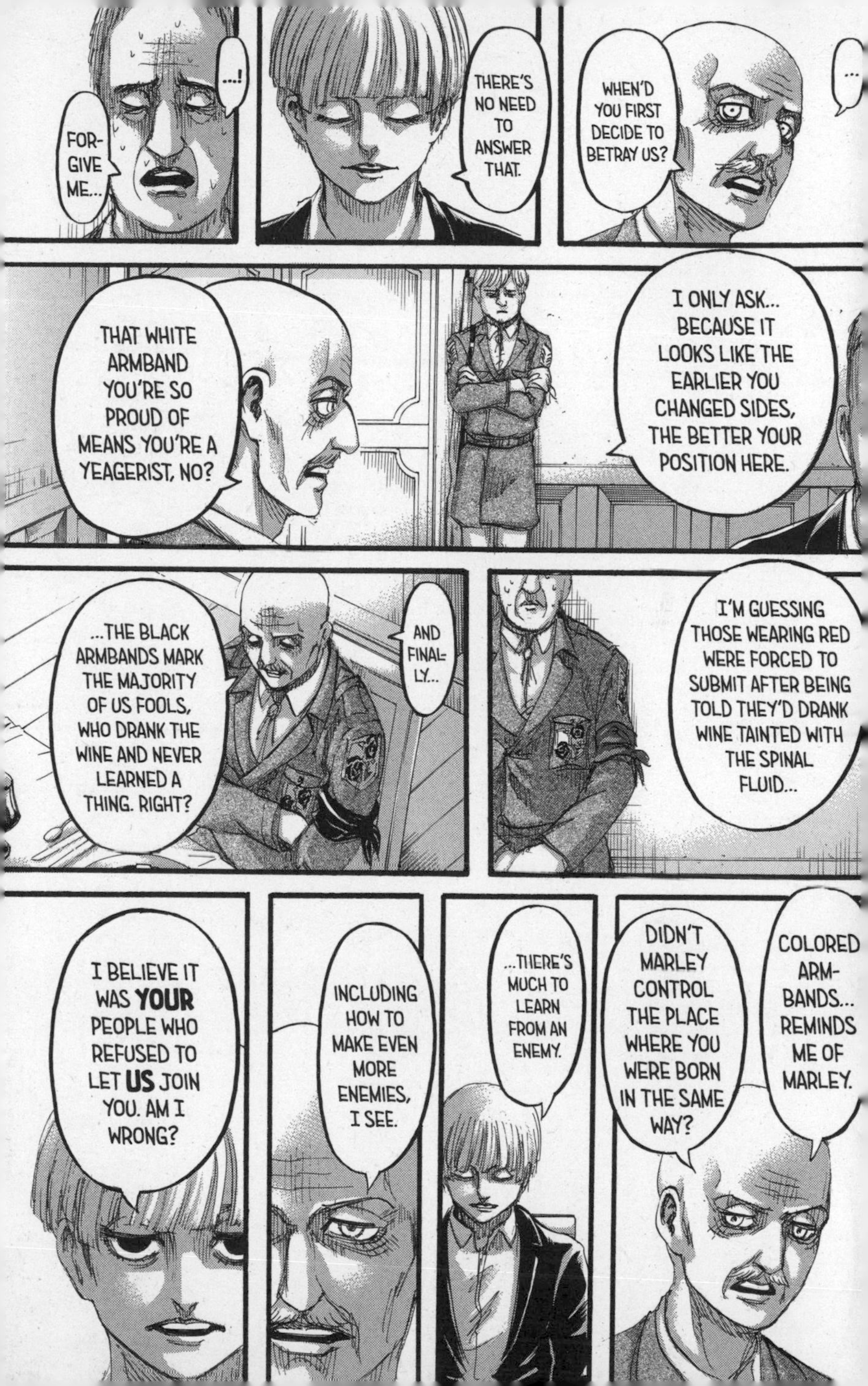
...
WHEN'D YOU FIRST DECIDE TO BETRAY US?
THERE'S NO NEED TO ANSWER THAT.
...!
FOR-GIVE ME...
I ONLY ASK... BECAUSE IT LOOKS LIKE THE EARLIER YOU CHANGED SIDES, THE BETTER YOUR POSITION HERE.
THAT WHITE ARMBAND YOU'RE SO PROUD OF MEANS YOU'RE A YEAGERIST, NO?
I'M GUESSING THOSE WEARING RED WERE FORCED TO SUBMIT AFTER BEING TOLD THEY'D DRANK WINE TAINTED WITH THE SPINAL FLUID...
AND FINAL-LY...
...THE BLACK ARMBANDS MARK THE MAJORITY OF US FOOLS, WHO DRANK THE WINE AND NEVER LEARNED A THING. RIGHT?
COLORED ARM-BANDS... REMINDS ME OF MARLEY.
DIDN'T MARLEY CONTROL THE PLACE WHERE YOU WERE BORN IN THE SAME WAY?
...THERE'S MUCH TO LEARN FROM AN ENEMY.
INCLUDING HOW TO MAKE EVEN MORE ENEMIES, I SEE.
I BELIEVE IT WAS **YOUR** PEOPLE WHO REFUSED TO LET **US** JOIN YOU. AM I WRONG?

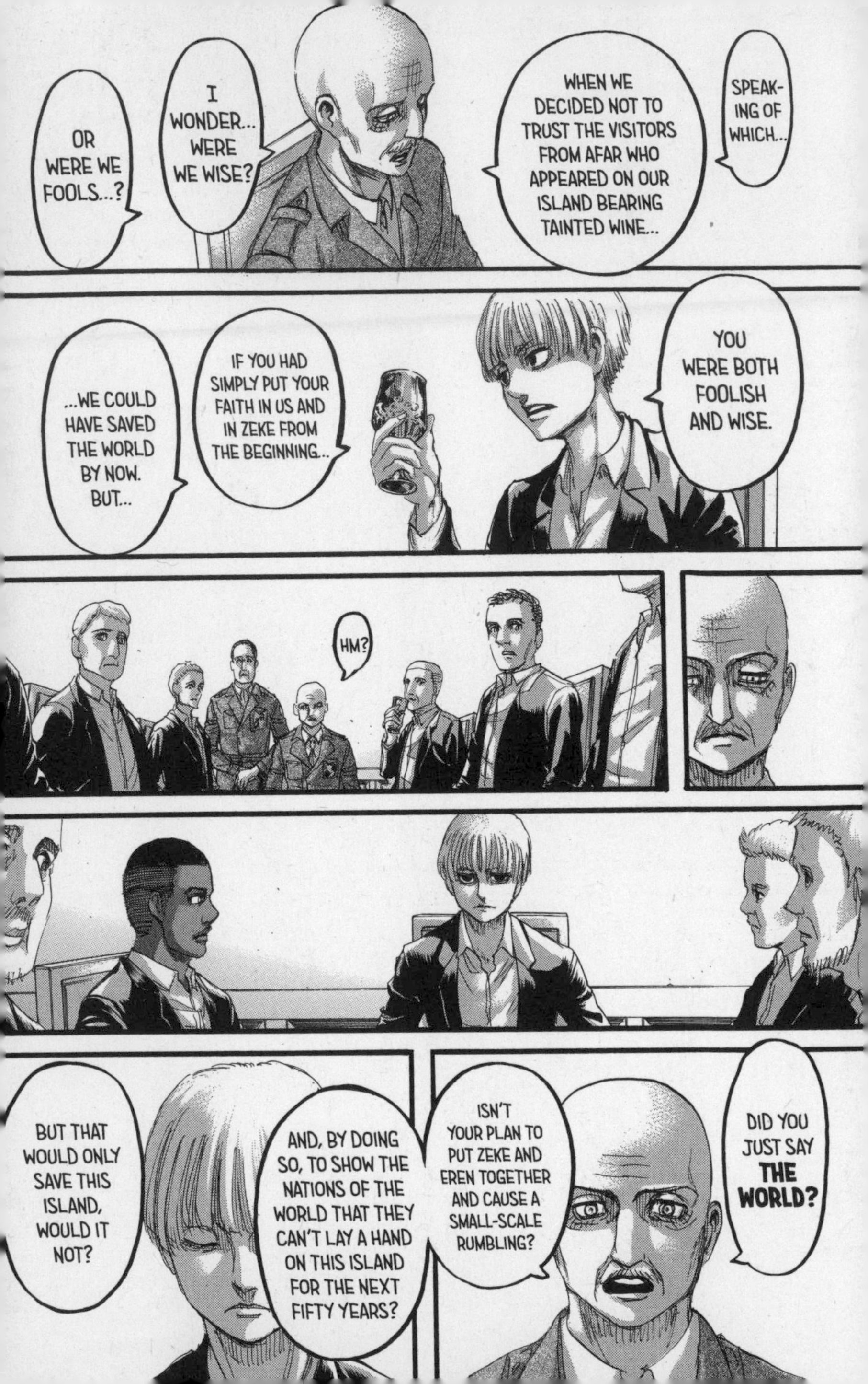
SPEAK-ING OF WHICH...
WHEN WE DECIDED NOT TO TRUST THE VISITORS FROM AFAR WHO APPEARED ON OUR ISLAND BEARING TAINTED WINE...
I WONDER... WERE WE WISE?
OR WERE WE FOOLS...?
YOU WERE BOTH FOOLISH AND WISE.
IF YOU HAD SIMPLY PUT YOUR FAITH IN US AND IN ZEKE FROM THE BEGINNING...
...WE COULD HAVE SAVED THE WORLD BY NOW. BUT...
HM?
DID YOU JUST SAY **THE WORLD?**
ISN'T YOUR PLAN TO PUT ZEKE AND EREN TOGETHER AND CAUSE A SMALL-SCALE RUMBLING?
AND, BY DOING SO, TO SHOW THE NATIONS OF THE WORLD THAT THEY CAN'T LAY A HAND ON THIS ISLAND FOR THE NEXT FIFTY YEARS?
BUT THAT WOULD ONLY SAVE THIS ISLAND, WOULD IT NOT?

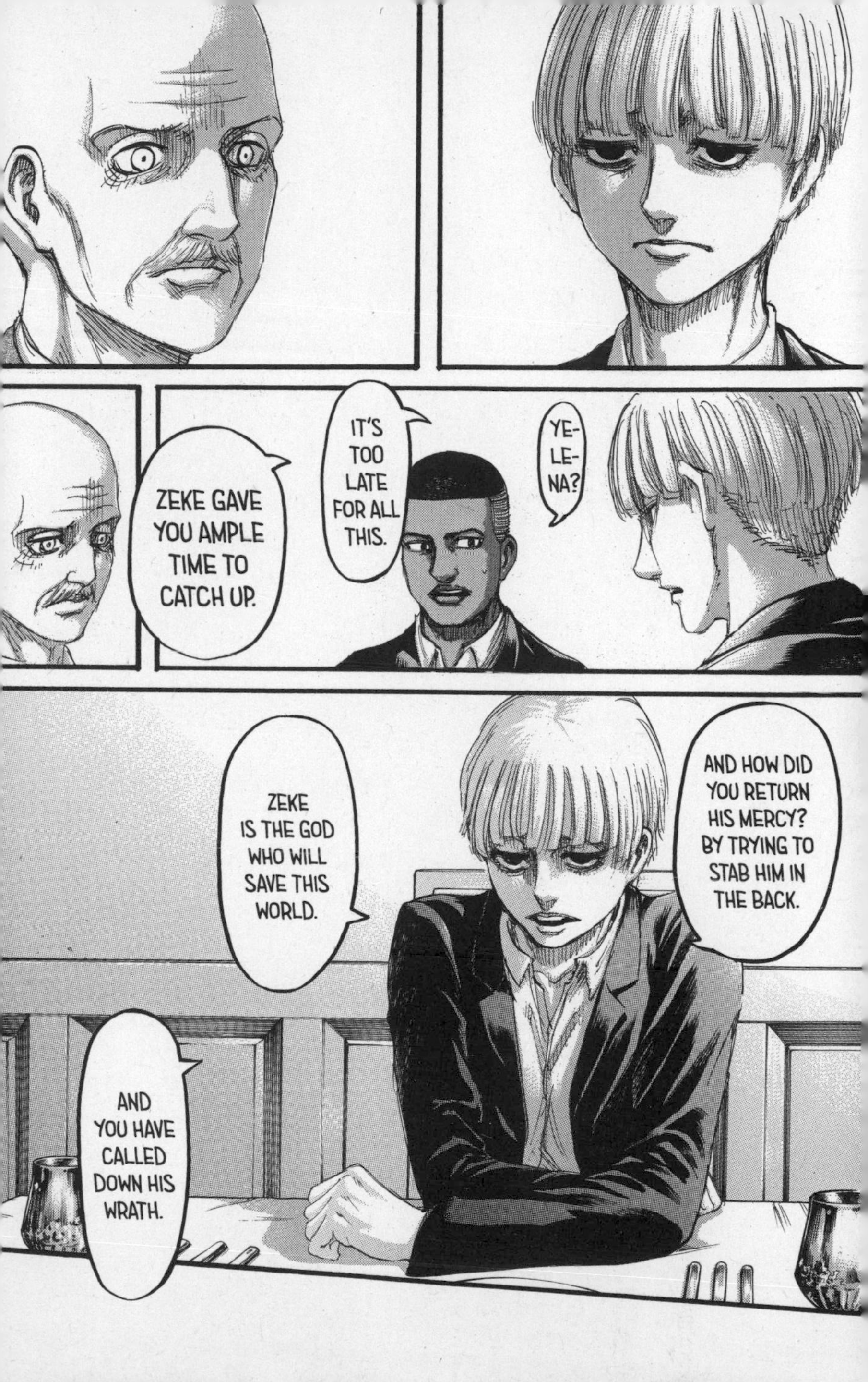
YE-LE-NA?
IT'S TOO LATE FOR ALL THIS.
ZEKE GAVE YOU AMPLE TIME TO CATCH UP.
AND HOW DID YOU RETURN HIS MERCY? BY TRYING TO STAB HIM IN THE BACK.
ZEKE IS THE GOD WHO WILL SAVE THIS WORLD.
AND YOU HAVE CALLED DOWN HIS WRATH.

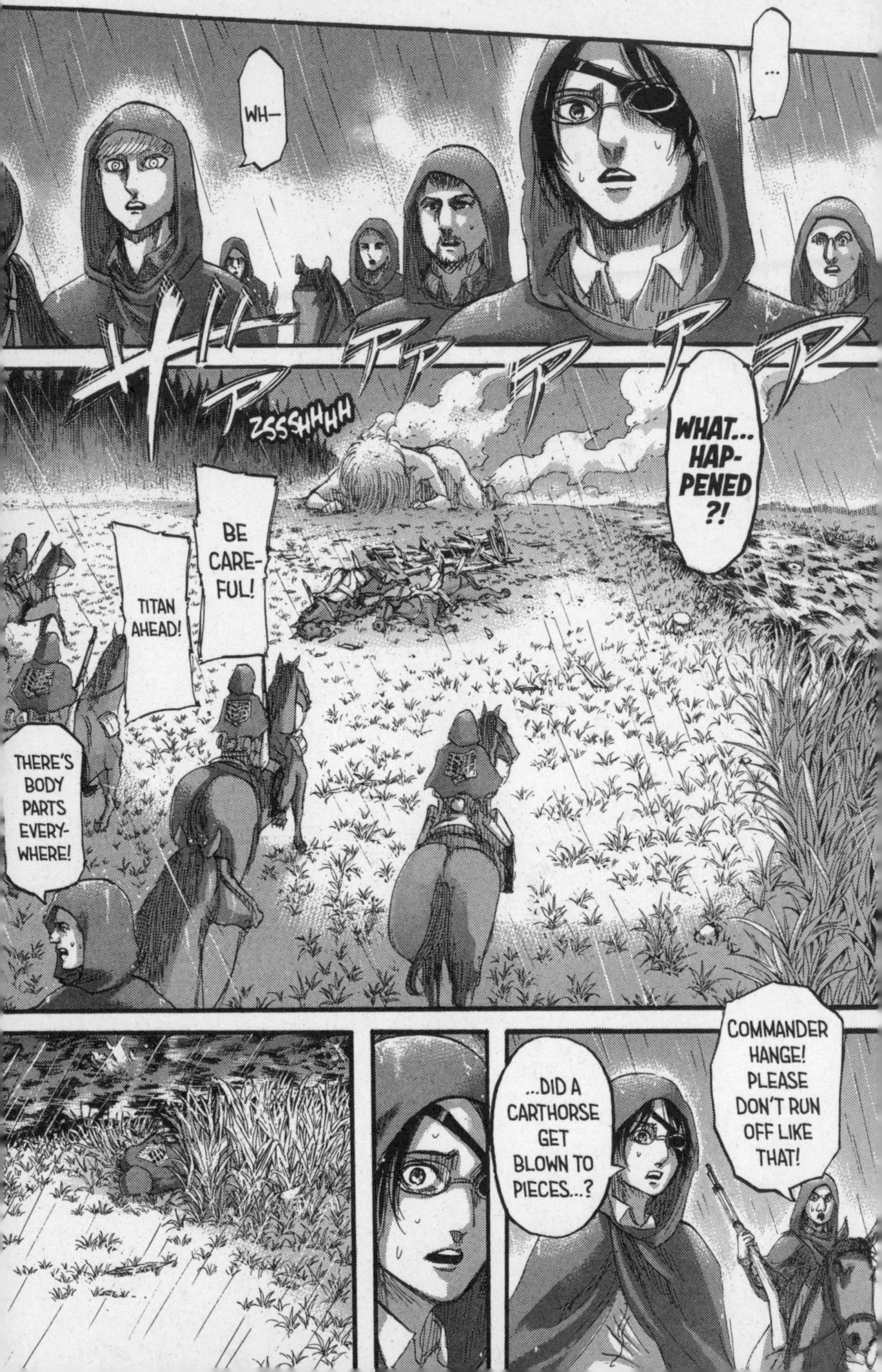
...
WH—
WHAT... HAP-PENED?!
ZSSSHHHH
BE CARE-FUL!
TITAN AHEAD!
THERE'S BODY PARTS EVERY-WHERE!
COMMANDER HANGE! PLEASE DON'T RUN OFF LIKE THAT!
...DID A CARTHORSE GET BLOWN TO PIECES...?

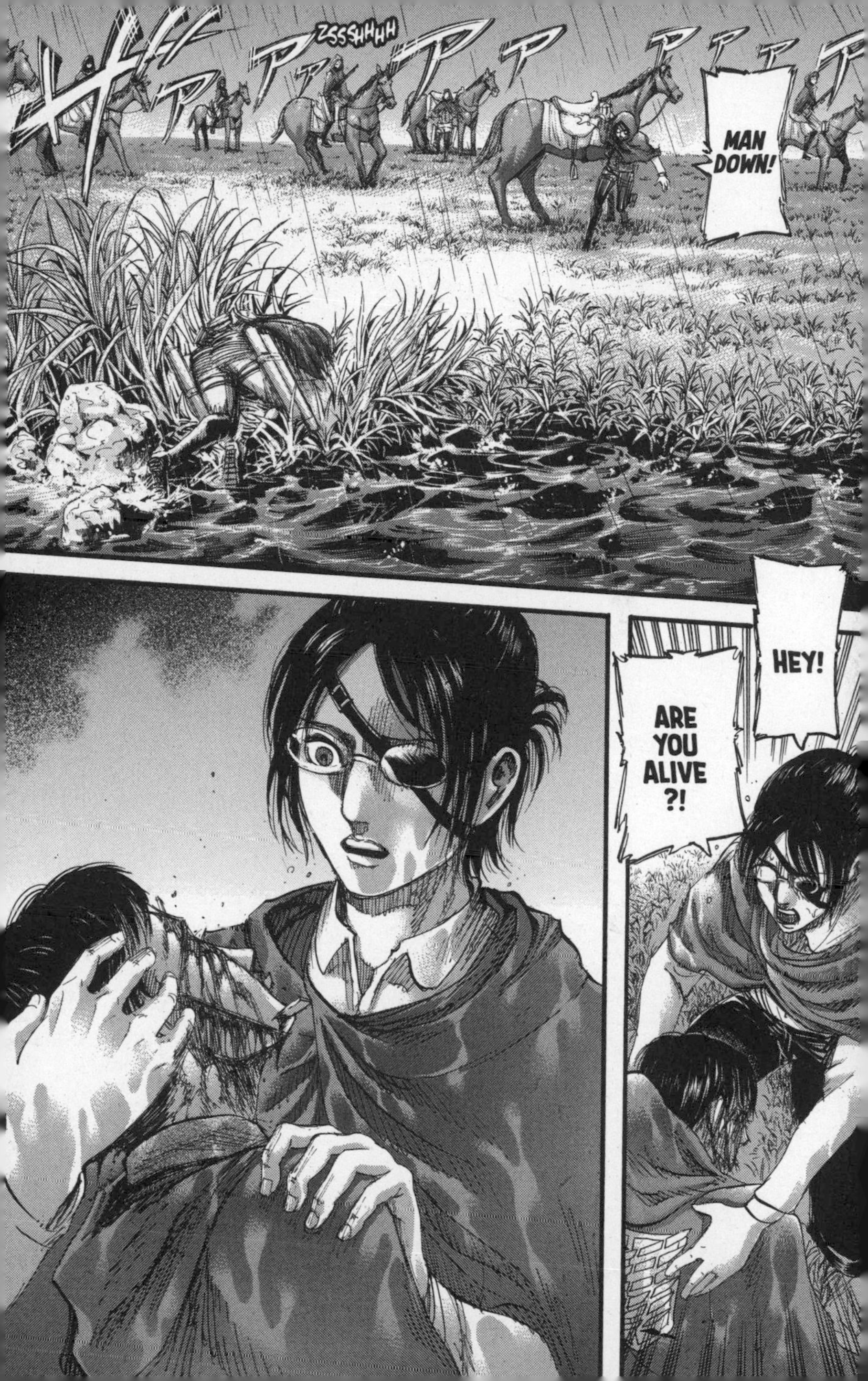
ZSSSHHHH
MAN DOWN!
HEY!
ARE YOU ALIVE ?!

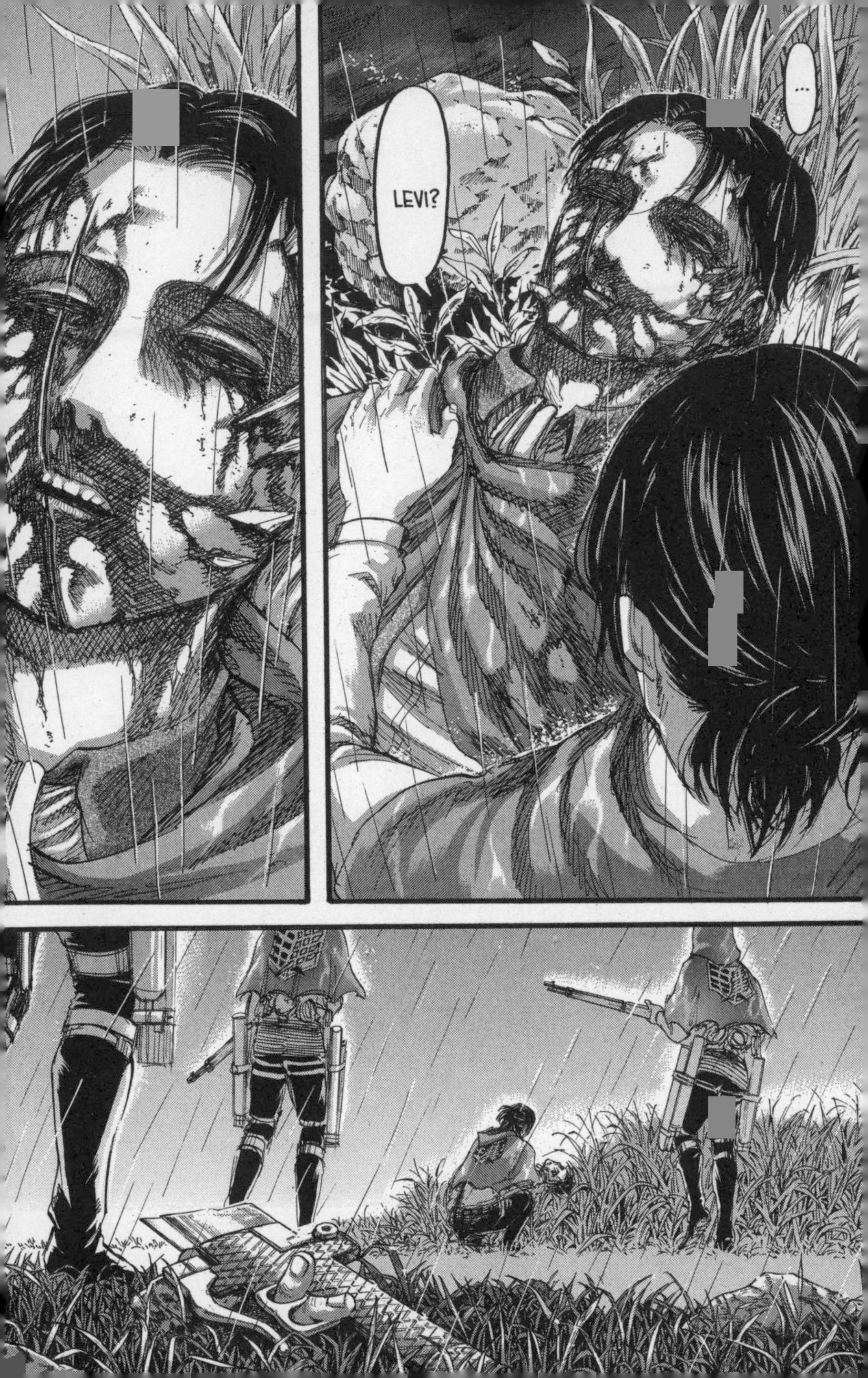
...
LEVI?

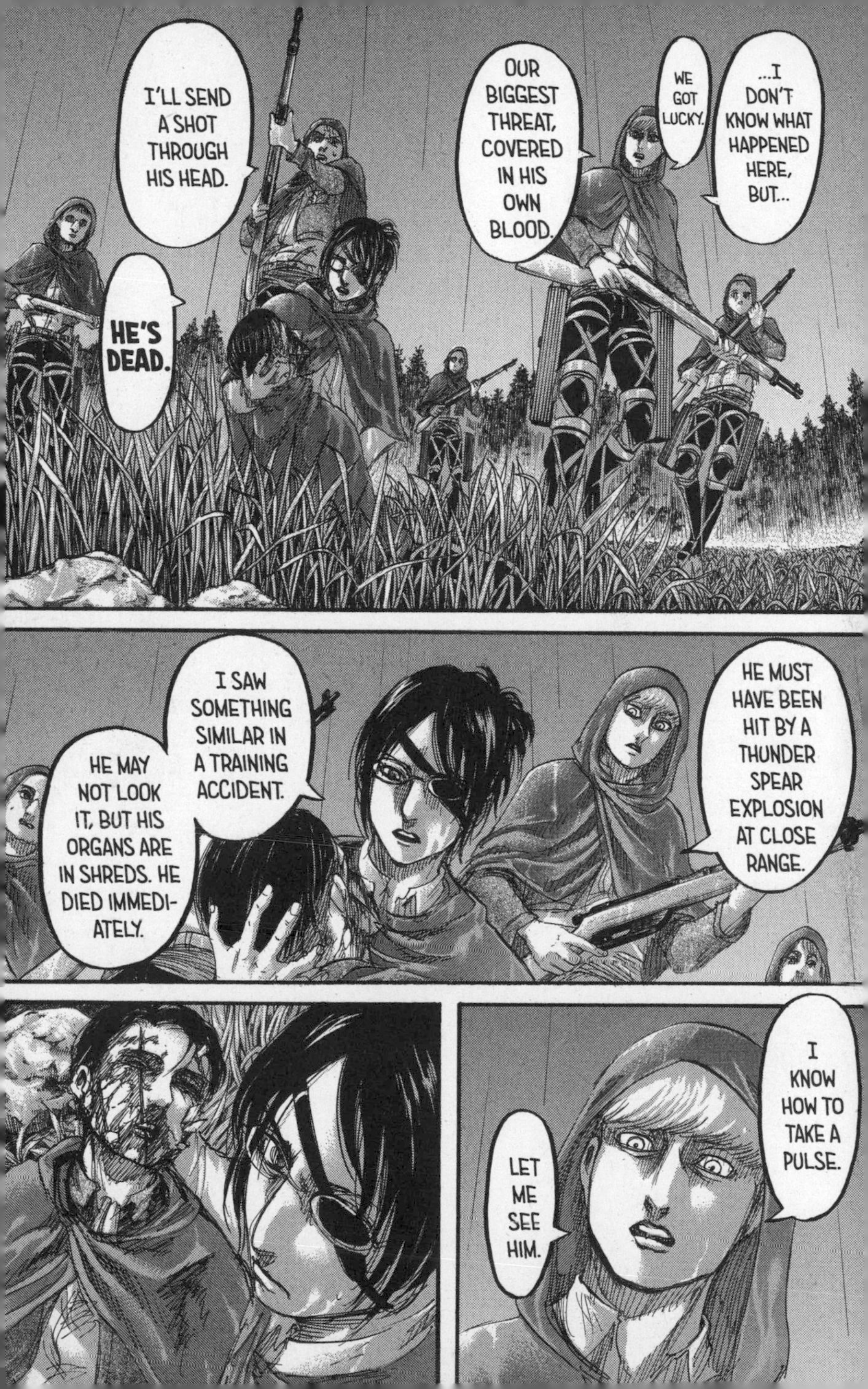
...I DON'T KNOW WHAT HAPPENED HERE, BUT...
WE GOT LUCKY.
OUR BIGGEST THREAT, COVERED IN HIS OWN BLOOD.
I'LL SEND A SHOT THROUGH HIS HEAD.
HE'S DEAD.
HE MUST HAVE BEEN HIT BY A THUNDER SPEAR EXPLOSION AT CLOSE RANGE.
I SAW SOMETHING SIMILAR IN A TRAINING ACCIDENT.
HE MAY NOT LOOK IT, BUT HIS ORGANS ARE IN SHREDS. HE DIED IMMEDI-ATELY.
I KNOW HOW TO TAKE A PULSE.
LET ME SEE HIM.

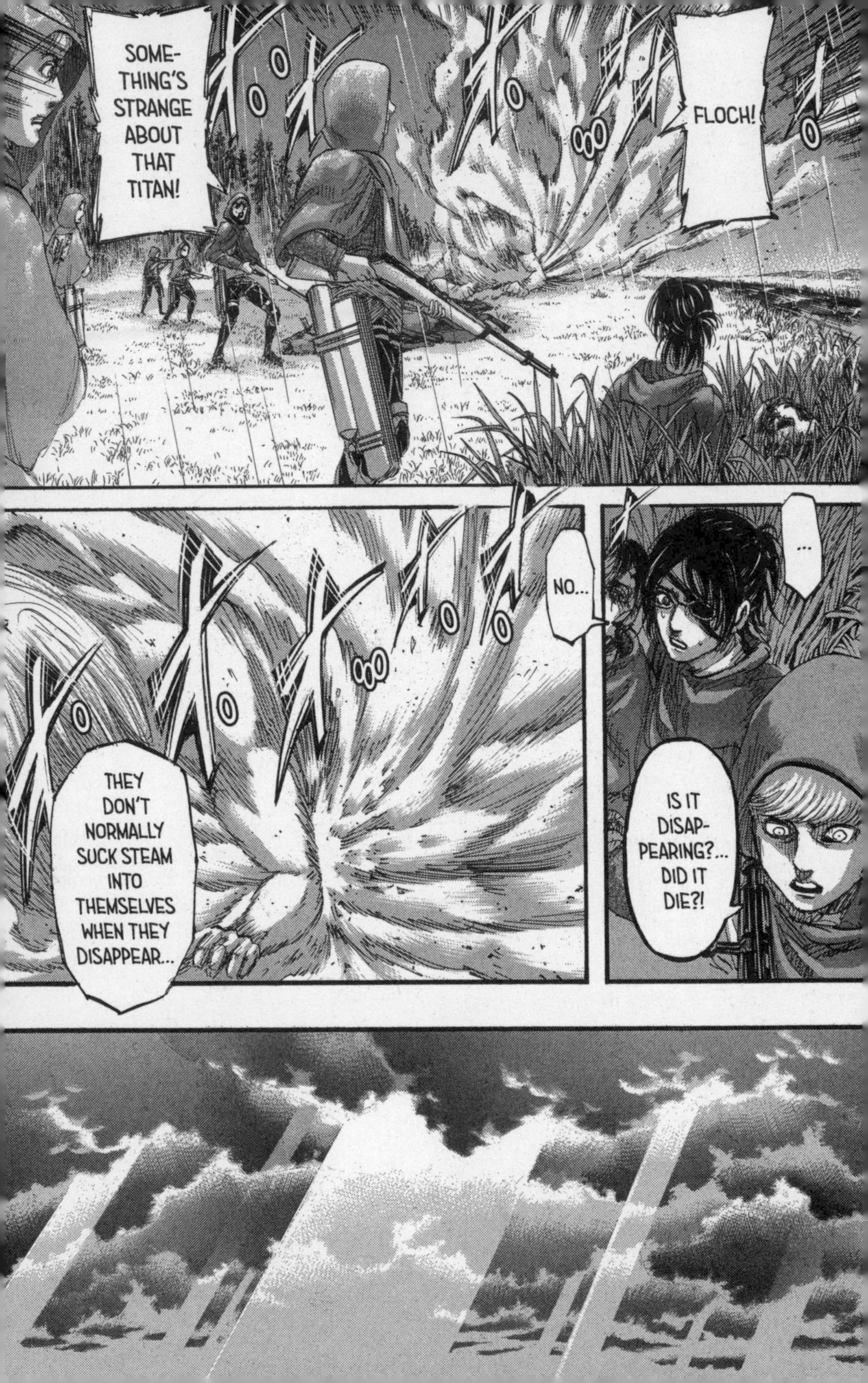
FLOCH!
SOME-THING'S STRANGE ABOUT THAT TITAN!
...
NO...
IS IT DISAP-PEARING?... DID IT DIE?!
THEY DON'T NORMALLY SUCK STEAM INTO THEMSELVES WHEN THEY DISAPPEAR...

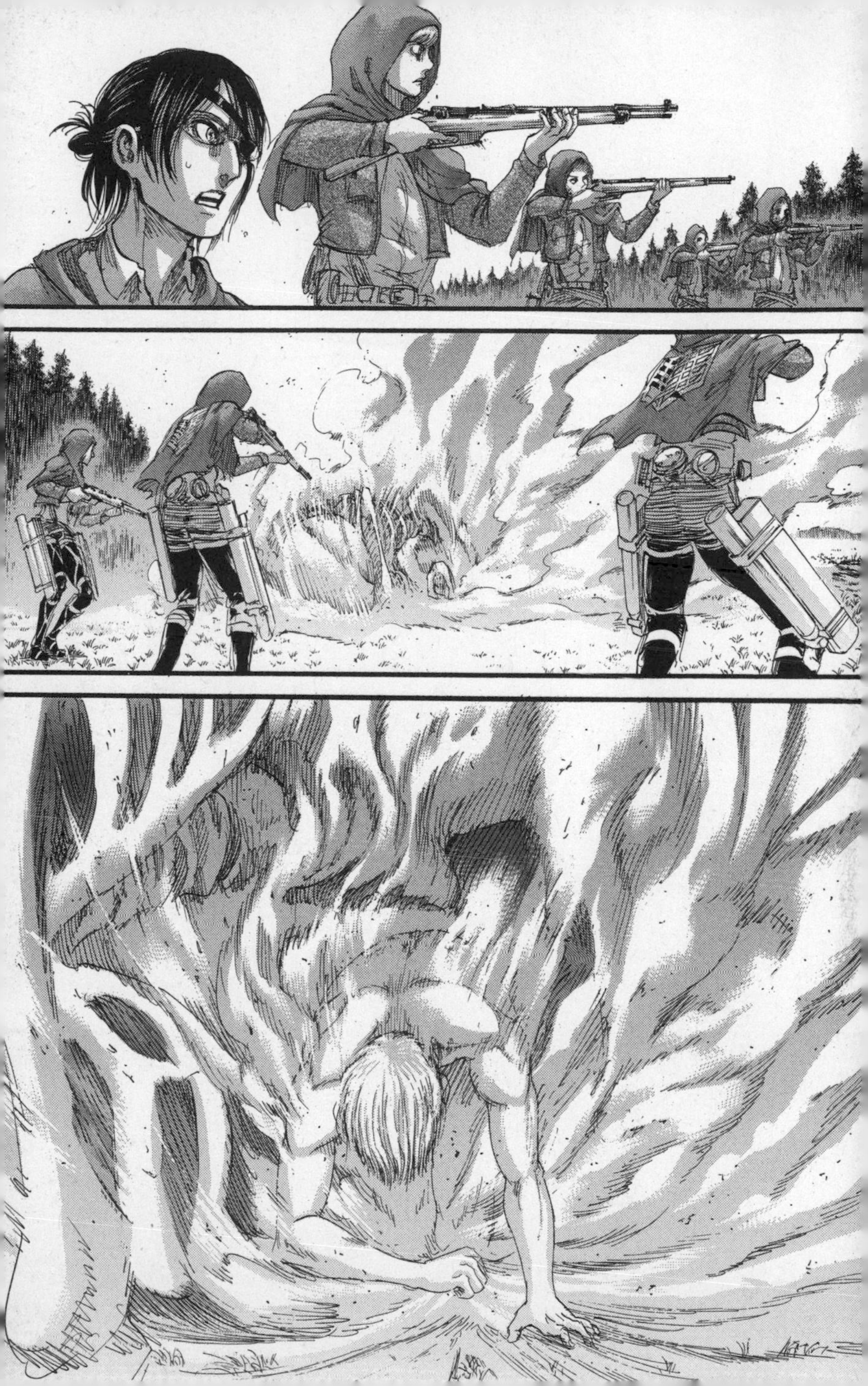

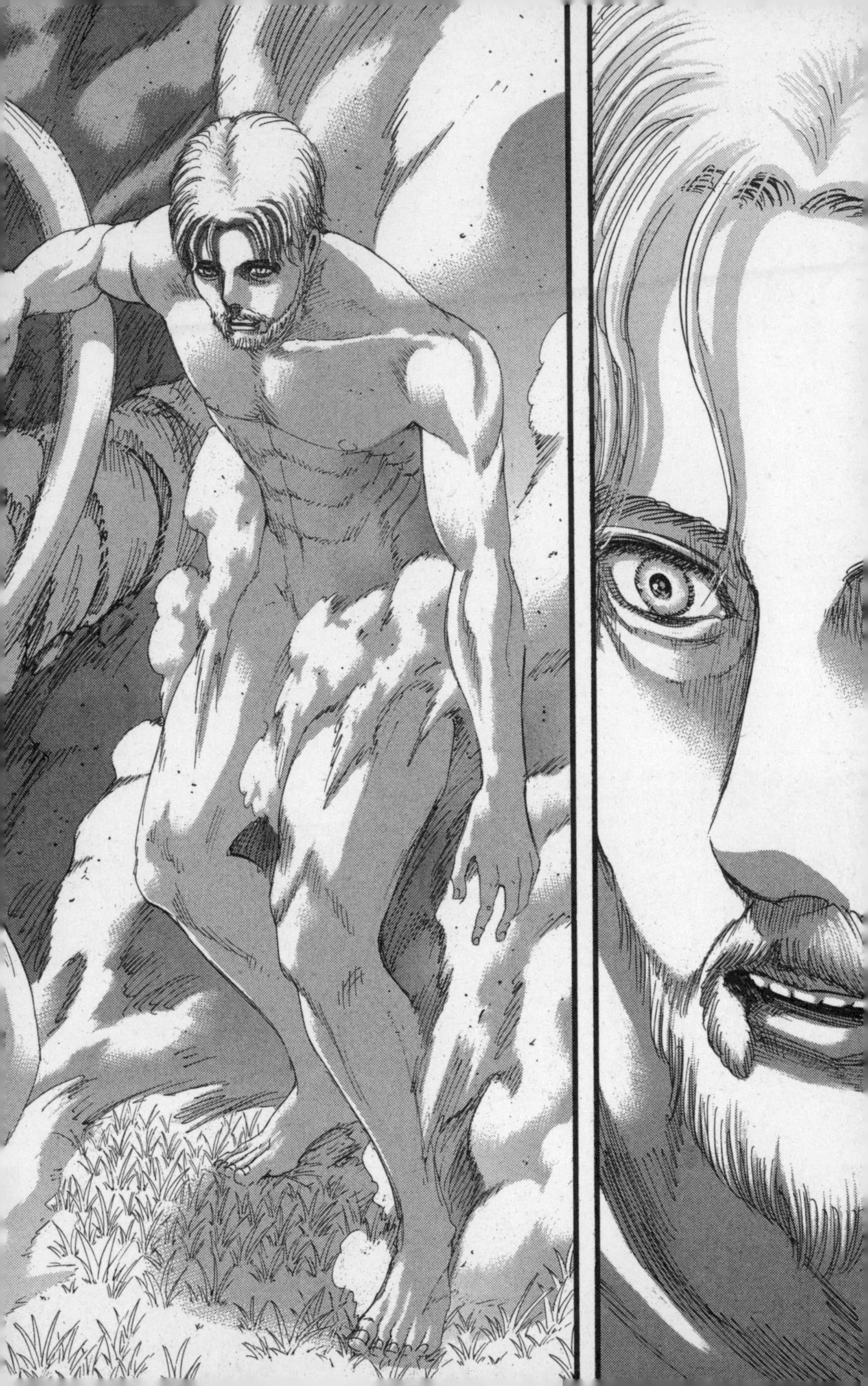

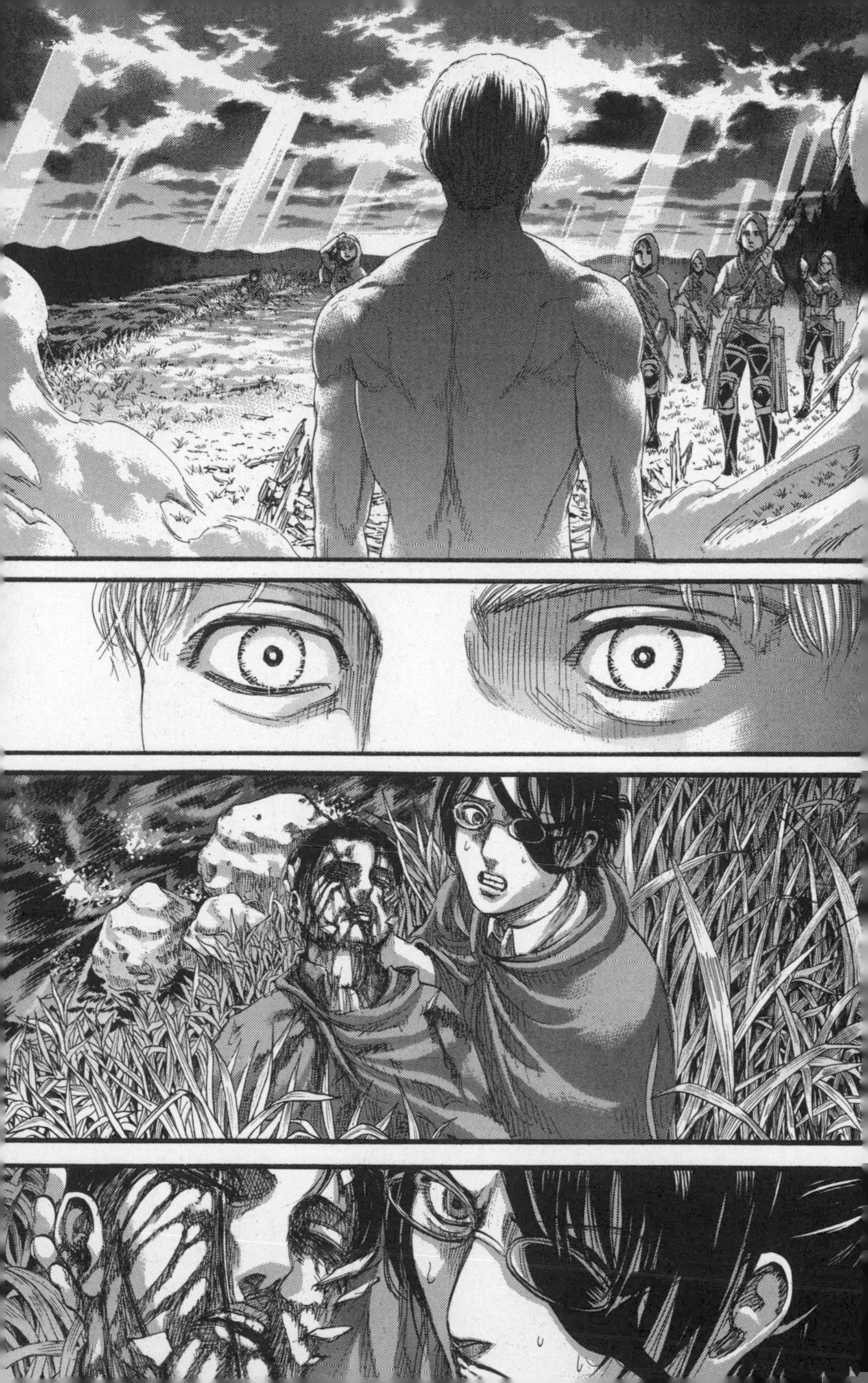

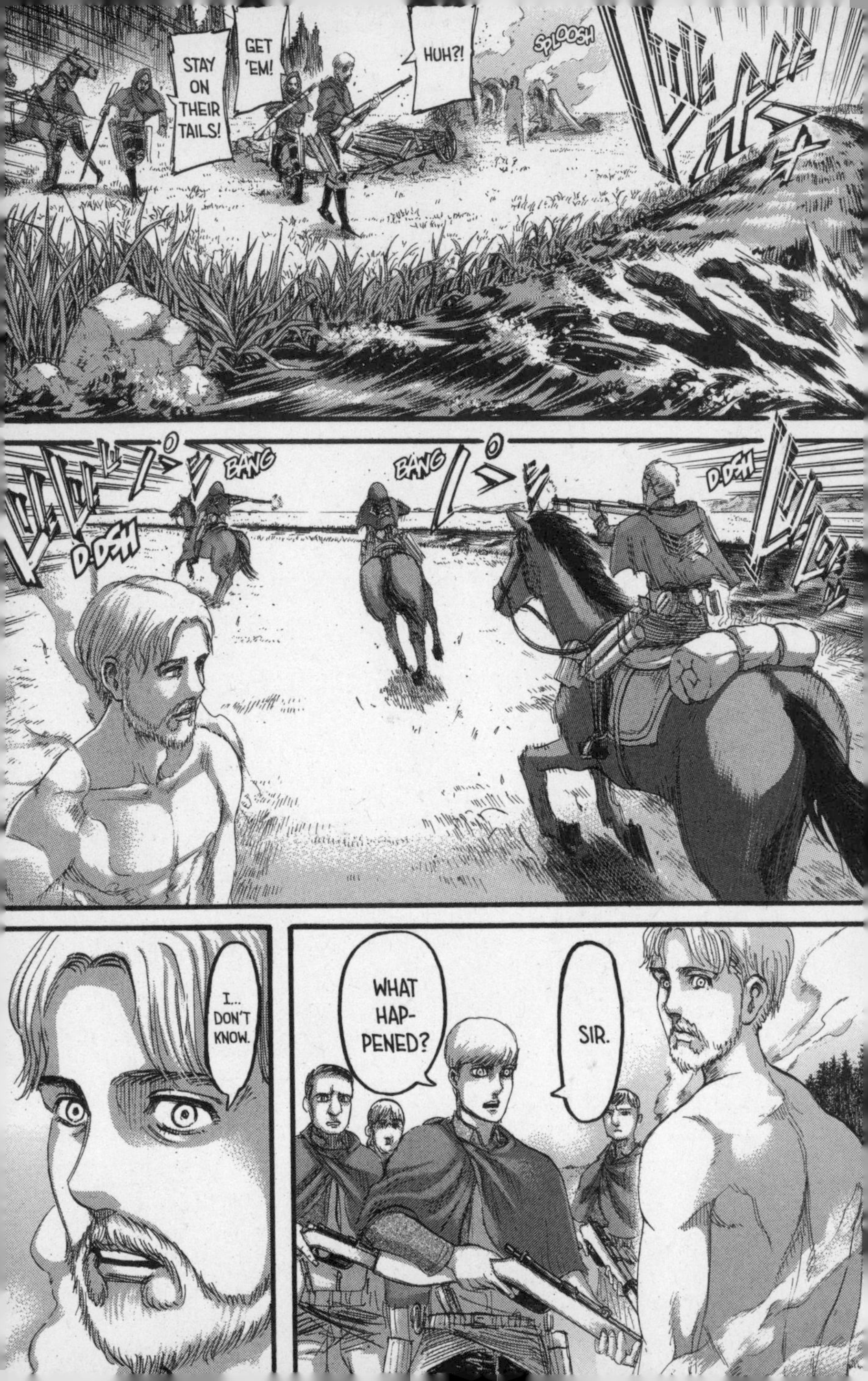
SPLOOSH
HUH?!
GET 'EM!
STAY ON THEIR TAILS!
D-DSH
BANG
BANG
D-DSH
SIR.
WHAT HAP-PENED?
I... DON'T KNOW.

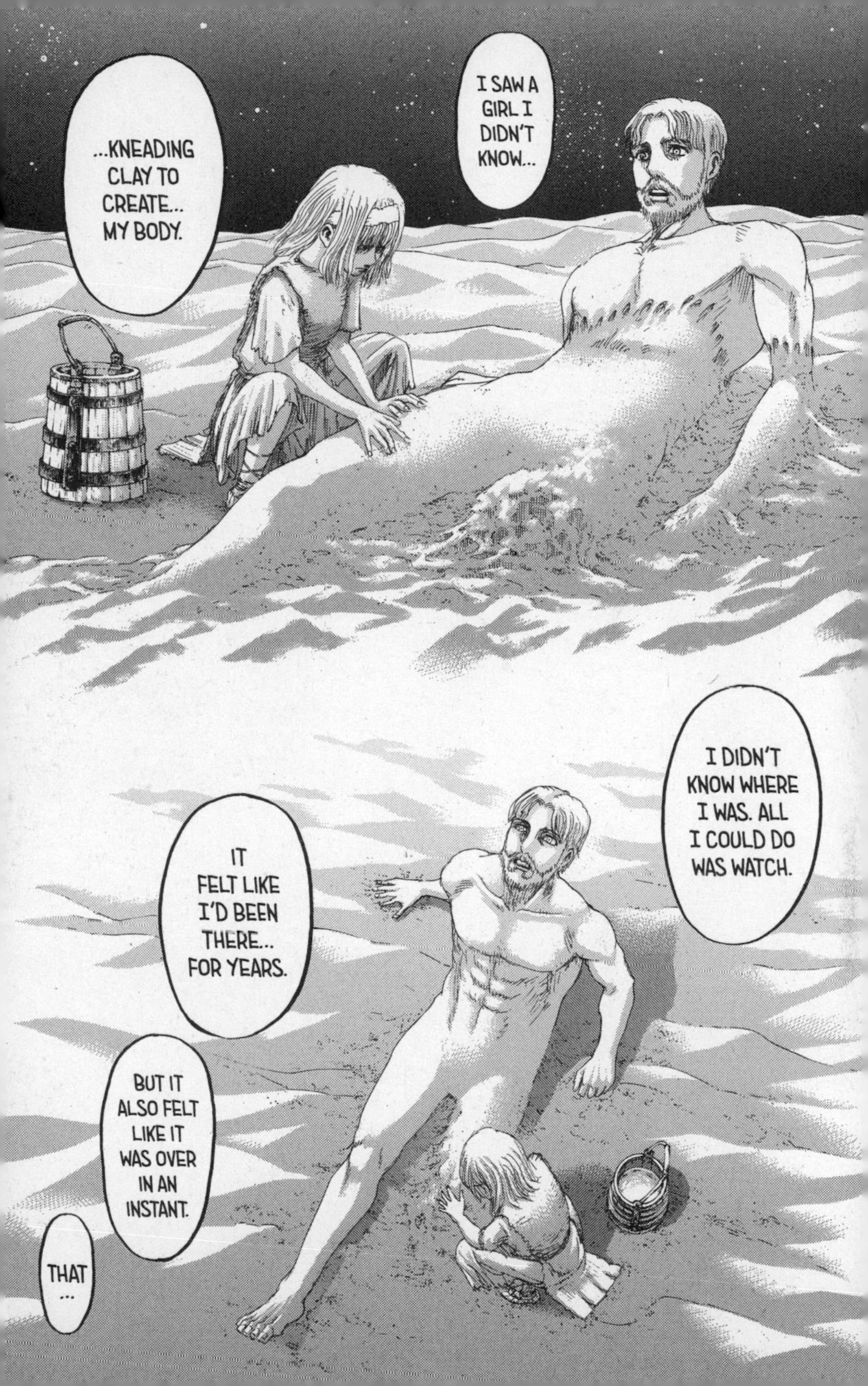
I SAW A GIRL I DIDN'T KNOW...
...KNEADING CLAY TO CREATE... MY BODY.
I DIDN'T KNOW WHERE I WAS. ALL I COULD DO WAS WATCH.
IT FELT LIKE I'D BEEN THERE... FOR YEARS.
BUT IT ALSO FELT LIKE IT WAS OVER IN AN INSTANT.
THAT...

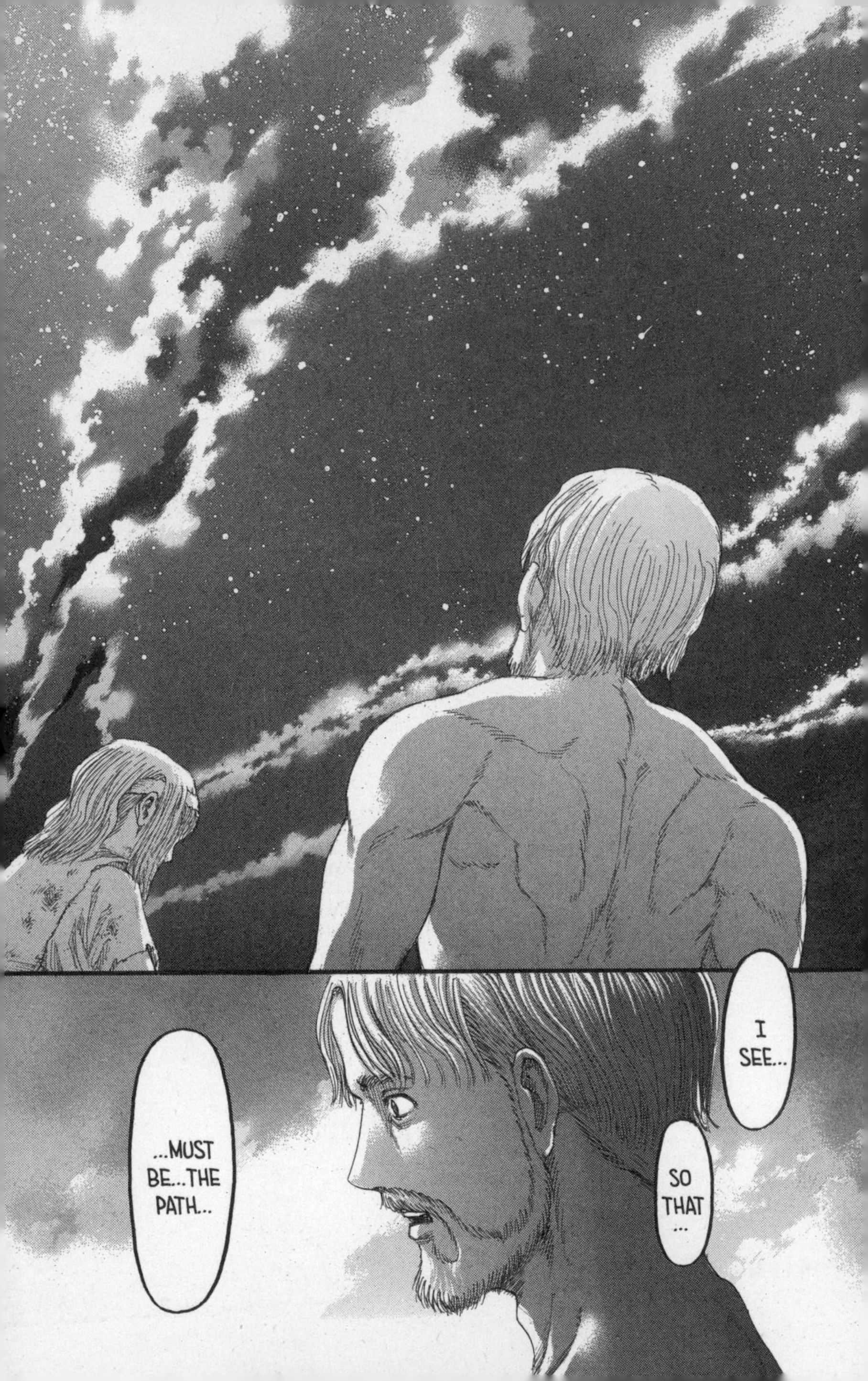
I SEE...
SO THAT ...
...MUST BE...THE PATH...

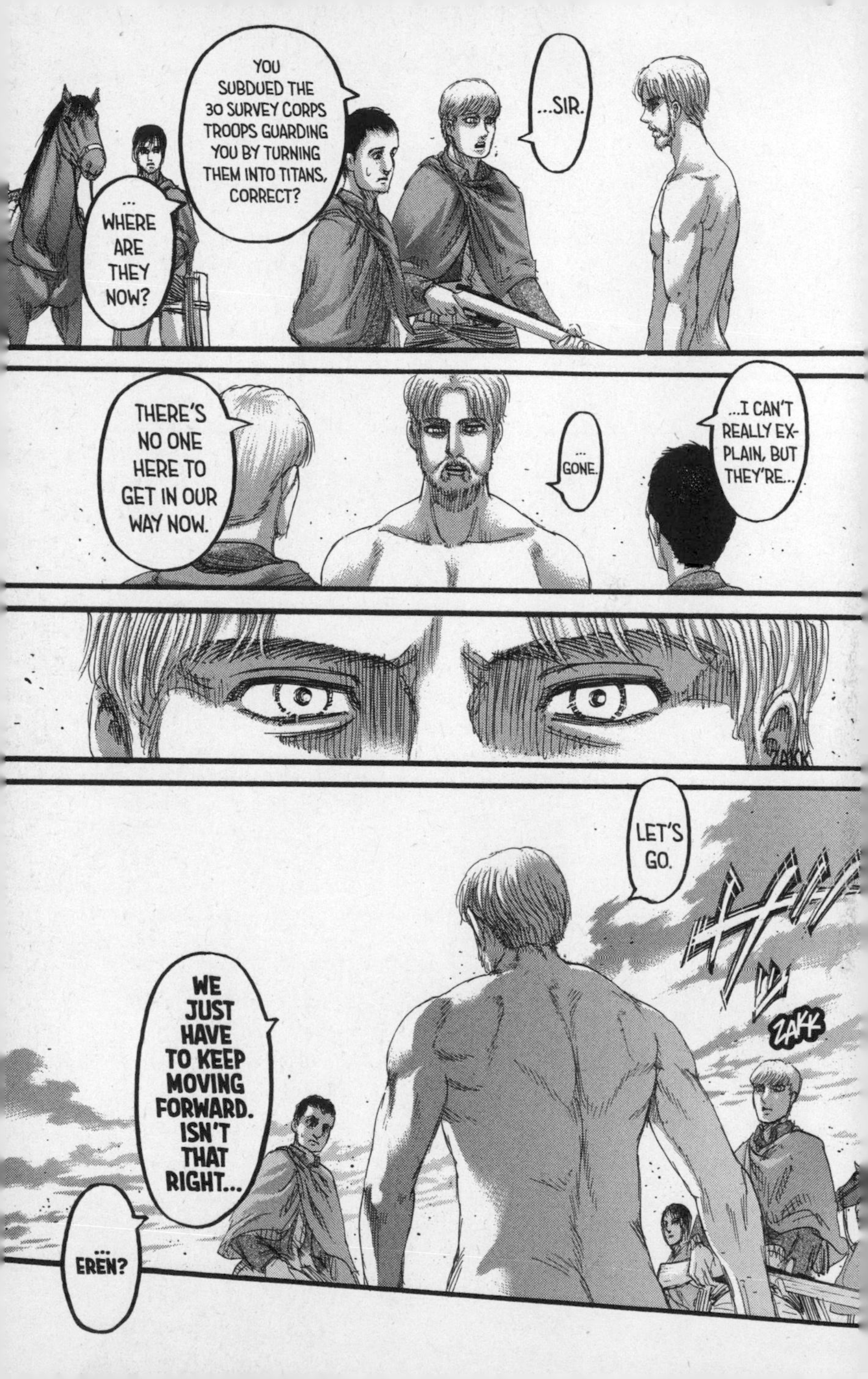
...SIR.
YOU SUBDUED THE 30 SURVEY CORPS TROOPS GUARDING YOU BY TURNING THEM INTO TITANS, CORRECT?
... WHERE ARE THEY NOW?
...I CAN'T REALLY EX-PLAIN, BUT THEY'RE...
... GONE.
THERE'S NO ONE HERE TO GET IN OUR WAY NOW.
ZAKK
LET'S GO.
ZAKK
WE JUST HAVE TO KEEP MOVING FORWARD. ISN'T THAT RIGHT...
... EREN?

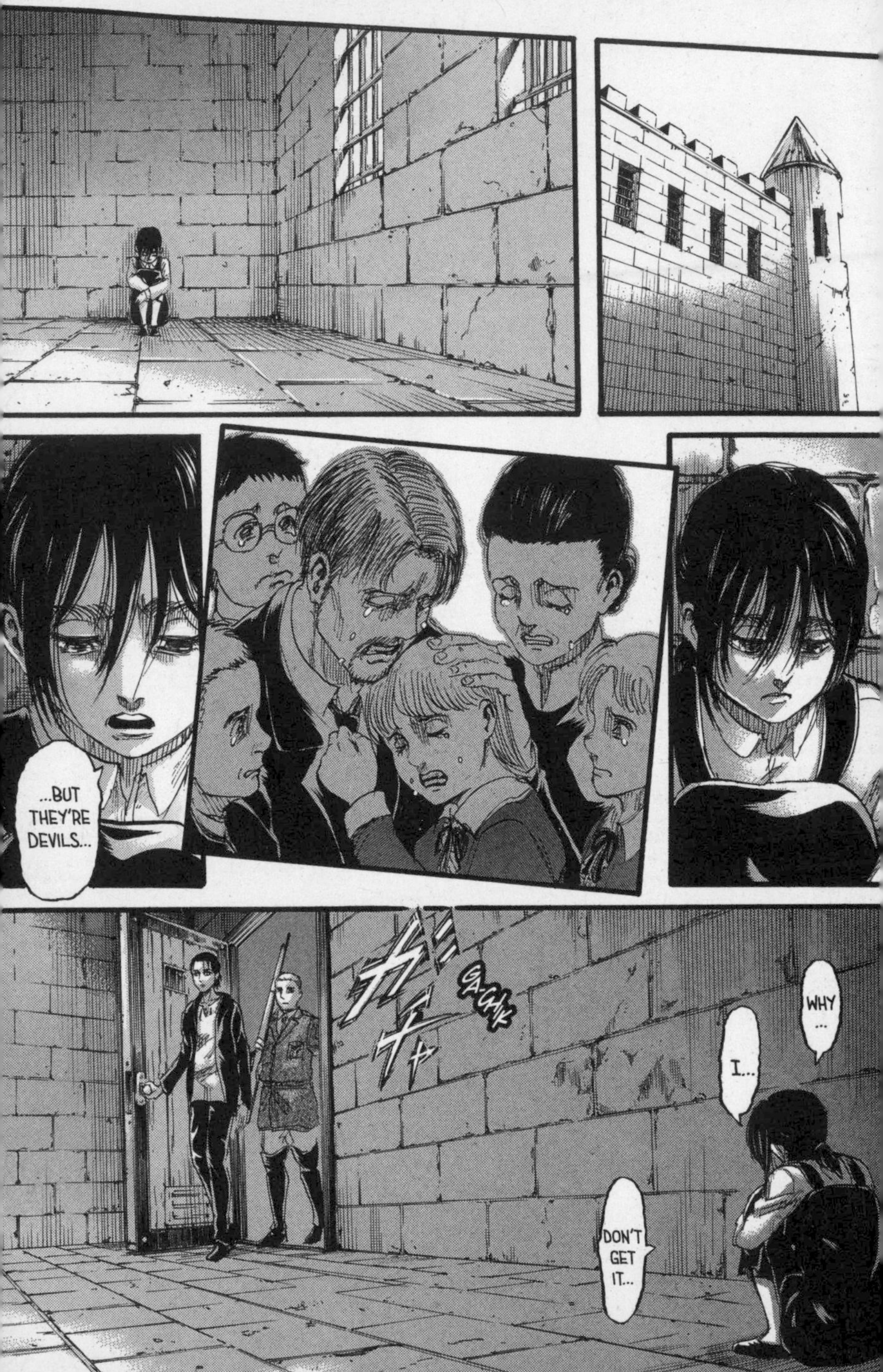
...BUT THEY'RE DEVILS...
WHY ...
I...
DON'T GET IT...
ガチャ
GA-CHAK

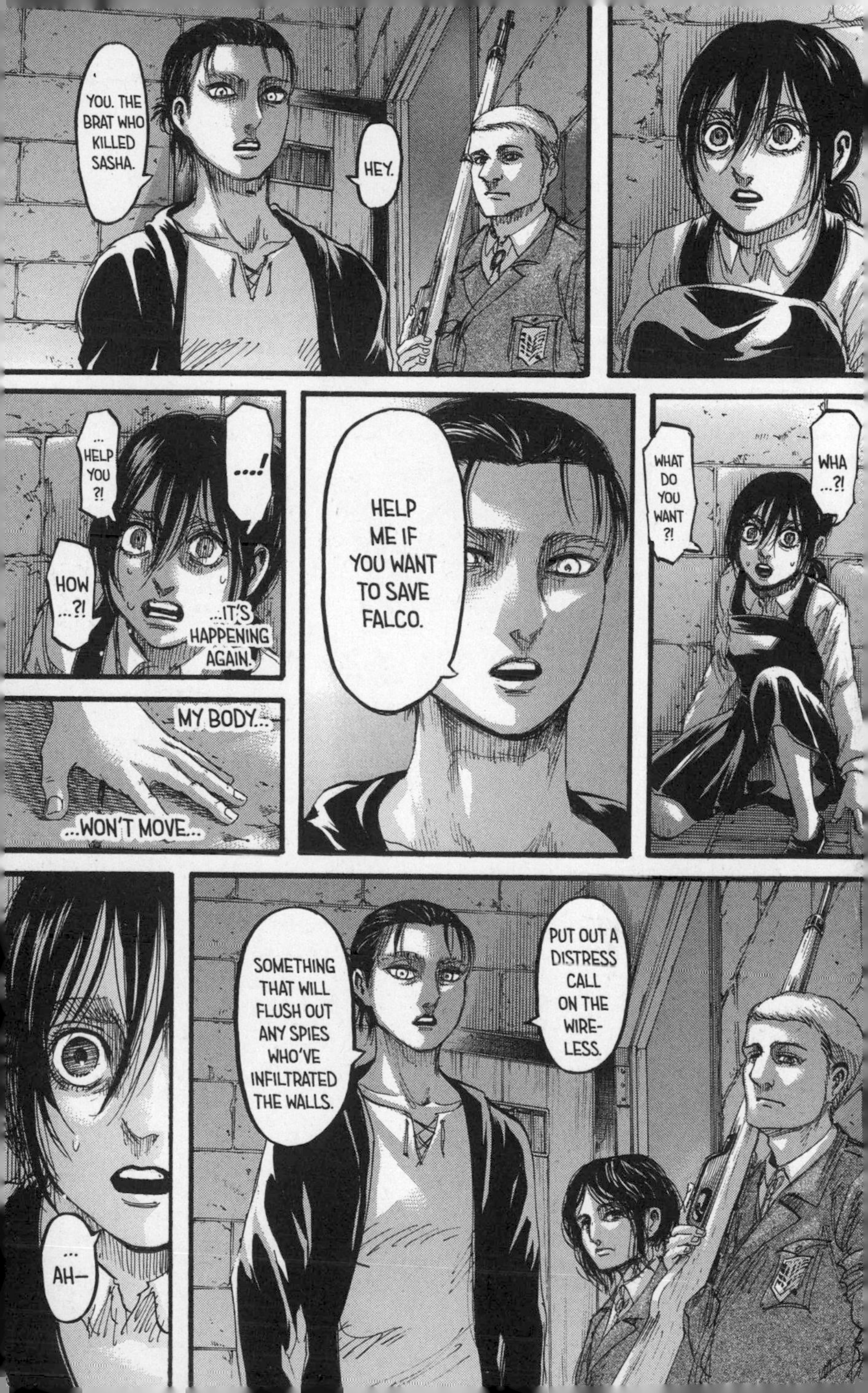
HEY.
YOU. THE BRAT WHO KILLED SASHA.
WHA ...?!
WHAT DO YOU WANT ?!
HELP ME IF YOU WANT TO SAVE FALCO.
...!
... HELP YOU ?!
HOW ...?!
...IT'S HAPPENING AGAIN.
MY BODY...
...WON'T MOVE...
PUT OUT A DISTRESS CALL ON THE WIRE-LESS.
SOMETHING THAT WILL FLUSH OUT ANY SPIES WHO'VE INFILTRATED THE WALLS.
... AH—

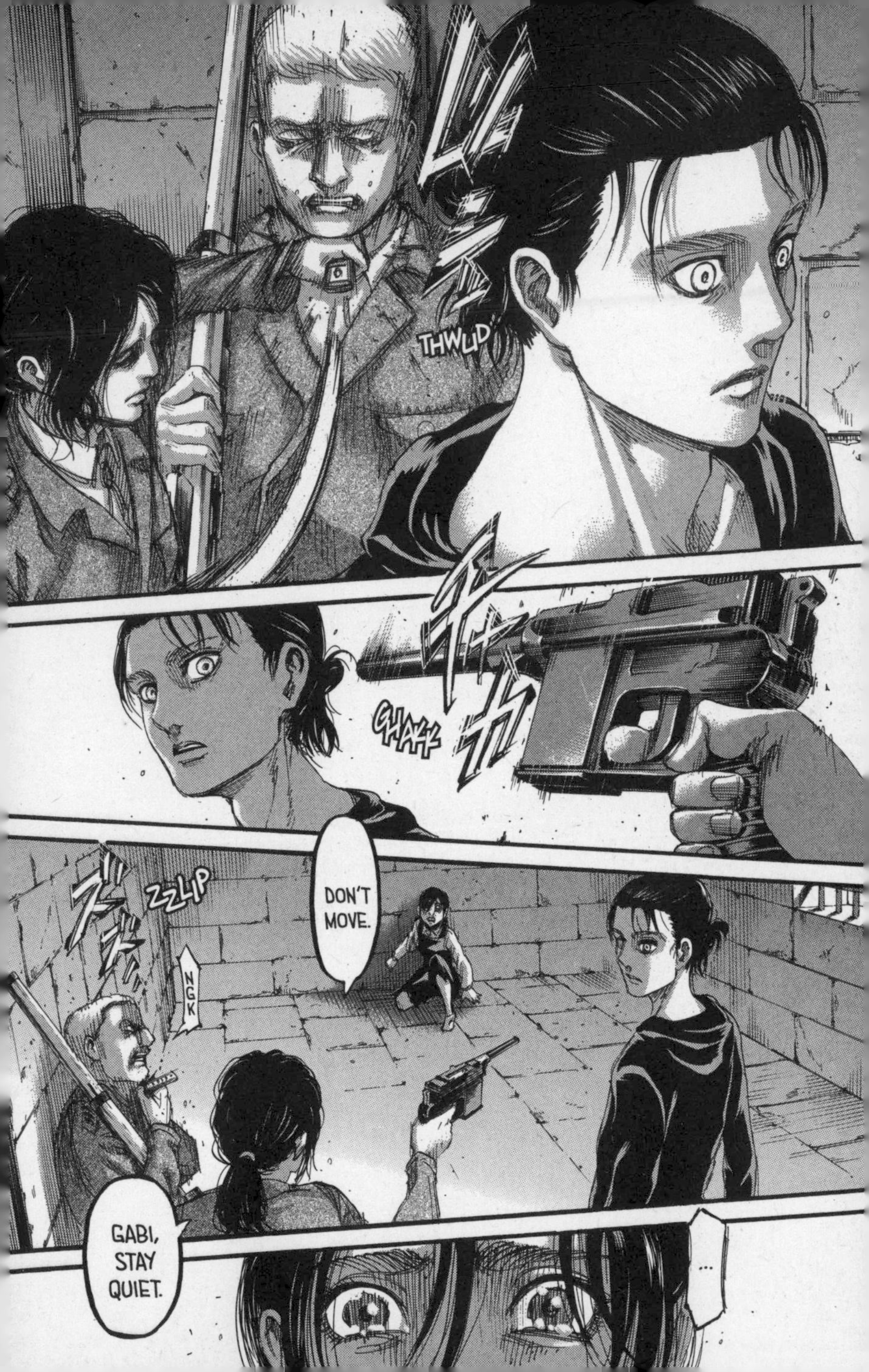
THWUD
CHAK
DON'T MOVE.
ZZLIP
NGK
...
GABI, STAY QUIET.

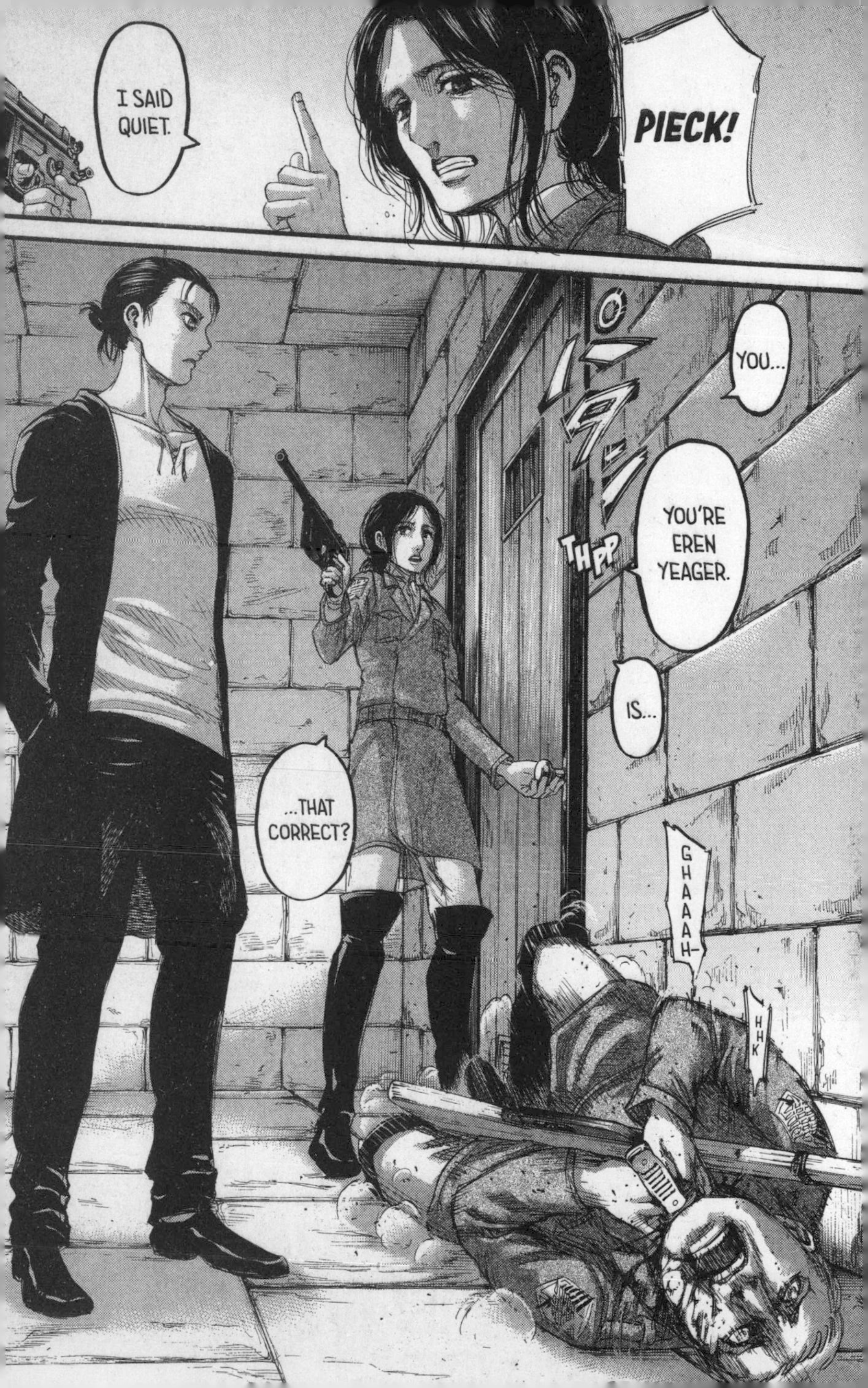
PIECK!
I SAID QUIET.
YOU...
THPP
YOU'RE EREN YEAGER.
IS...
...THAT CORRECT?
GHAAAH-
HHK

ATTACK
on TITAN

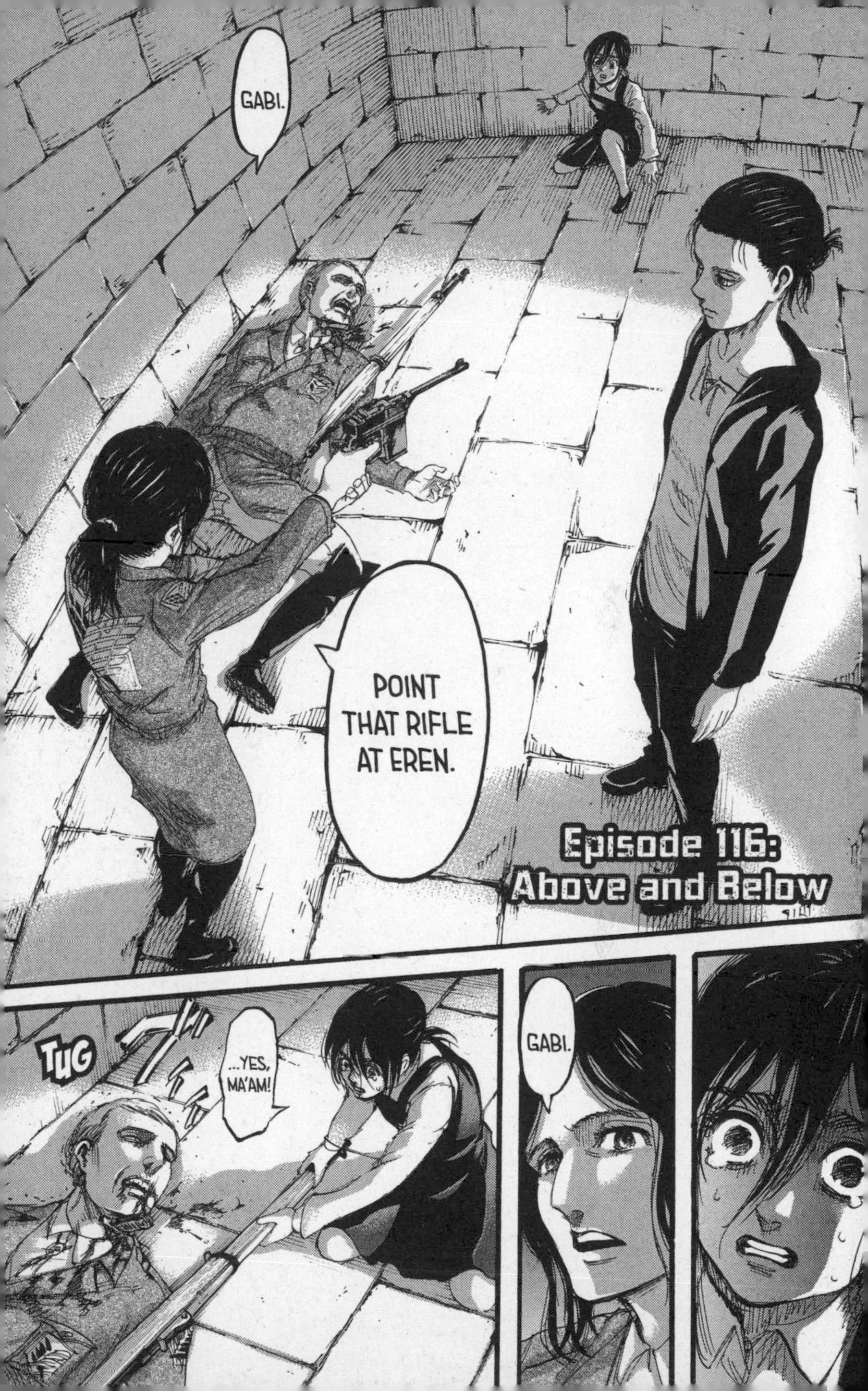
GABI.
POINT THAT RIFLE AT EREN.
Episode 116: Above and Below
GABI.
...YES, MA'AM!
TUG

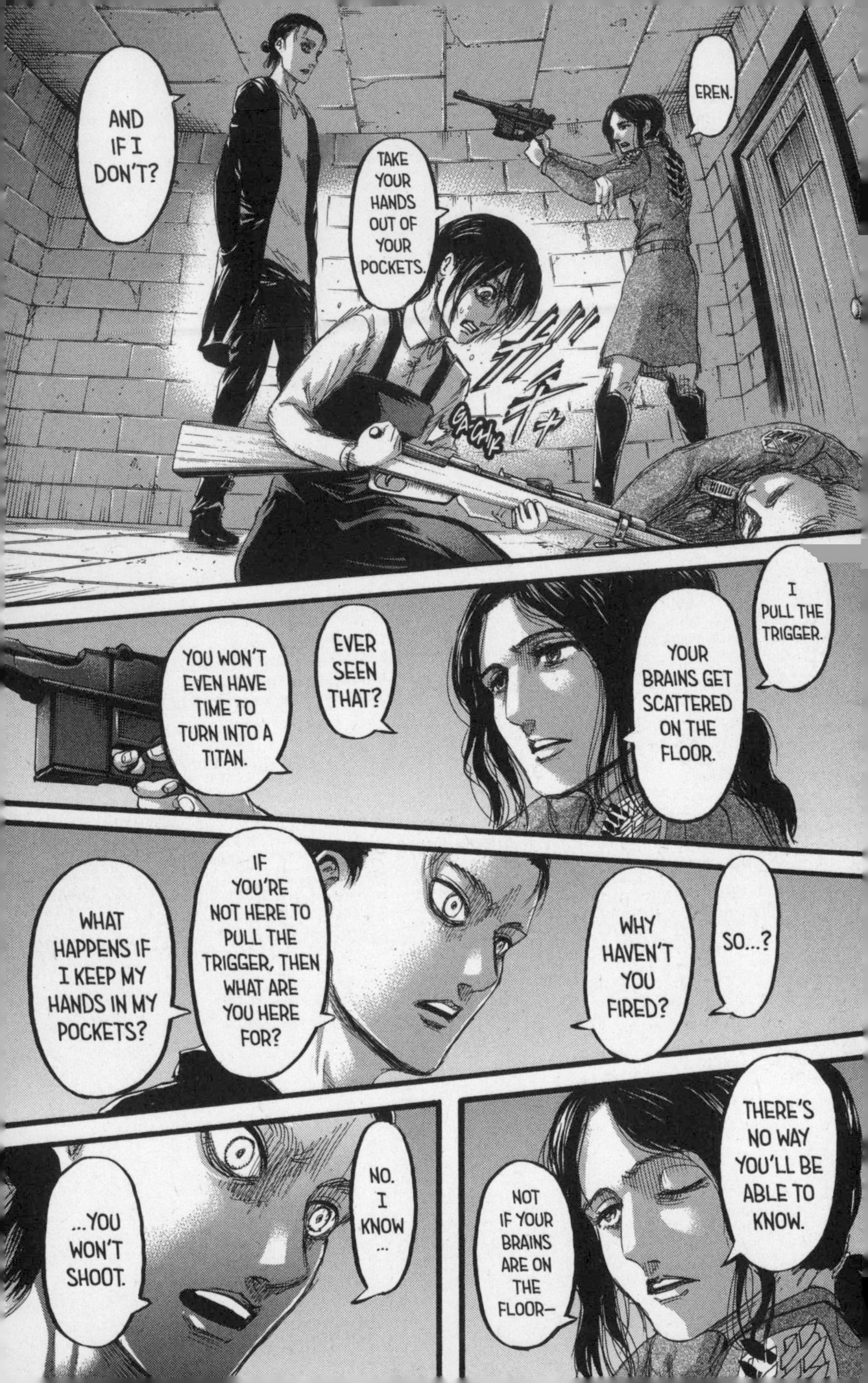
EREN.
TAKE YOUR HANDS OUT OF YOUR POCKETS.
AND IF I DON'T?
GA-CHAK
I PULL THE TRIGGER.
YOUR BRAINS GET SCATTERED ON THE FLOOR.
EVER SEEN THAT?
YOU WON'T EVEN HAVE TIME TO TURN INTO A TITAN.
SO...?
WHY HAVEN'T YOU FIRED?
IF YOU'RE NOT HERE TO PULL THE TRIGGER, THEN WHAT ARE YOU HERE FOR?
WHAT HAPPENS IF I KEEP MY HANDS IN MY POCKETS?
THERE'S NO WAY YOU'LL BE ABLE TO KNOW.
NOT IF YOUR BRAINS ARE ON THE FLOOR—
NO. I KNOW ...
...YOU WON'T SHOOT.

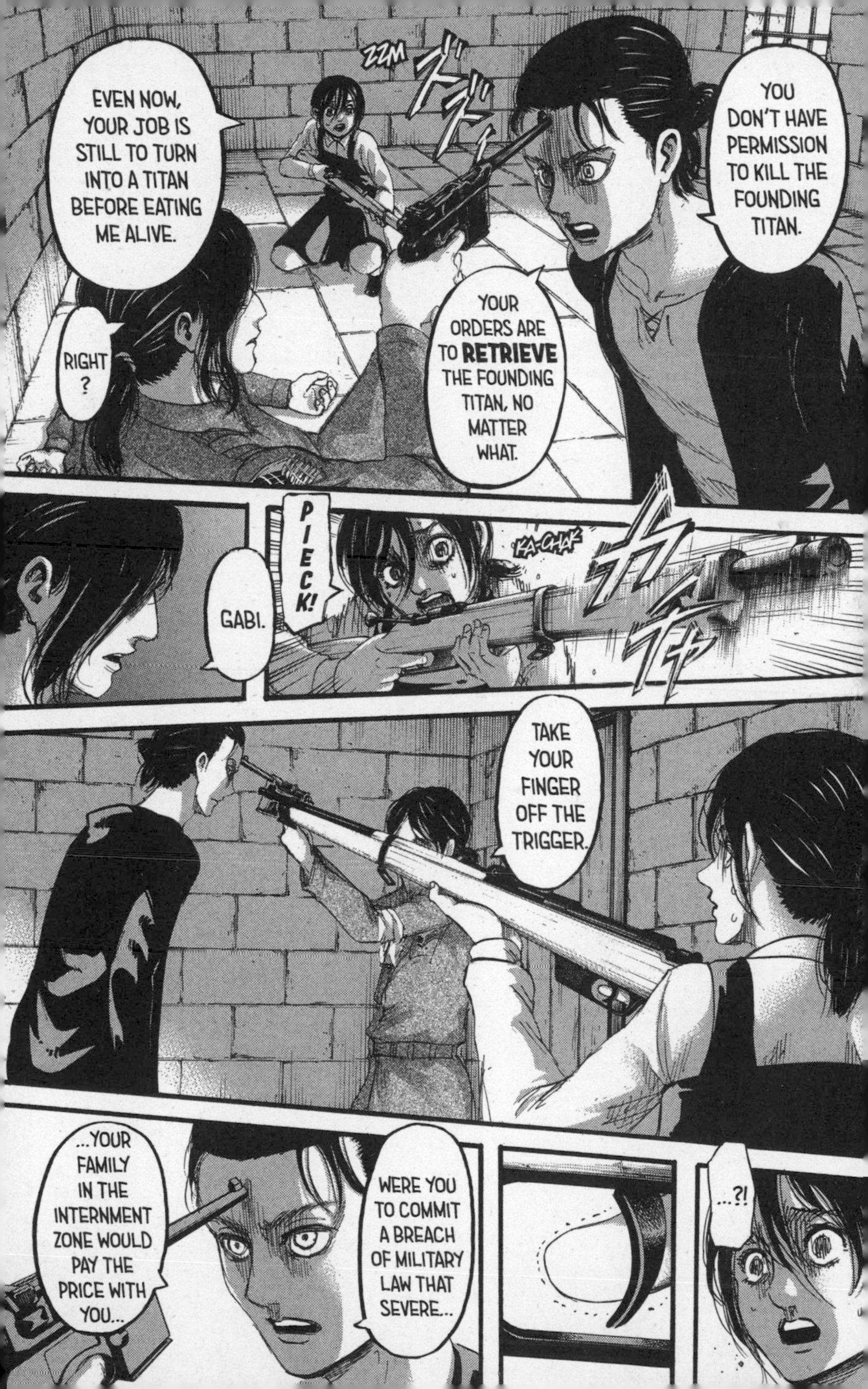
ZZM
YOU DON'T HAVE PERMISSION TO KILL THE FOUNDING TITAN.
YOUR ORDERS ARE TO **RETRIEVE** THE FOUNDING TITAN, NO MATTER WHAT.
EVEN NOW, YOUR JOB IS STILL TO TURN INTO A TITAN BEFORE EATING ME ALIVE.
RIGHT?
KA-CHAK
PIECK!
GABI.
TAKE YOUR FINGER OFF THE TRIGGER.
...?!
WERE YOU TO COMMIT A BREACH OF MILITARY LAW THAT SEVERE...
...YOUR FAMILY IN THE INTERNMENT ZONE WOULD PAY THE PRICE WITH YOU...

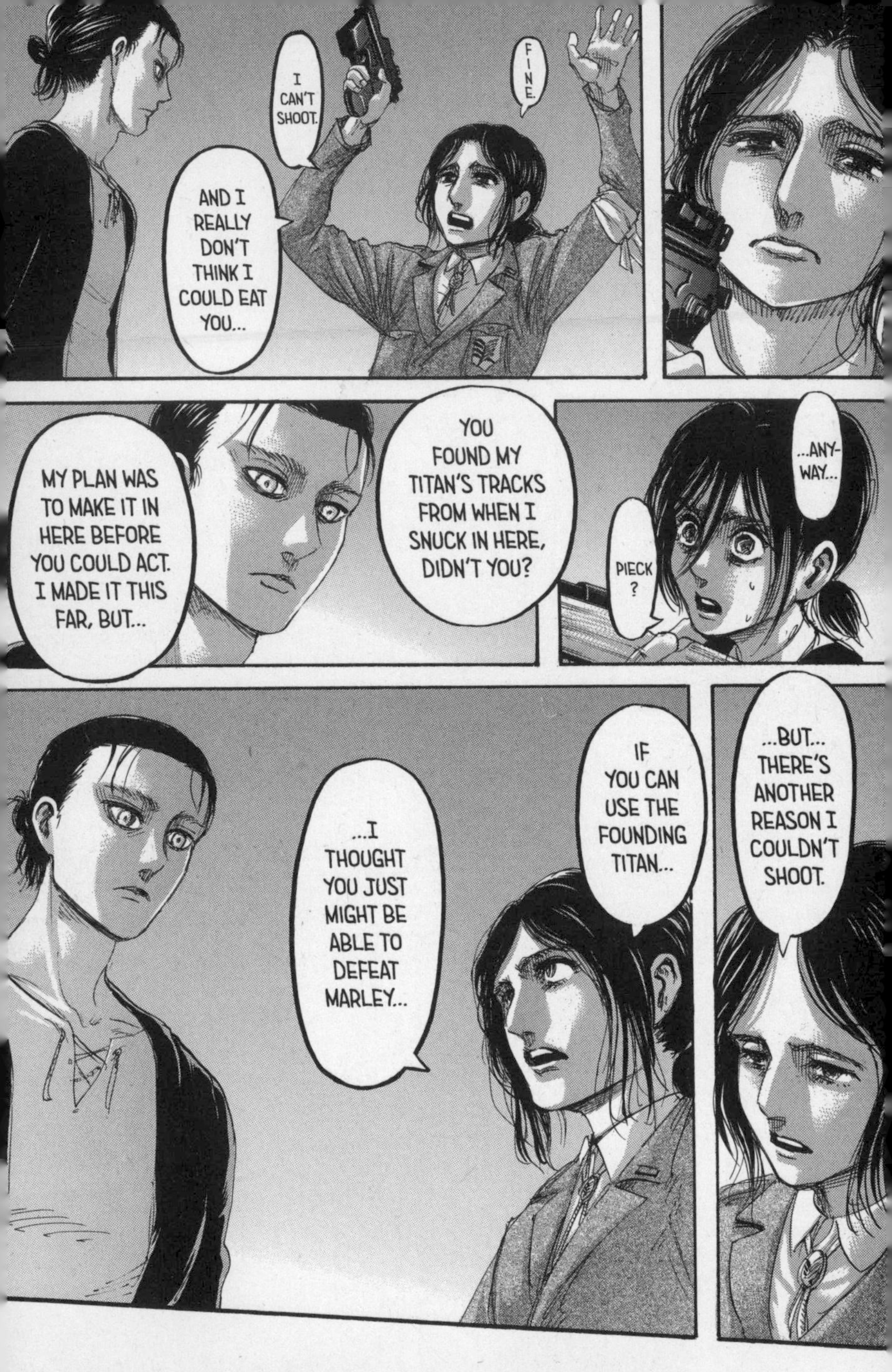
FINE.
I CAN'T SHOOT.
AND I REALLY DON'T THINK I COULD EAT YOU...
...ANYWAY...
PIECK?
YOU FOUND MY TITAN'S TRACKS FROM WHEN I SNUCK IN HERE, DIDN'T YOU?
MY PLAN WAS TO MAKE IT IN HERE BEFORE YOU COULD ACT. I MADE IT THIS FAR, BUT...
...BUT... THERE'S ANOTHER REASON I COULDN'T SHOOT.
IF YOU CAN USE THE FOUNDING TITAN...
...I THOUGHT YOU JUST MIGHT BE ABLE TO DEFEAT MARLEY...

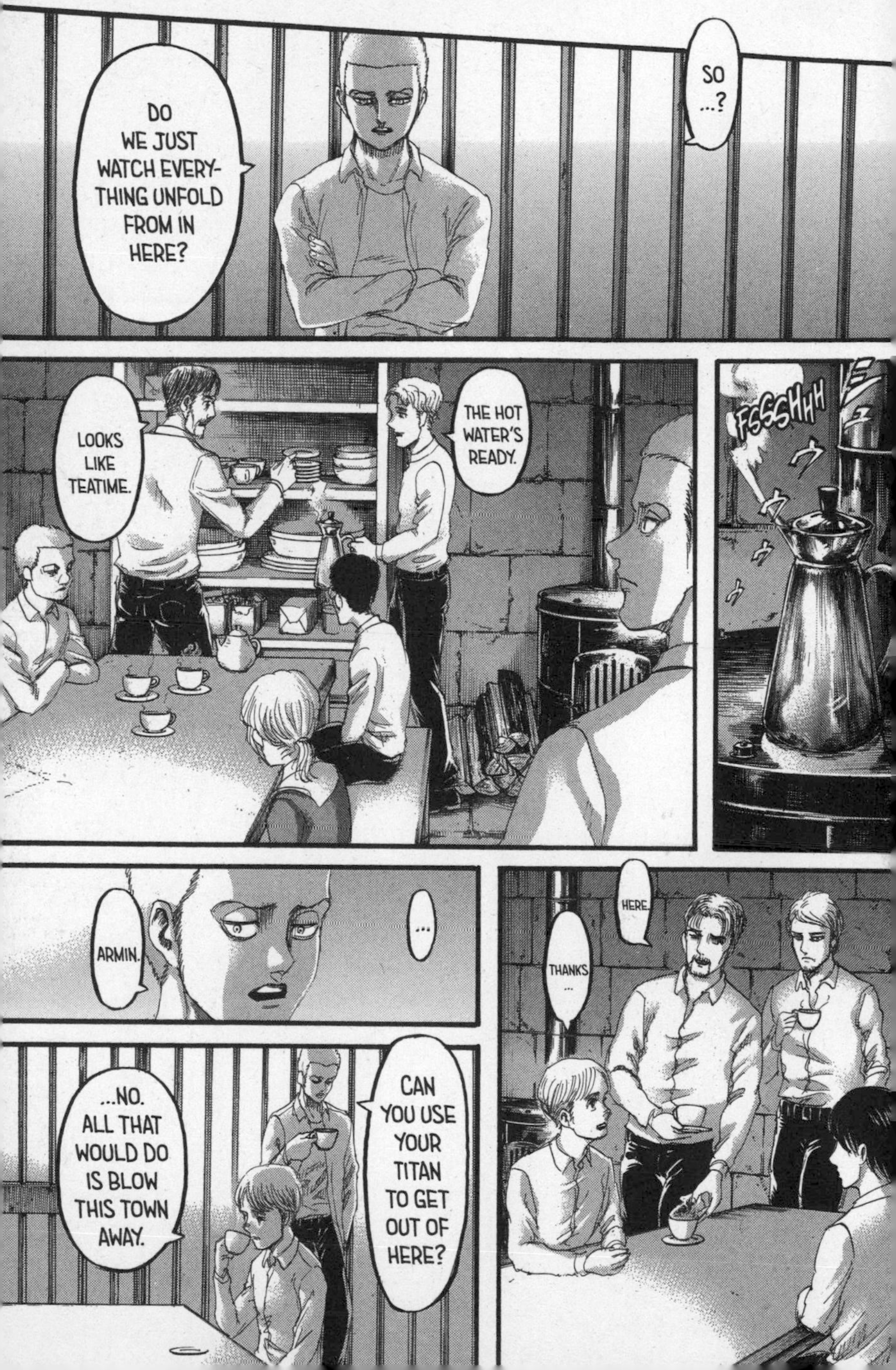
SO ...?
DO WE JUST WATCH EVERY-THING UNFOLD FROM IN HERE?
FSSSHHH
THE HOT WATER'S READY.
LOOKS LIKE TEATIME.
HERE.
THANKS ...
...
ARMIN.
CAN YOU USE YOUR TITAN TO GET OUT OF HERE?
...NO. ALL THAT WOULD DO IS BLOW THIS TOWN AWAY.

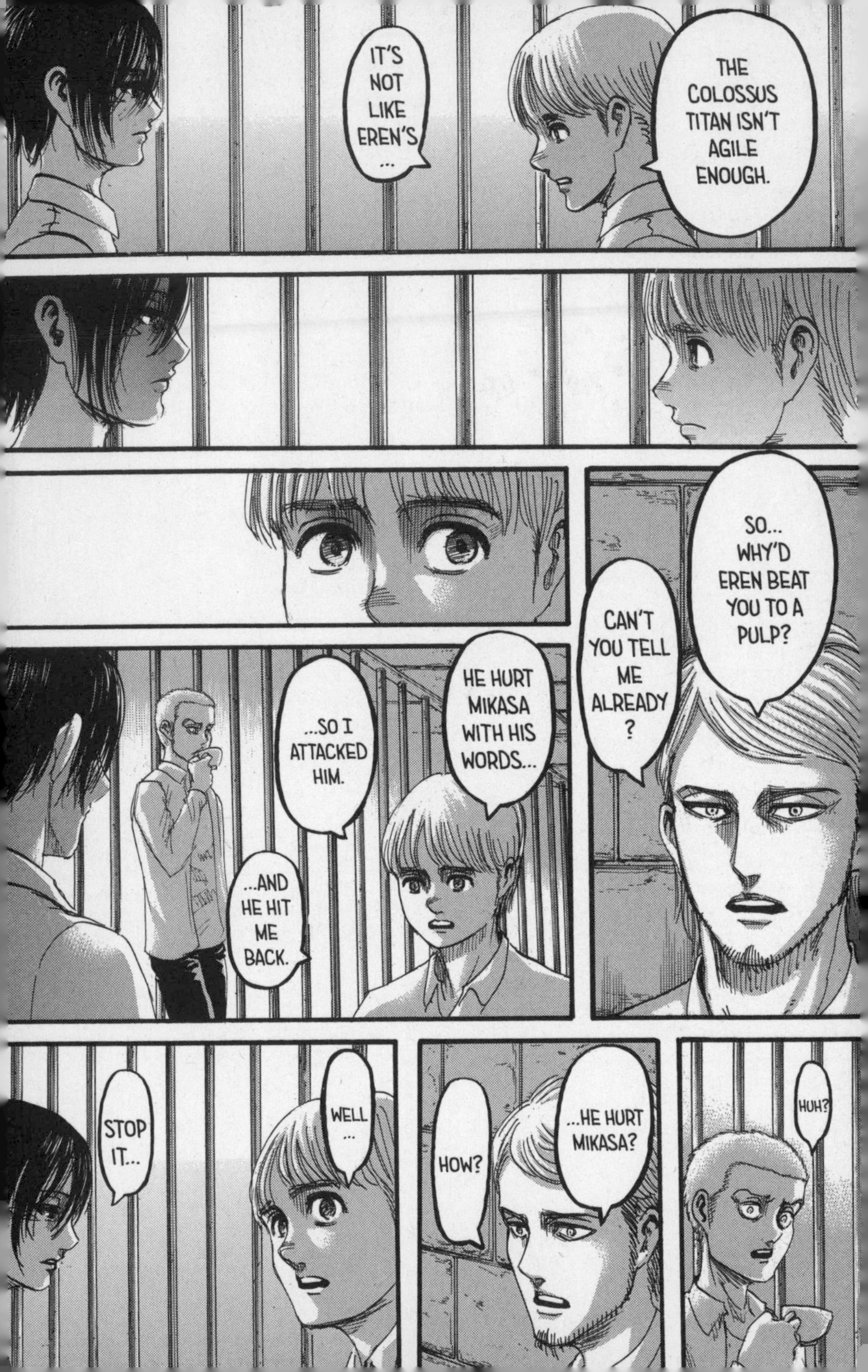
THE COLOSSUS TITAN ISN'T AGILE ENOUGH.
IT'S NOT LIKE EREN'S ...
SO... WHY'D EREN BEAT YOU TO A PULP?
CAN'T YOU TELL ME ALREADY ?
HE HURT MIKASA WITH HIS WORDS...
...SO I ATTACKED HIM.
...AND HE HIT ME BACK.
HUH?
...HE HURT MIKASA?
HOW?
WELL ...
STOP IT...

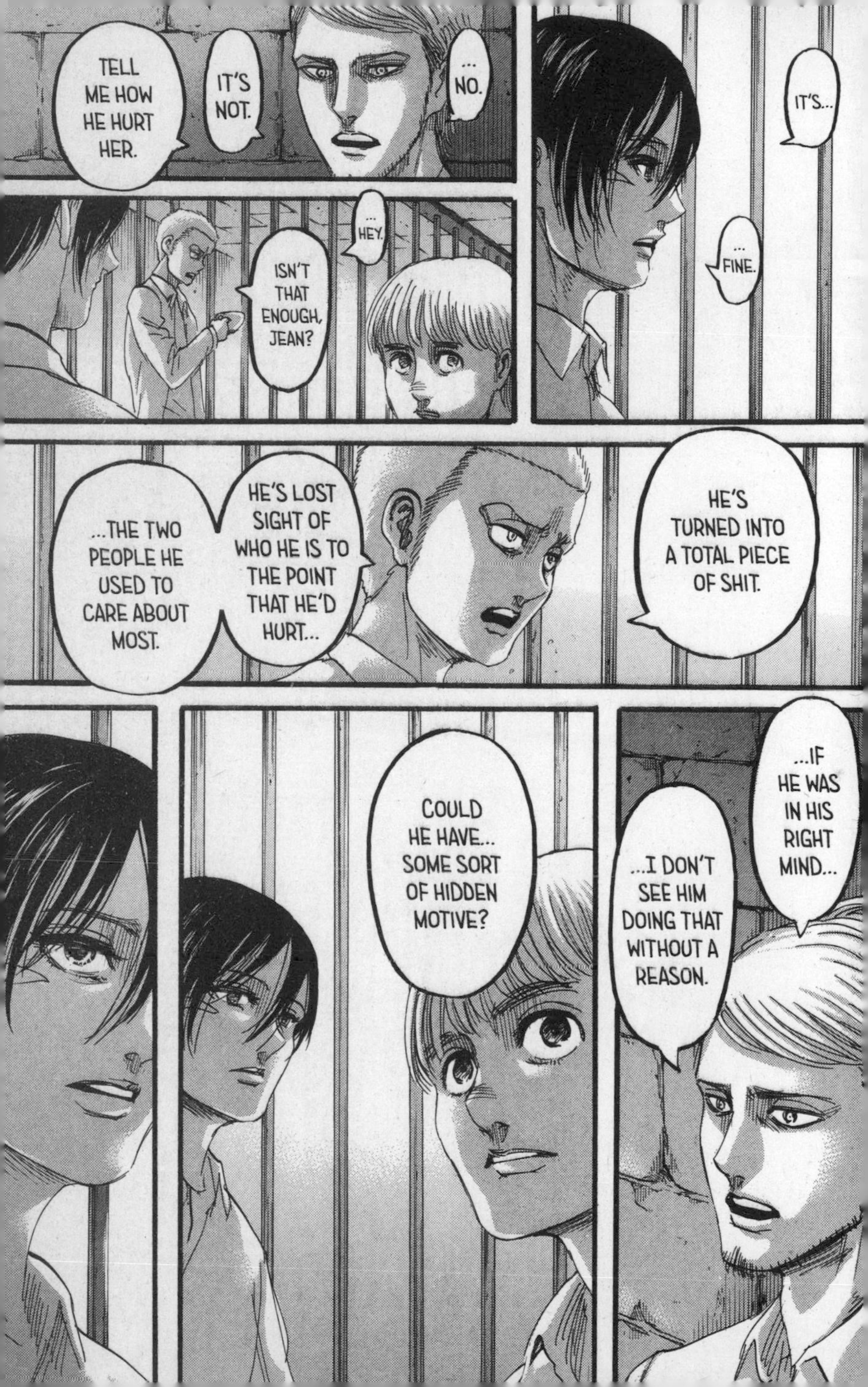
IT'S...
... FINE.
... NO.
IT'S NOT.
TELL ME HOW HE HURT HER.
... HEY.
ISN'T THAT ENOUGH, JEAN?
HE'S TURNED INTO A TOTAL PIECE OF SHIT.
HE'S LOST SIGHT OF WHO HE IS TO THE POINT THAT HE'D HURT...
...THE TWO PEOPLE HE USED TO CARE ABOUT MOST.
...IF HE WAS IN HIS RIGHT MIND...
...I DON'T SEE HIM DOING THAT WITHOUT A REASON.
COULD HE HAVE... SOME SORT OF HIDDEN MOTIVE?

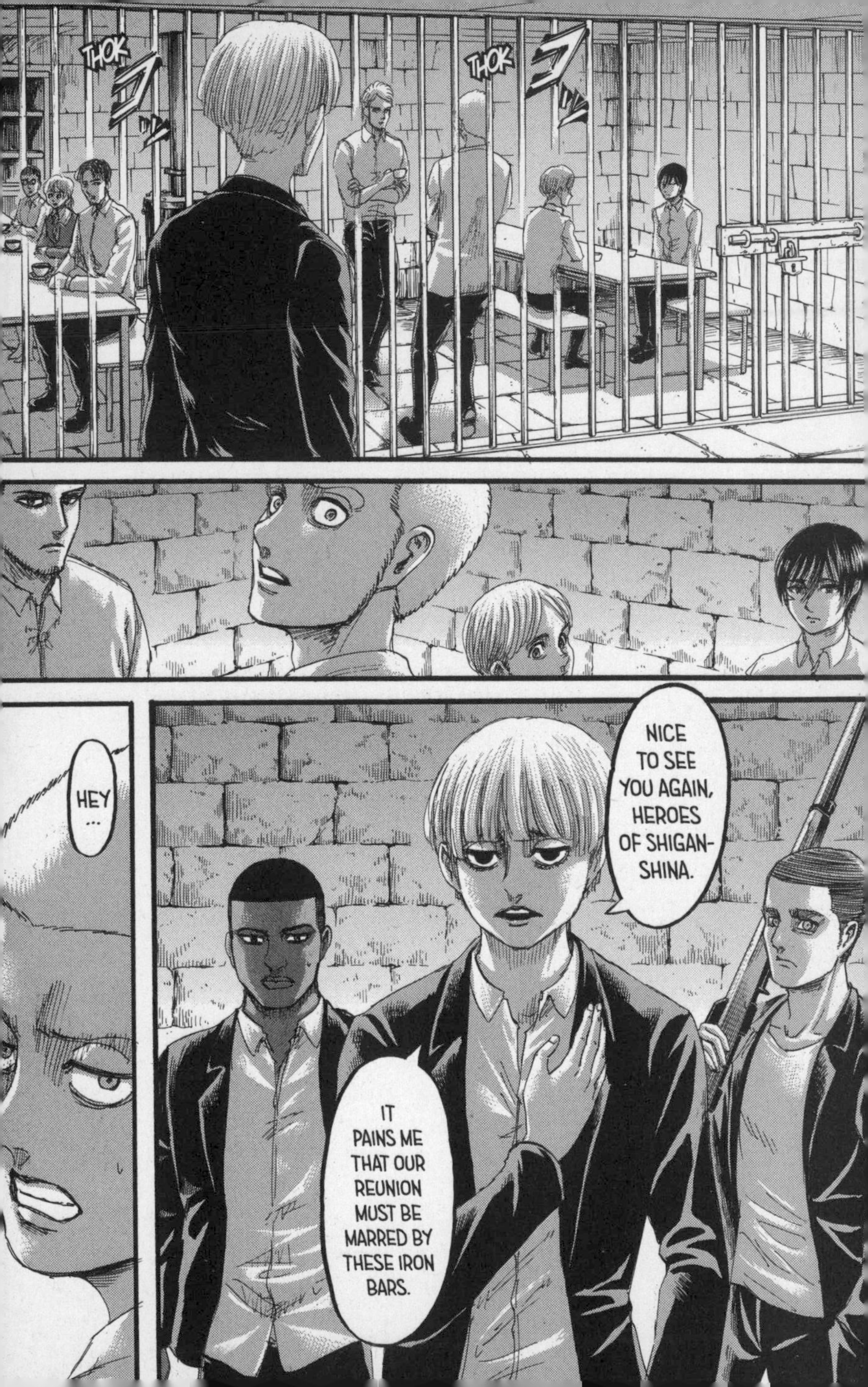
THOK
THOK
NICE TO SEE YOU AGAIN, HEROES OF SHIGAN-SHINA.
IT PAINS ME THAT OUR REUNION MUST BE MARRED BY THESE IRON BARS.
HEY ...

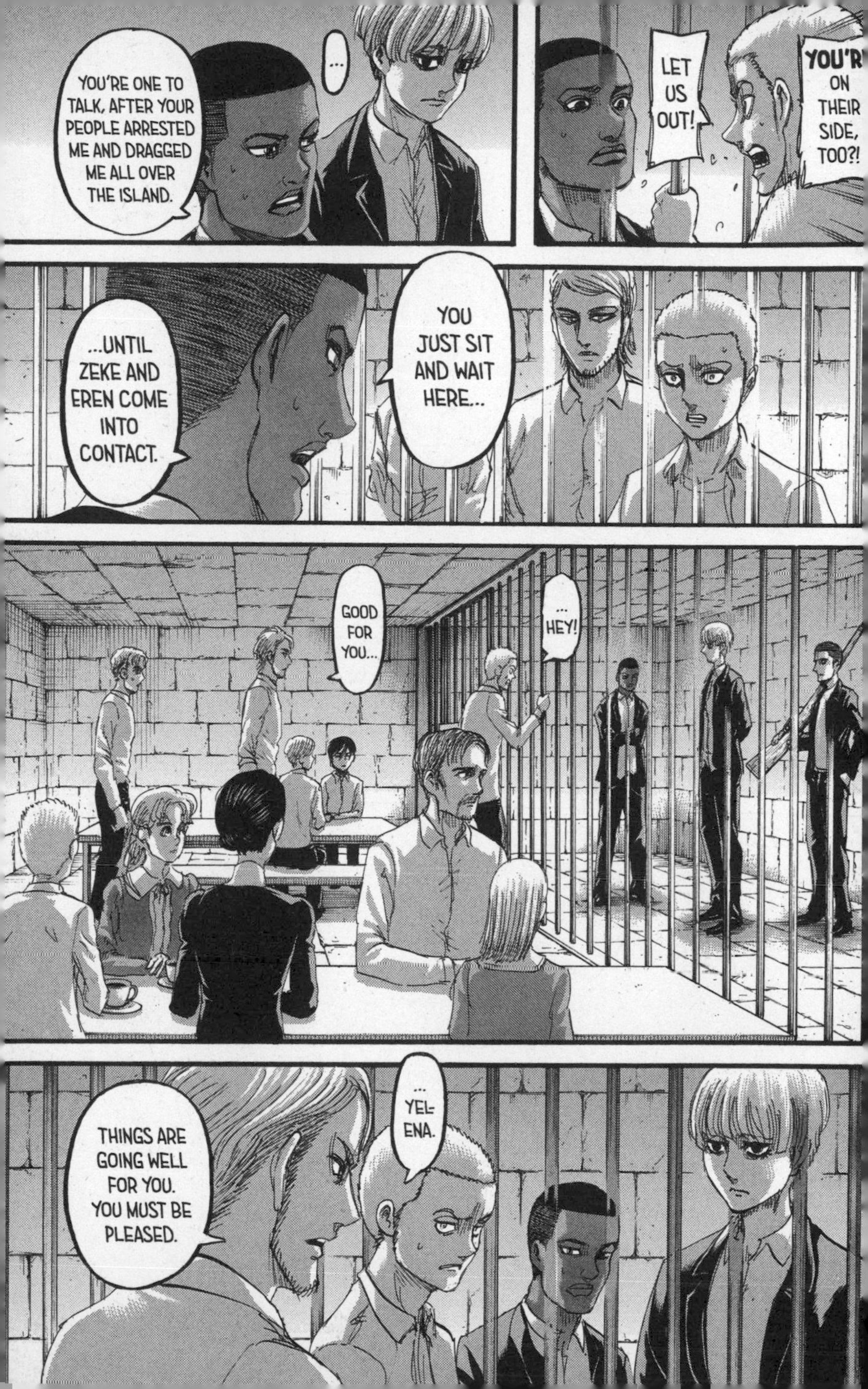
YOU'R ON THEIR SIDE, TOO?!
LET US OUT!
...
YOU'RE ONE TO TALK, AFTER YOUR PEOPLE ARRESTED ME AND DRAGGED ME ALL OVER THE ISLAND.
YOU JUST SIT AND WAIT HERE...
...UNTIL ZEKE AND EREN COME INTO CONTACT.
... HEY!
GOOD FOR YOU...
... YEL- ENA.
THINGS ARE GOING WELL FOR YOU. YOU MUST BE PLEASED.

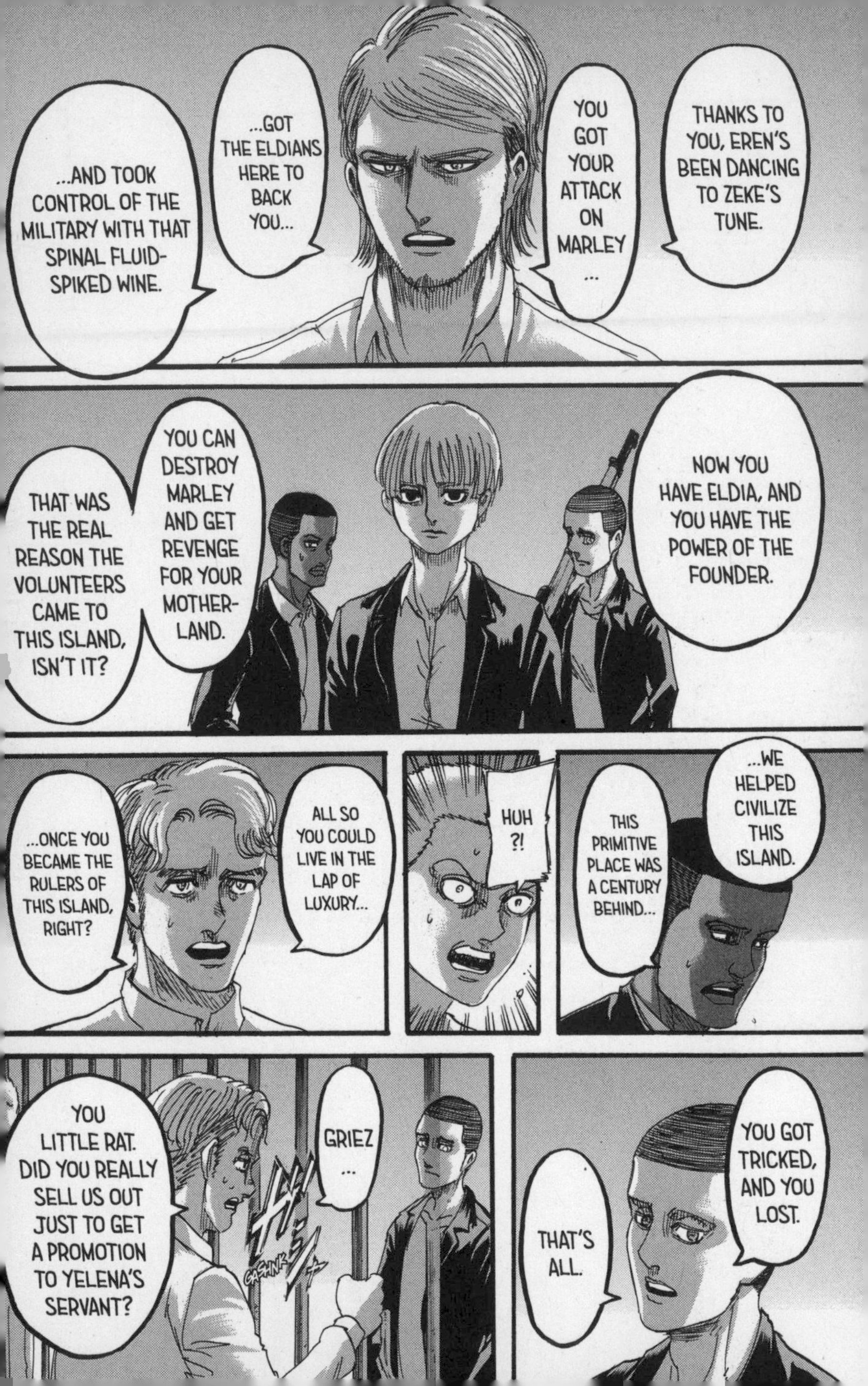
THANKS TO YOU, EREN'S BEEN DANCING TO ZEKE'S TUNE.
YOU GOT YOUR ATTACK ON MARLEY ...
...GOT THE ELDIANS HERE TO BACK YOU...
...AND TOOK CONTROL OF THE MILITARY WITH THAT SPINAL FLUID-SPIKED WINE.
NOW YOU HAVE ELDIA, AND YOU HAVE THE POWER OF THE FOUNDER.
YOU CAN DESTROY MARLEY AND GET REVENGE FOR YOUR MOTHER-LAND.
THAT WAS THE REAL REASON THE VOLUNTEERS CAME TO THIS ISLAND, ISN'T IT?
...WE HELPED CIVILIZE THIS ISLAND.
THIS PRIMITIVE PLACE WAS A CENTURY BEHIND...
HUH ?!
ALL SO YOU COULD LIVE IN THE LAP OF LUXURY...
...ONCE YOU BECAME THE RULERS OF THIS ISLAND, RIGHT?
YOU GOT TRICKED, AND YOU LOST.
THAT'S ALL.
GRIEZ ...
YOU LITTLE RAT. DID YOU REALLY SELL US OUT JUST TO GET A PROMOTION TO YELENA'S SERVANT?
GASHNK

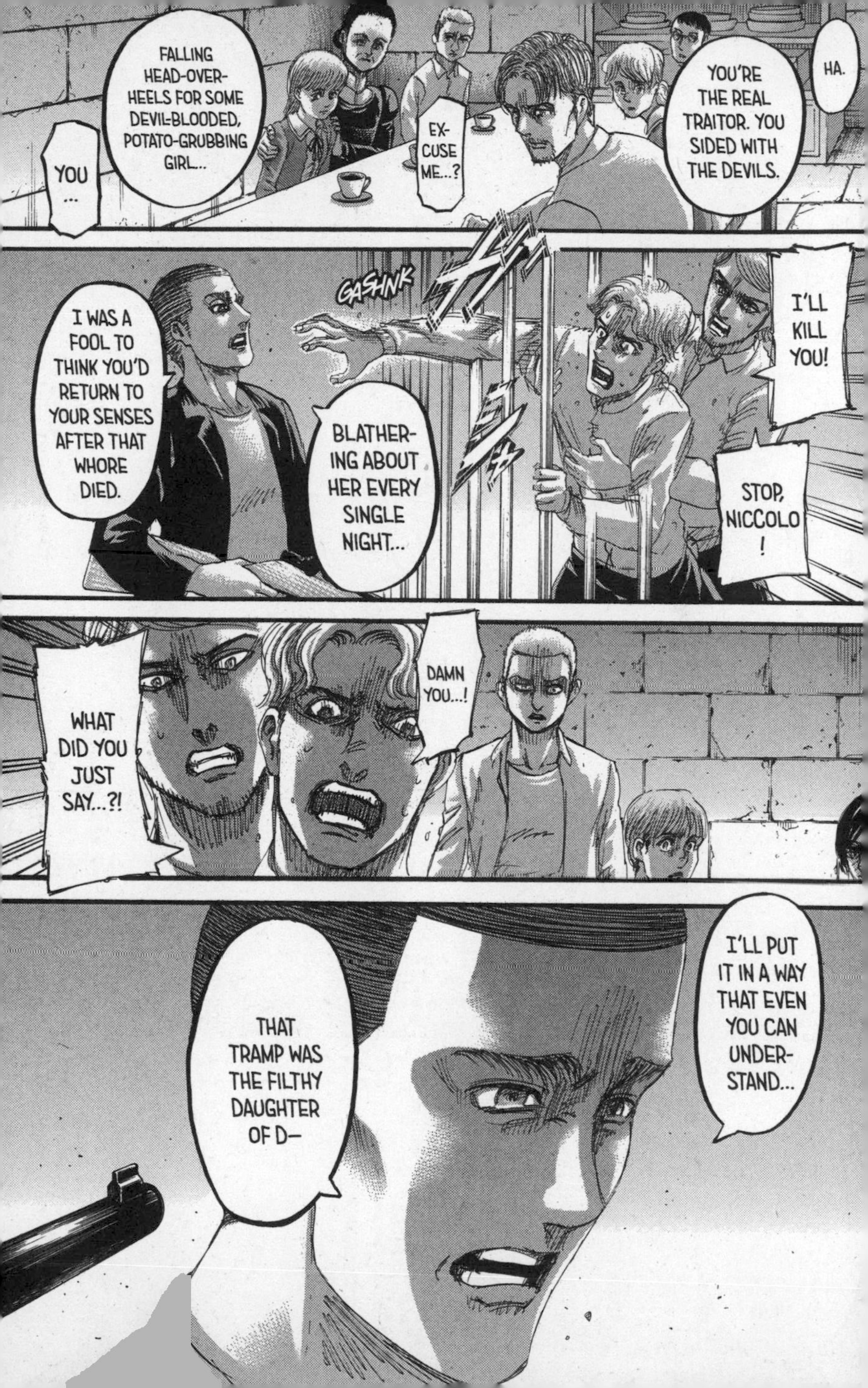
HA.
YOU'RE THE REAL TRAITOR. YOU SIDED WITH THE DEVILS.
EX-CUSE ME...?
FALLING HEAD-OVER-HEELS FOR SOME DEVIL-BLOODED, POTATO-GRUBBING GIRL...
YOU ...
I'LL KILL YOU!
STOP, NICCOLO!
GASHINK
I WAS A FOOL TO THINK YOU'D RETURN TO YOUR SENSES AFTER THAT WHORE DIED.
BLATHER-ING ABOUT HER EVERY SINGLE NIGHT...
DAMN YOU...!
WHAT DID YOU JUST SAY...?!
I'LL PUT IT IN A WAY THAT EVEN YOU CAN UNDER-STAND...
THAT TRAMP WAS THE FILTHY DAUGHTER OF D—

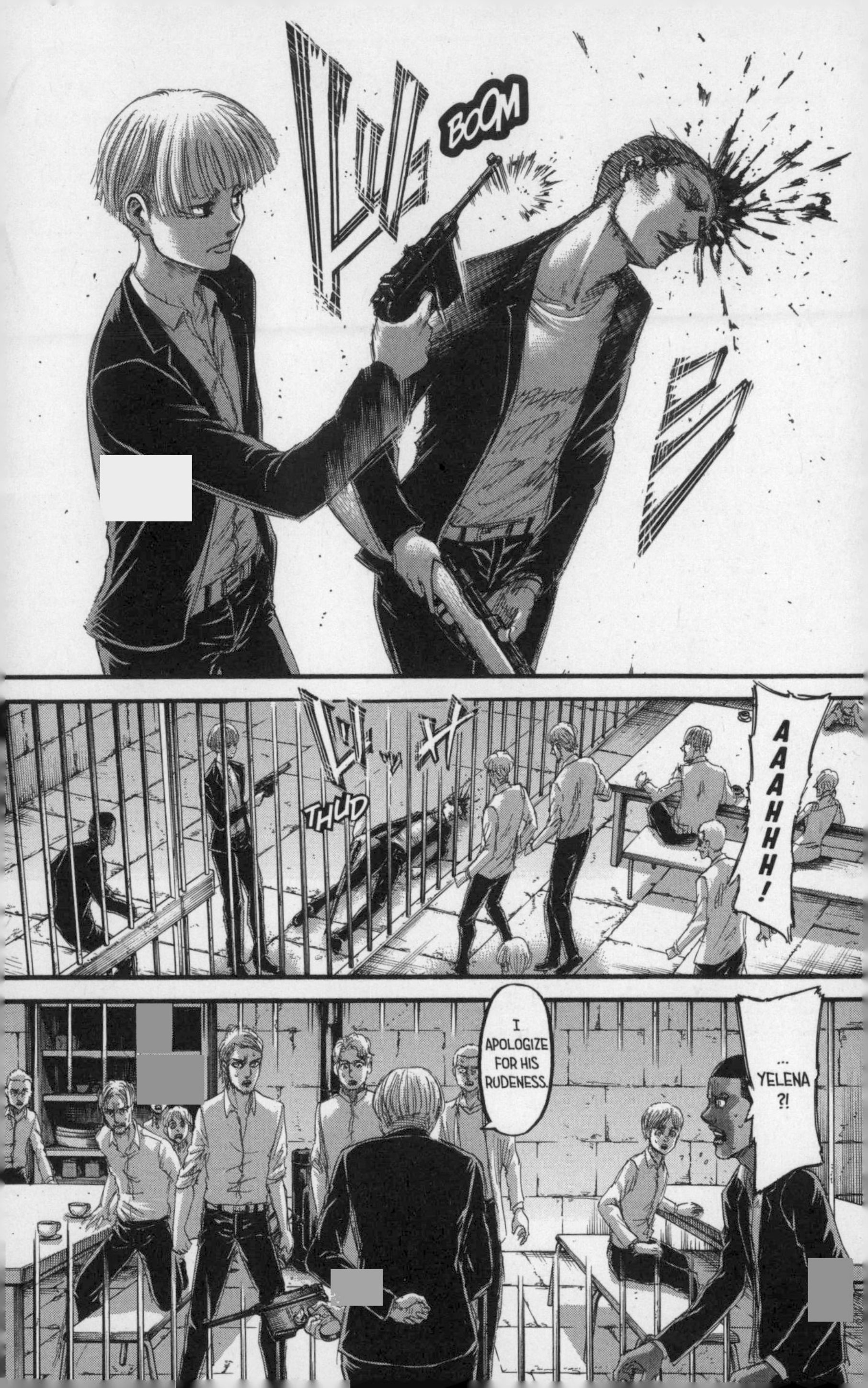
BOOM
AAAAHHH!
THUD
...YELENA?!
I APOLOGIZE FOR HIS RUDENESS.

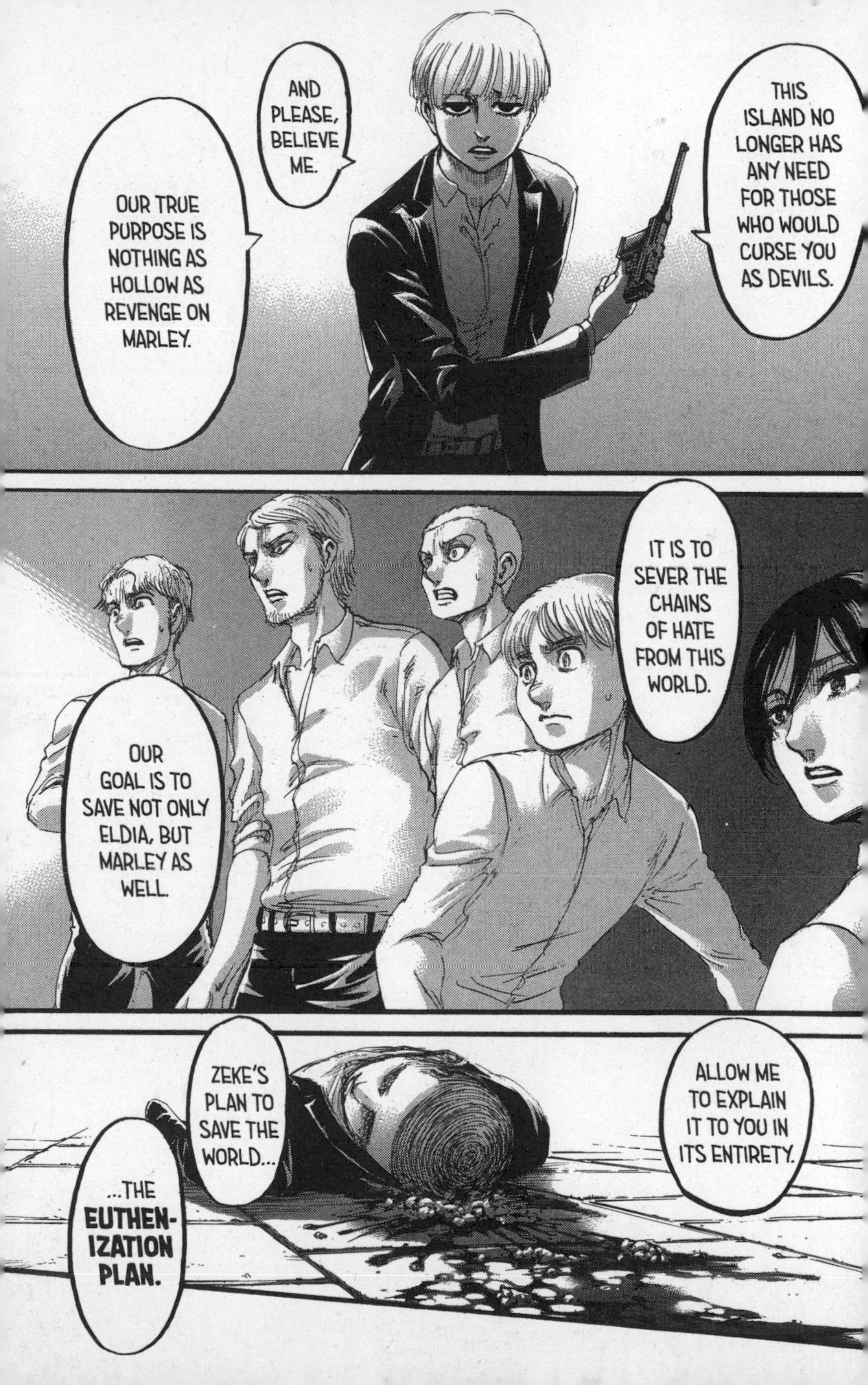
THIS ISLAND NO LONGER HAS ANY NEED FOR THOSE WHO WOULD CURSE YOU AS DEVILS.
AND PLEASE, BELIEVE ME.
OUR TRUE PURPOSE IS NOTHING AS HOLLOW AS REVENGE ON MARLEY.
IT IS TO SEVER THE CHAINS OF HATE FROM THIS WORLD.
OUR GOAL IS TO SAVE NOT ONLY ELDIA, BUT MARLEY AS WELL.
ALLOW ME TO EXPLAIN IT TO YOU IN ITS ENTIRETY.
ZEKE'S PLAN TO SAVE THE WORLD...
...THE **EUTHENIZATION PLAN.**

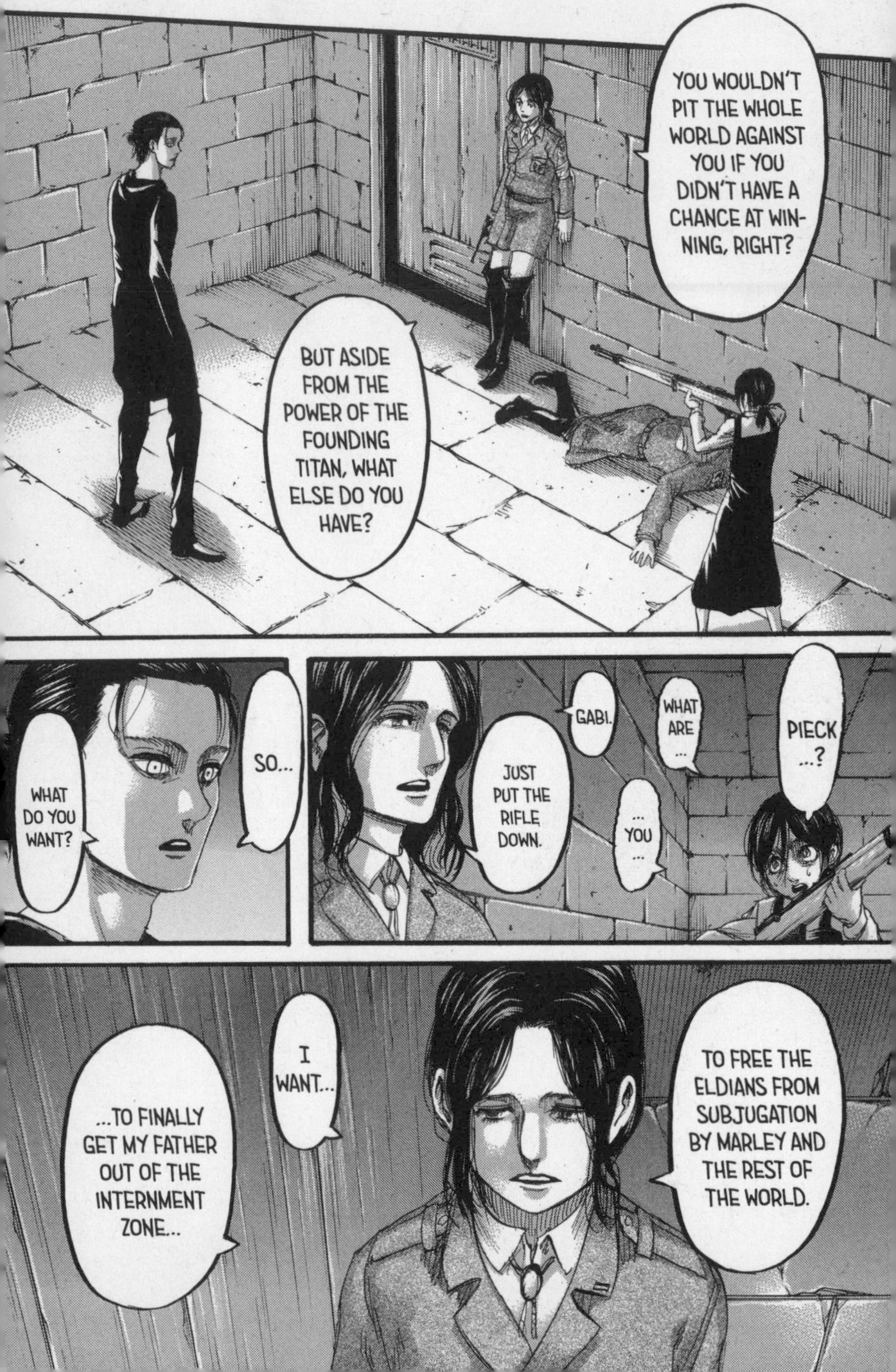
YOU WOULDN'T PIT THE WHOLE WORLD AGAINST YOU IF YOU DIDN'T HAVE A CHANCE AT WIN-NING, RIGHT?
BUT ASIDE FROM THE POWER OF THE FOUNDING TITAN, WHAT ELSE DO YOU HAVE?
PIECK ...?
WHAT ARE ...
GABI.
... YOU ...
JUST PUT THE RIFLE DOWN.
SO...
WHAT DO YOU WANT?
TO FREE THE ELDIANS FROM SUBJUGATION BY MARLEY AND THE REST OF THE WORLD.
I WANT...
...TO FINALLY GET MY FATHER OUT OF THE INTERNMENT ZONE...

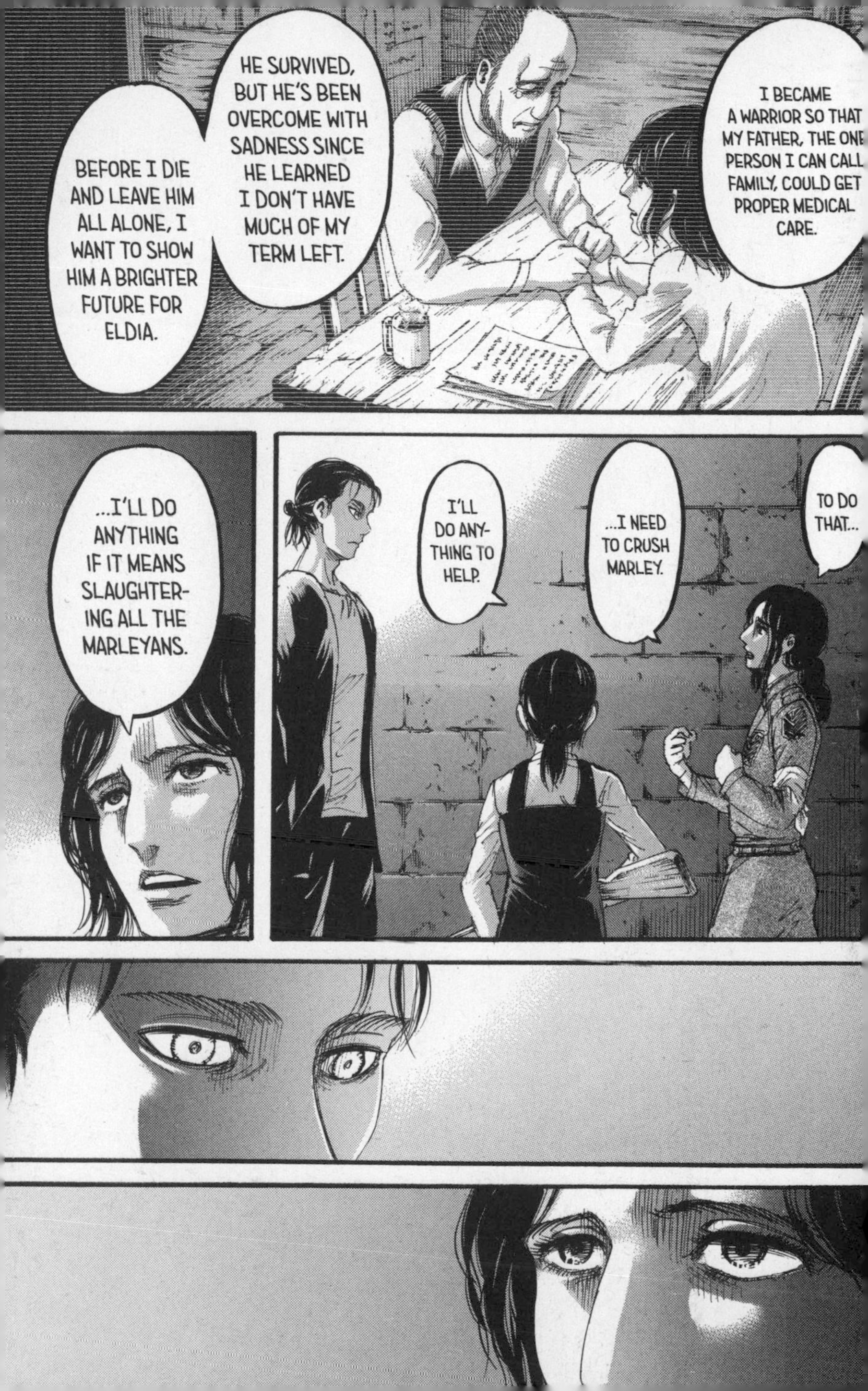
I BECAME A WARRIOR SO THAT MY FATHER, THE ONE PERSON I CAN CALL FAMILY, COULD GET PROPER MEDICAL CARE.
HE SURVIVED, BUT HE'S BEEN OVERCOME WITH SADNESS SINCE HE LEARNED I DON'T HAVE MUCH OF MY TERM LEFT.
BEFORE I DIE AND LEAVE HIM ALL ALONE, I WANT TO SHOW HIM A BRIGHTER FUTURE FOR ELDIA.
TO DO THAT...
...I NEED TO CRUSH MARLEY.
I'LL DO ANYTHING TO HELP.
...I'LL DO ANYTHING IF IT MEANS SLAUGHTERING ALL THE MARLEYANS.

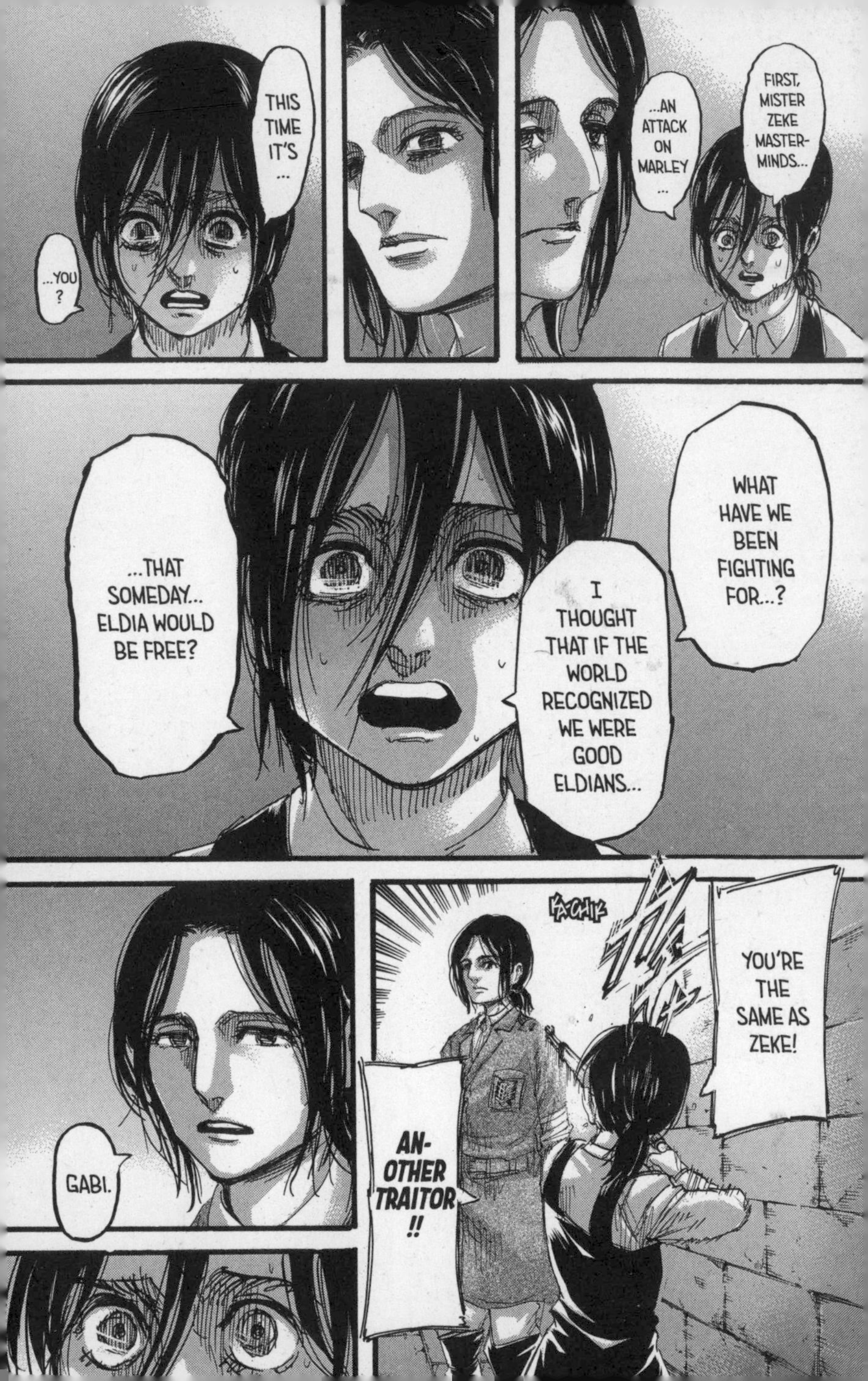
FIRST, MISTER ZEKE MASTER-MINDS...
...AN ATTACK ON MARLEY ...
THIS TIME IT'S ...
...YOU ?
WHAT HAVE WE BEEN FIGHTING FOR...?
I THOUGHT THAT IF THE WORLD RECOGNIZED WE WERE GOOD ELDIANS...
...THAT SOMEDAY... ELDIA WOULD BE FREE?
KACHIK
YOU'RE THE SAME AS ZEKE!
AN-OTHER TRAITOR !!
GABI.

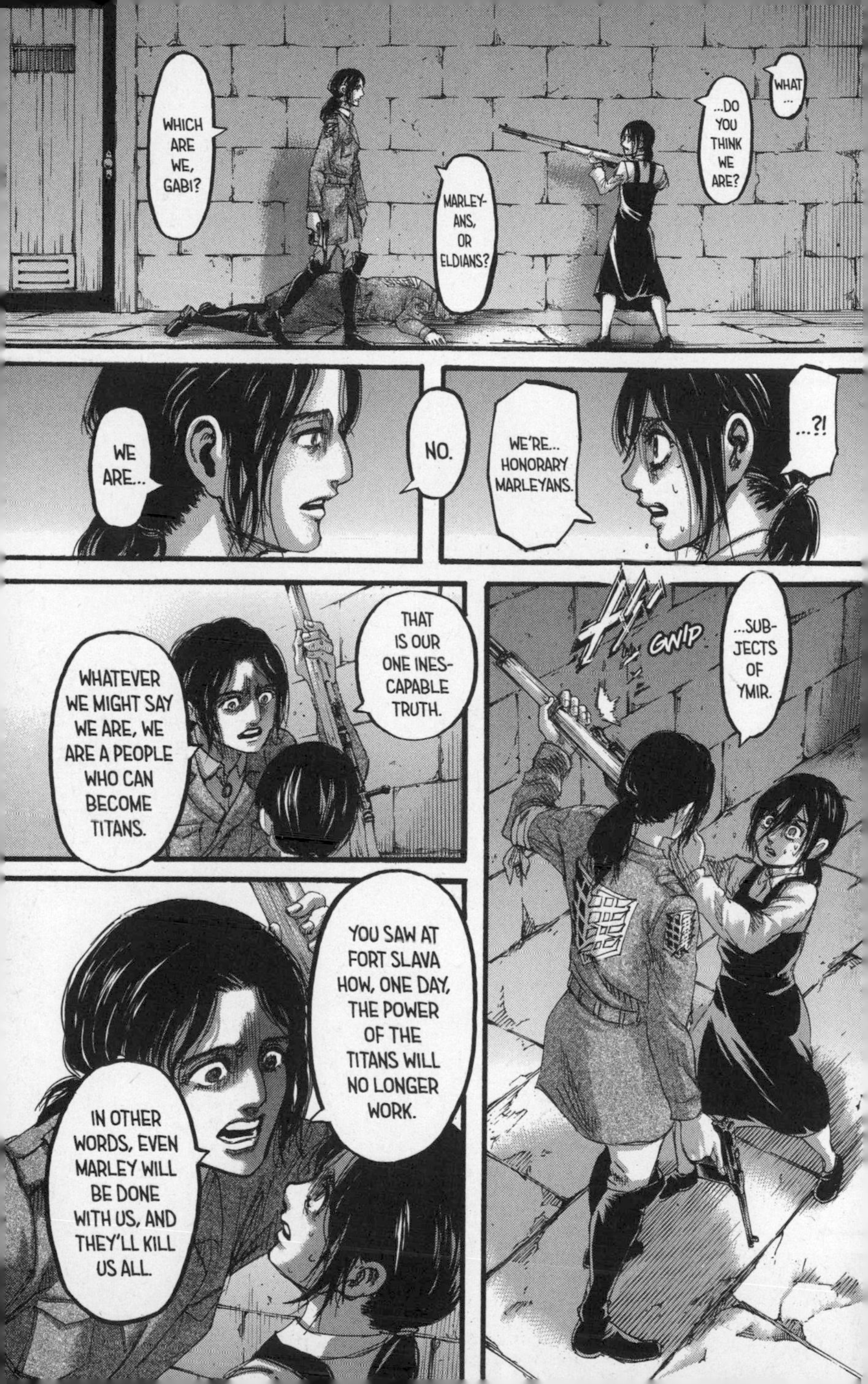
WHAT...
...DO YOU THINK WE ARE?
MARLEY-ANS, OR ELDIANS?
WHICH ARE WE, GABI?
...?!
WE'RE... HONORARY MARLEYANS.
NO.
WE ARE...
...SUB-JECTS OF YMIR.
GWIP
THAT IS OUR ONE INES-CAPABLE TRUTH.
WHATEVER WE MIGHT SAY WE ARE, WE ARE A PEOPLE WHO CAN BECOME TITANS.
YOU SAW AT FORT SLAVA HOW, ONE DAY, THE POWER OF THE TITANS WILL NO LONGER WORK.
IN OTHER WORDS, EVEN MARLEY WILL BE DONE WITH US, AND THEY'LL KILL US ALL.

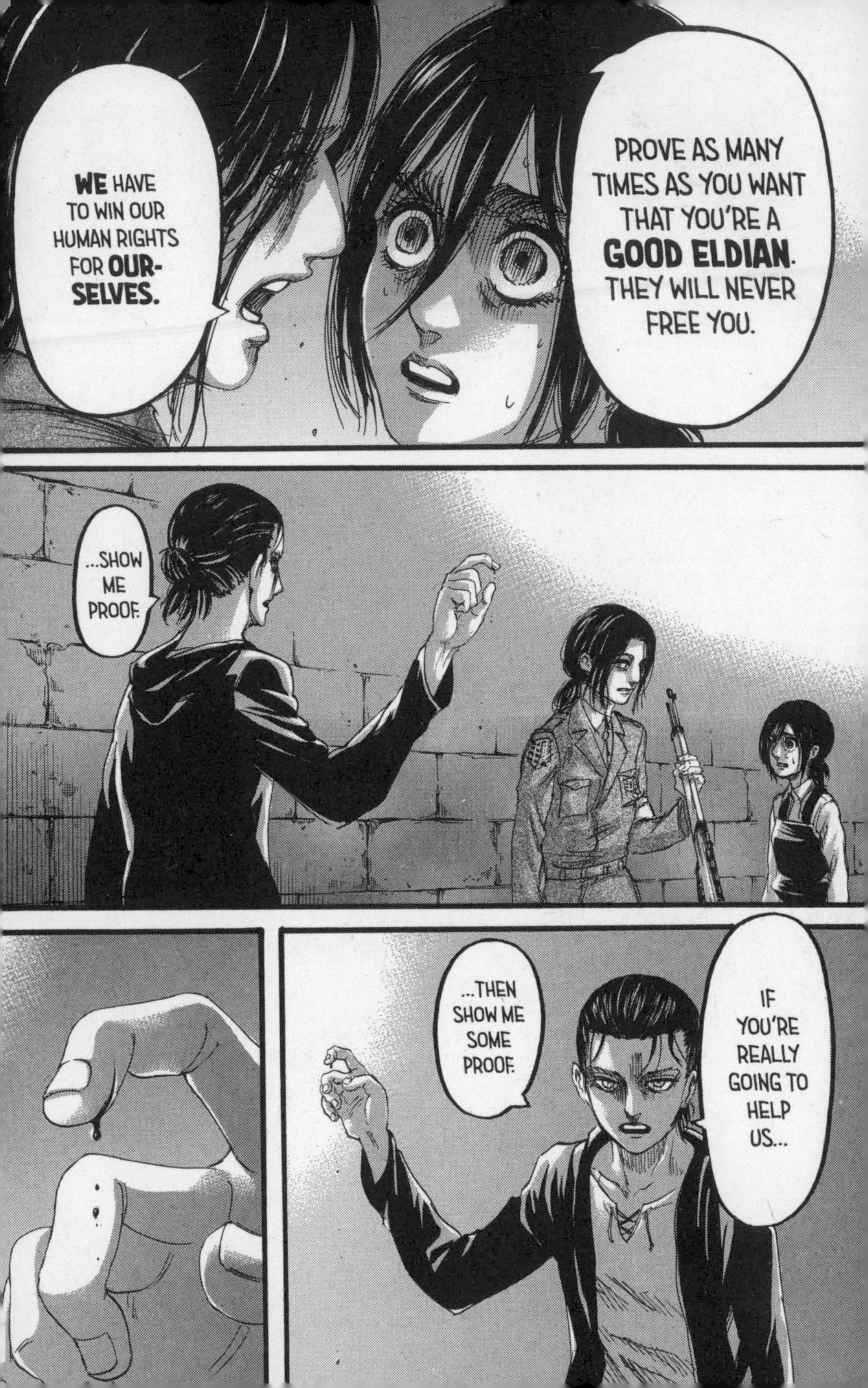
PROVE AS MANY TIMES AS YOU WANT THAT YOU'RE A **GOOD ELDIAN**. THEY WILL NEVER FREE YOU.
WE HAVE TO WIN OUR HUMAN RIGHTS FOR **OURSELVES.**
...SHOW ME PROOF.
IF YOU'RE REALLY GOING TO HELP US...
...THEN SHOW ME SOME PROOF.

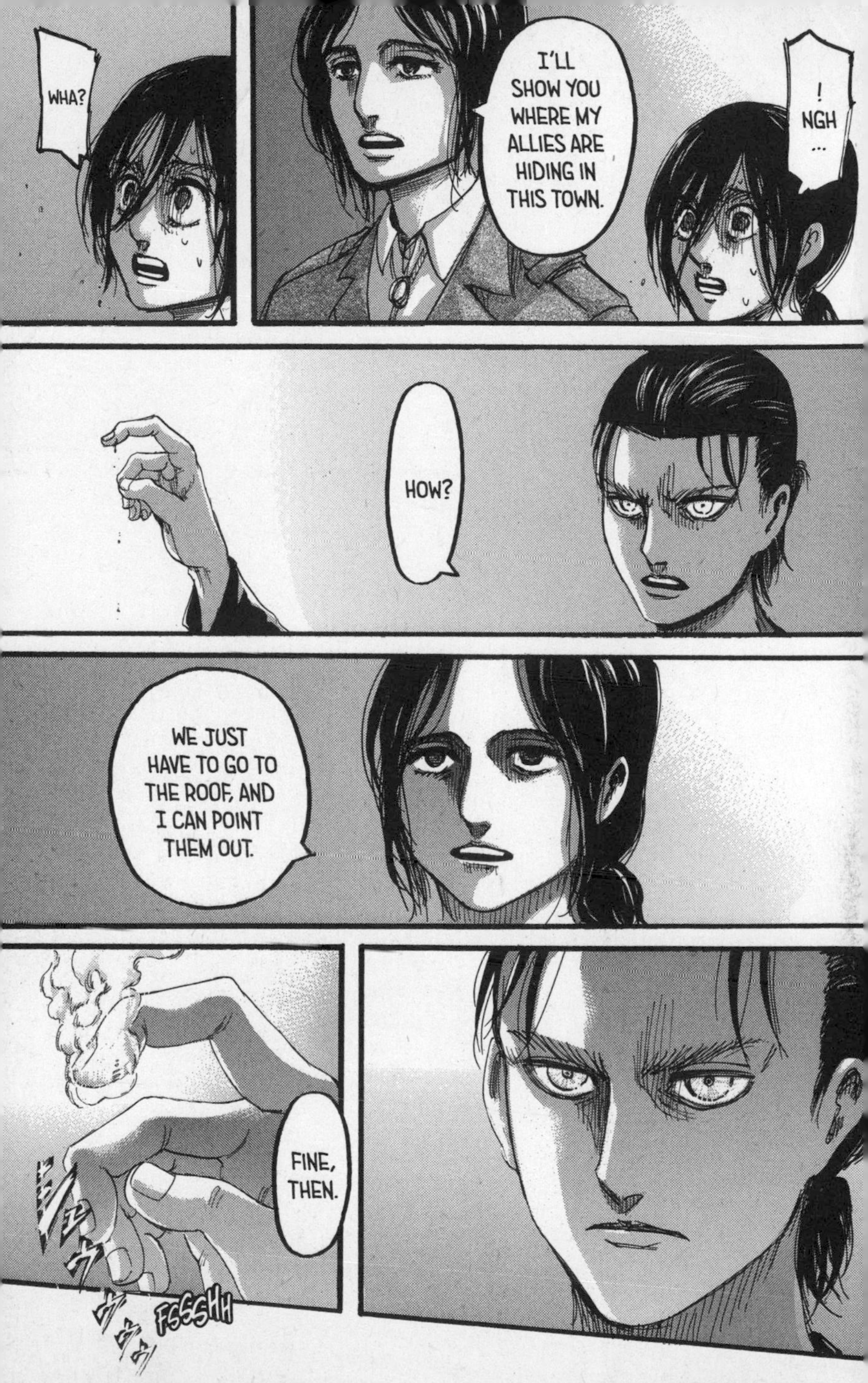
! NGH ...
I'LL SHOW YOU WHERE MY ALLIES ARE HIDING IN THIS TOWN.
WHA?
HOW?
WE JUST HAVE TO GO TO THE ROOF, AND I CAN POINT THEM OUT.
FINE, THEN.
FSSSHH

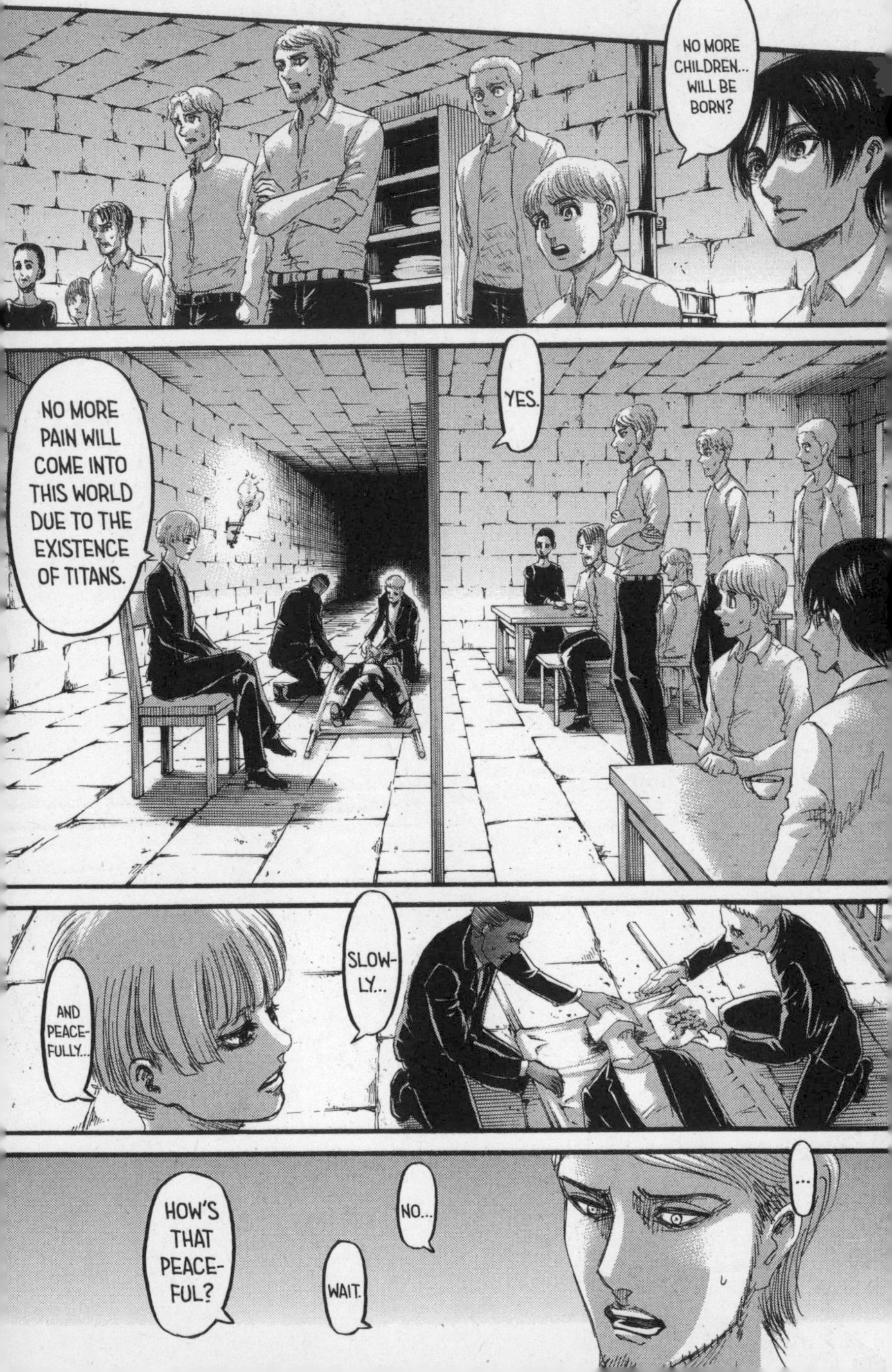
NO MORE CHILDREN... WILL BE BORN?
YES.
NO MORE PAIN WILL COME INTO THIS WORLD DUE TO THE EXISTENCE OF TITANS.
SLOW-LY...
AND PEACE-FULLY...
...
NO...
WAIT.
HOW'S THAT PEACE-FUL?

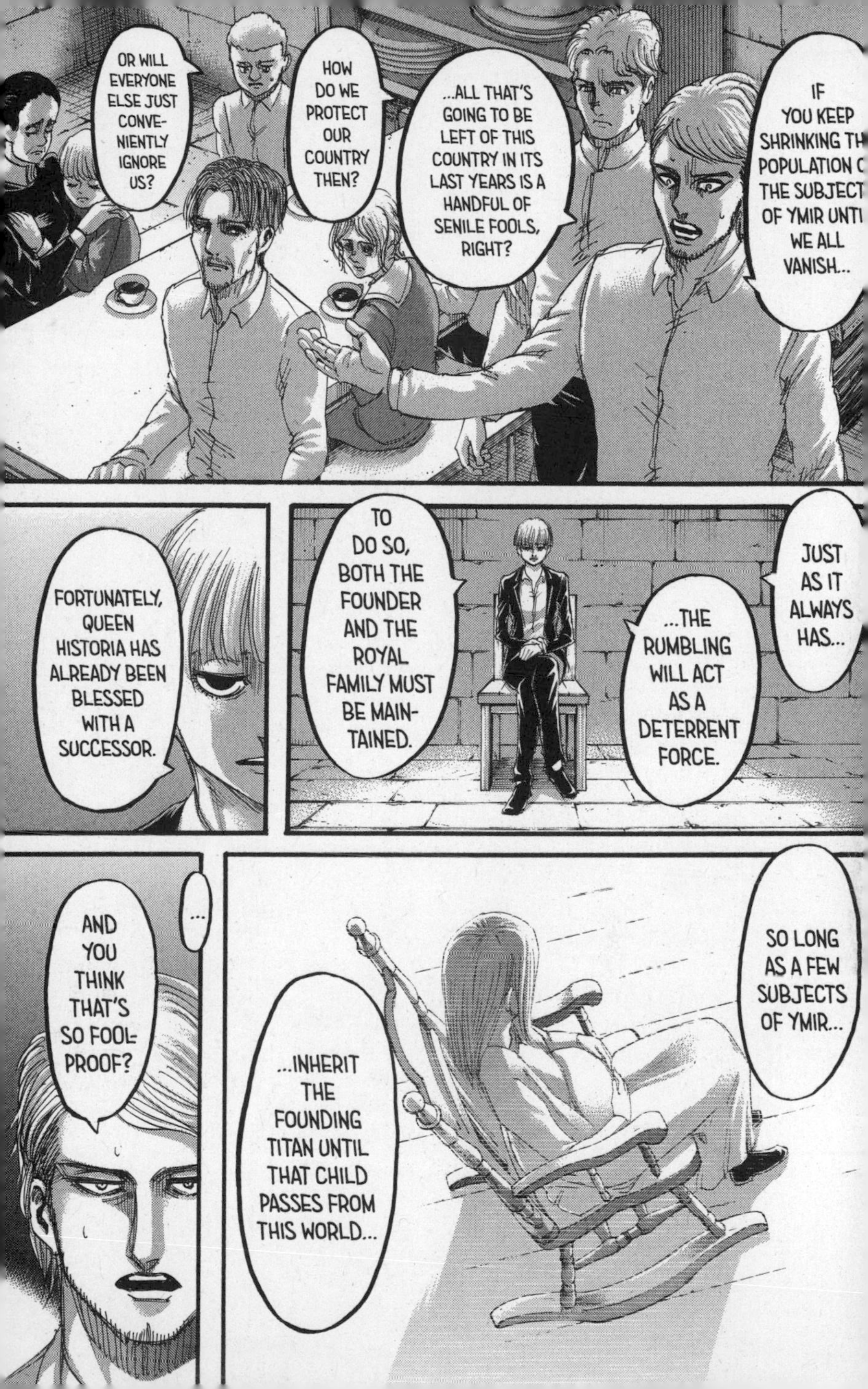
IF YOU KEEP SHRINKING TH POPULATION C THE SUBJECT OF YMIR UNTI WE ALL VANISH...
...ALL THAT'S GOING TO BE LEFT OF THIS COUNTRY IN ITS LAST YEARS IS A HANDFUL OF SENILE FOOLS, RIGHT?
HOW DO WE PROTECT OUR COUNTRY THEN?
OR WILL EVERYONE ELSE JUST CONVENIENTLY IGNORE US?
JUST AS IT ALWAYS HAS...
...THE RUMBLING WILL ACT AS A DETERRENT FORCE.
TO DO SO, BOTH THE FOUNDER AND THE ROYAL FAMILY MUST BE MAINTAINED.
FORTUNATELY, QUEEN HISTORIA HAS ALREADY BEEN BLESSED WITH A SUCCESSOR.
SO LONG AS A FEW SUBJECTS OF YMIR...
...INHERIT THE FOUNDING TITAN UNTIL THAT CHILD PASSES FROM THIS WORLD...
...
AND YOU THINK THAT'S SO FOOLPROOF?

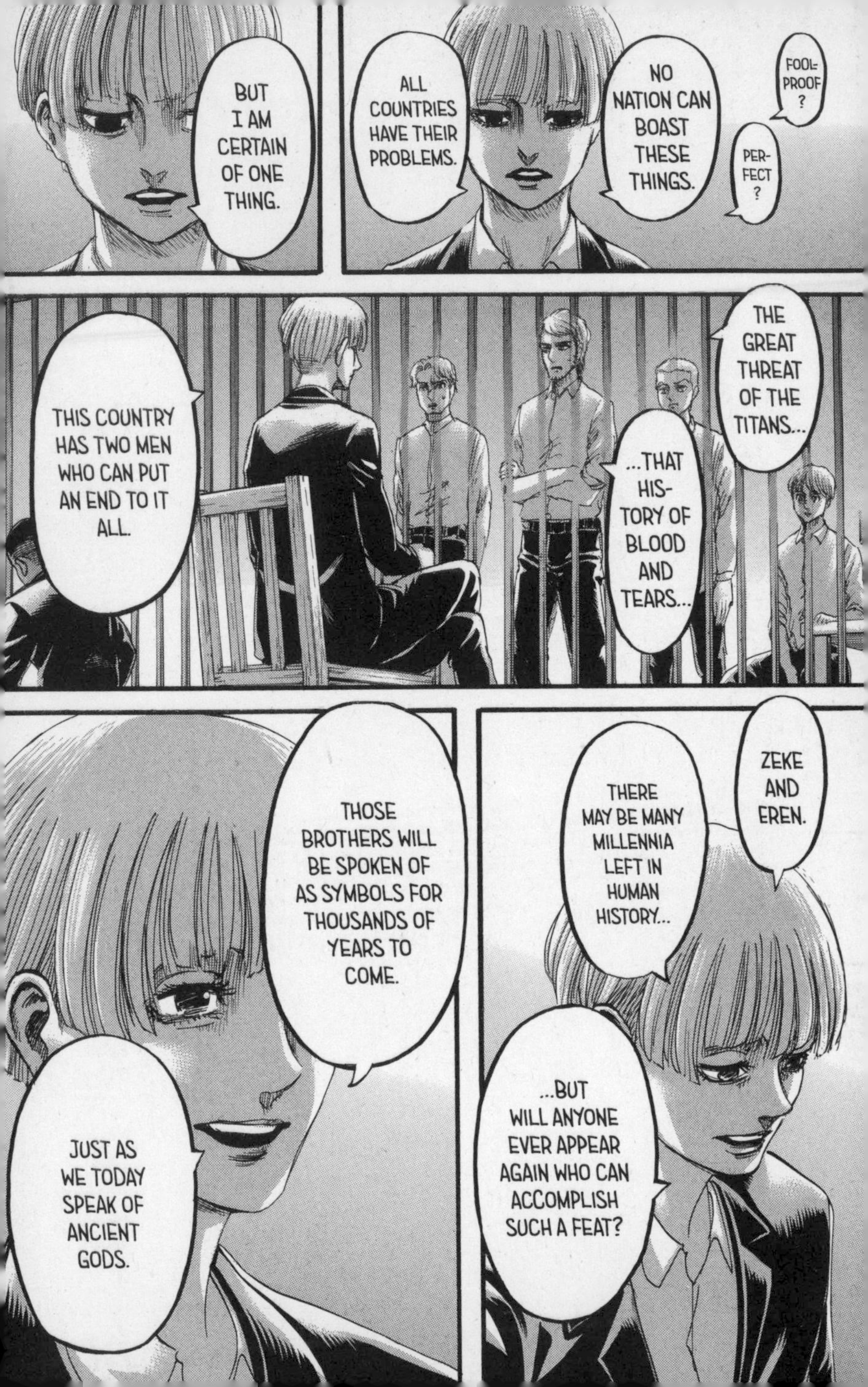
FOOL-PROOF?
PER-FECT?
NO NATION CAN BOAST THESE THINGS.
ALL COUNTRIES HAVE THEIR PROBLEMS.
BUT I AM CERTAIN OF ONE THING.
THE GREAT THREAT OF THE TITANS...
...THAT HIS-TORY OF BLOOD AND TEARS...
THIS COUNTRY HAS TWO MEN WHO CAN PUT AN END TO IT ALL.
ZEKE AND EREN.
THERE MAY BE MANY MILLENNIA LEFT IN HUMAN HISTORY...
...BUT WILL ANYONE EVER APPEAR AGAIN WHO CAN ACCOMPLISH SUCH A FEAT?
THOSE BROTHERS WILL BE SPOKEN OF AS SYMBOLS FOR THOUSANDS OF YEARS TO COME.
JUST AS WE TODAY SPEAK OF ANCIENT GODS.

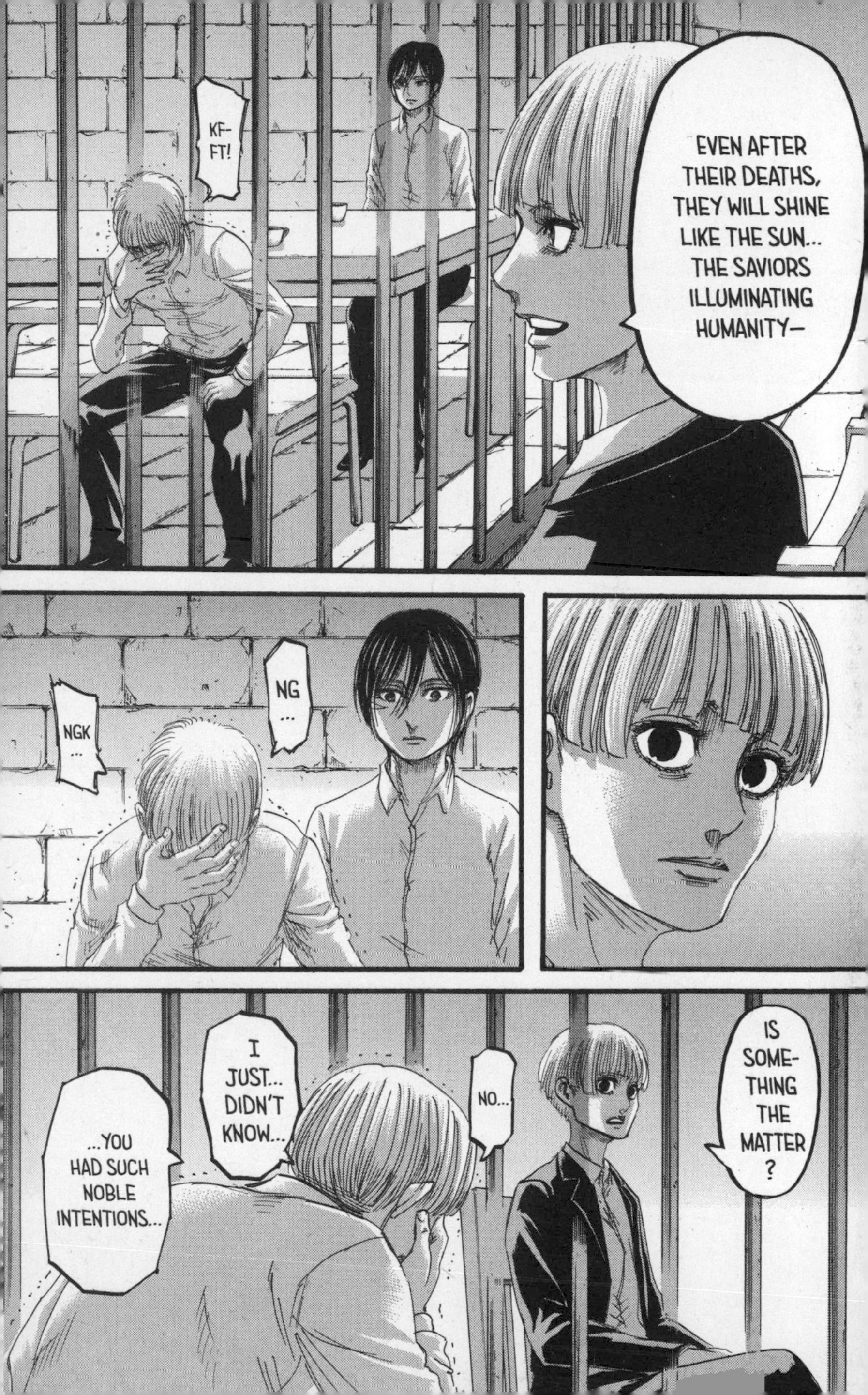
EVEN AFTER THEIR DEATHS, THEY WILL SHINE LIKE THE SUN... THE SAVIORS ILLUMINATING HUMANITY—
KF-FT!
NG...
NGK...
IS SOMETHING THE MATTER?
NO...
I JUST... DIDN'T KNOW...
...YOU HAD SUCH NOBLE INTENTIONS...

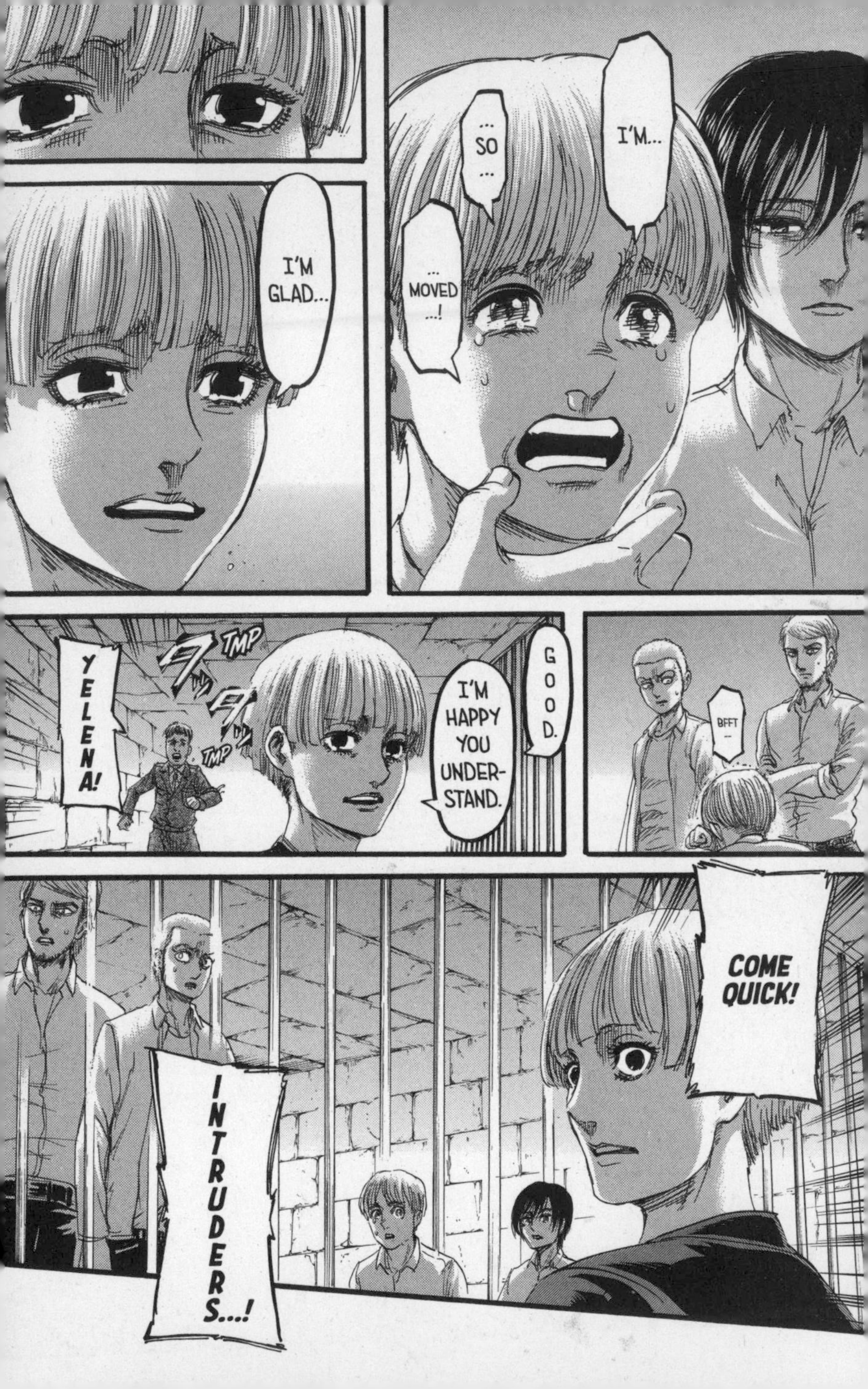
I'M...
...SO...
...MOVED...!
I'M GLAD...
BFFT--
GOOD.
I'M HAPPY YOU UNDERSTAND.
TMP
TMP
YELENA!
COME QUICK!
INTRUDERS...!

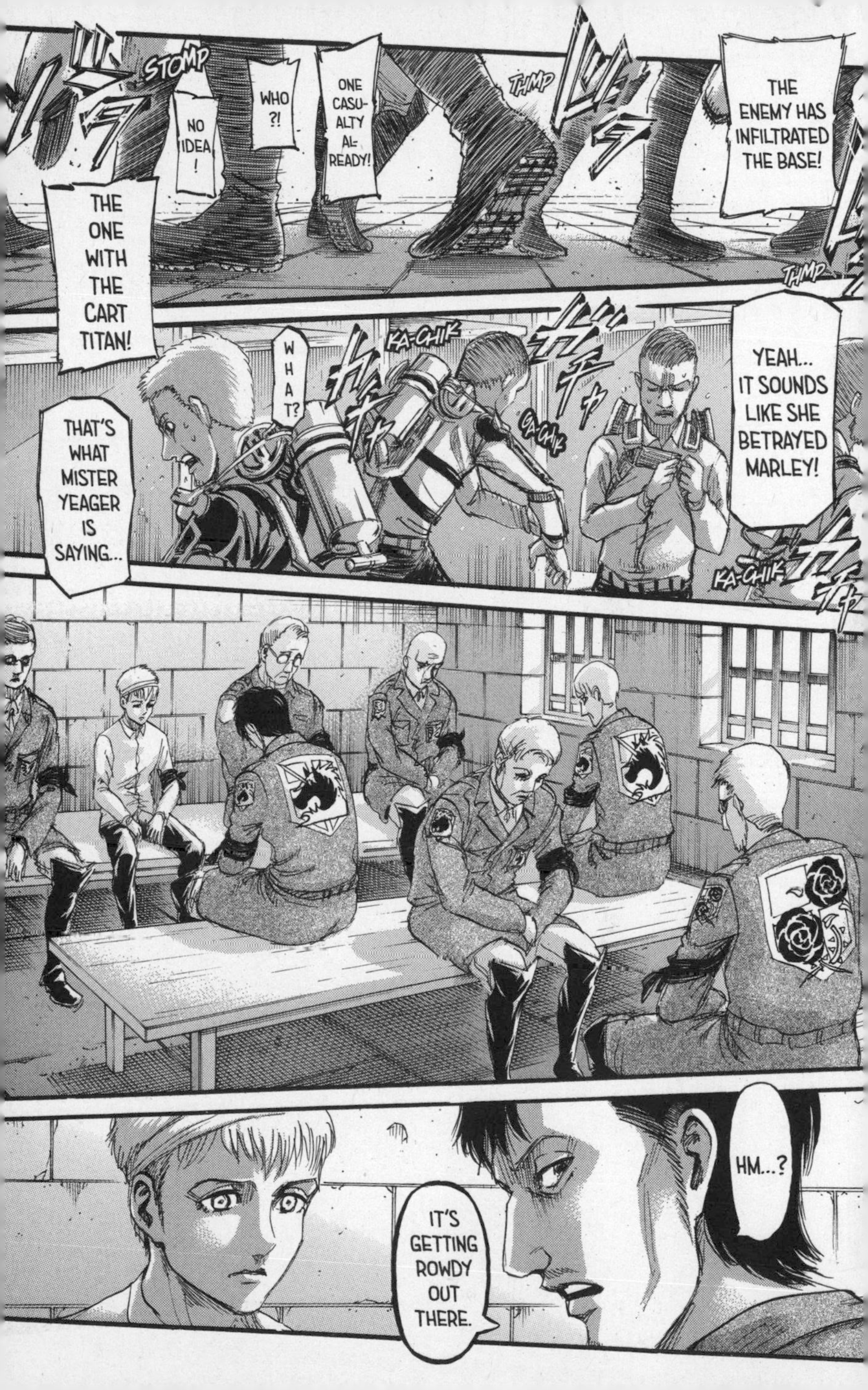
THE ENEMY HAS INFILTRATED THE BASE!
THMP
THMP
ONE CASUALTY ALREADY!
WHO?!
NO IDEA!
STOMP
THE ONE WITH THE CART TITAN!
YEAH... IT SOUNDS LIKE SHE BETRAYED MARLEY!
KA-CHIK
GA-CHIK
KA-CHIK
WHAT?
THAT'S WHAT MISTER YEAGER IS SAYING...
HM...?
IT'S GETTING ROWDY OUT THERE.

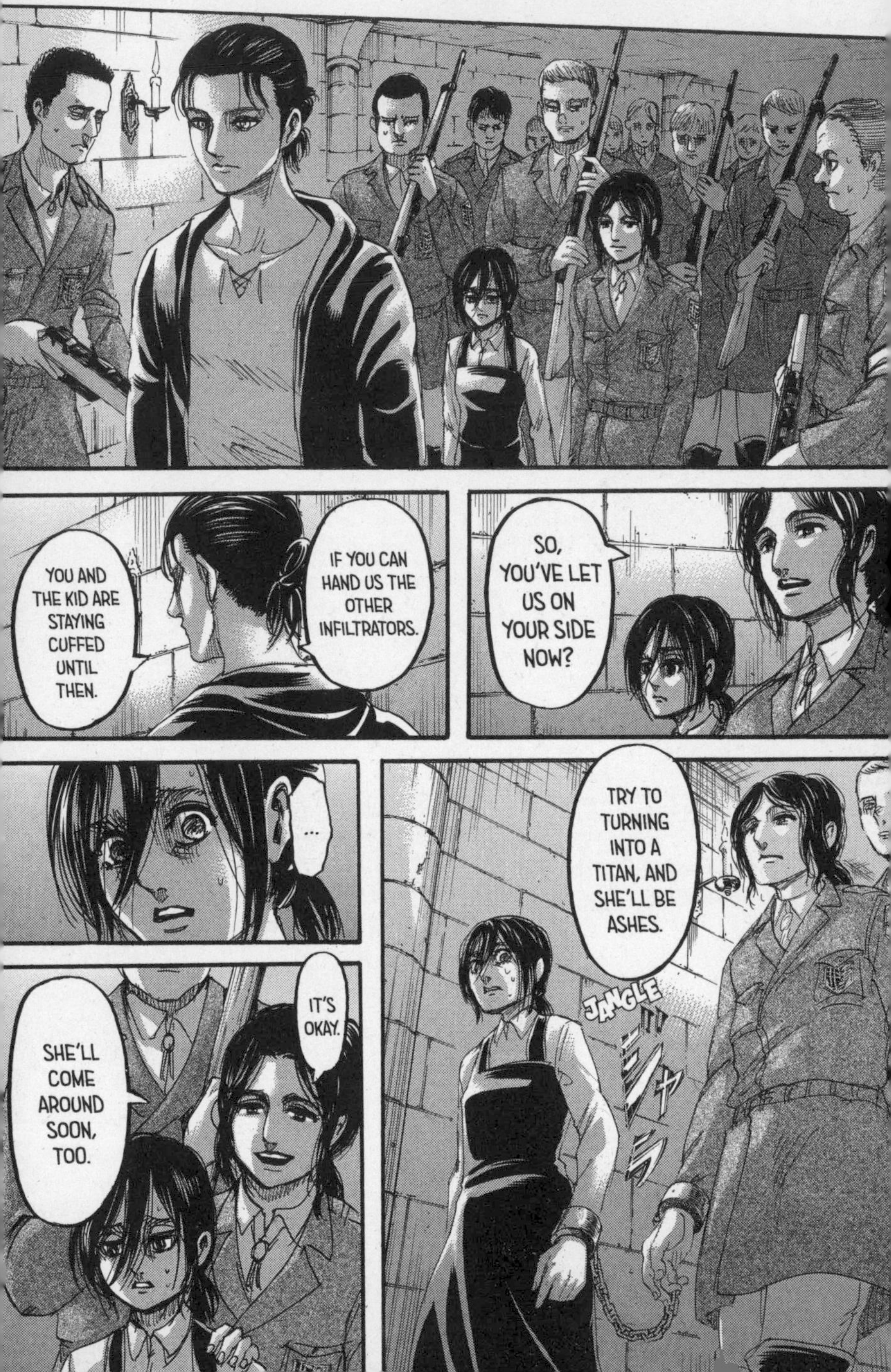
SO, YOU'VE LET US ON YOUR SIDE NOW?
IF YOU CAN HAND US THE OTHER INFILTRATORS.
YOU AND THE KID ARE STAYING CUFFED UNTIL THEN.
TRY TO TURNING INTO A TITAN, AND SHE'LL BE ASHES.
JANGLE
...
IT'S OKAY.
SHE'LL COME AROUND SOON, TOO.

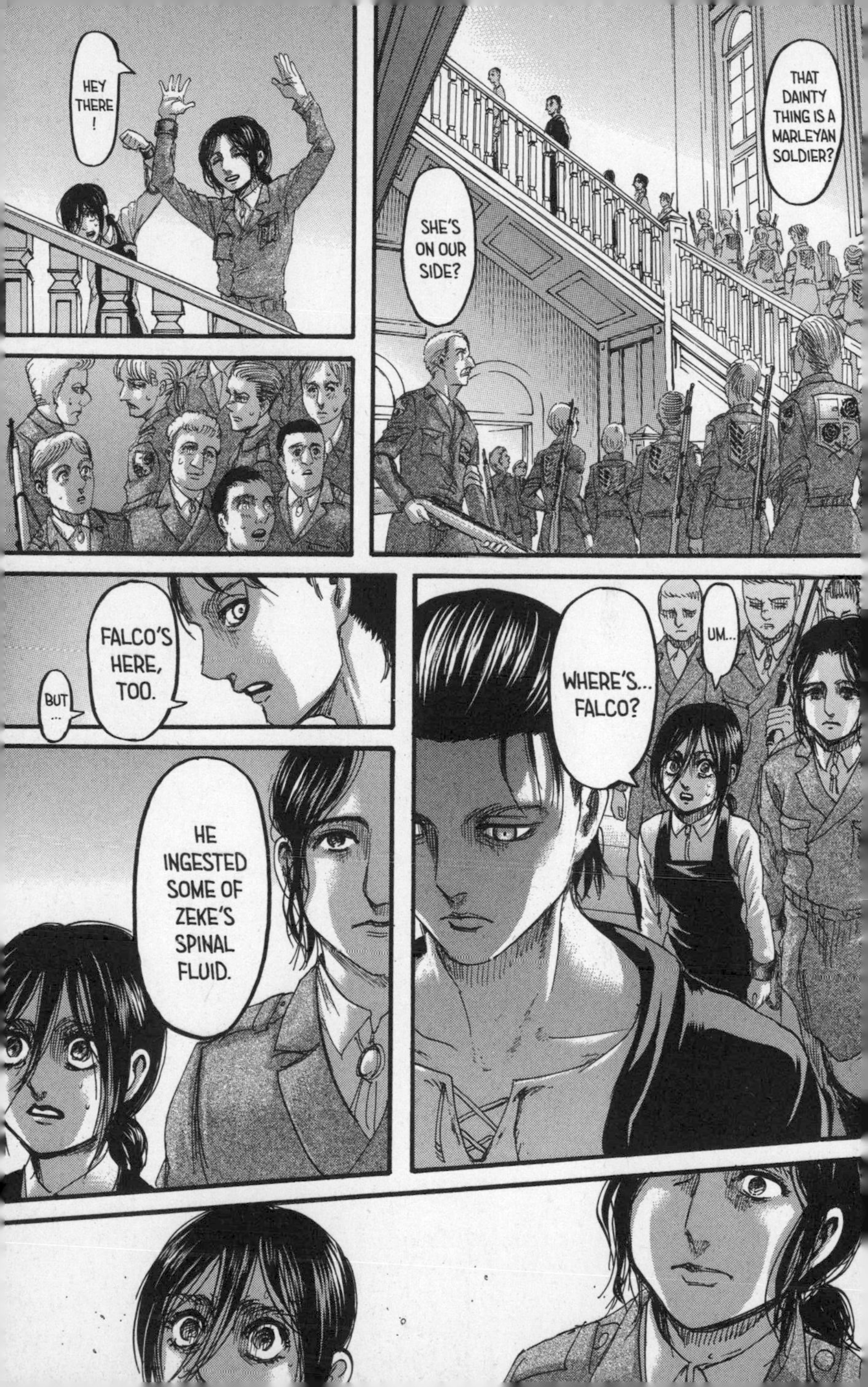
THAT DAINTY THING IS A MARLEYAN SOLDIER?
SHE'S ON OUR SIDE?
HEY THERE!
UM...
WHERE'S... FALCO?
FALCO'S HERE, TOO.
BUT...
HE INGESTED SOME OF ZEKE'S SPINAL FLUID.

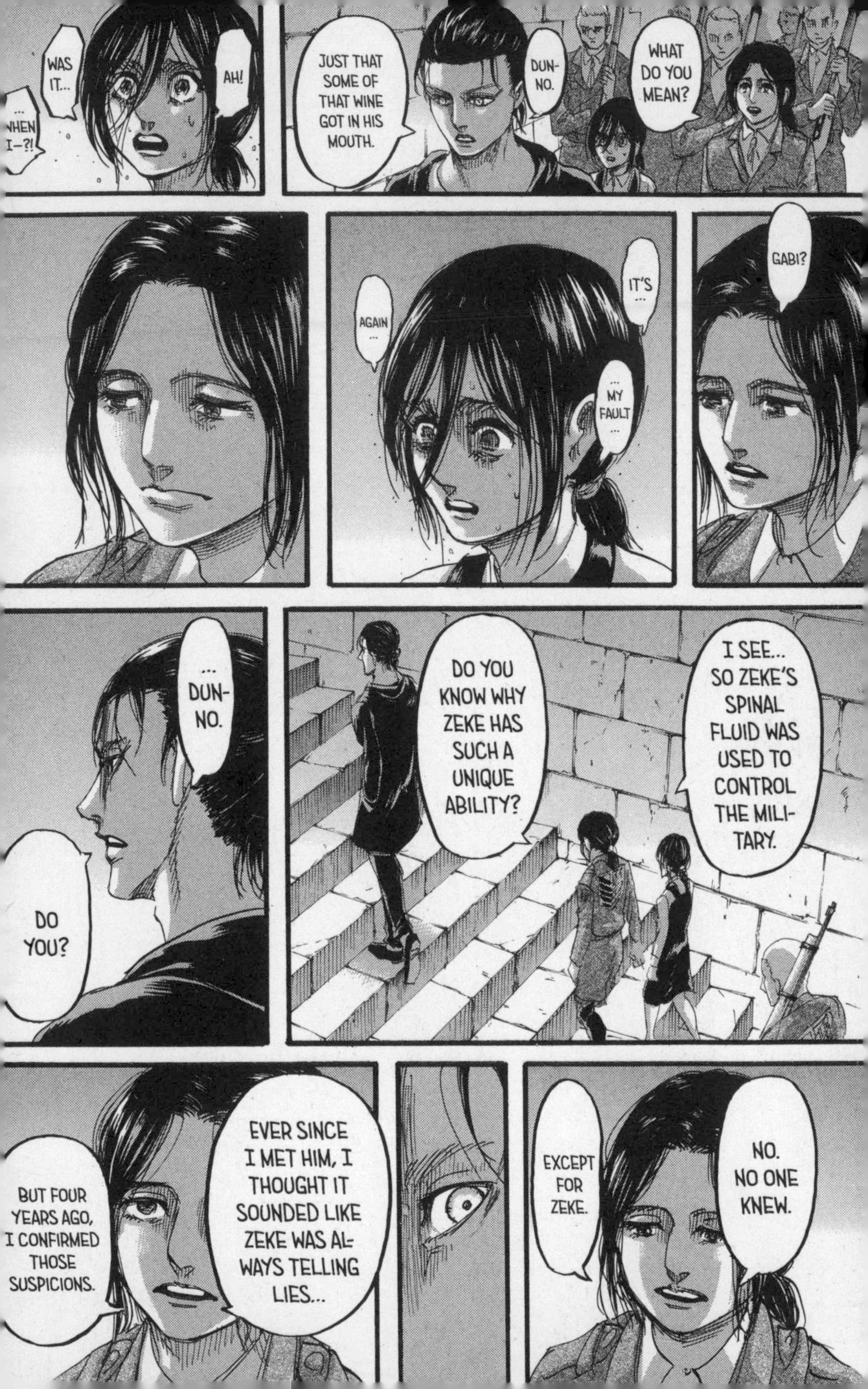
WHAT DO YOU MEAN?
DUN-NO.
JUST THAT SOME OF THAT WINE GOT IN HIS MOUTH.
AH!
WAS IT...
...WHEN I—?!
GABI?
IT'S...
...MY FAULT...
AGAIN...
I SEE... SO ZEKE'S SPINAL FLUID WAS USED TO CONTROL THE MILITARY.
DO YOU KNOW WHY ZEKE HAS SUCH A UNIQUE ABILITY?
...DUN-NO.
DO YOU?
NO. NO ONE KNEW.
EXCEPT FOR ZEKE.
EVER SINCE I MET HIM, I THOUGHT IT SOUNDED LIKE ZEKE WAS AL-WAYS TELLING LIES...
BUT FOUR YEARS AGO, I CONFIRMED THOSE SUSPICIONS.

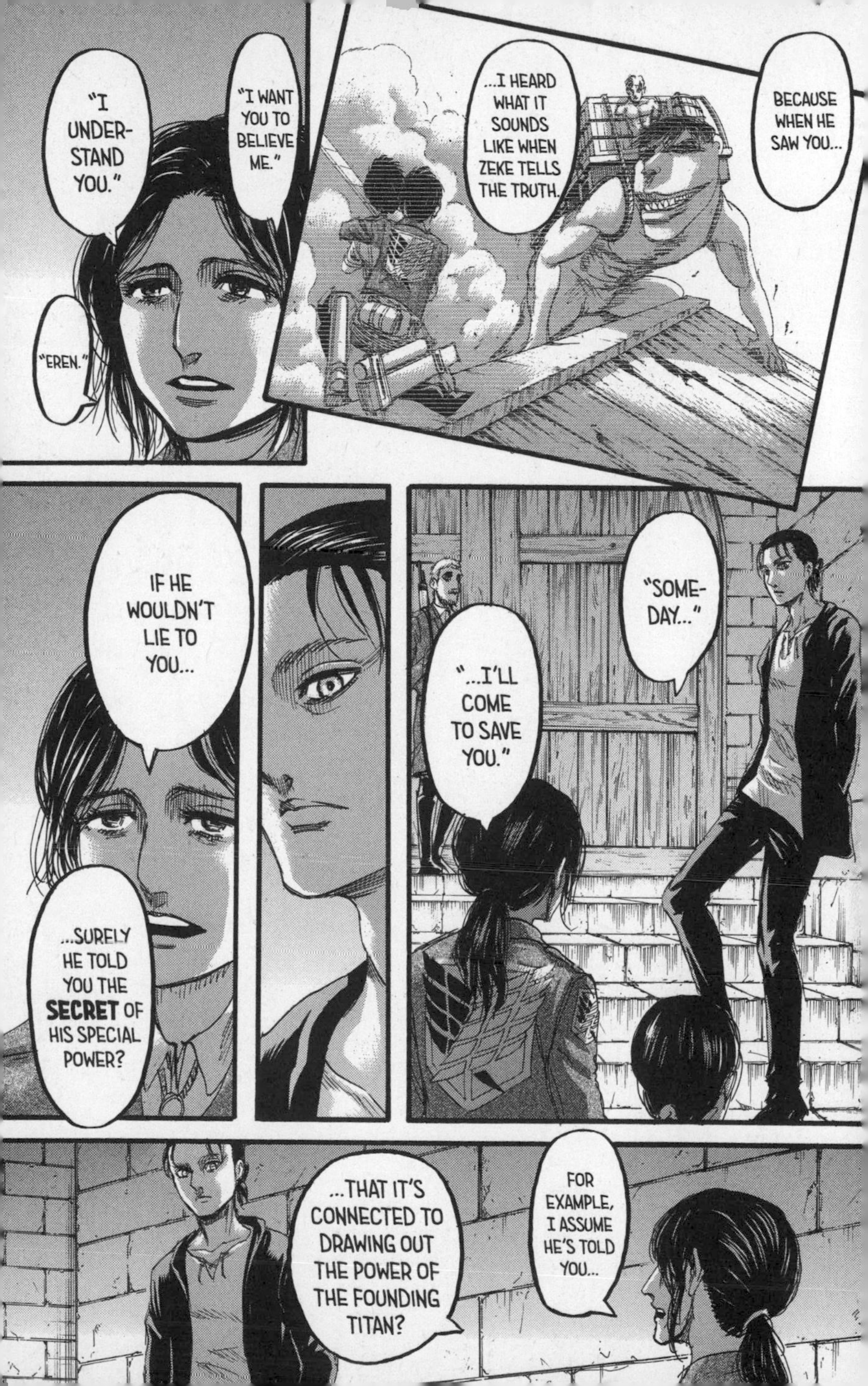
BECAUSE WHEN HE SAW YOU...
...I HEARD WHAT IT SOUNDS LIKE WHEN ZEKE TELLS THE TRUTH.
"I WANT YOU TO BELIEVE ME."
"I UNDERSTAND YOU."
"EREN."
"SOMEDAY..."
"...I'LL COME TO SAVE YOU."
IF HE WOULDN'T LIE TO YOU...
...SURELY HE TOLD YOU THE **SECRET** OF HIS SPECIAL POWER?
FOR EXAMPLE, I ASSUME HE'S TOLD YOU...
...THAT IT'S CONNECTED TO DRAWING OUT THE POWER OF THE FOUNDING TITAN?

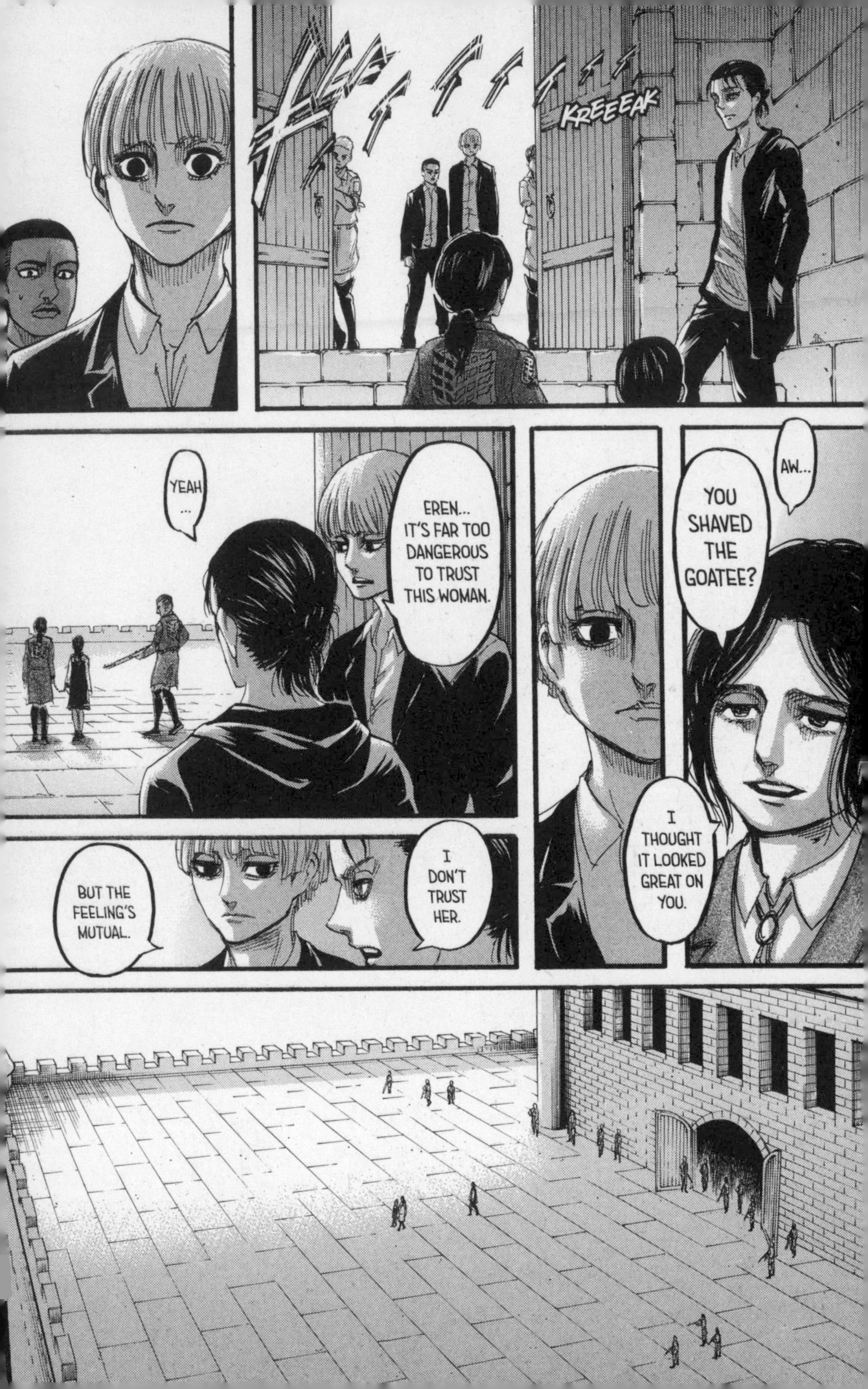
KREEEAK
AW...
YOU SHAVED THE GOATEE?
I THOUGHT IT LOOKED GREAT ON YOU.
EREN... IT'S FAR TOO DANGEROUS TO TRUST THIS WOMAN.
YEAH ...
I DON'T TRUST HER.
BUT THE FEELING'S MUTUAL.

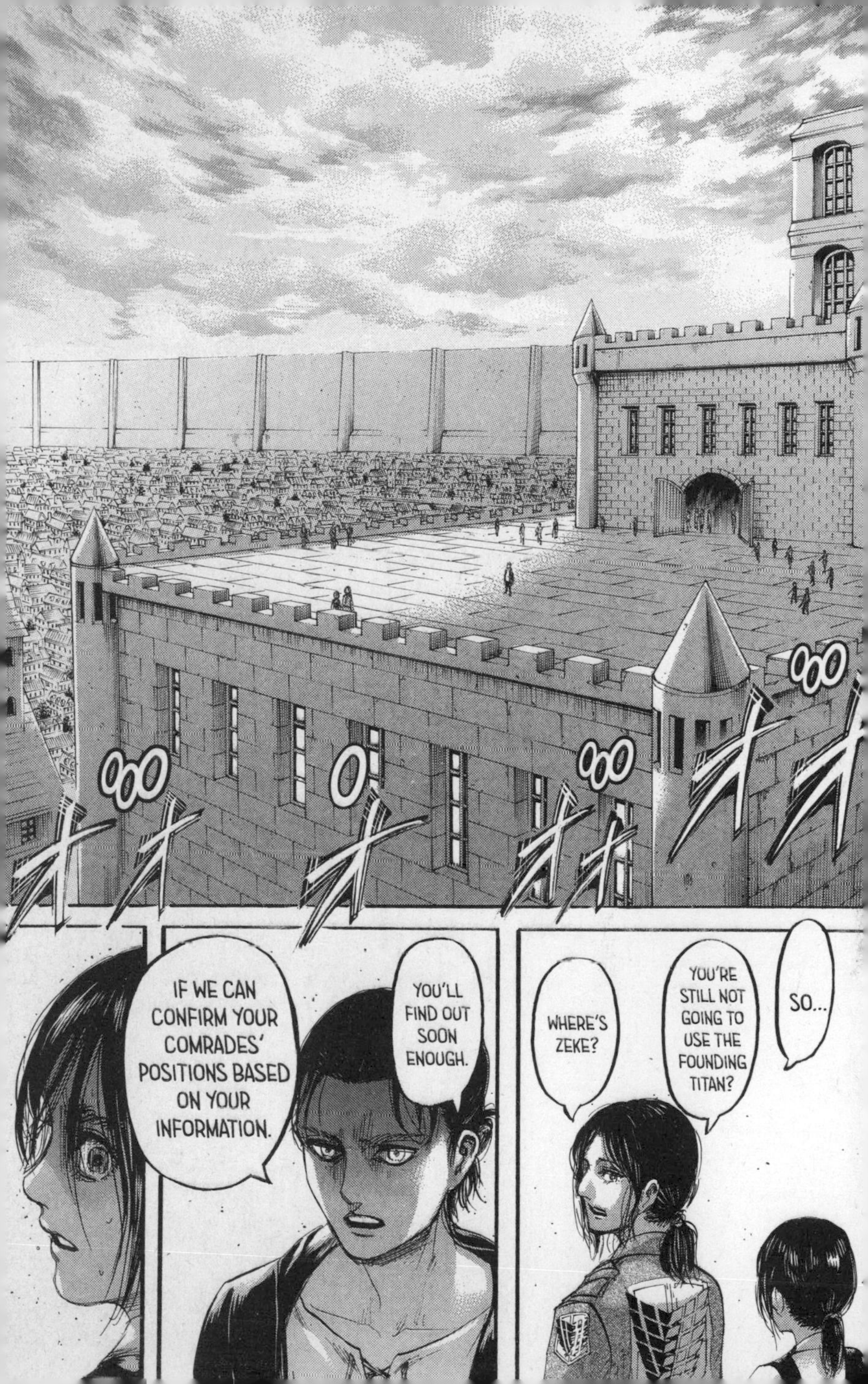
OOO
OOO
O
OOO
SO...
YOU'RE STILL NOT GOING TO USE THE FOUNDING TITAN?
WHERE'S ZEKE?
YOU'LL FIND OUT SOON ENOUGH.
IF WE CAN CONFIRM YOUR COMRADES' POSITIONS BASED ON YOUR INFORMATION.

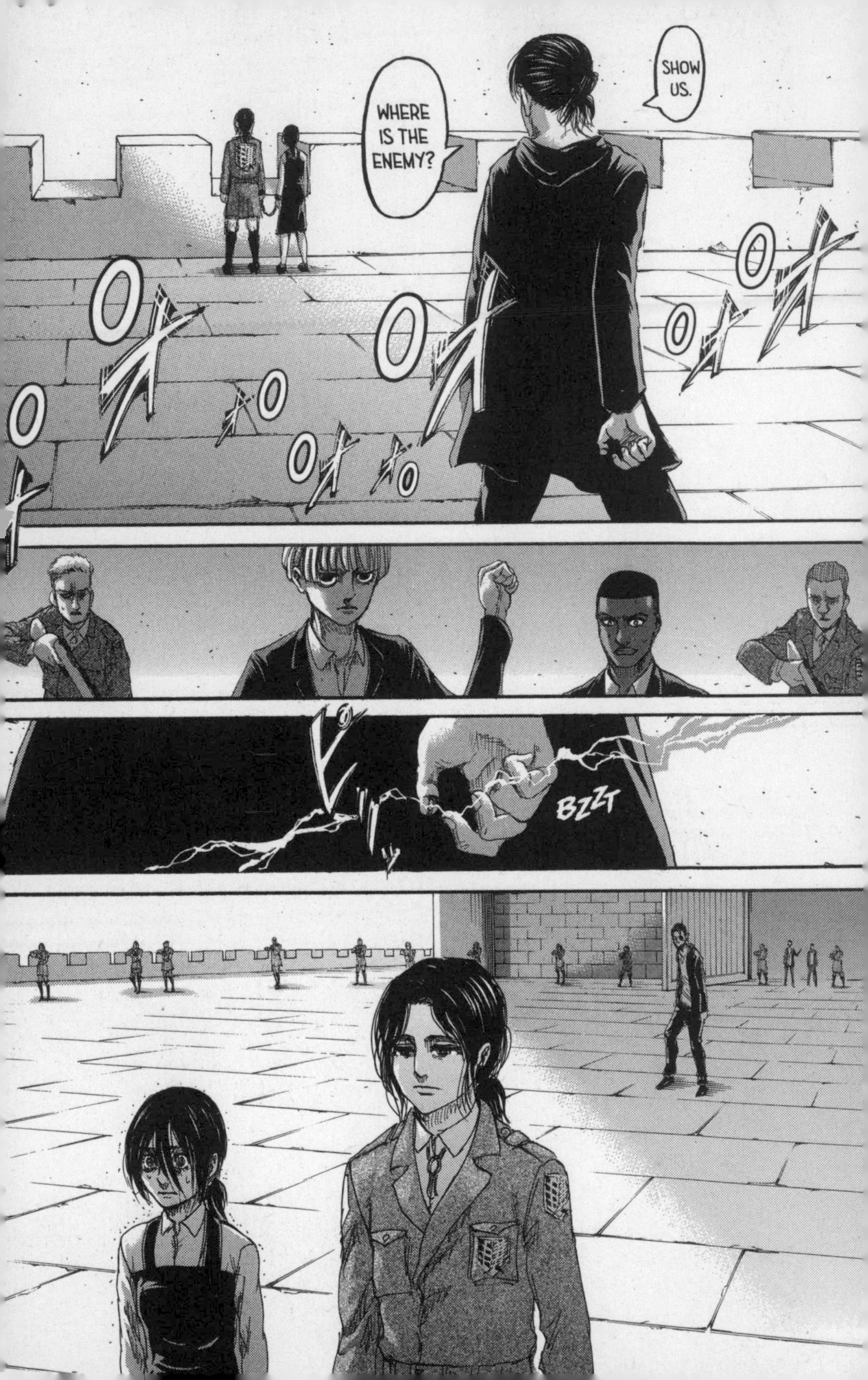
SHOW US.
WHERE IS THE ENEMY?
BZZT

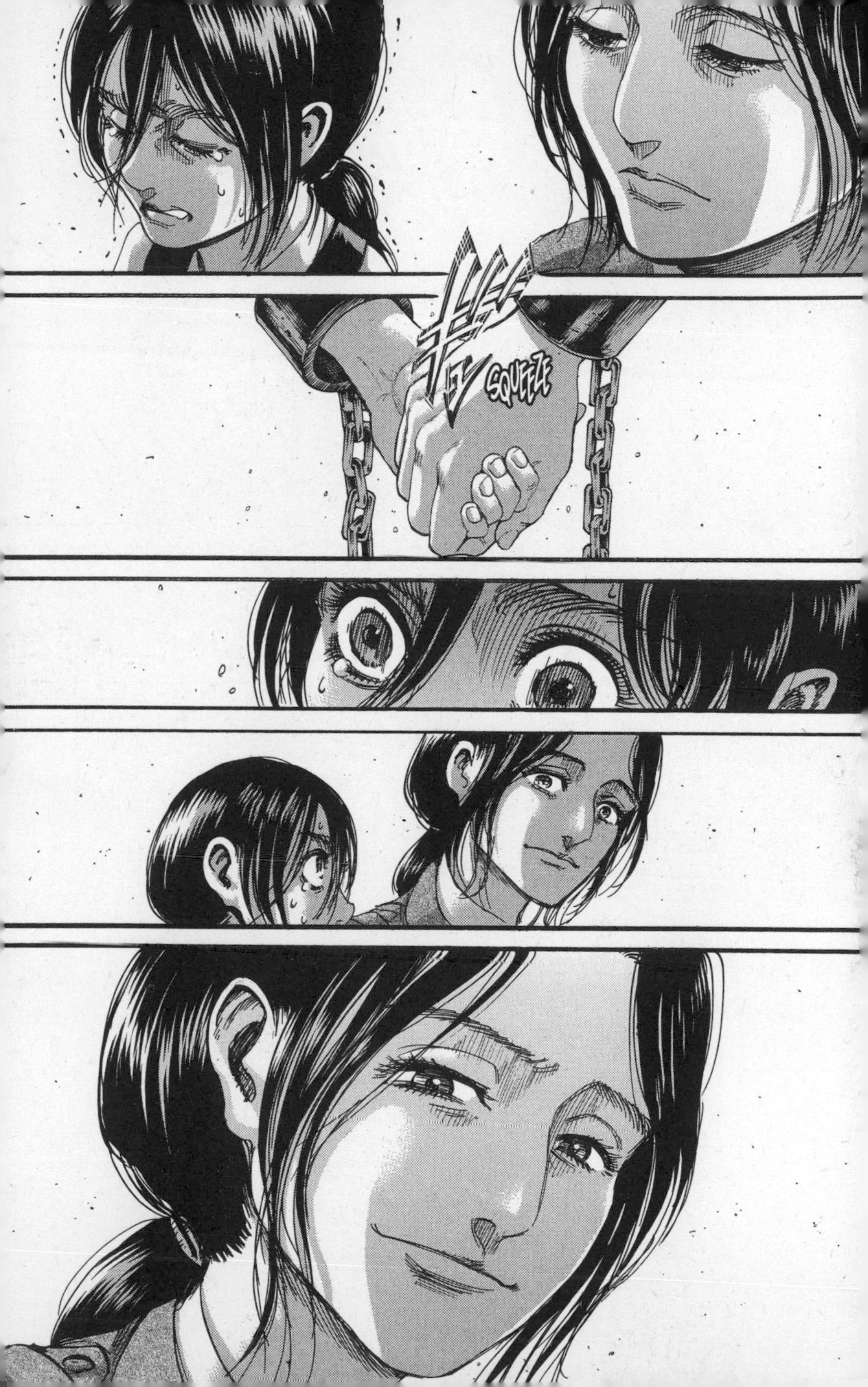
SQUEEZE

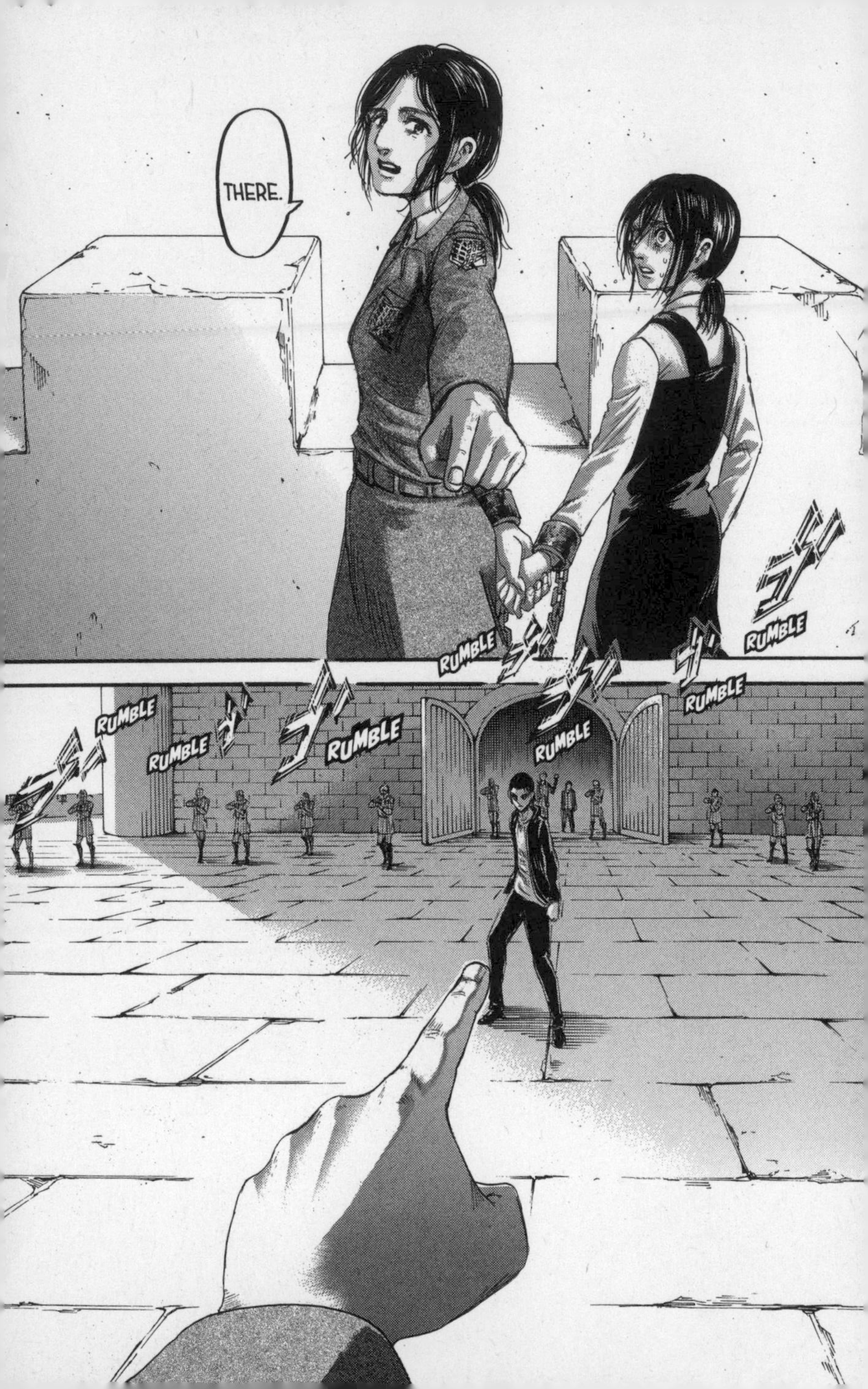
THERE.
RUMBLE
RUMBLE
RUMBLE
RUMBLE
RUMBLE
RUMBLE
RUMBLE

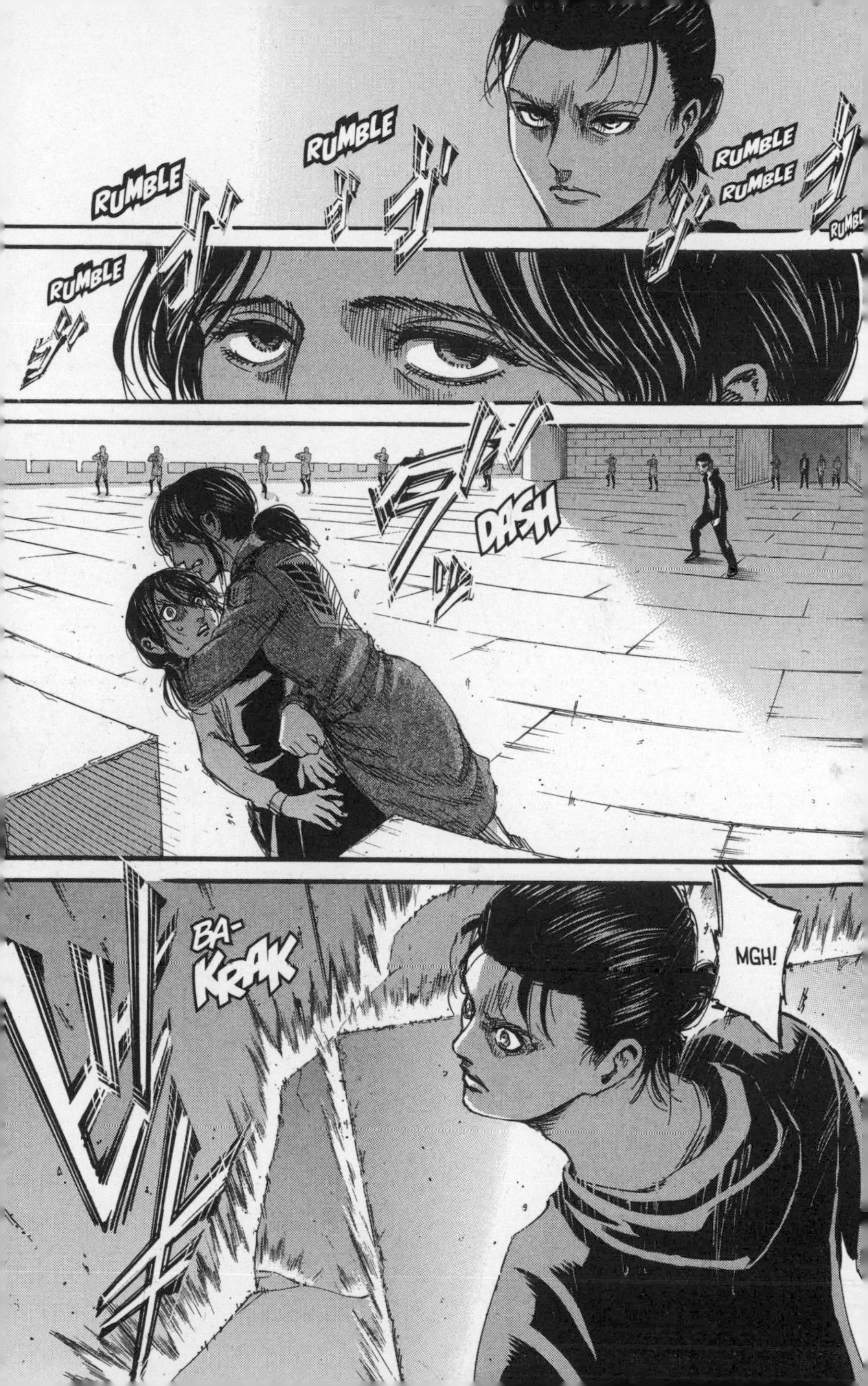
RUMBLE
RUMBLE
RUMBLE
RUMBLE
RUMBLE
DASH
MGH!
BA-KRAK

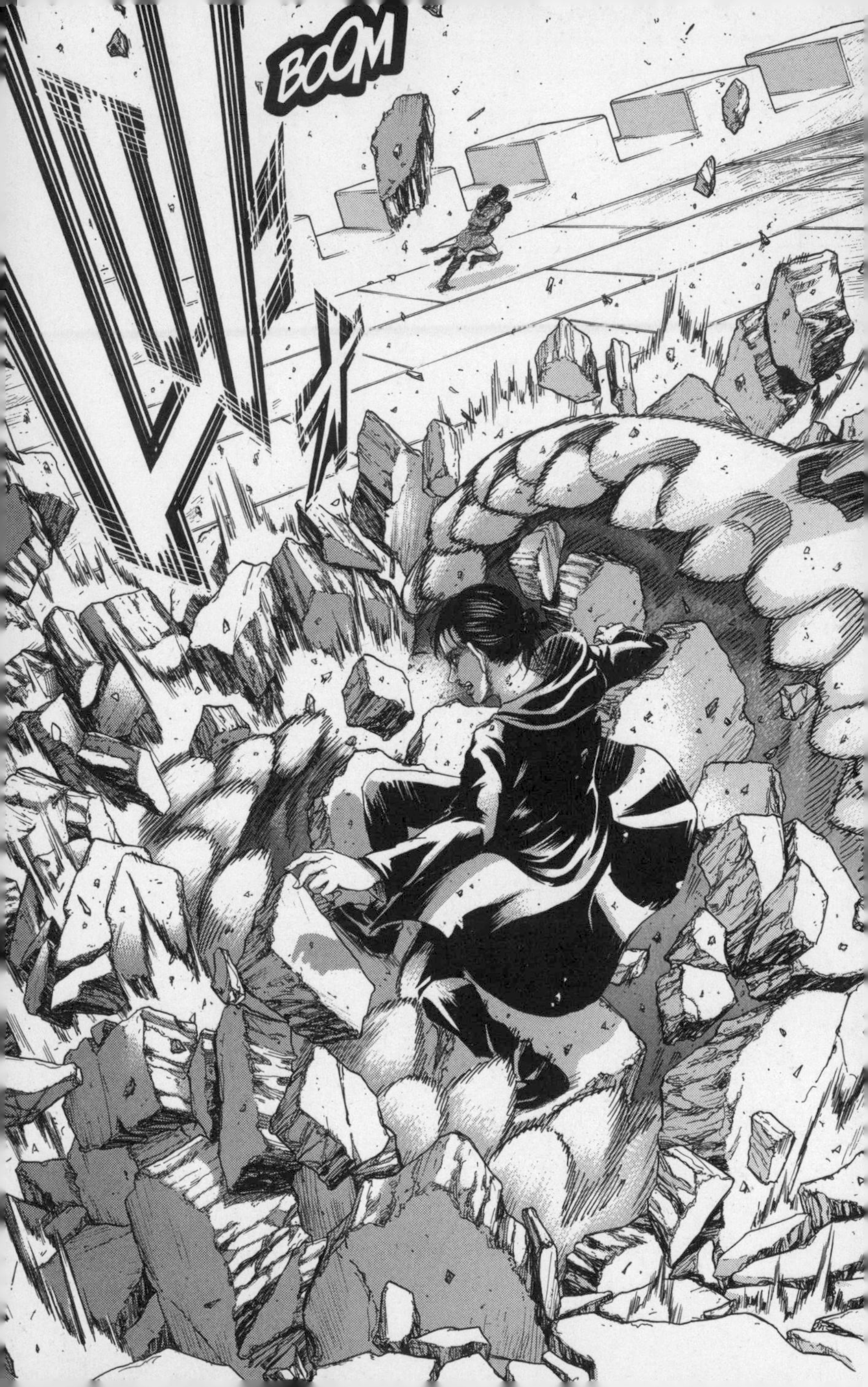
BOOM

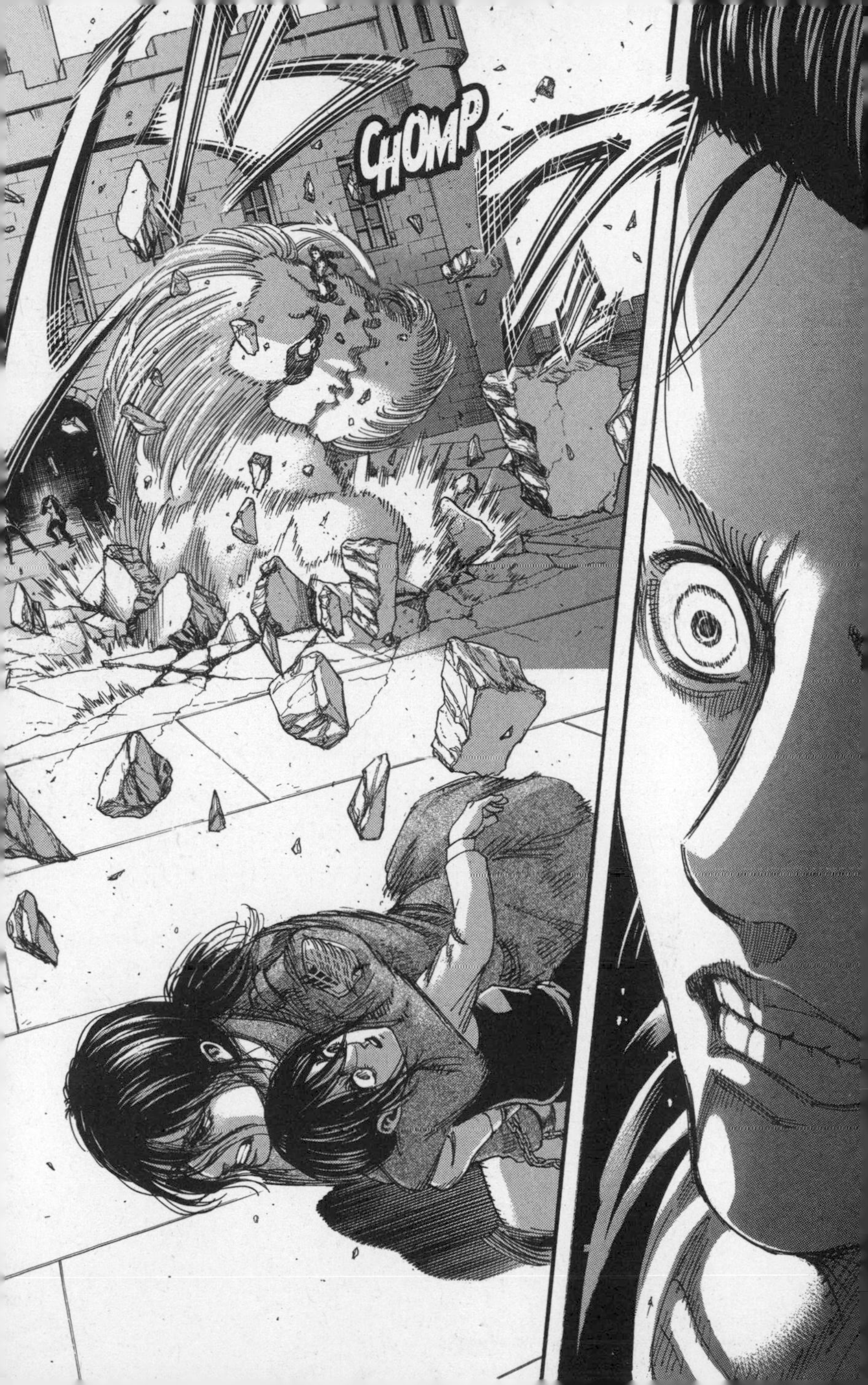
CHOMP

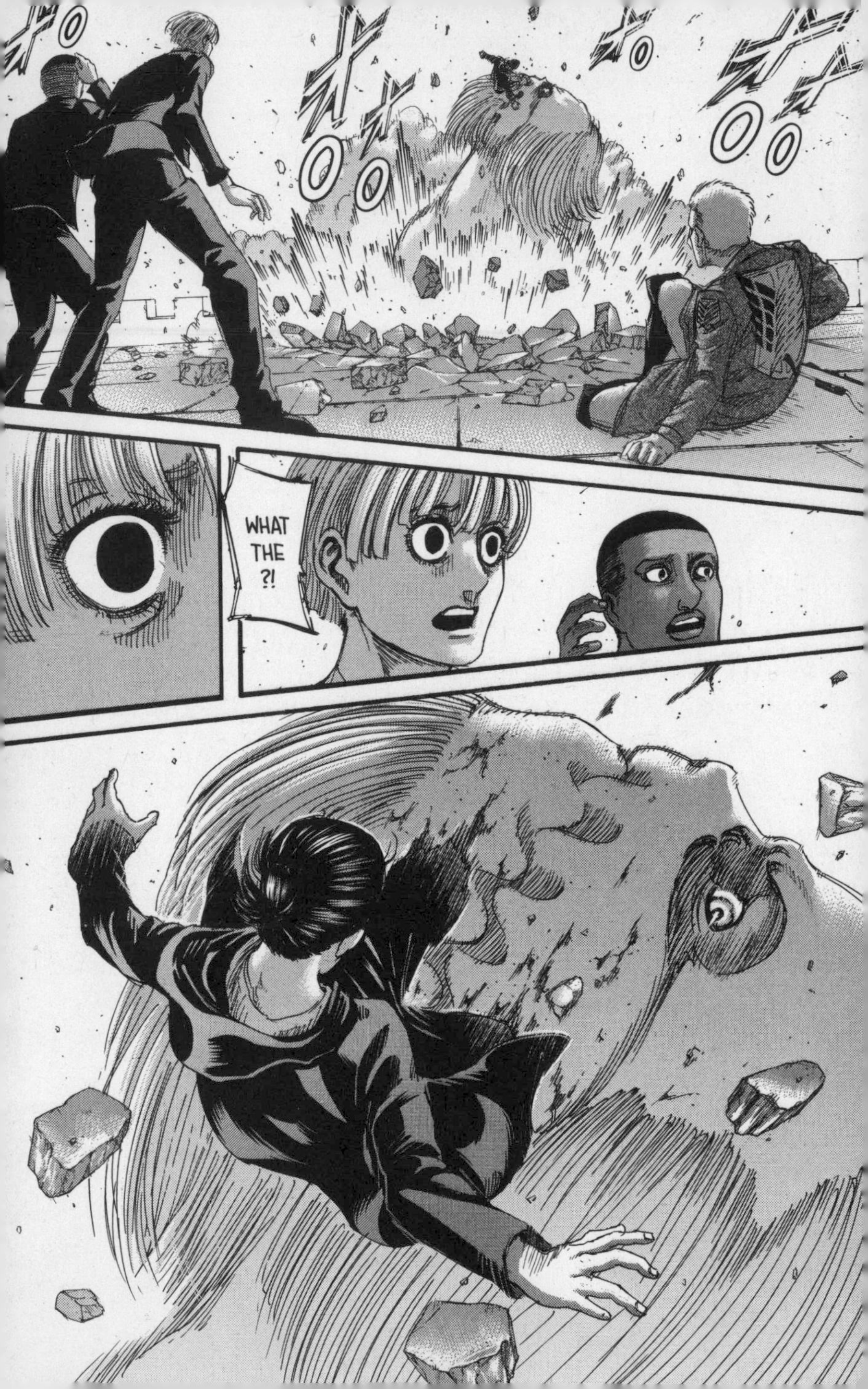
WHAT THE ?!

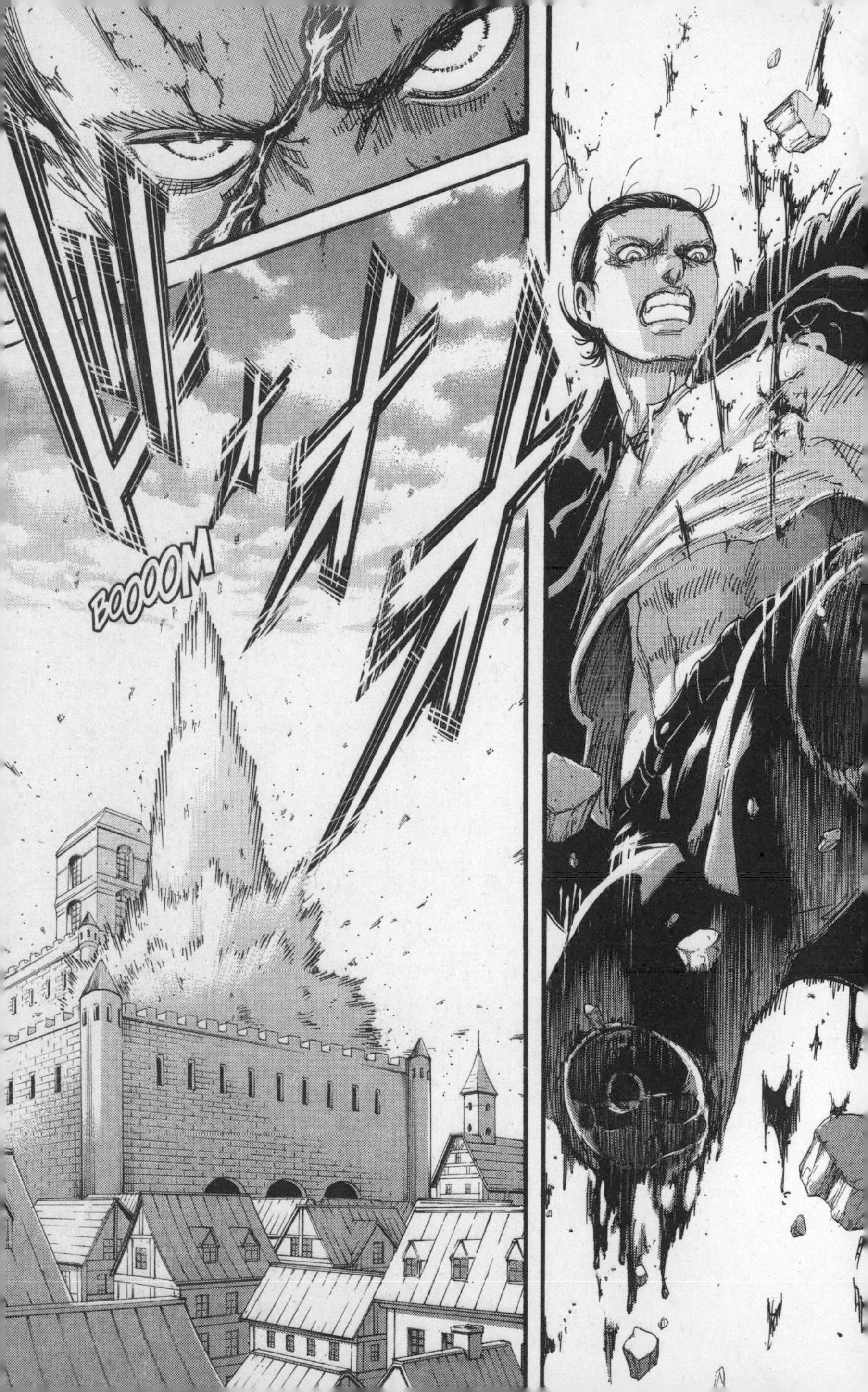
BOOOOM

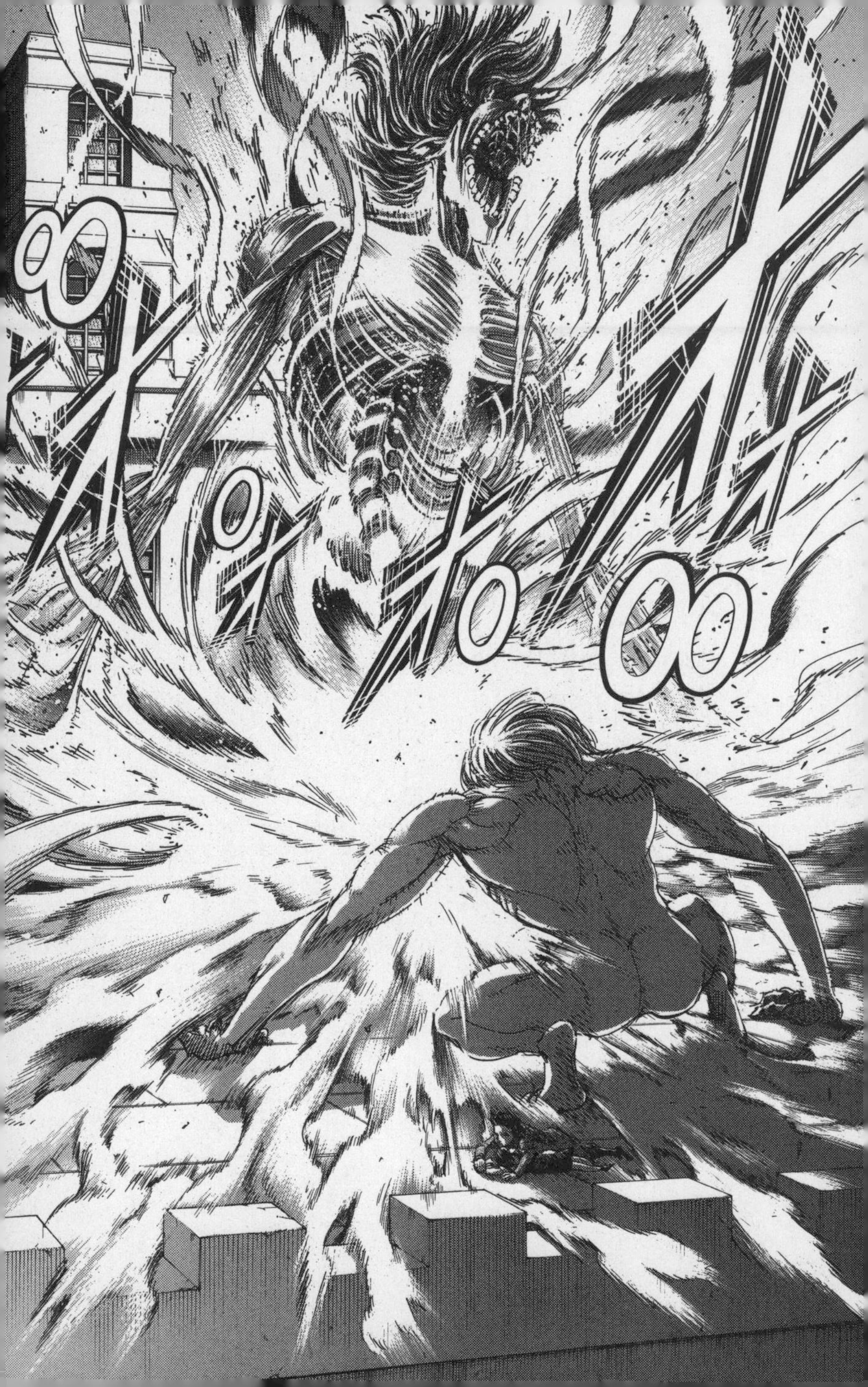

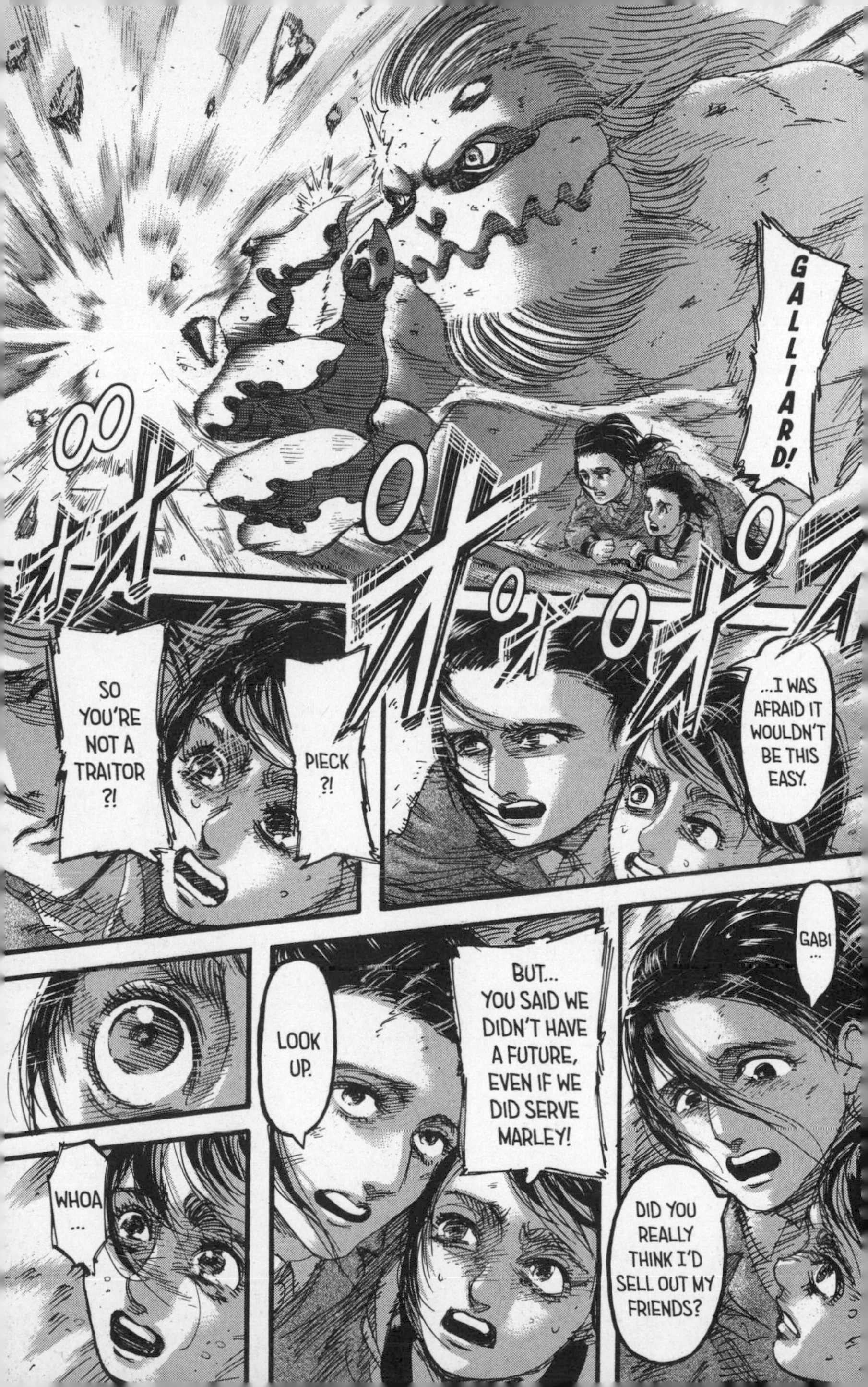
GALLIARD!
...I WAS AFRAID IT WOULDN'T BE THIS EASY.
PIECK ?!
SO YOU'RE NOT A TRAITOR ?!
GABI ...
DID YOU REALLY THINK I'D SELL OUT MY FRIENDS?
BUT... YOU SAID WE DIDN'T HAVE A FUTURE, EVEN IF WE DID SERVE MARLEY!
LOOK UP.
WHOA ...

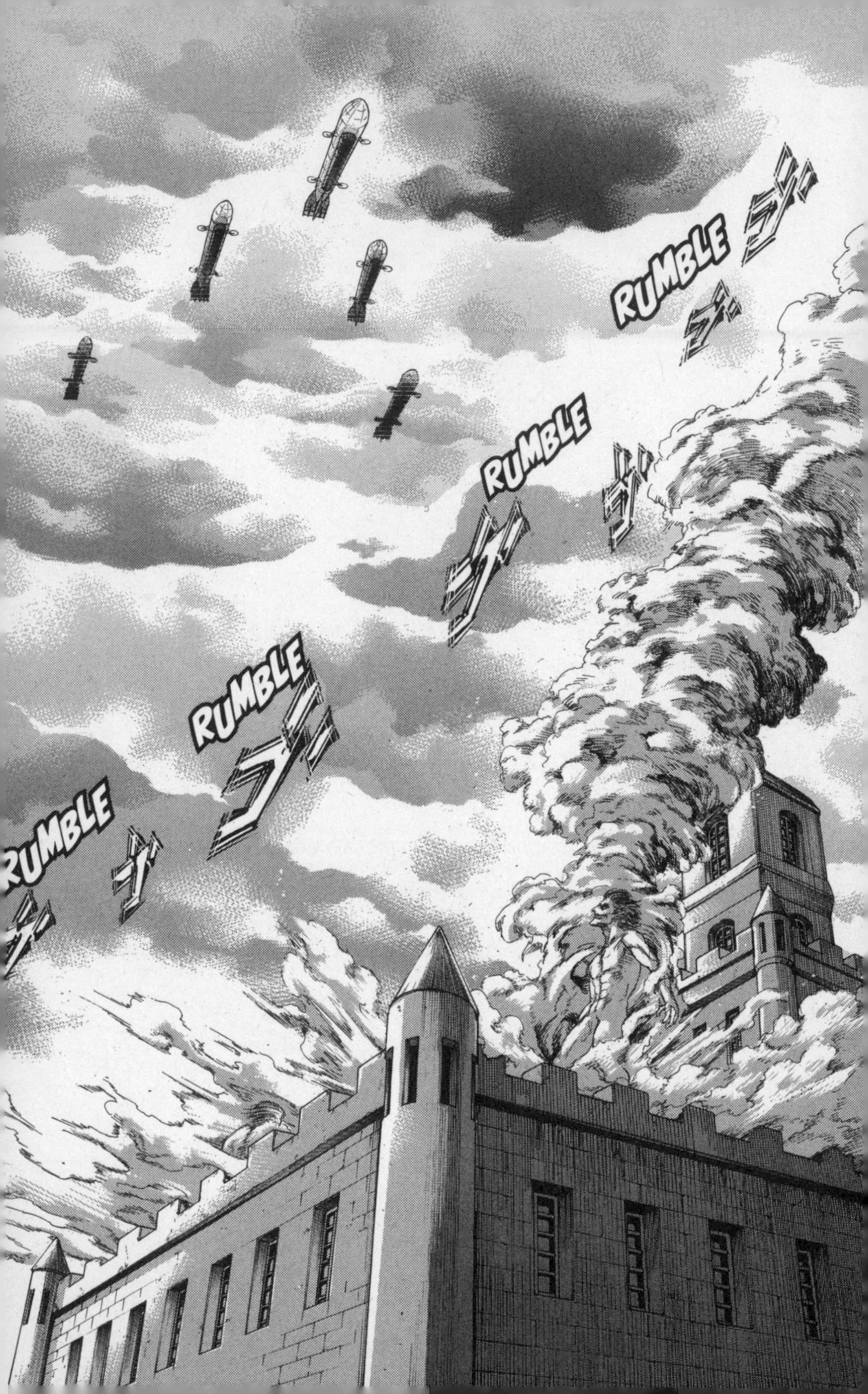
RUMBLE
RUMBLE
RUMBLE
RUMBLE

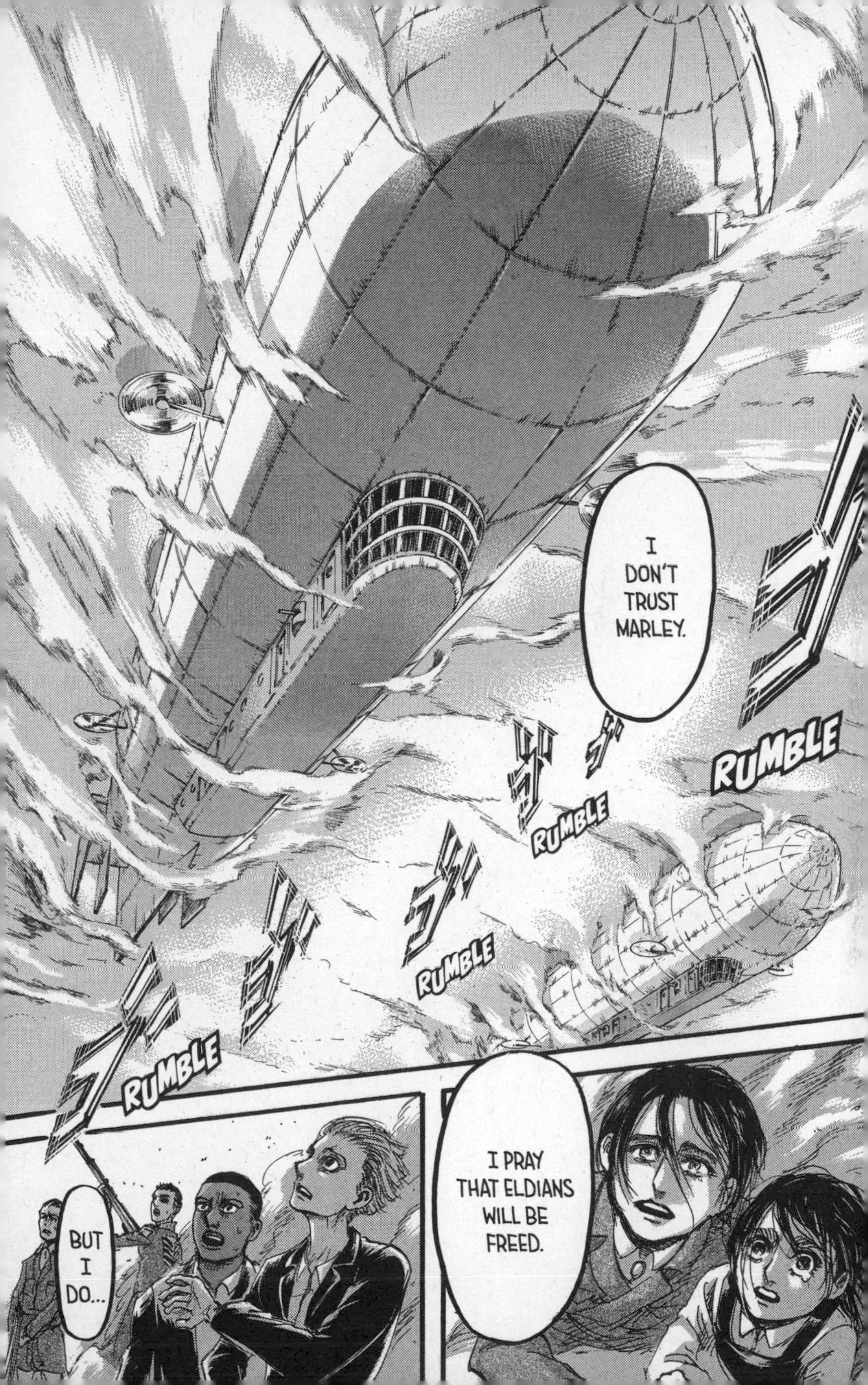
I DON'T TRUST MARLEY.
RUMBLE
RUMBLE
RUMBLE
RUMBLE
I PRAY THAT ELDIANS WILL BE FREED.
BUT I DO...

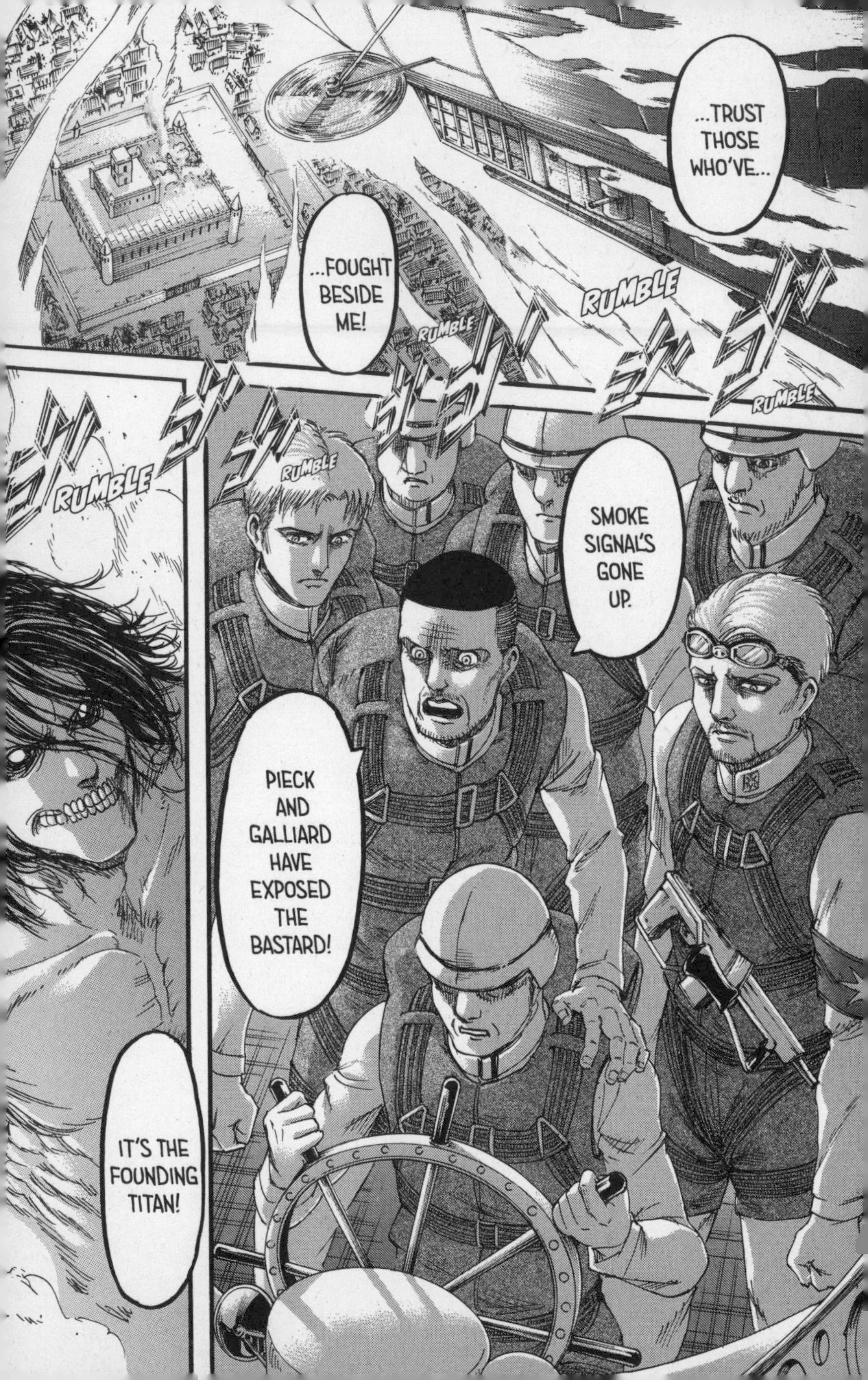
...TRUST THOSE WHO'VE...
RUMBLE
...FOUGHT BESIDE ME!
RUMBLE
RUMBLE
SMOKE SIGNAL'S GONE UP.
RUMBLE
PIECK AND GALLIARD HAVE EXPOSED THE BASTARD!
RUMBLE
IT'S THE FOUNDING TITAN!

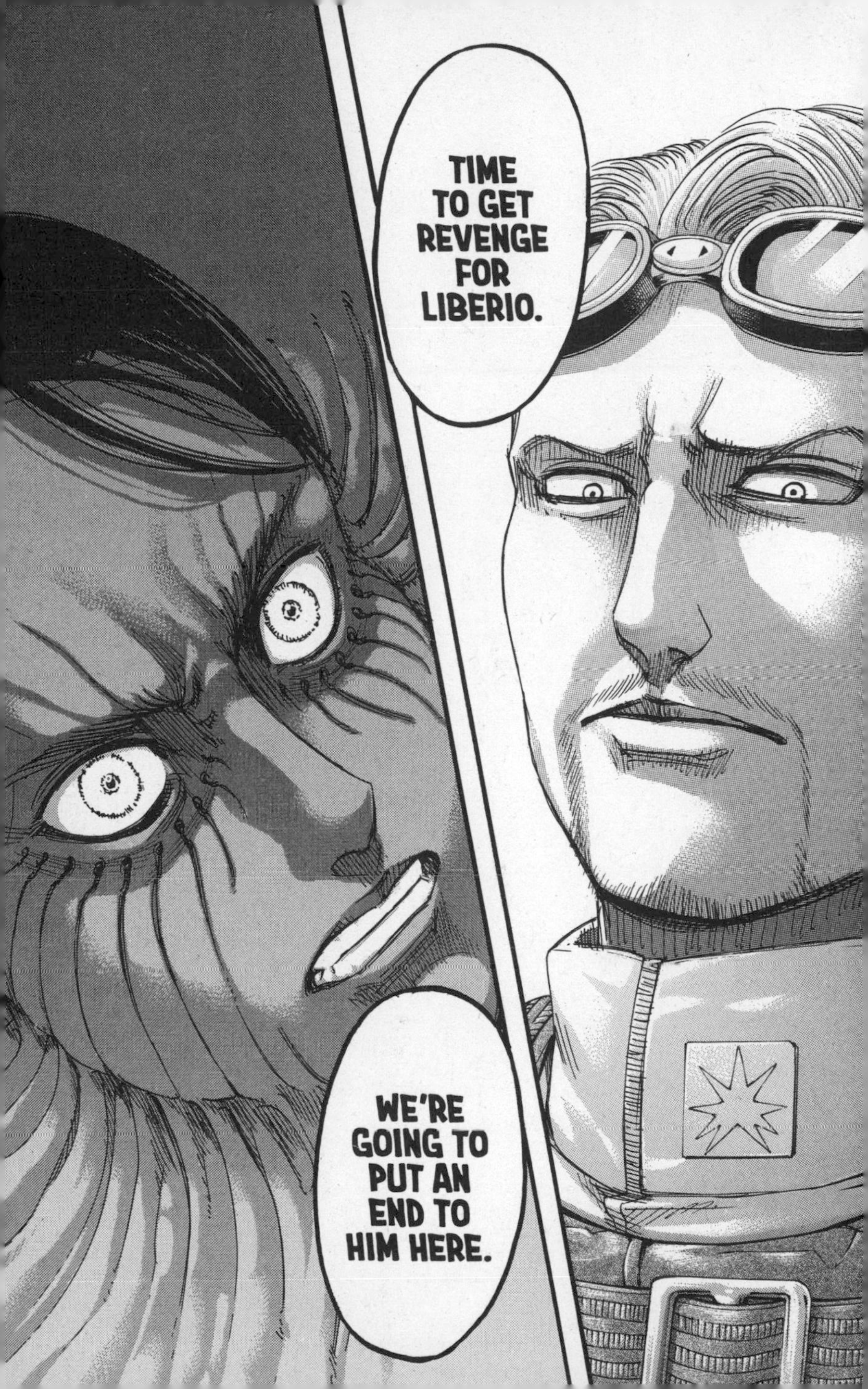
TIME TO GET REVENGE FOR LIBERIO.
WE'RE GOING TO PUT AN END TO HIM HERE.

ATTACK on TITAN

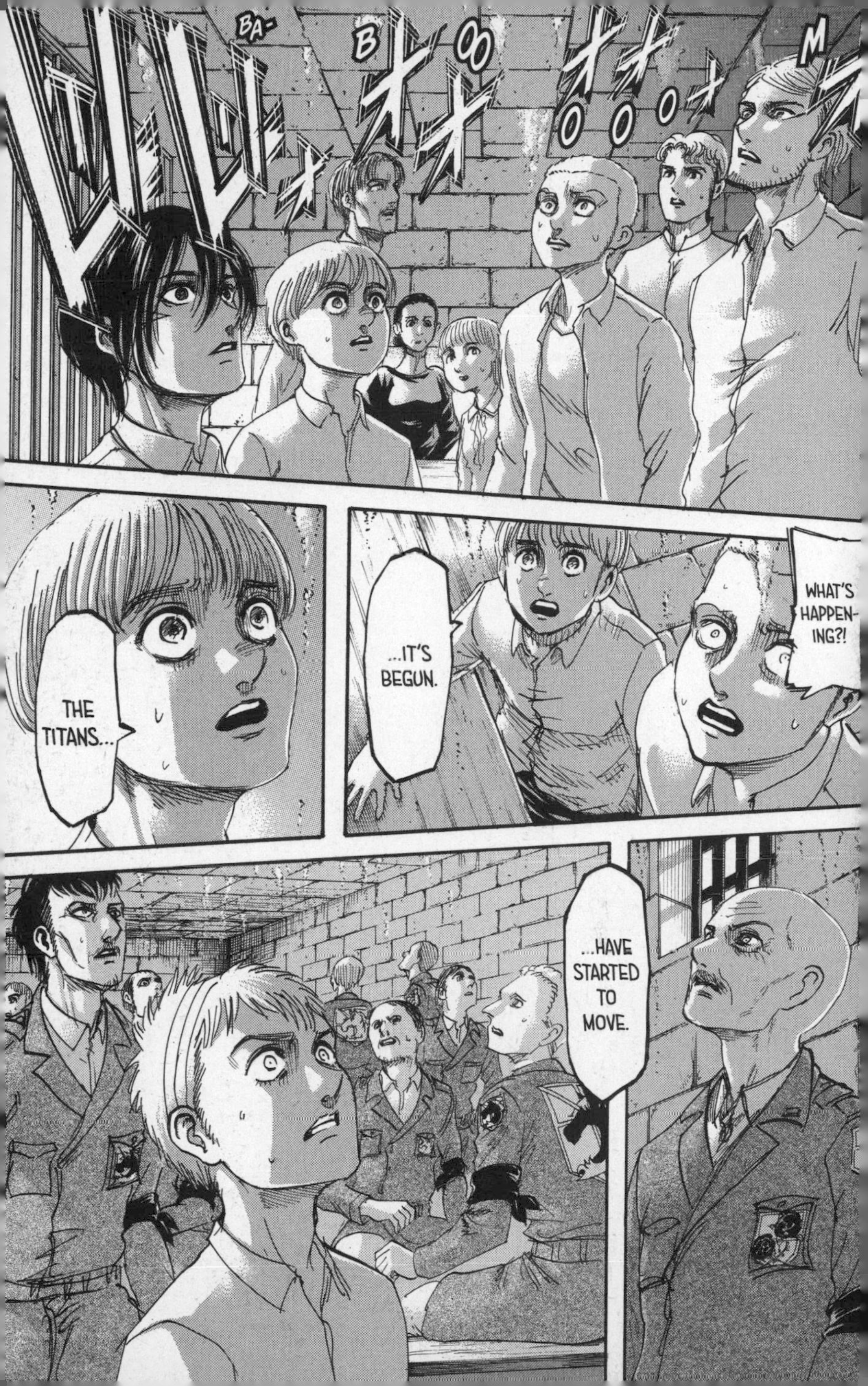
BA-BOOOOOM
WHAT'S HAPPEN-ING?!
...IT'S BEGUN.
THE TITANS...
...HAVE STARTED TO MOVE.

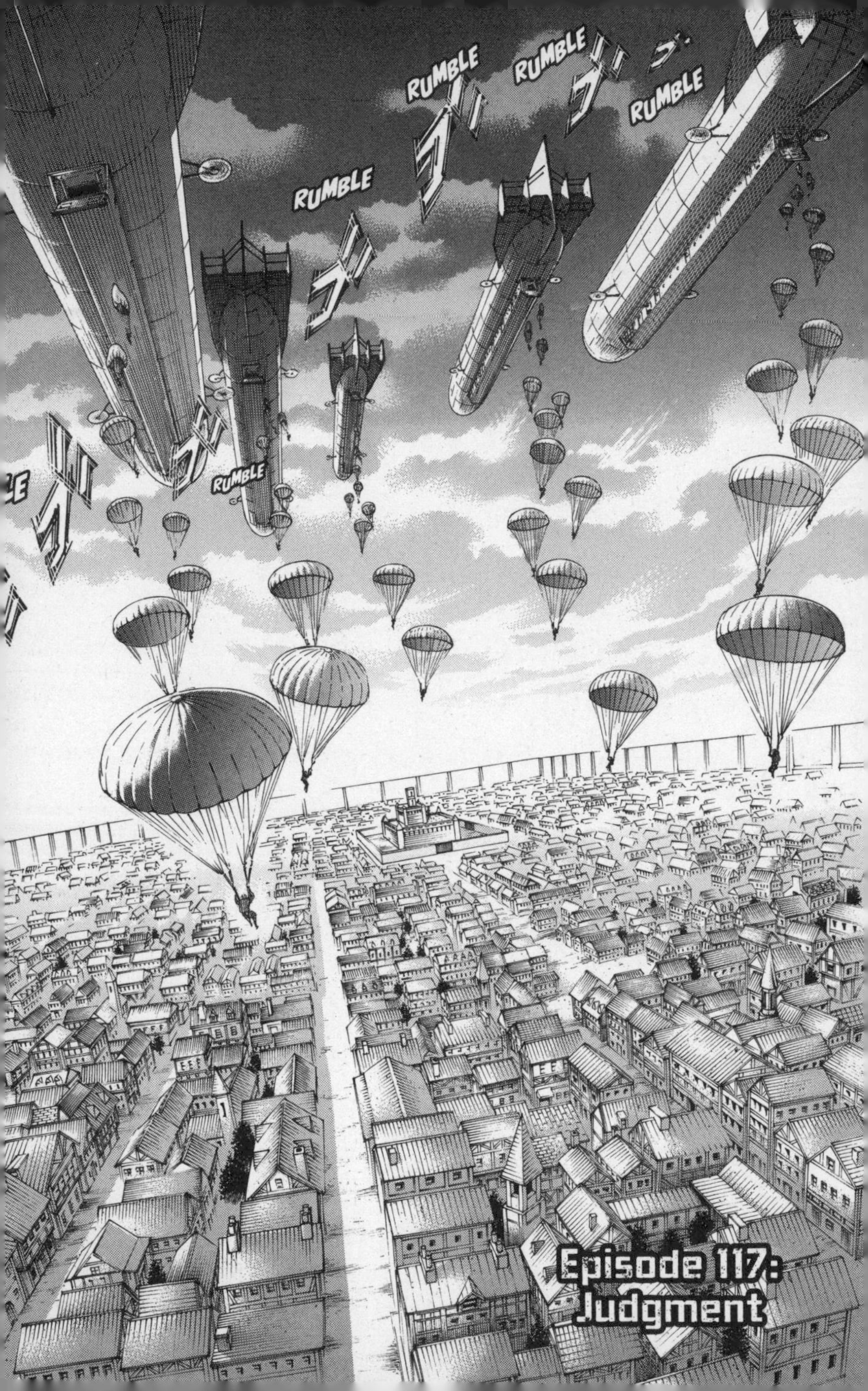
RUMBLE
RUMBLE
RUMBLE
RUMBLE
RUMBLE
Episode 117: Judgment

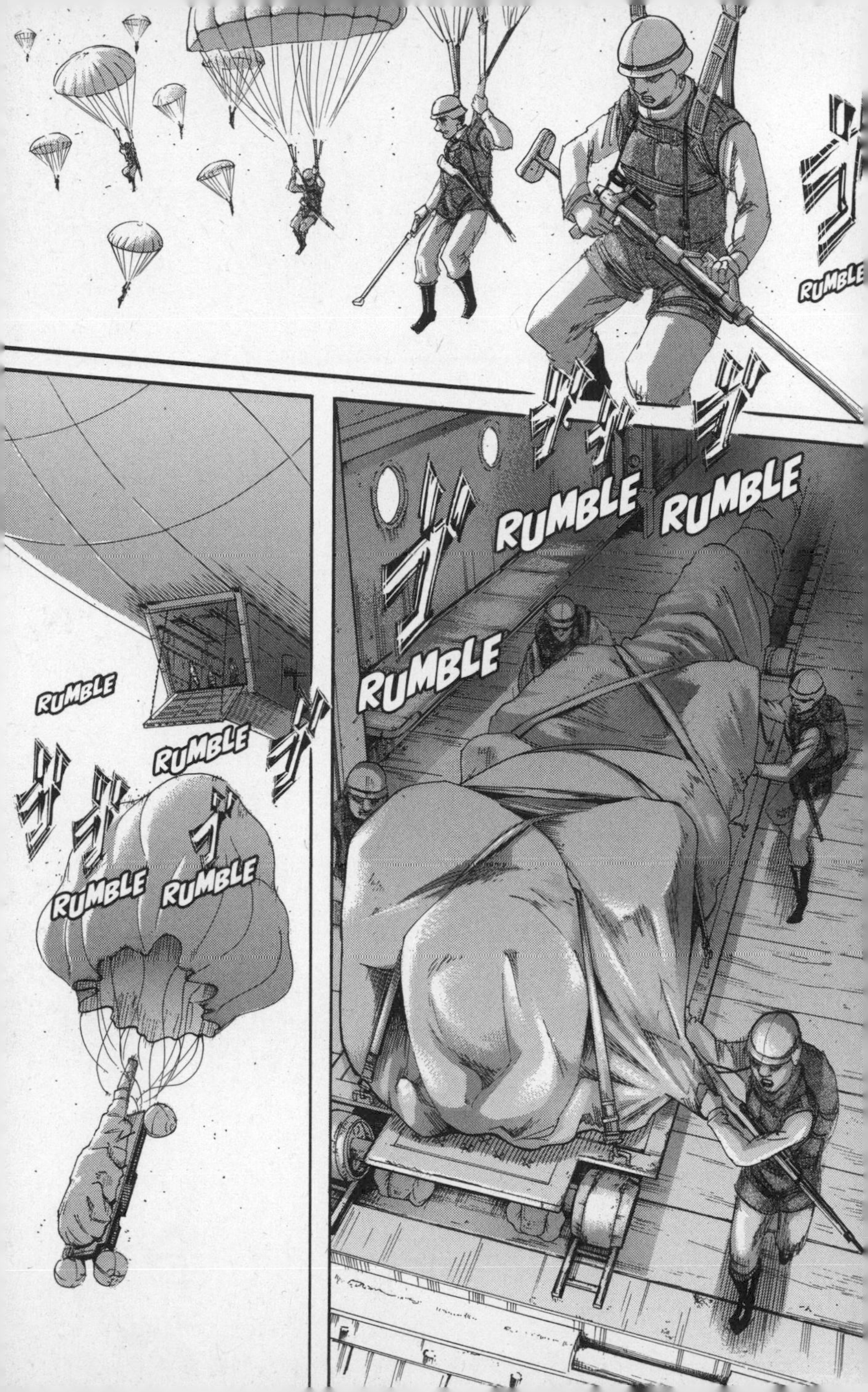
RUMBLE
RUMBLE
RUMBLE
RUMBLE
RUMBLE
RUMBLE
RUMBLE
RUMBLE
RUMBLE

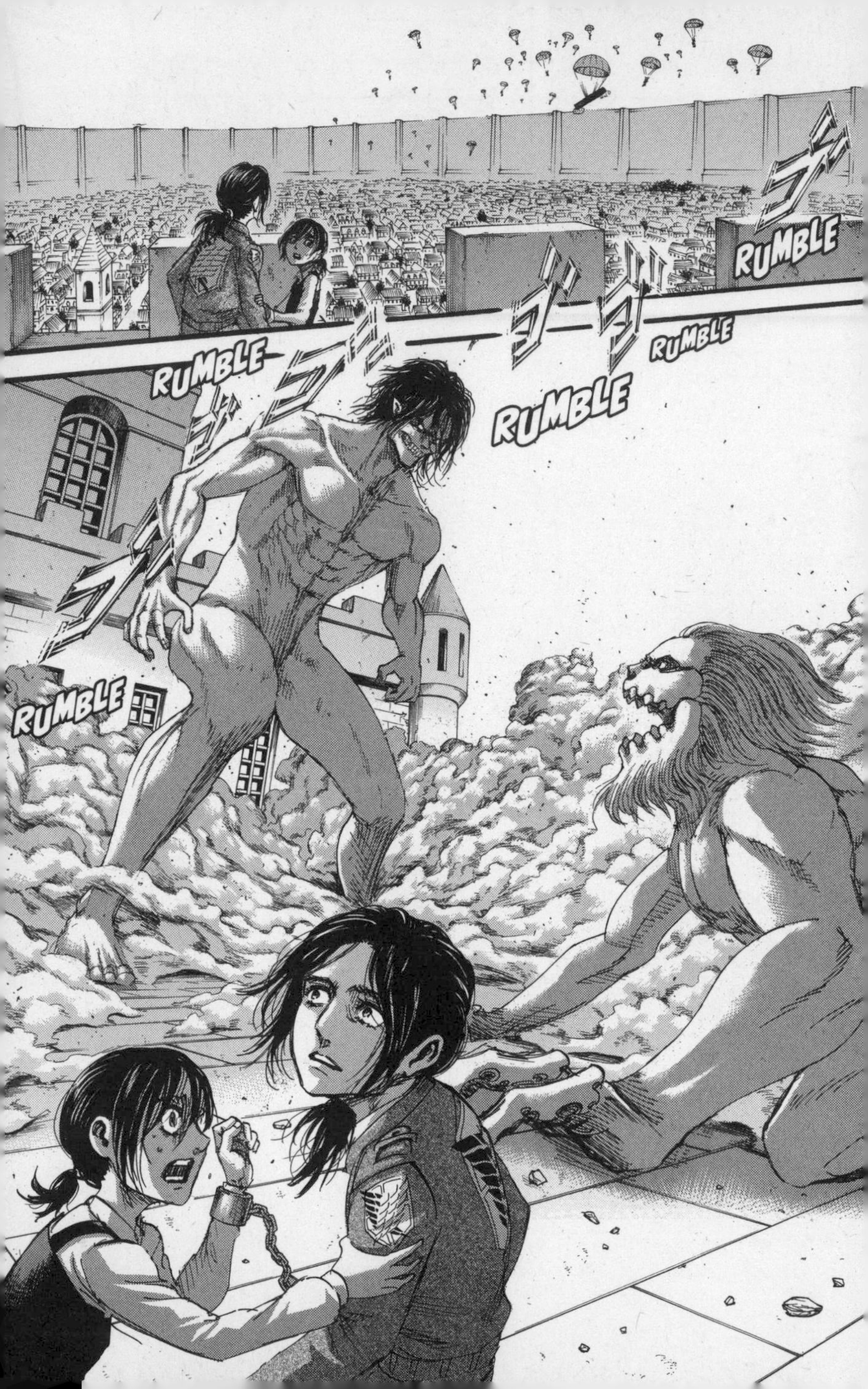
RUMBLE
RUMBLE
RUMBLE
RUMBLE
RUMBLE

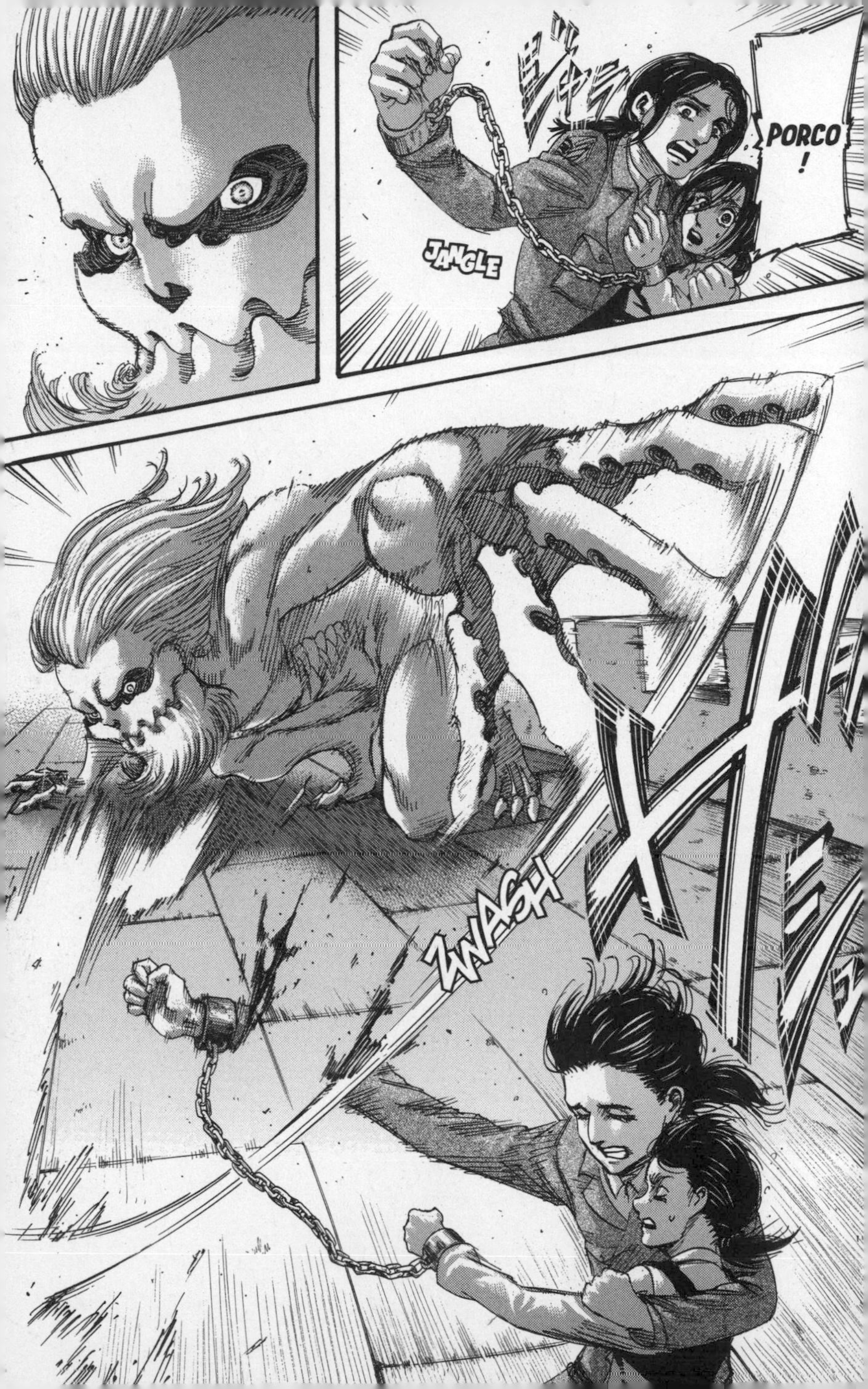
PORCO!
JANGLE
ZWASH

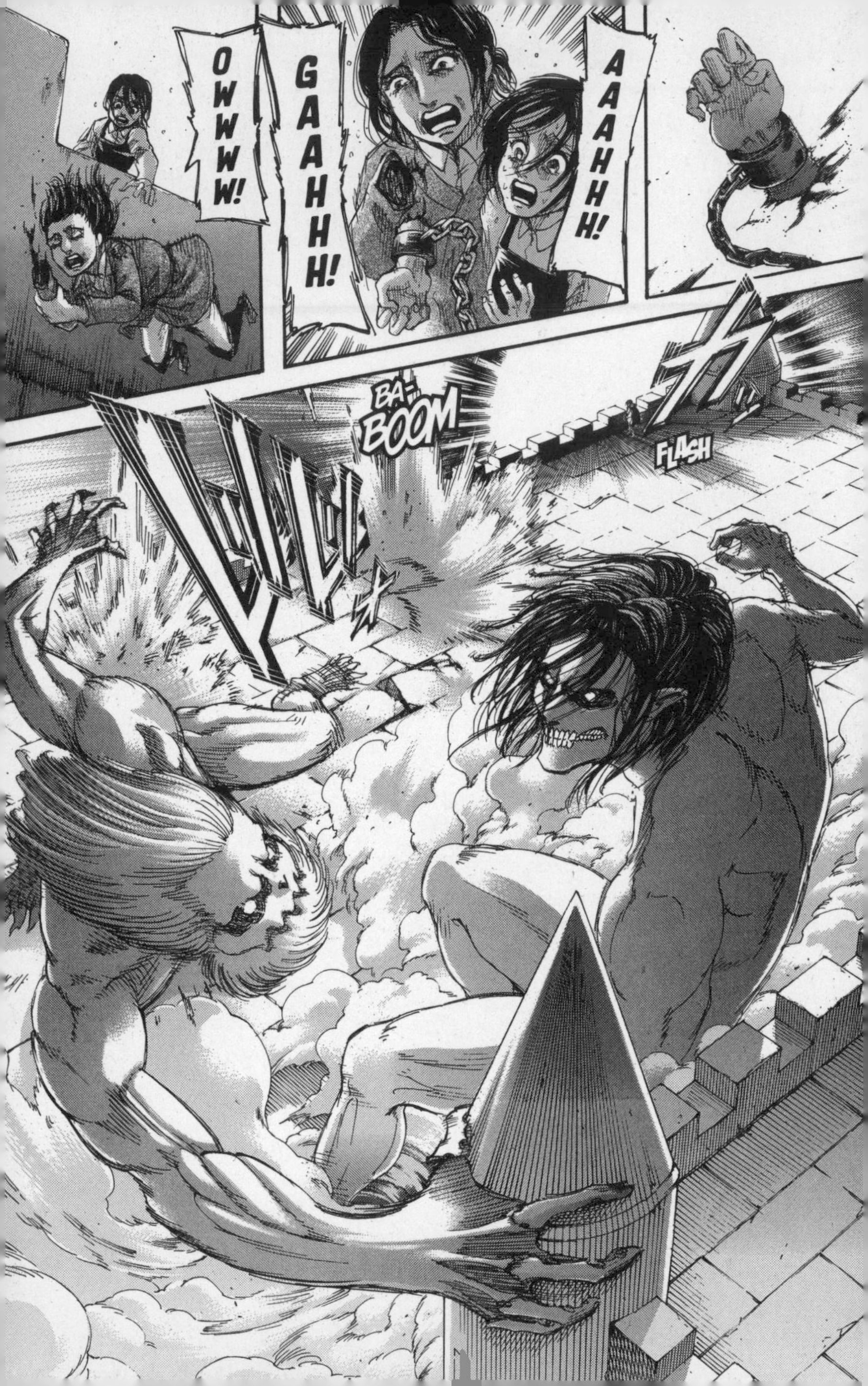
AAAAHHH!
GAAHHH!
OWWWW!
FLASH
BA-BOOM

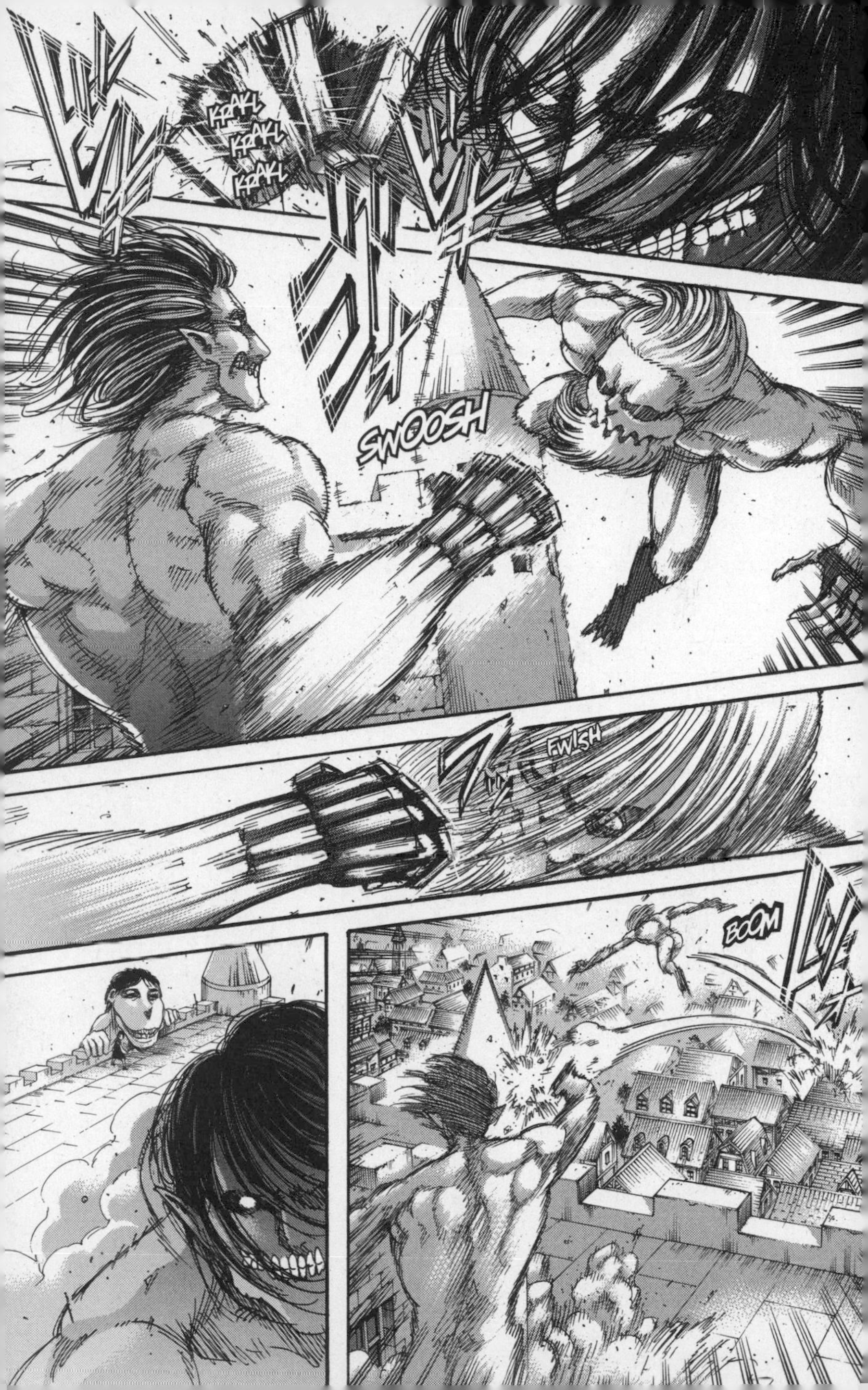
KRAKL
KRAKL
KRAKL
SWOOSH
FWISH
BOOM

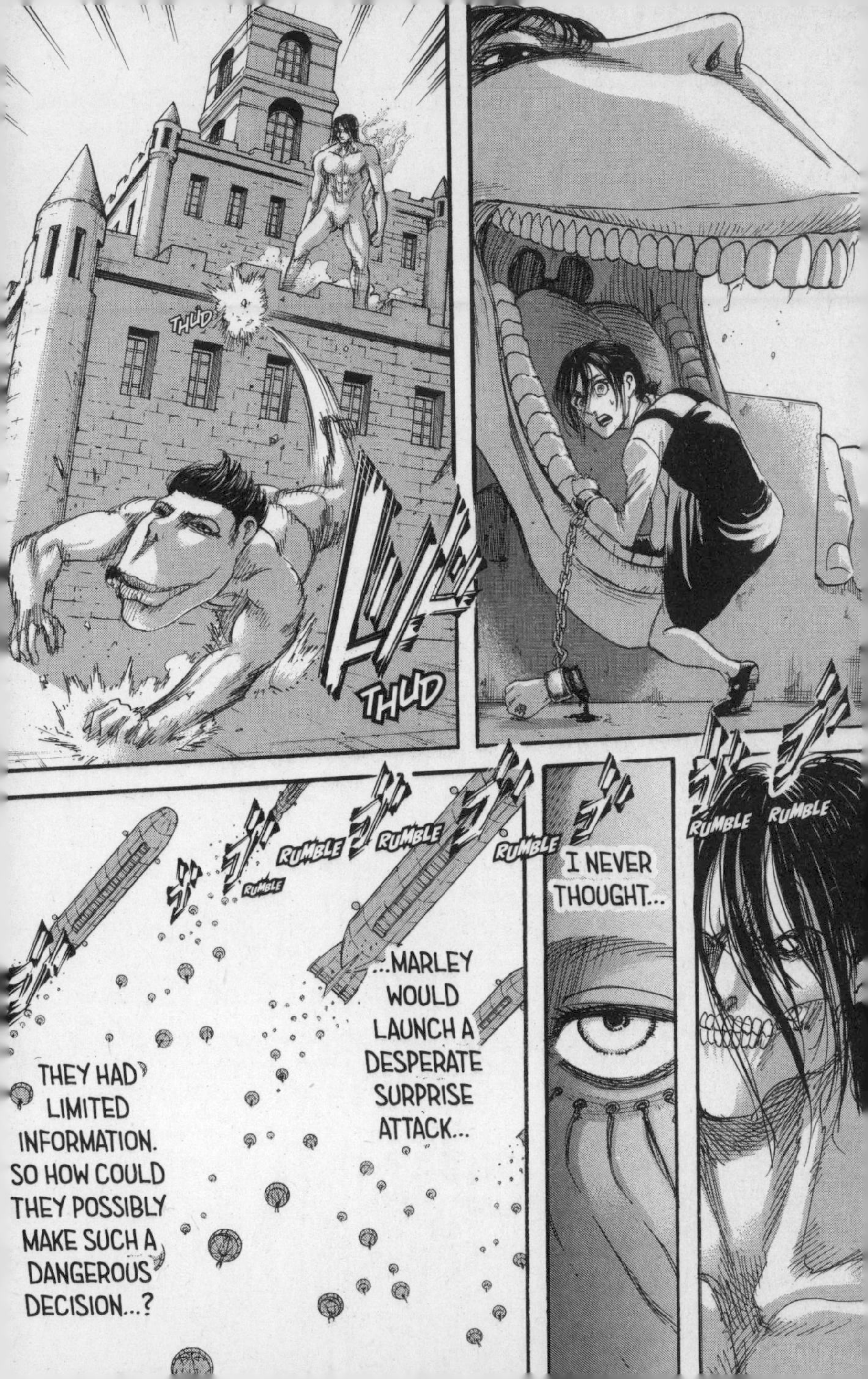
THUD
THUD
RUMBLE
RUMBLE
I NEVER THOUGHT...
RUMBLE
RUMBLE
RUMBLE
RUMBLE
...MARLEY WOULD LAUNCH A DESPERATE SURPRISE ATTACK...
THEY HAD LIMITED INFORMATION. SO HOW COULD THEY POSSIBLY MAKE SUCH A DANGEROUS DECISION...?

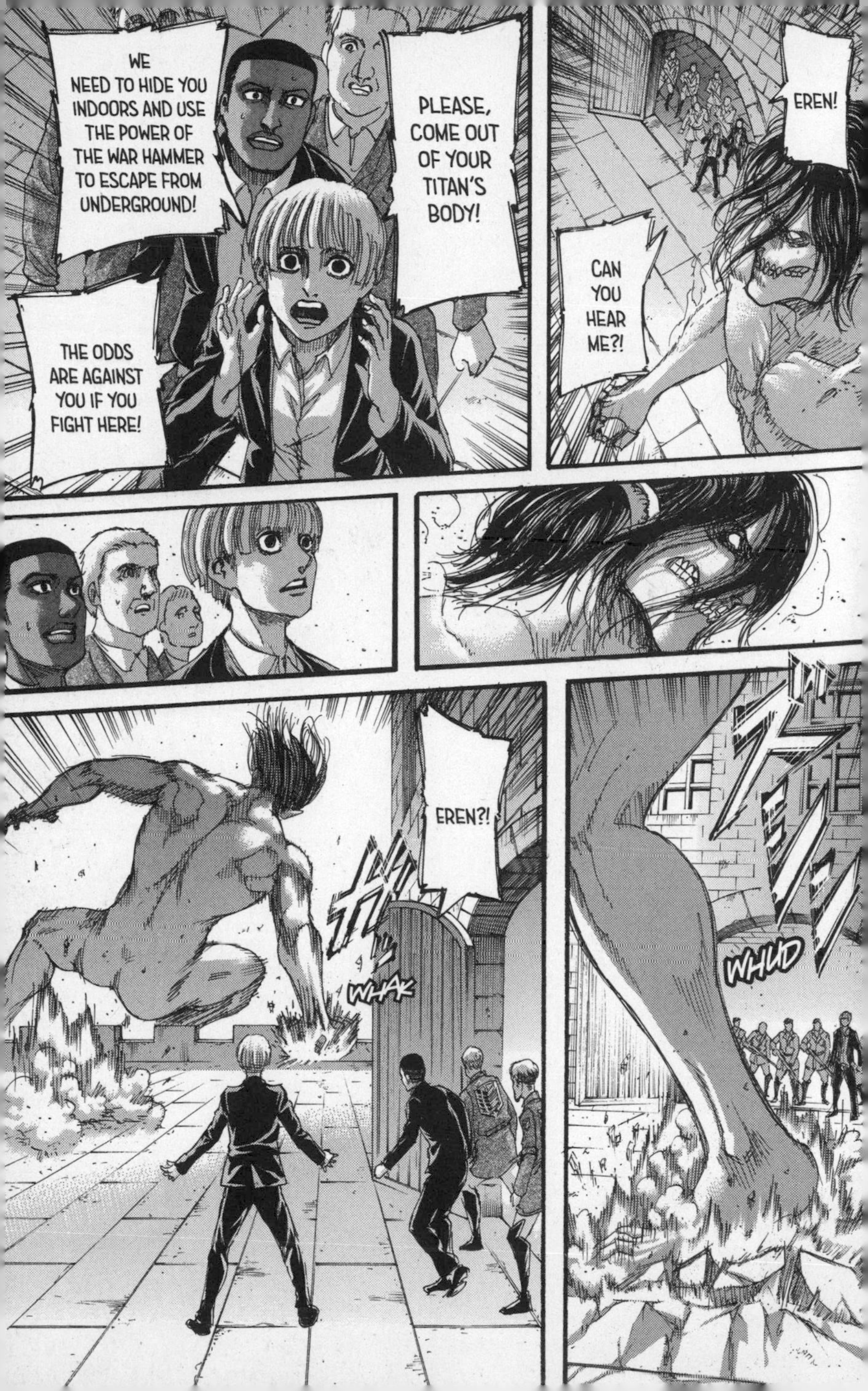
EREN!
CAN YOU HEAR ME?!
PLEASE, COME OUT OF YOUR TITAN'S BODY!
WE NEED TO HIDE YOU INDOORS AND USE THE POWER OF THE WAR HAMMER TO ESCAPE FROM UNDERGROUND!
THE ODDS ARE AGAINST YOU IF YOU FIGHT HERE!
WHUD
EREN?!
WHAK

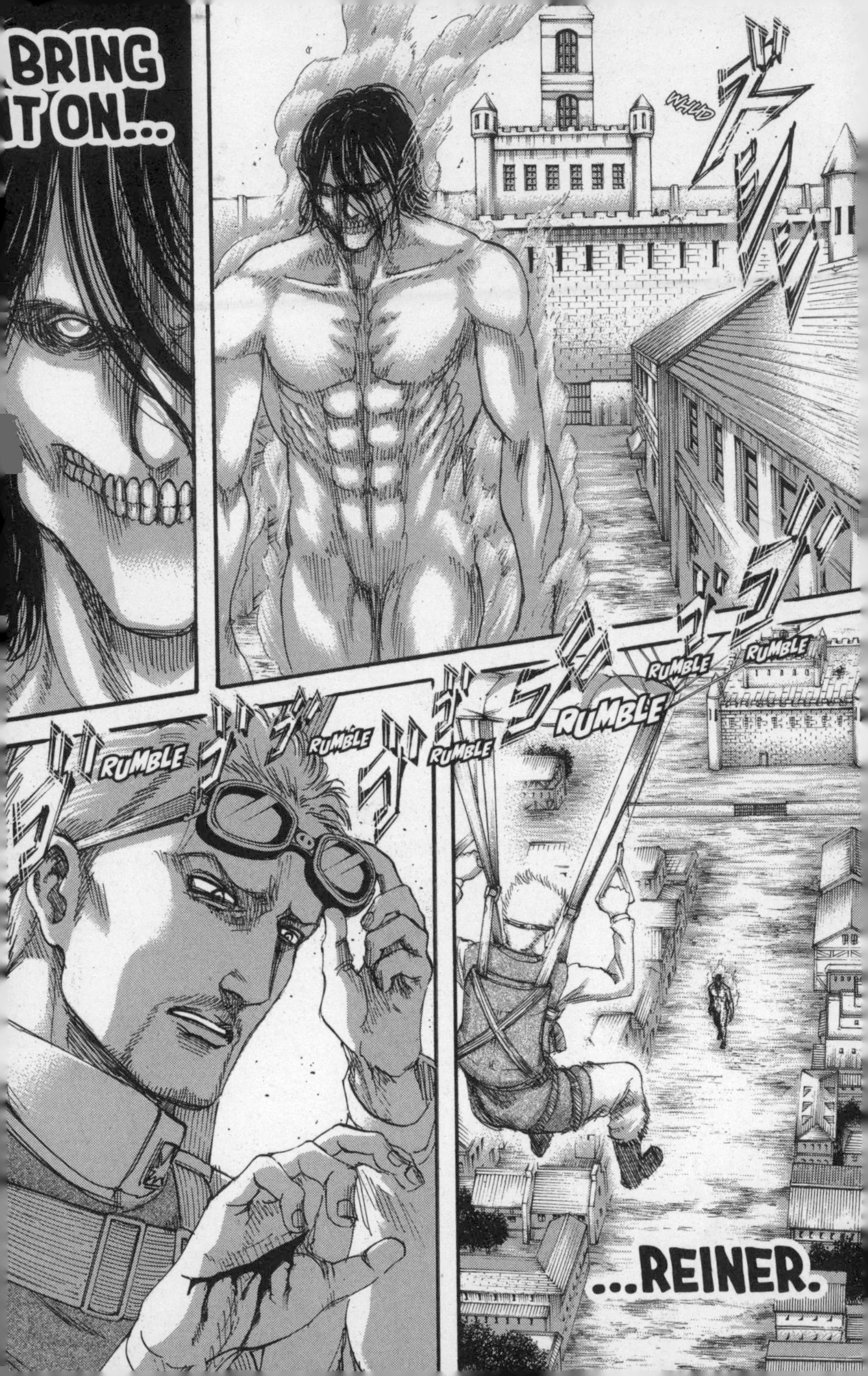
WHUD
BRING
T ON...
RUMBLE
RUMBLE
RUMBLE
...REINER.
RUMBLE
RUMBLE
RUMBLE

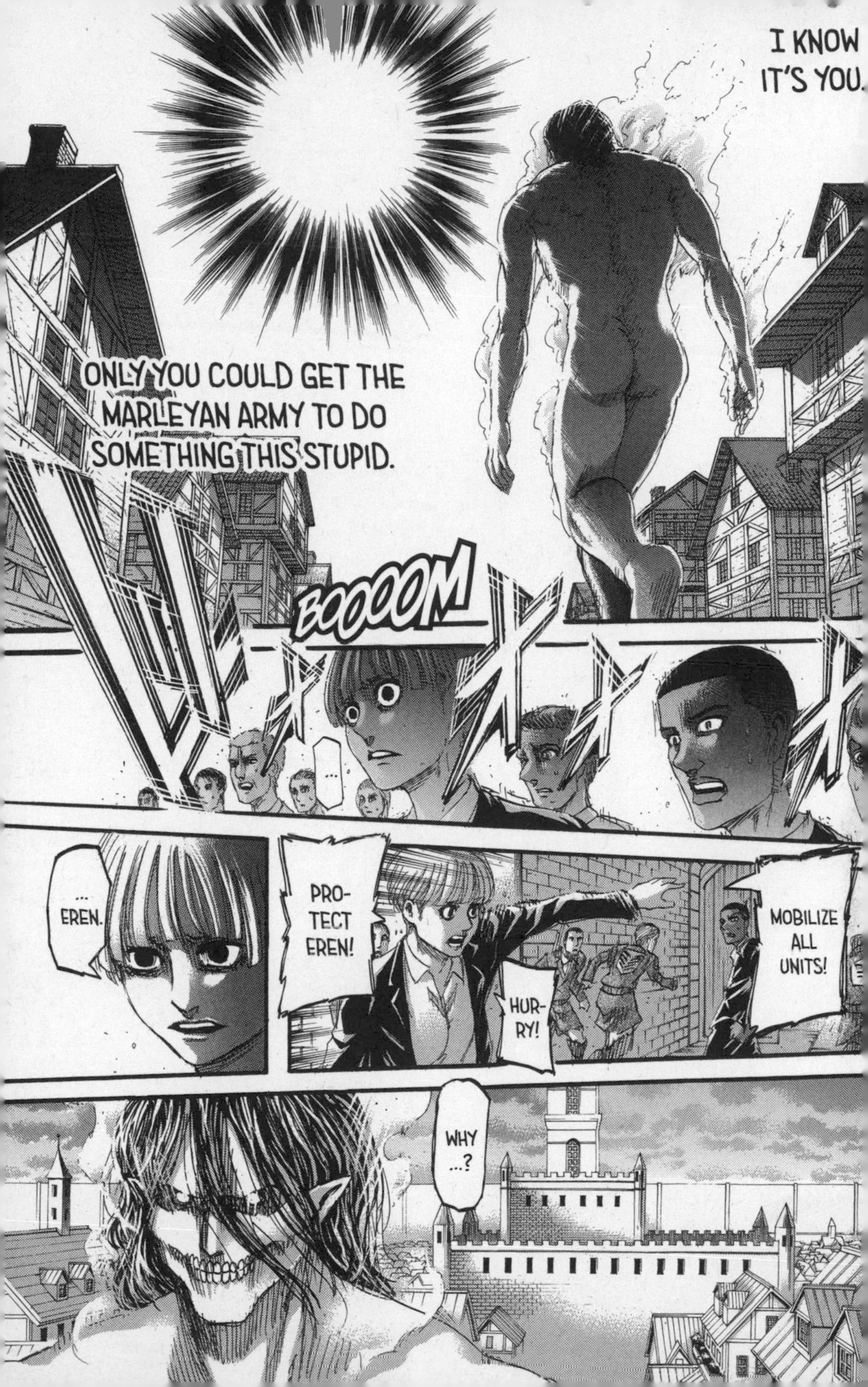
I KNOW IT'S YOU.
ONLY YOU COULD GET THE MARLEYAN ARMY TO DO SOMETHING THIS STUPID.
BOOOOOM
...
MOBILIZE ALL UNITS!
HURRY!
PROTECT EREN!
... EREN.
WHY ...?

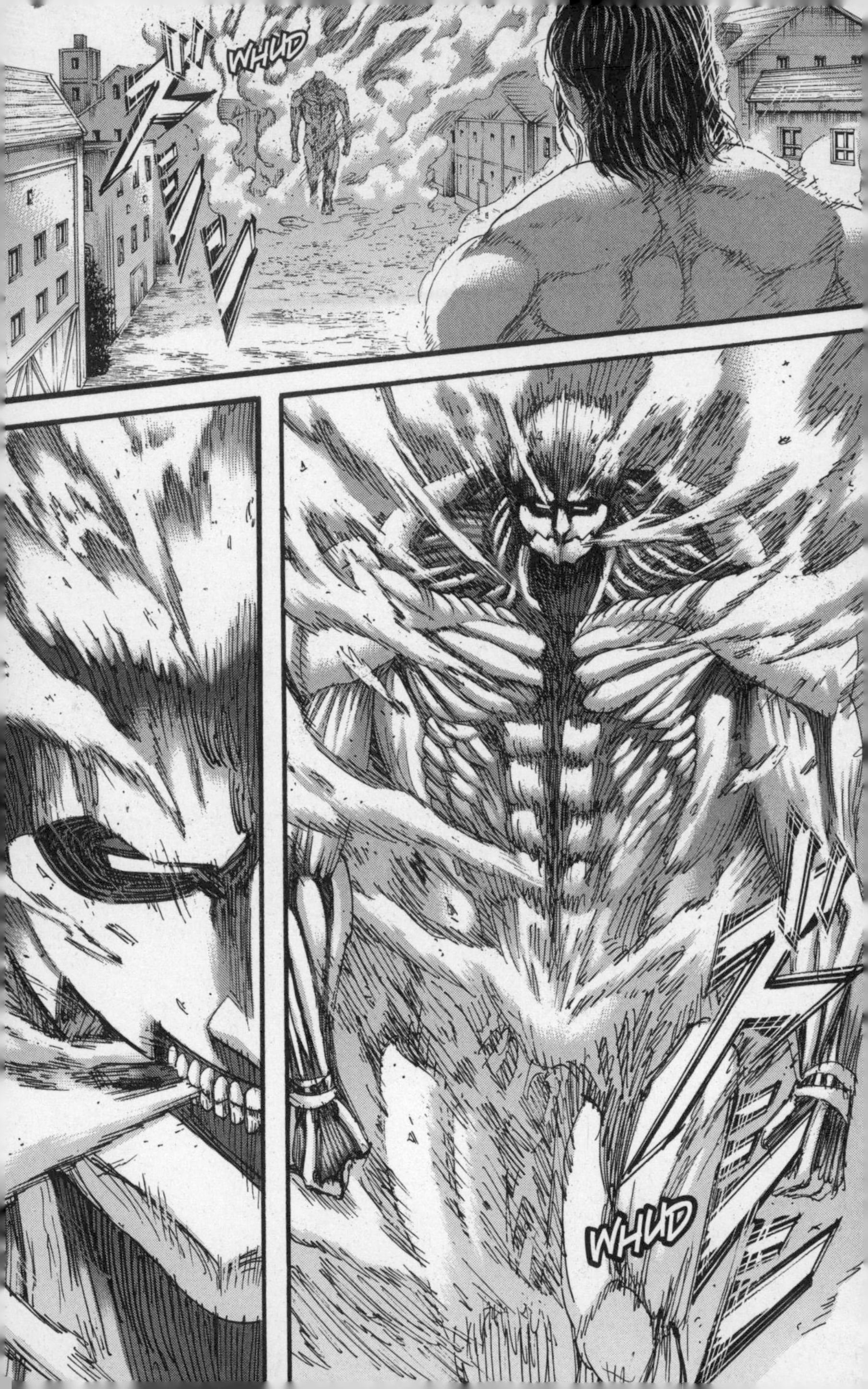
WHUD
WHUD

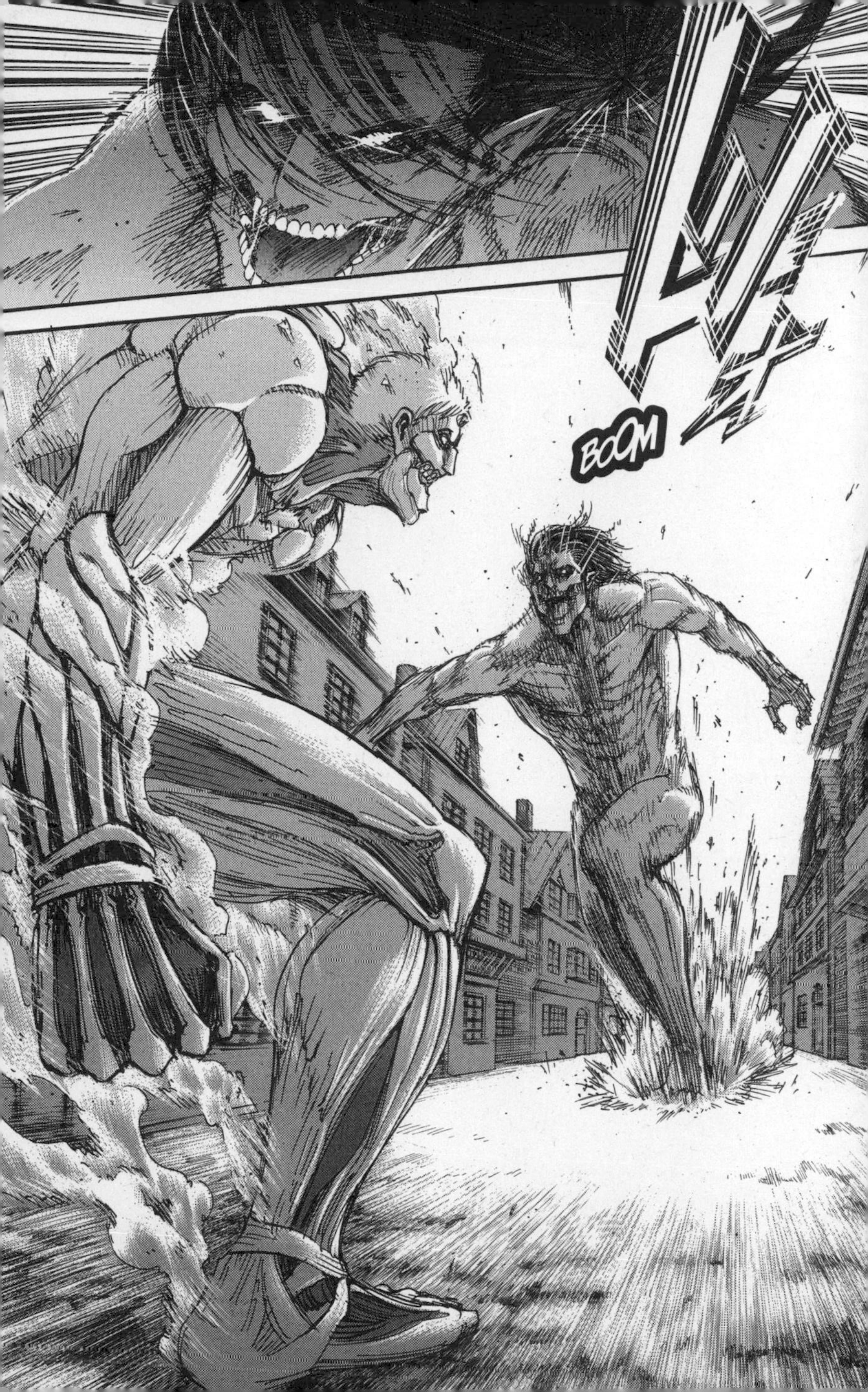
BOOM

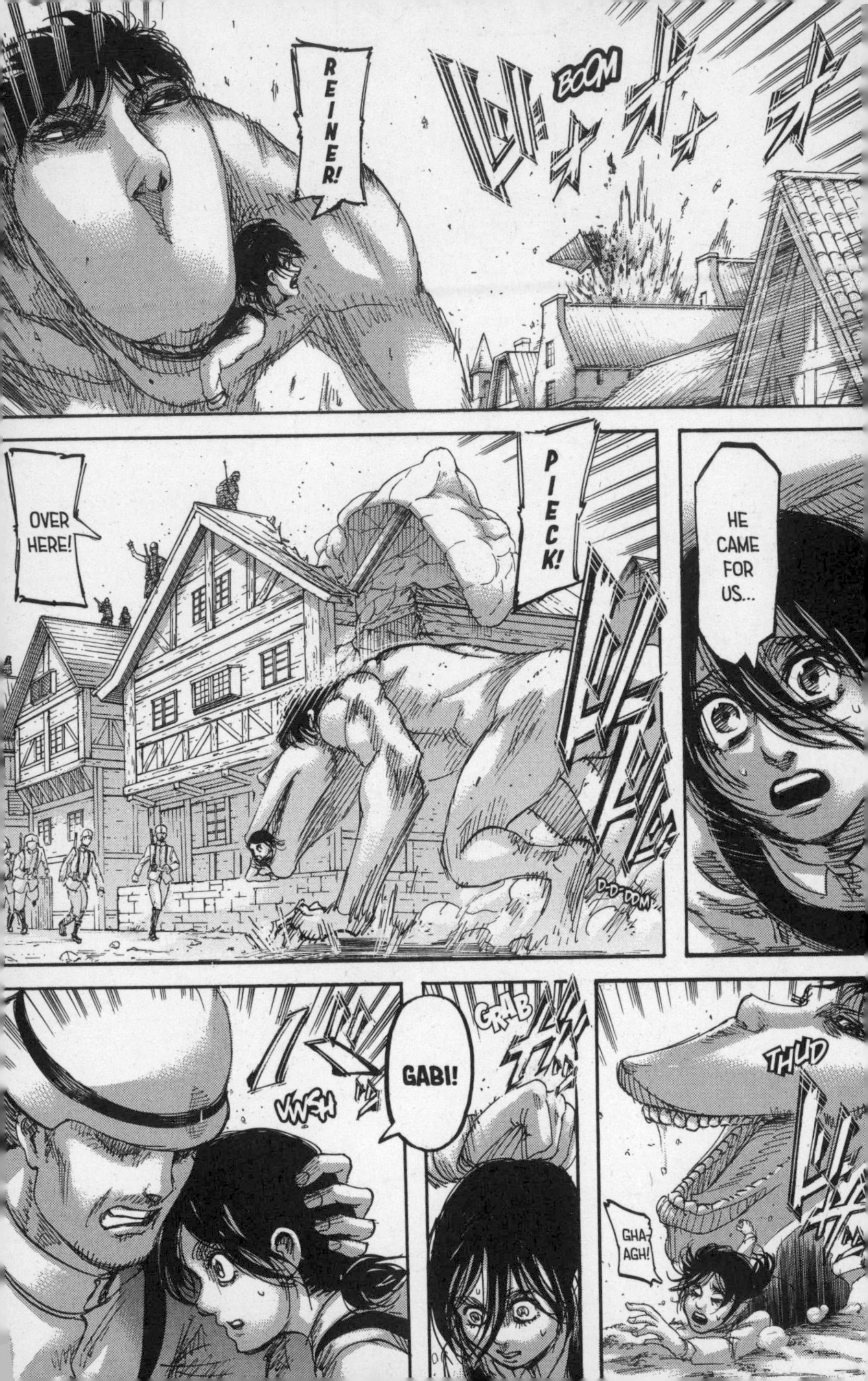
BOOM
REINER!
HE CAME FOR US...
PIECK!
D-D-DDM
OVER HERE!
THUD
GHA-AGH!
GRAB
GABI!
VWSH

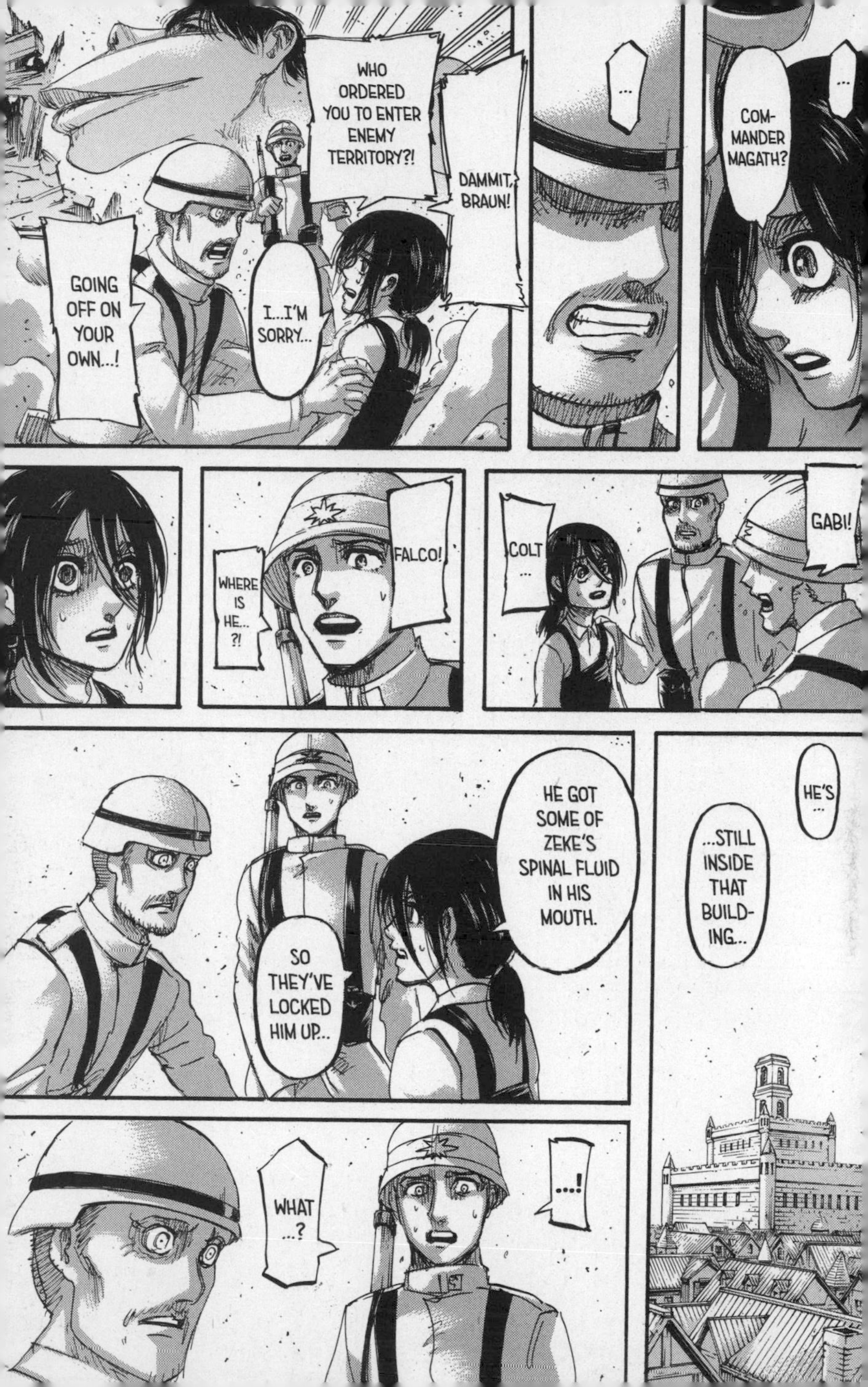
...
COM-MANDER MAGATH?
...
DAMMIT, BRAUN!
WHO ORDERED YOU TO ENTER ENEMY TERRITORY?!
GOING OFF ON YOUR OWN...!
I...I'M SORRY...
GABI!
COLT...
FALCO!
WHERE IS HE...?!
HE'S...
...STILL INSIDE THAT BUILD-ING...
HE GOT SOME OF ZEKE'S SPINAL FLUID IN HIS MOUTH.
SO THEY'VE LOCKED HIM UP...
...!
WHAT...?

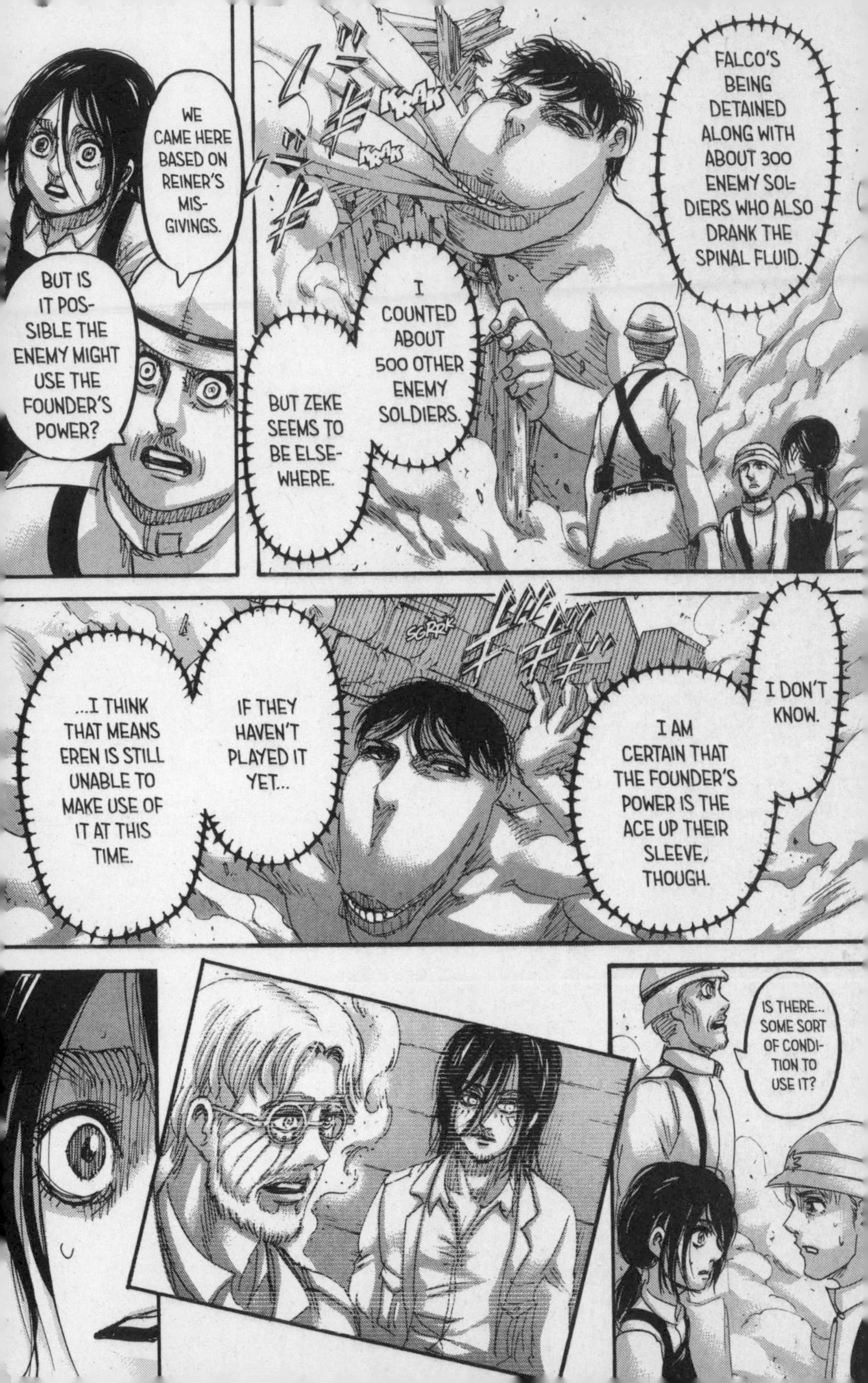
FALCO'S BEING DETAINED ALONG WITH ABOUT 300 ENEMY SOLDIERS WHO ALSO DRANK THE SPINAL FLUID.
KRAK
KRAK
I COUNTED ABOUT 500 OTHER ENEMY SOLDIERS.
BUT ZEKE SEEMS TO BE ELSEWHERE.
WE CAME HERE BASED ON REINER'S MISGIVINGS.
BUT IS IT POSSIBLE THE ENEMY MIGHT USE THE FOUNDER'S POWER?
I DON'T KNOW.
I AM CERTAIN THAT THE FOUNDER'S POWER IS THE ACE UP THEIR SLEEVE, THOUGH.
SCRRK
IF THEY HAVEN'T PLAYED IT YET...
...I THINK THAT MEANS EREN IS STILL UNABLE TO MAKE USE OF IT AT THIS TIME.
IS THERE... SOME SORT OF CONDITION TO USE IT?

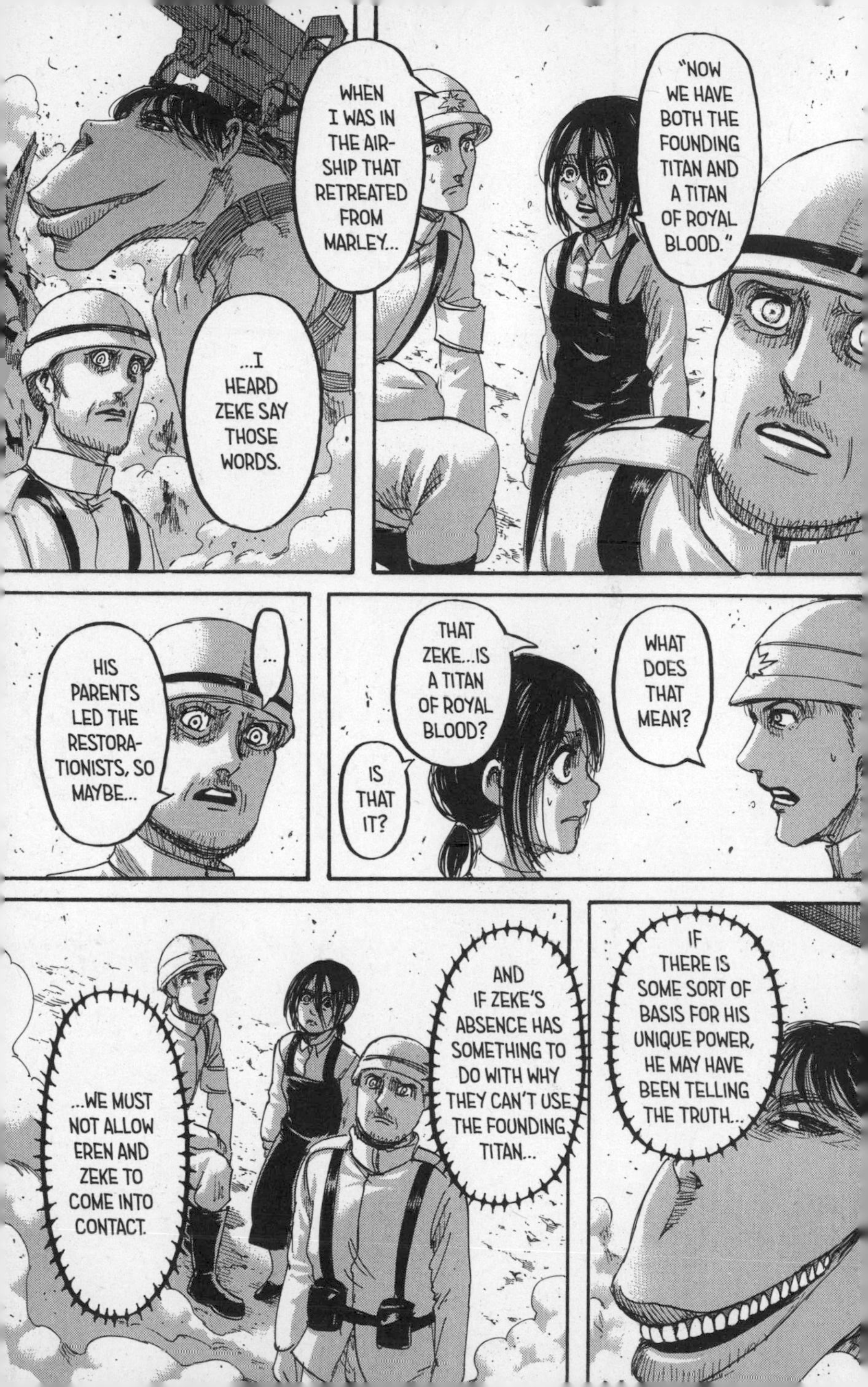
"NOW WE HAVE BOTH THE FOUNDING TITAN AND A TITAN OF ROYAL BLOOD."
WHEN I WAS IN THE AIR-SHIP THAT RETREATED FROM MARLEY...
...I HEARD ZEKE SAY THOSE WORDS.
WHAT DOES THAT MEAN?
THAT ZEKE...IS A TITAN OF ROYAL BLOOD?
IS THAT IT?
...
HIS PARENTS LED THE RESTORA-TIONISTS, SO MAYBE...
IF THERE IS SOME SORT OF BASIS FOR HIS UNIQUE POWER, HE MAY HAVE BEEN TELLING THE TRUTH...
AND IF ZEKE'S ABSENCE HAS SOMETHING TO DO WITH WHY THEY CAN'T USE THE FOUNDING TITAN...
...WE MUST NOT ALLOW EREN AND ZEKE TO COME INTO CONTACT.

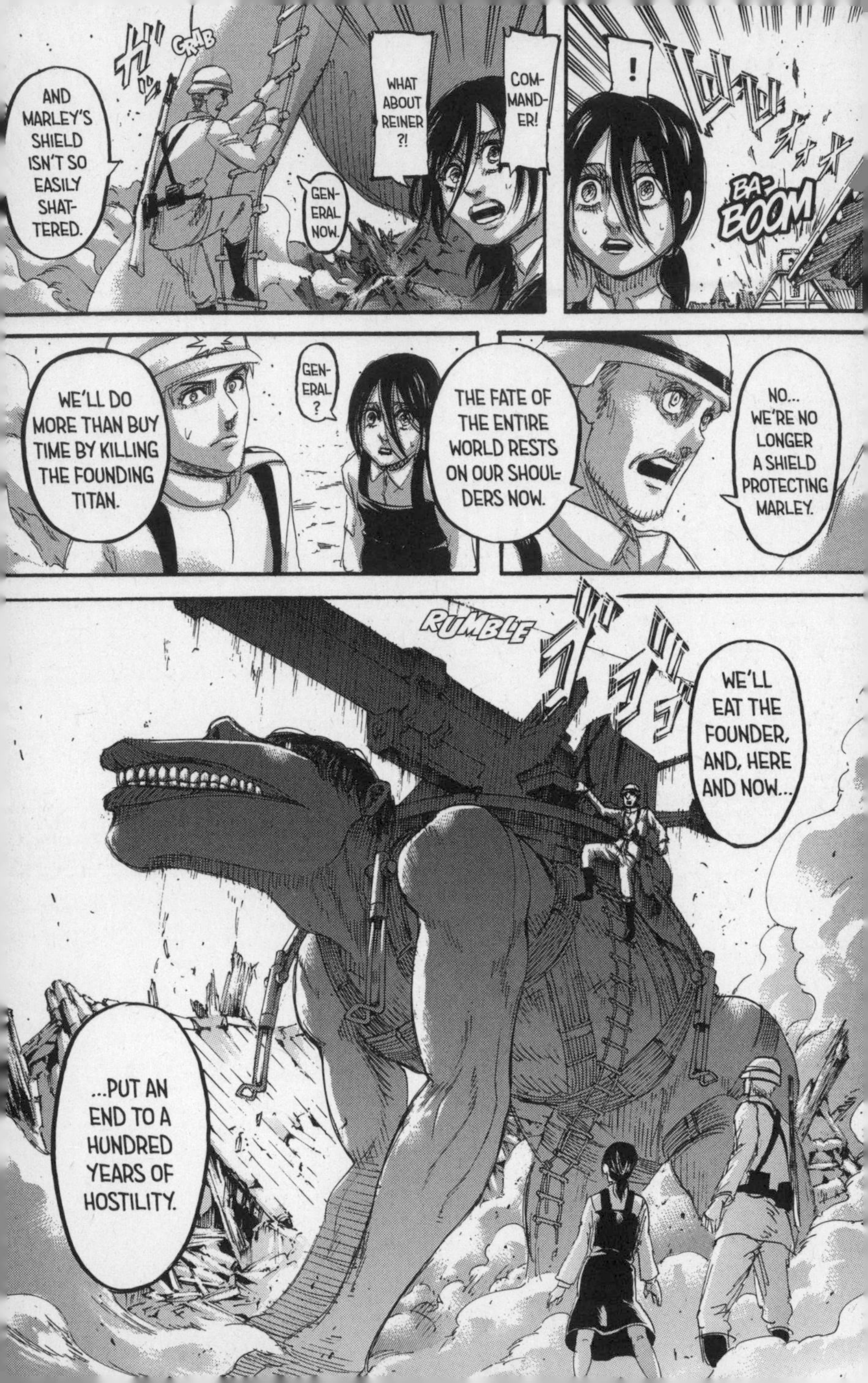
!
BA-BOOM
COM-MAND-ER!
WHAT ABOUT REINER?!
GEN-ERAL NOW.
GRAB
AND MARLEY'S SHIELD ISN'T SO EASILY SHAT-TERED.
NO... WE'RE NO LONGER A SHIELD PROTECTING MARLEY.
THE FATE OF THE ENTIRE WORLD RESTS ON OUR SHOUL-DERS NOW.
GEN-ERAL?
WE'LL DO MORE THAN BUY TIME BY KILLING THE FOUNDING TITAN.
RUMBLE
WE'LL EAT THE FOUNDER, AND, HERE AND NOW...
...PUT AN END TO A HUNDRED YEARS OF HOSTILITY.

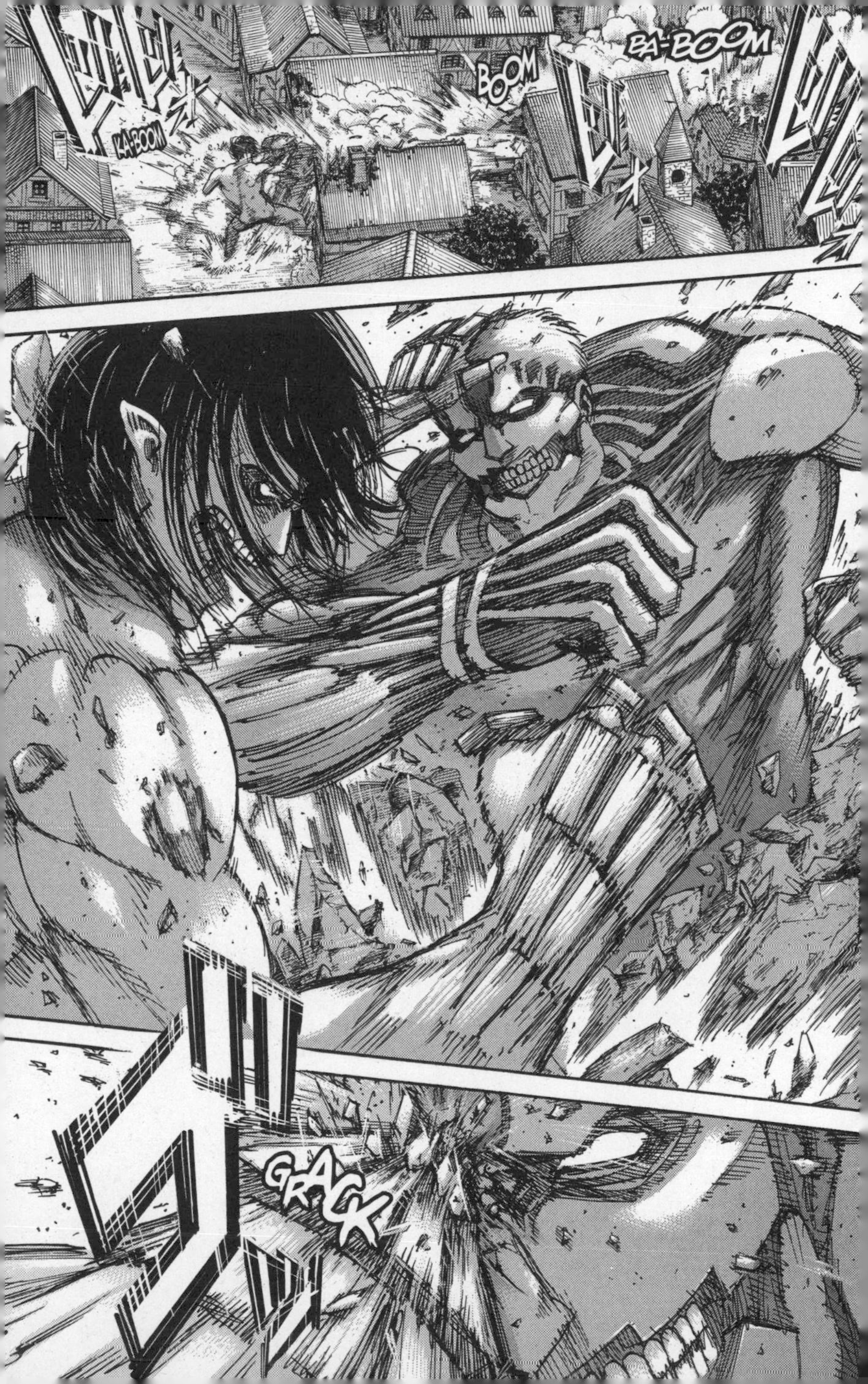
BA-BOOM
BOOM
KA-BOOM
GRACK

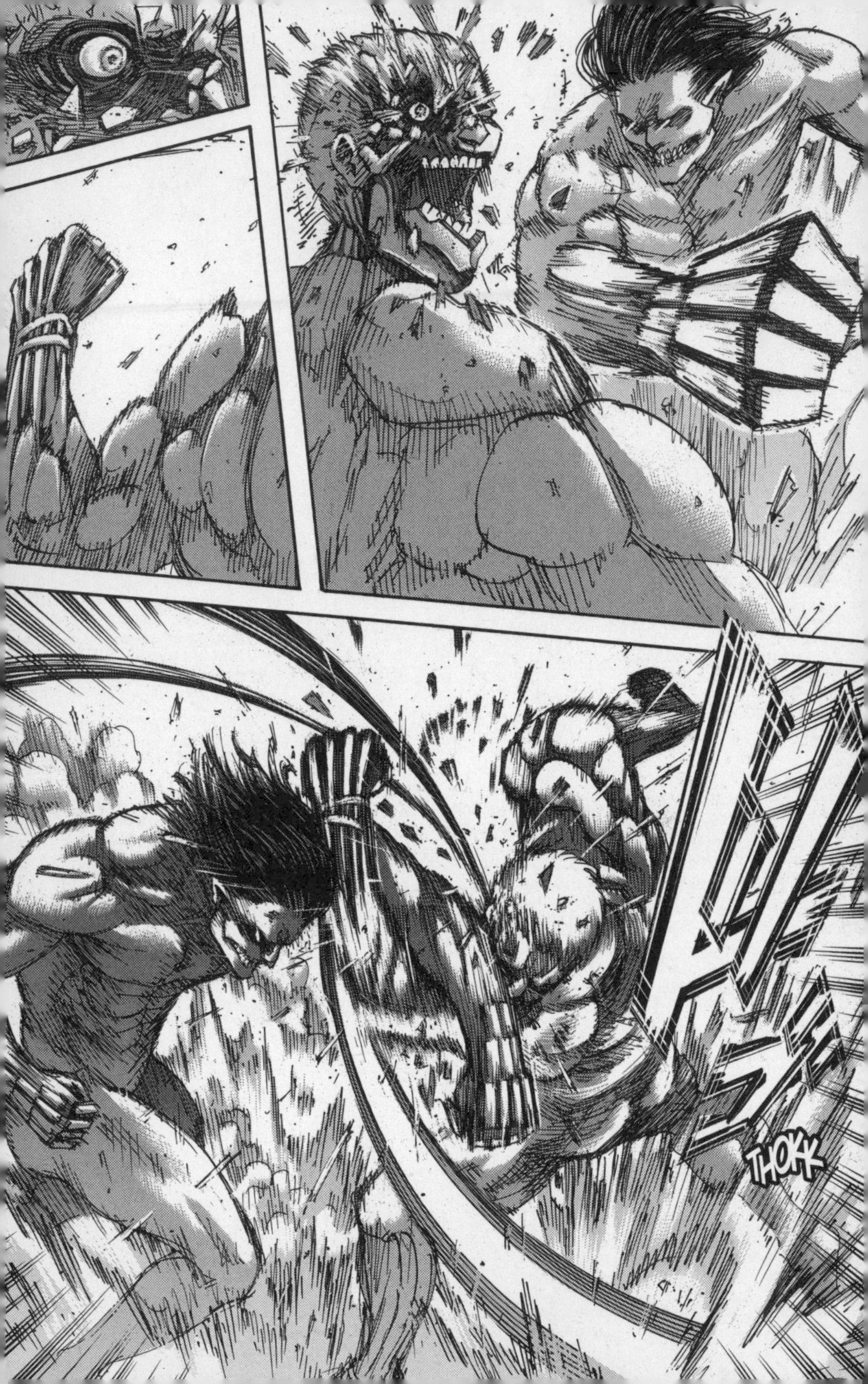
THOKK

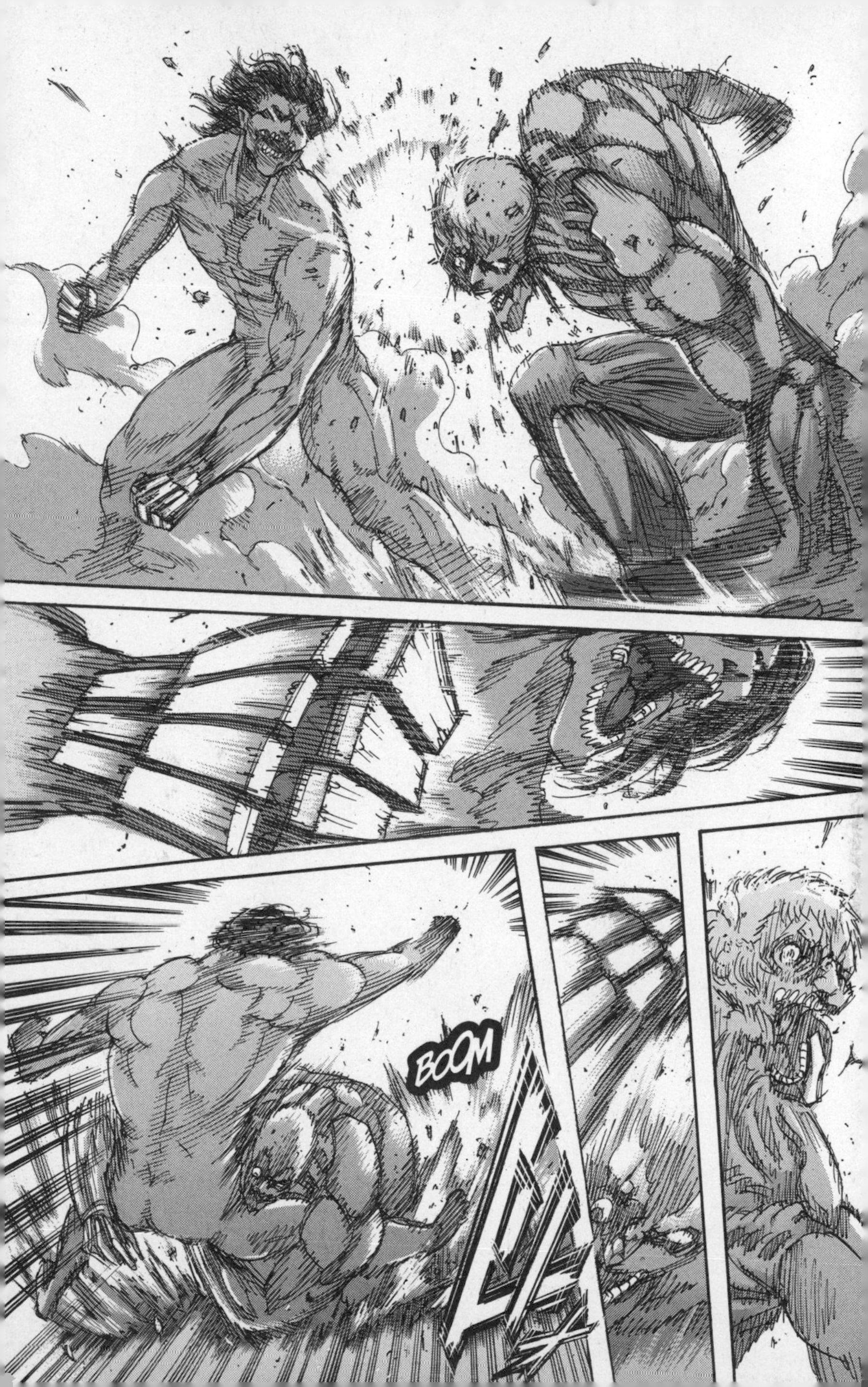
BOOM

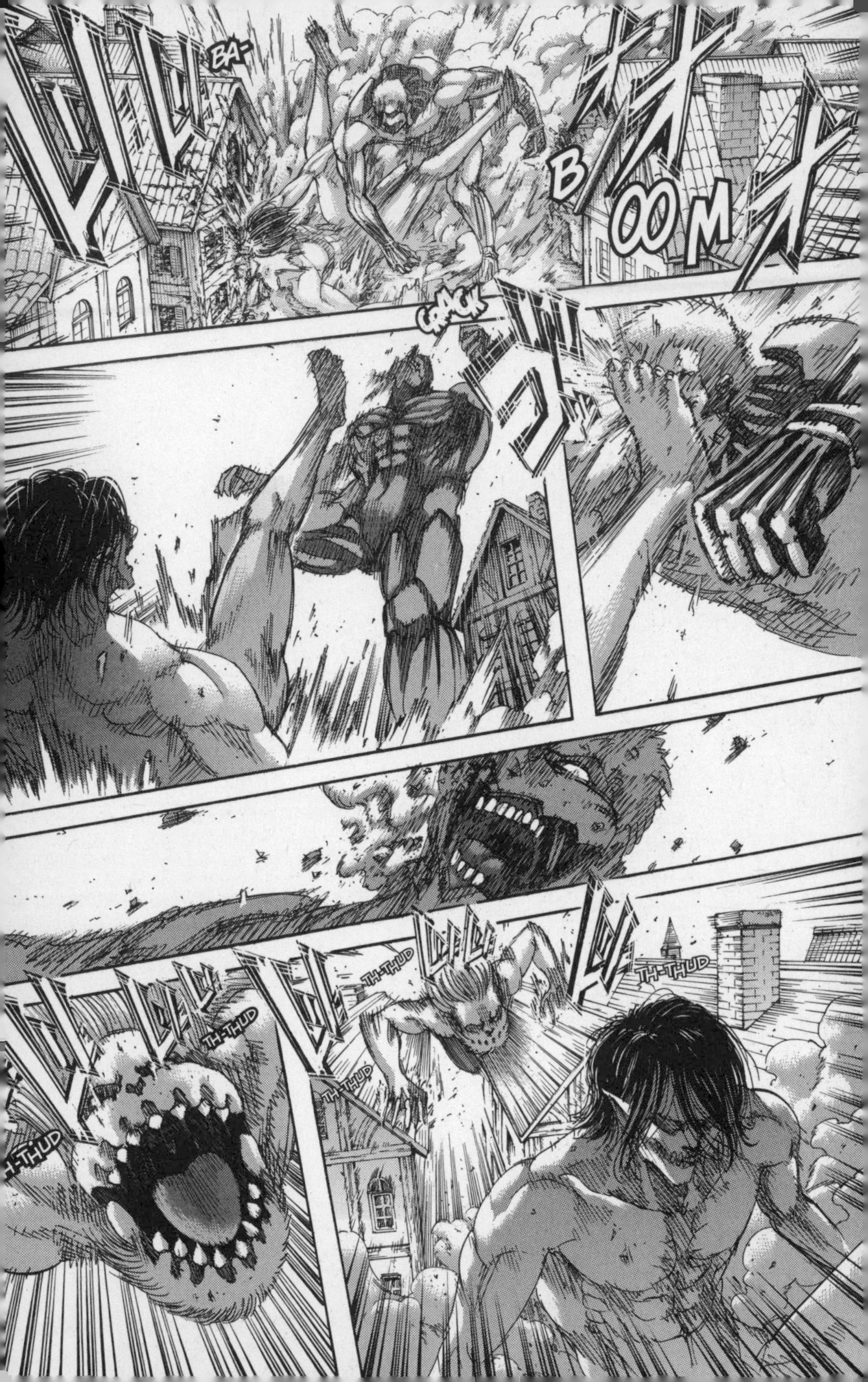
BOOM
BA-
CRACK
TH-THUD
TH-THUD
TH-THUD
TH-THUD
TH-THUD

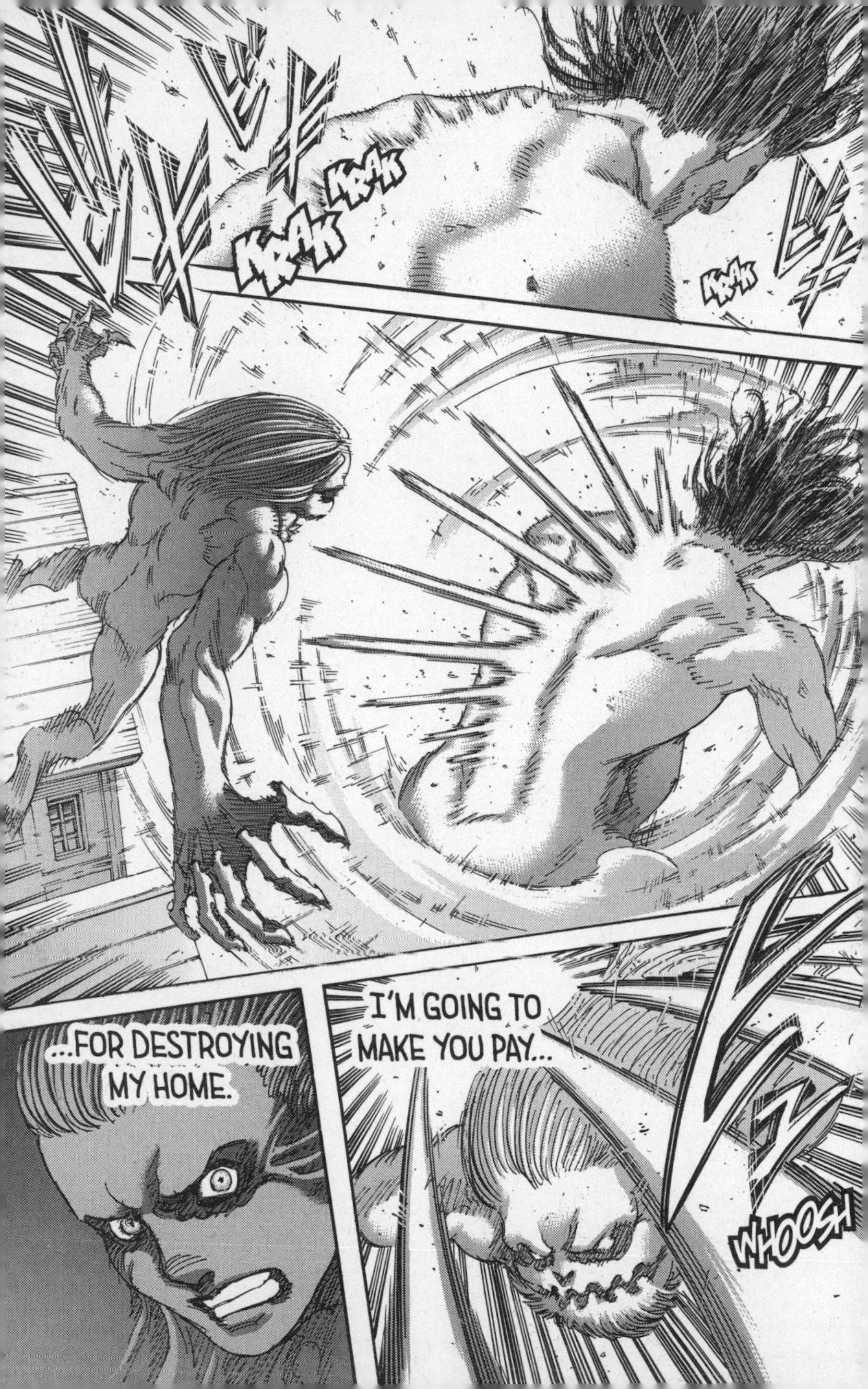
KRAK
KRAK KRAK
I'M GOING TO MAKE YOU PAY...
WHOOSH
...FOR DESTROYING MY HOME.

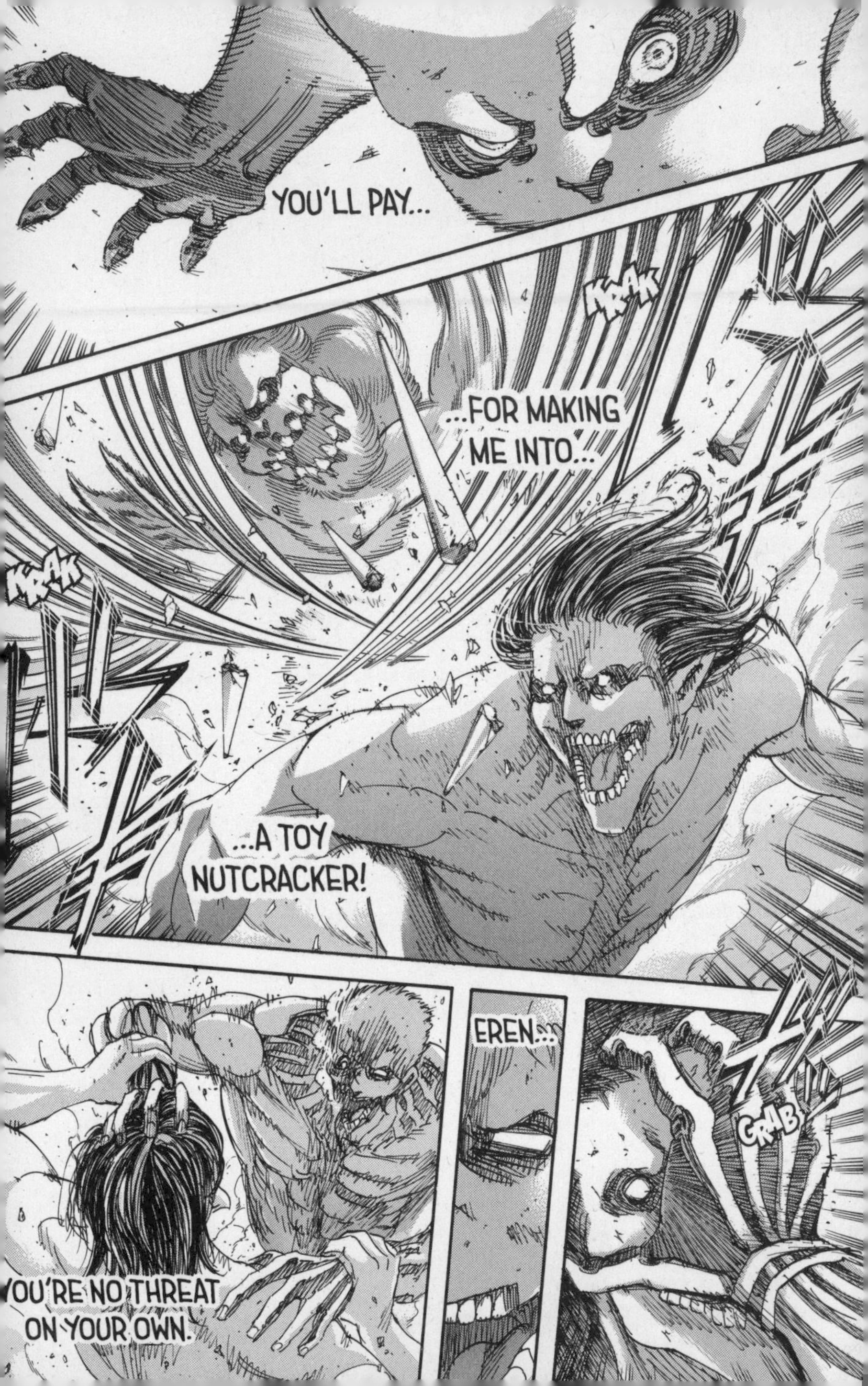
YOU'LL PAY...
KRAK
...FOR MAKING ME INTO...
KRAK
...A TOY NUTCRACKER!
GRAB
EREN...
YOU'RE NO THREAT ON YOUR OWN.

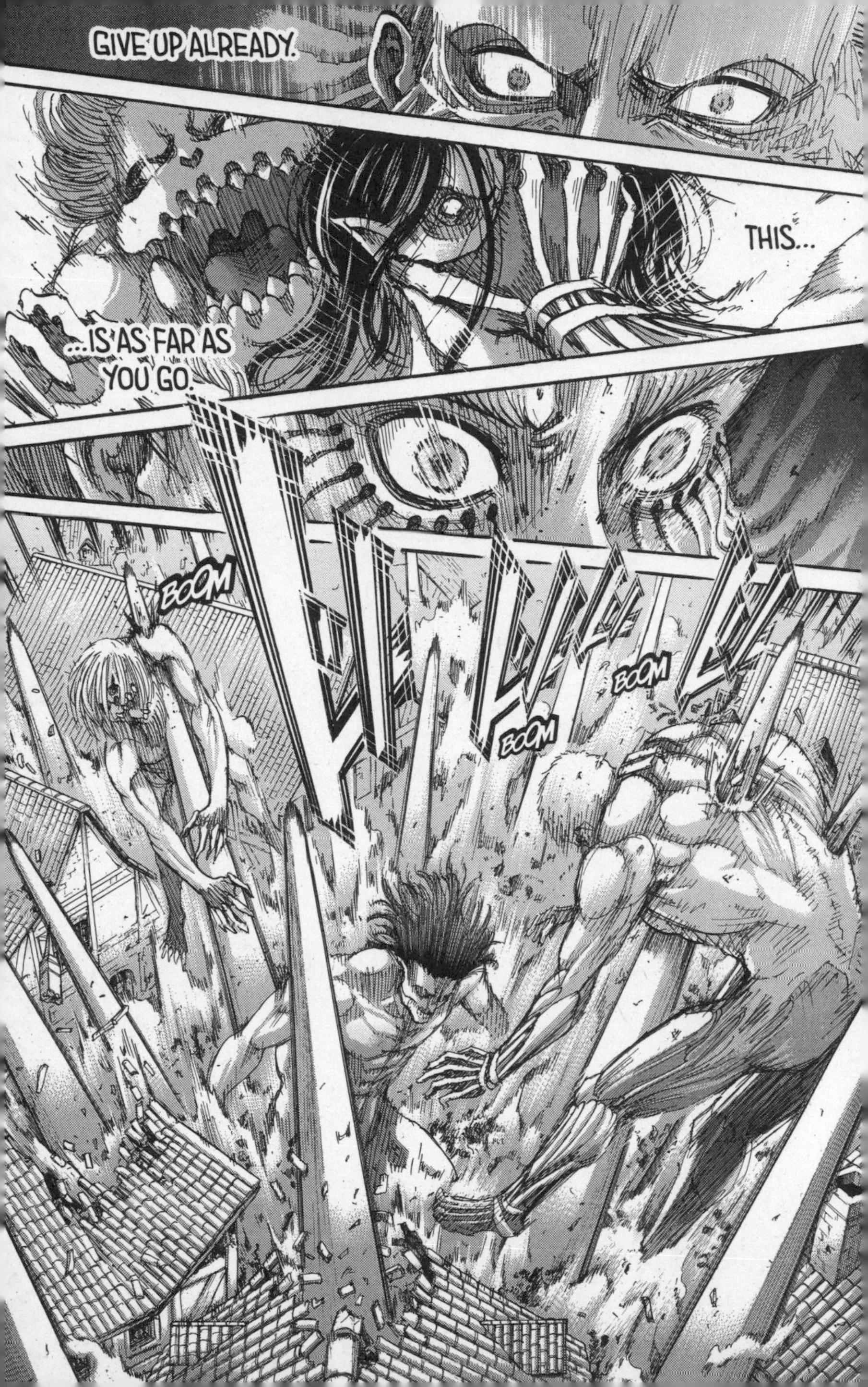
GIVE UP ALREADY.
THIS...
...IS AS FAR AS YOU GO.
BOOM
BOOM
BOOM

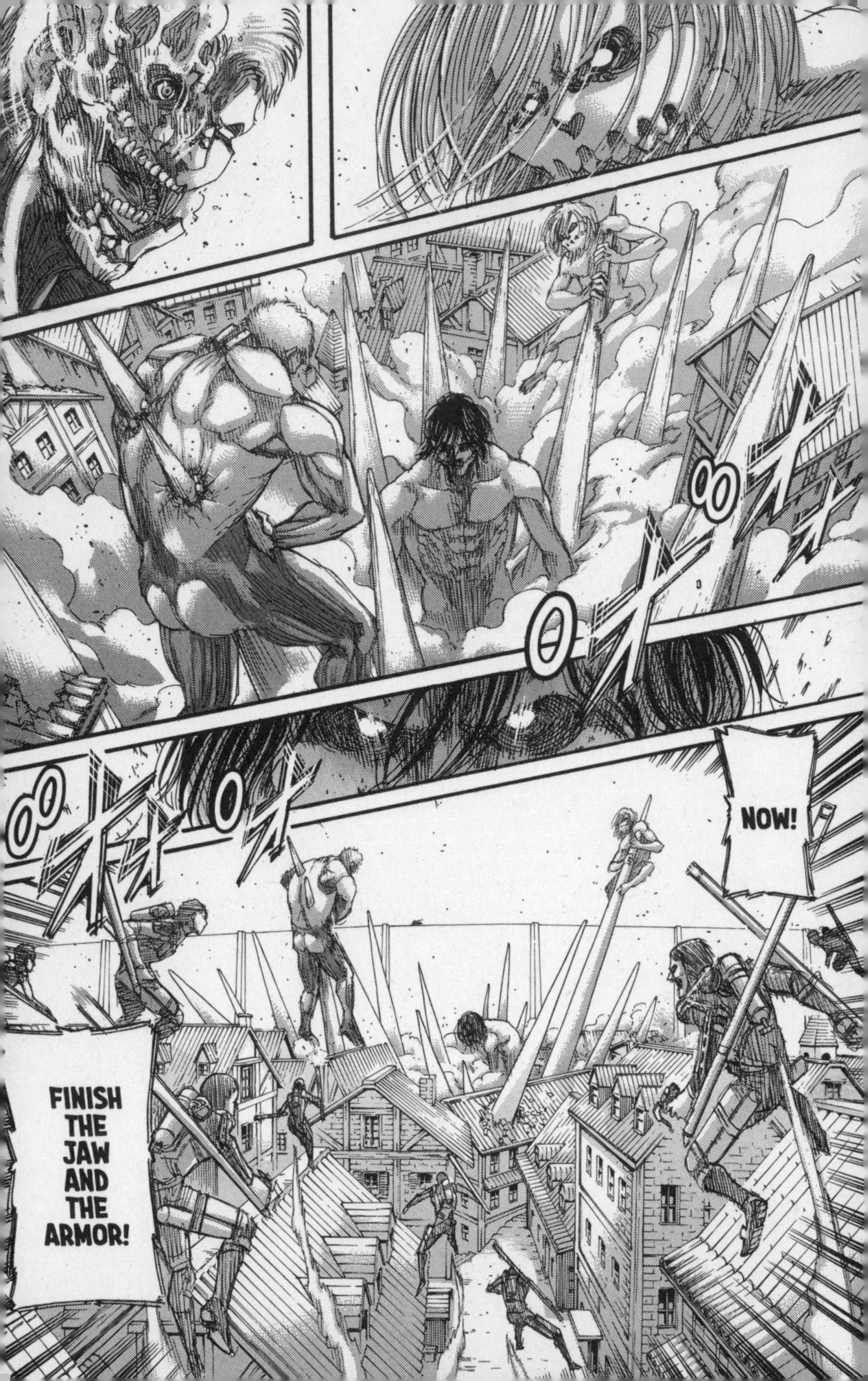
NOW!
FINISH THE JAW AND THE ARMOR!

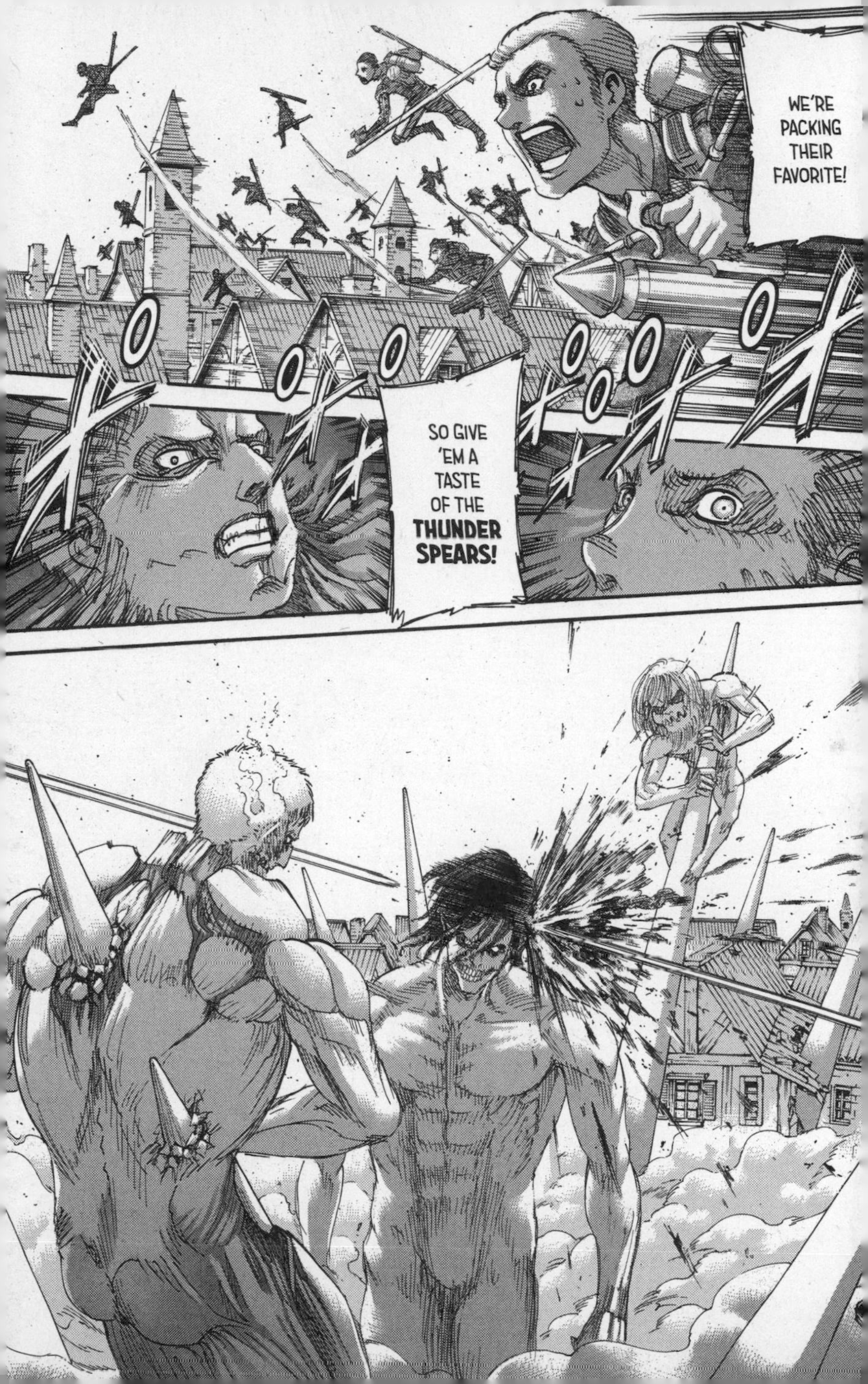
WE'RE PACKING THEIR FAVORITE!
SO GIVE 'EM A TASTE OF THE **THUNDER SPEARS!**

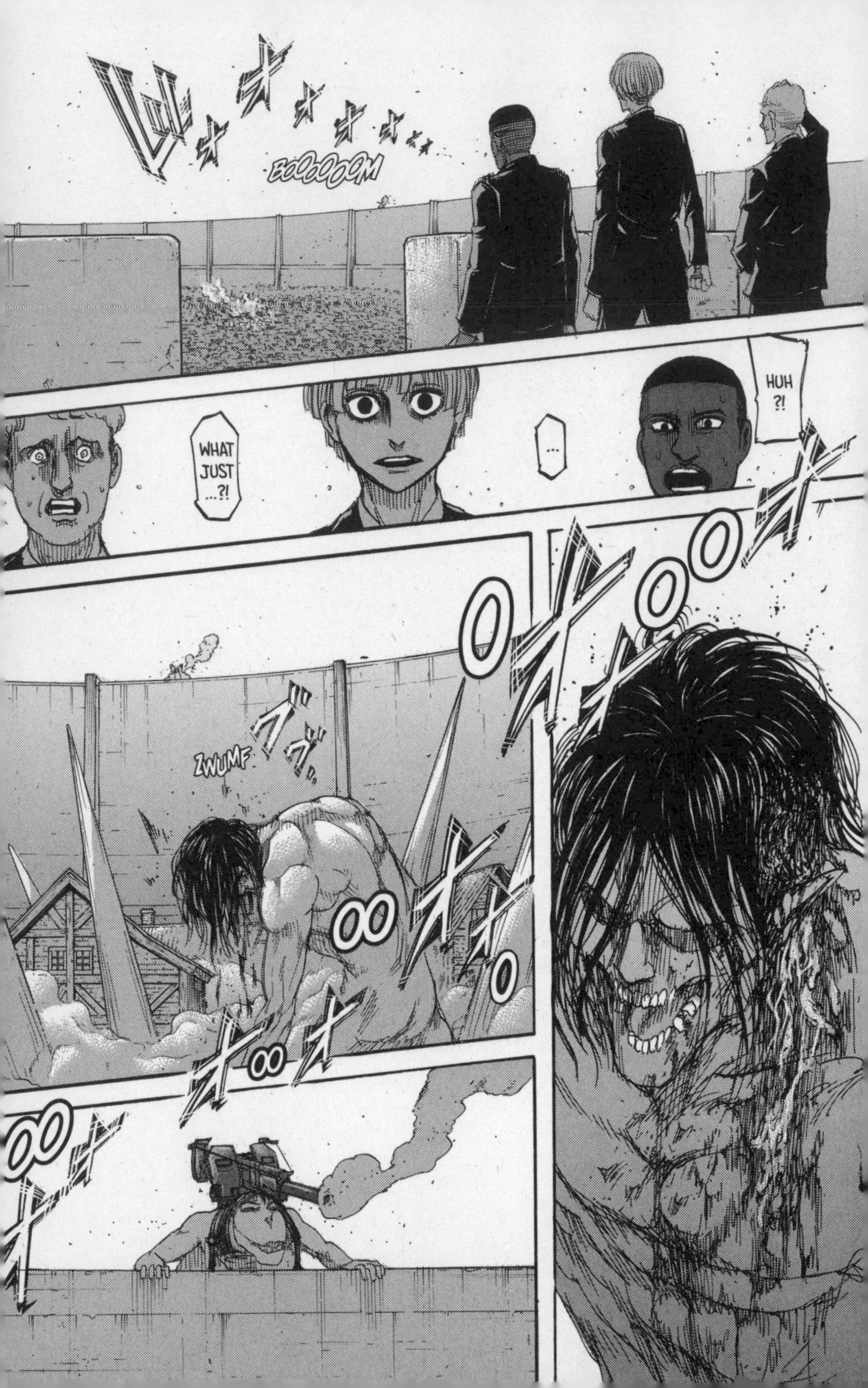
BOOOOOOOM
HUH ?!
...
WHAT JUST ...?!
ZWUMF

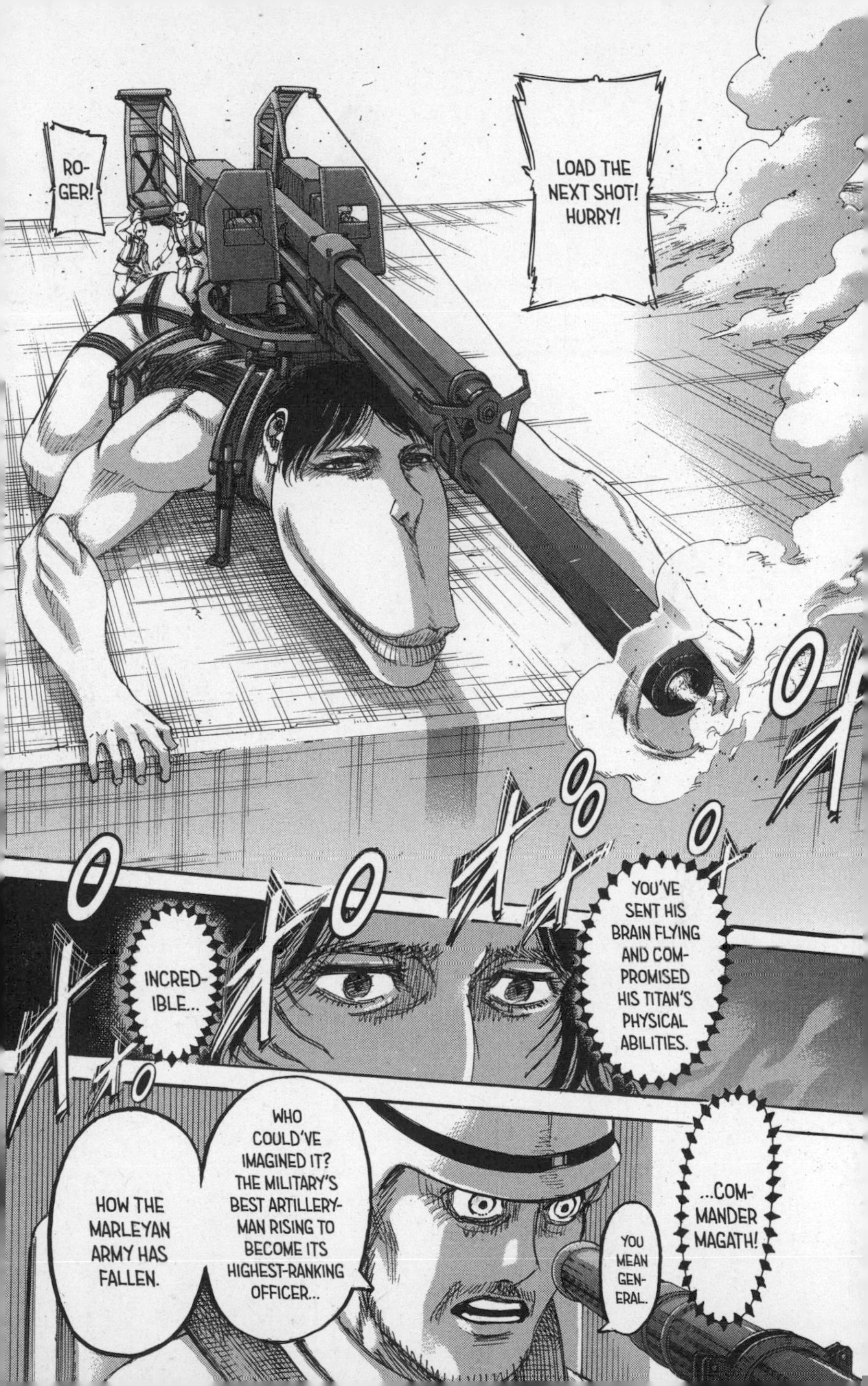
LOAD THE NEXT SHOT! HURRY!
RO-GER!
YOU'VE SENT HIS BRAIN FLYING AND COM-PROMISED HIS TITAN'S PHYSICAL ABILITIES.
INCRED-IBLE...
...COM-MANDER MAGATH!
YOU MEAN GEN-ERAL.
WHO COULD'VE IMAGINED IT? THE MILITARY'S BEST ARTILLERY-MAN RISING TO BECOME ITS HIGHEST-RANKING OFFICER...
HOW THE MARLEYAN ARMY HAS FALLEN.

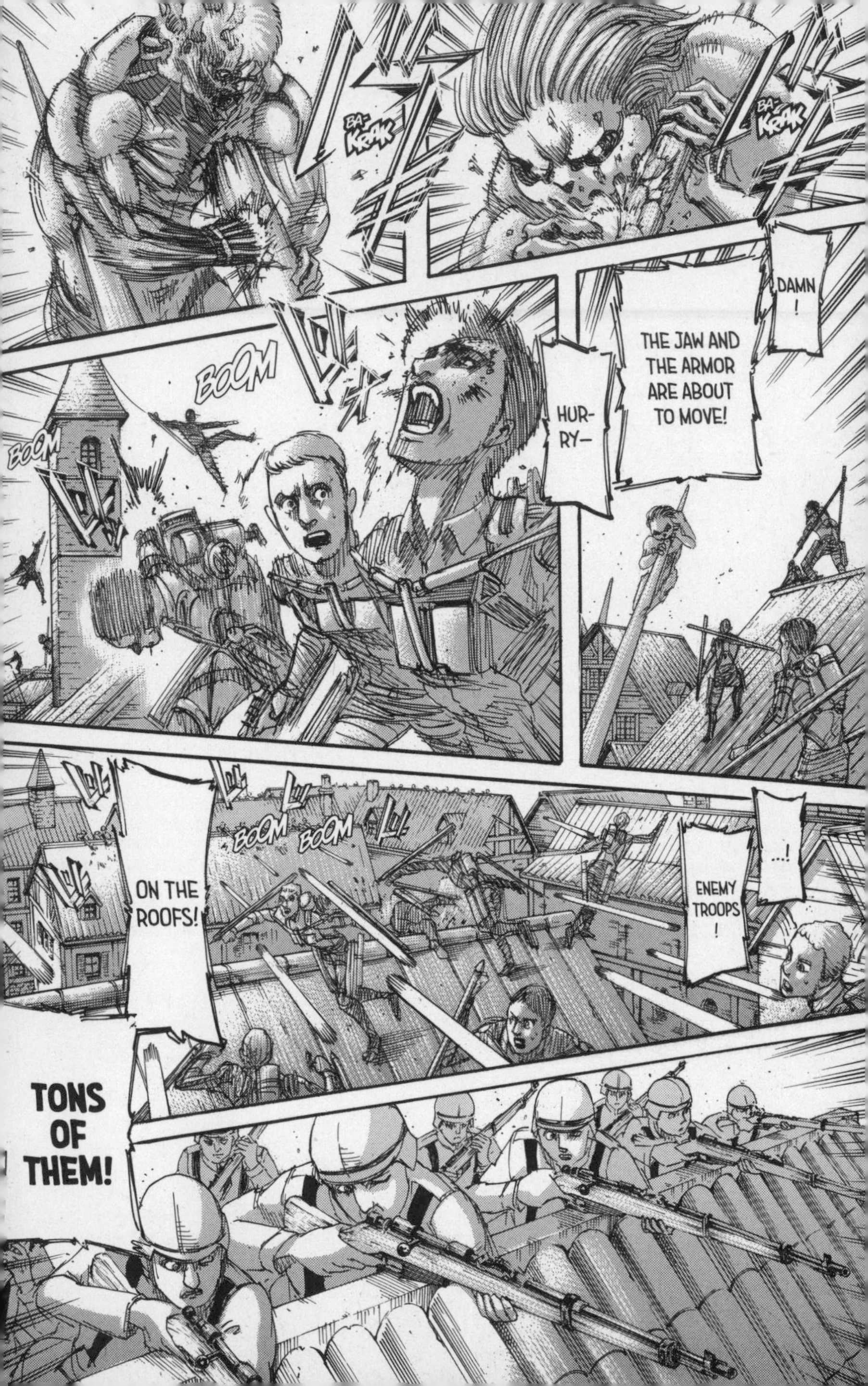
BA-KRAK
BA-KRAK
DAMN!
THE JAW AND THE ARMOR ARE ABOUT TO MOVE!
HURRY—
BOOM
BOOM
...!
ENEMY TROOPS!
BOOM
BOOM
ON THE ROOFS!
TONS OF THEM!

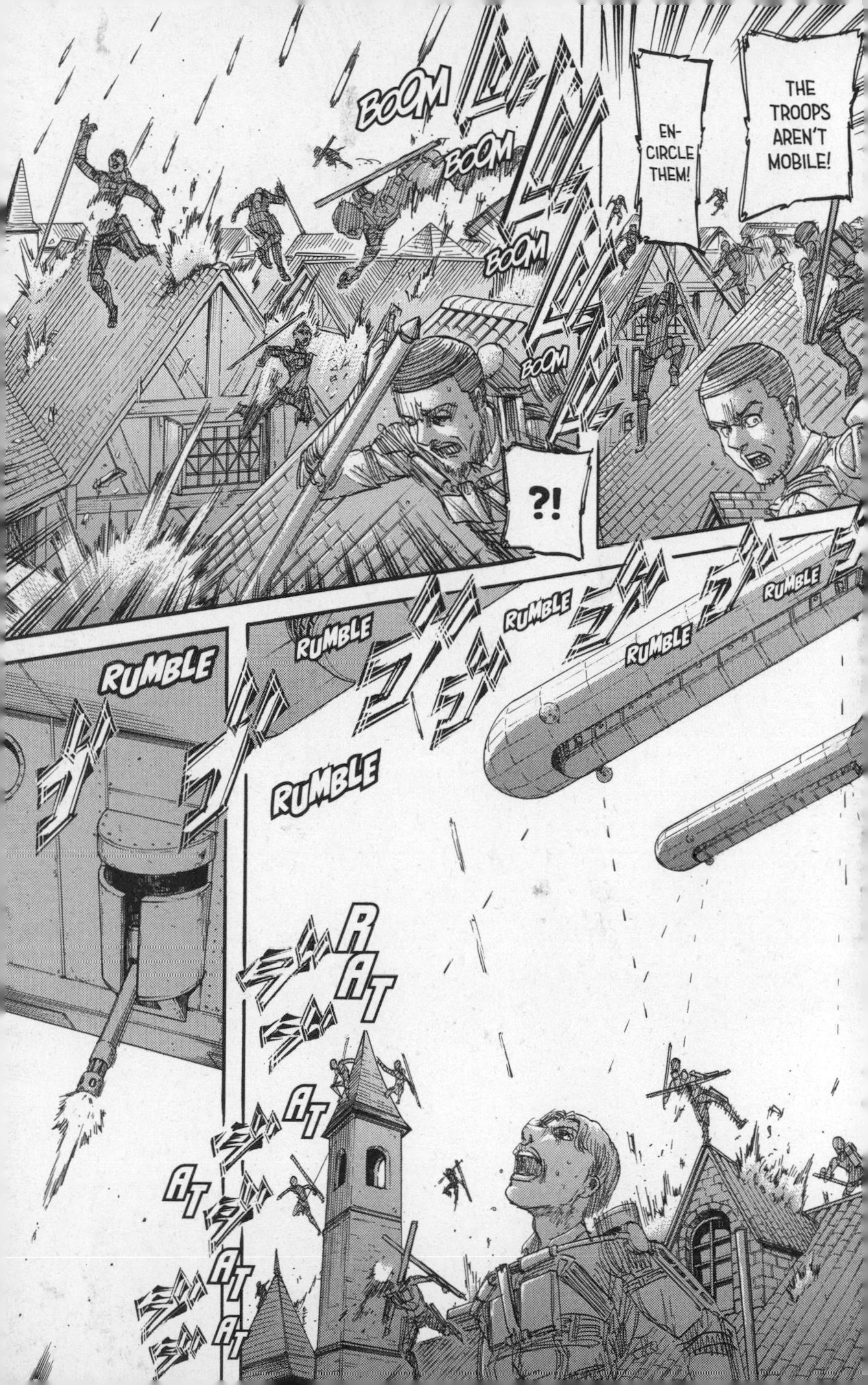
THE TROOPS AREN'T MOBILE!
EN-CIRCLE THEM!
BOOM
BOOM
BOOM
BOOM
?!
RUMBLE
RUMBLE
RUMBLE
RUMBLE
RUMBLE
RUMBLE
RAT
AT
AT
AT
AT

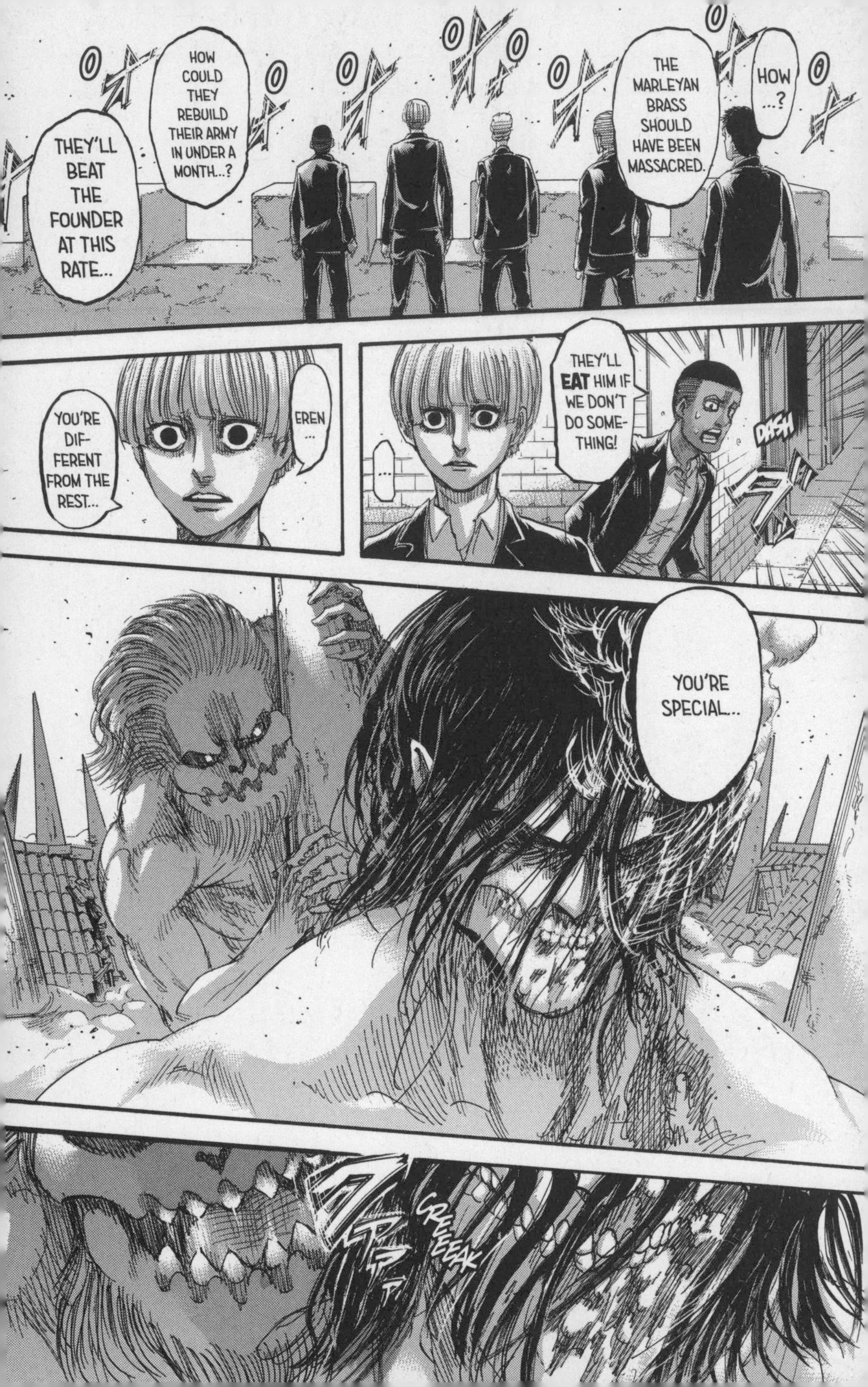
HOW ...?
THE MARLEYAN BRASS SHOULD HAVE BEEN MASSACRED.
HOW COULD THEY REBUILD THEIR ARMY IN UNDER A MONTH...?
THEY'LL BEAT THE FOUNDER AT THIS RATE...
THEY'LL **EAT** HIM IF WE DON'T DO SOME-THING!
DASH
...
EREN ...
YOU'RE DIF-FERENT FROM THE REST...
YOU'RE SPECIAL...
GREEEAK

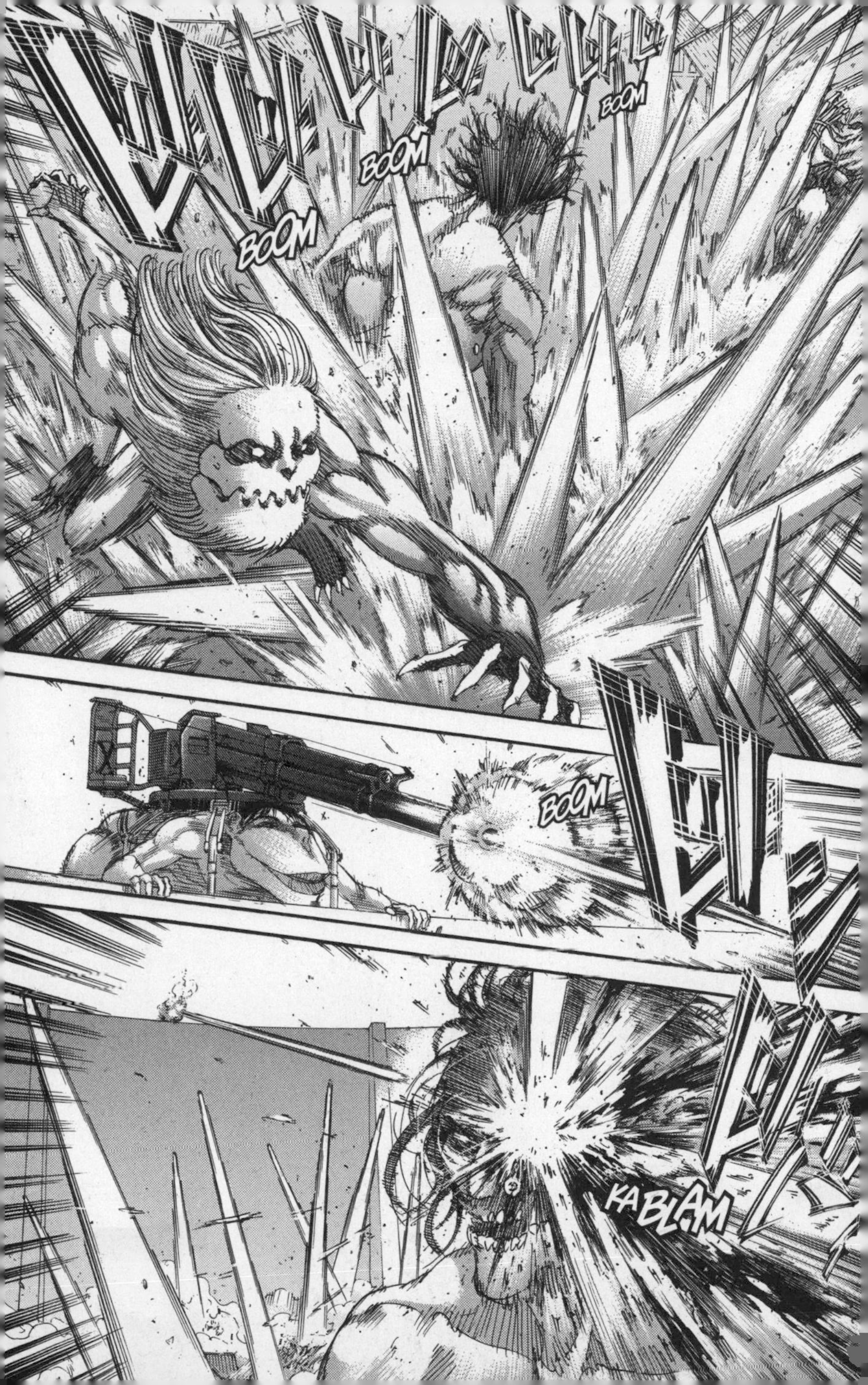
BOOM
BOOM
BOOM
BOOM
KABLAM

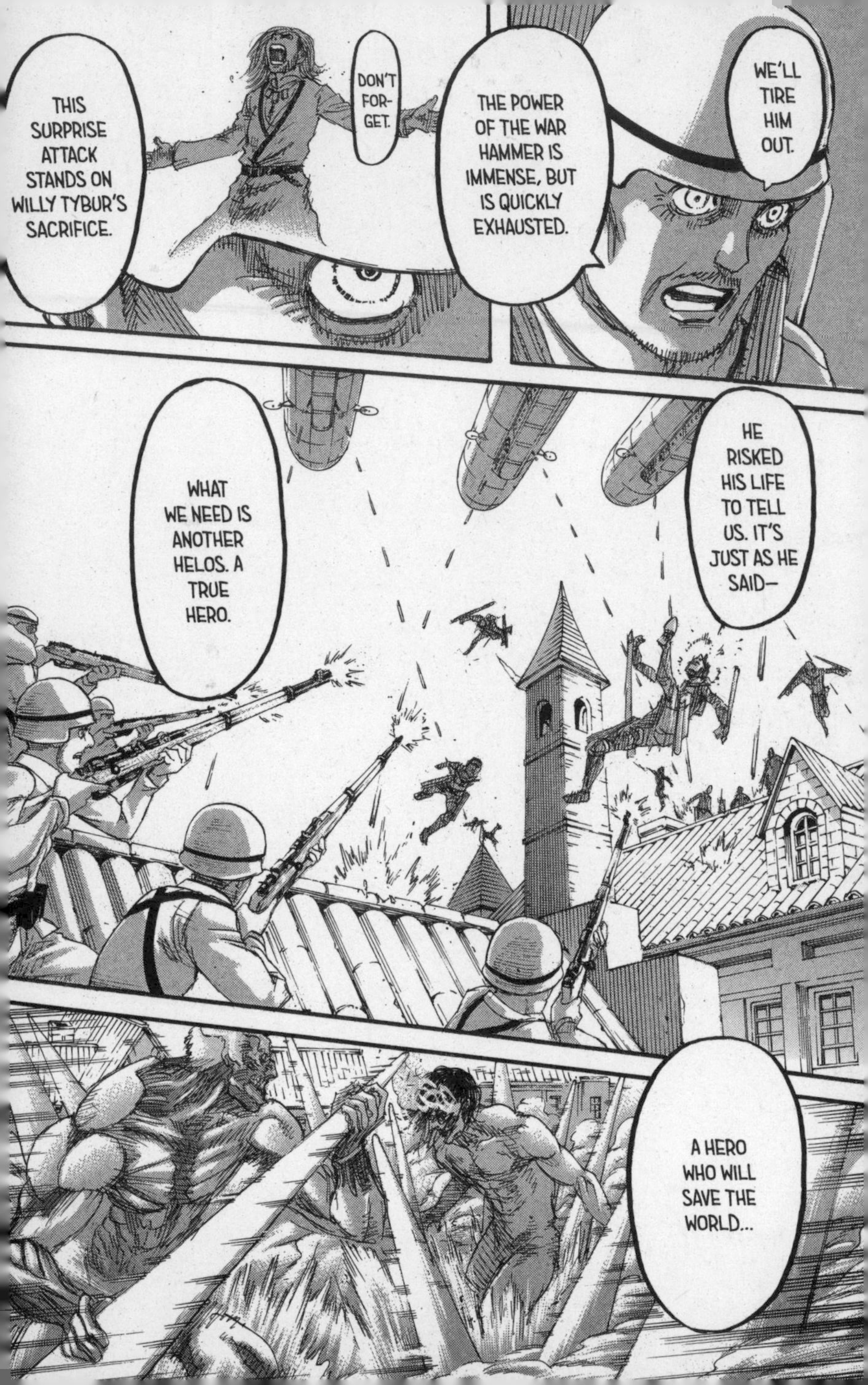
THE POWER OF THE WAR HAMMER IS IMMENSE, BUT IS QUICKLY EXHAUSTED.
WE'LL TIRE HIM OUT.
DON'T FOR-GET.
THIS SURPRISE ATTACK STANDS ON WILLY TYBUR'S SACRIFICE.
HE RISKED HIS LIFE TO TELL US. IT'S JUST AS HE SAID—
WHAT WE NEED IS ANOTHER HELOS. A TRUE HERO.
A HERO WHO WILL SAVE THE WORLD...

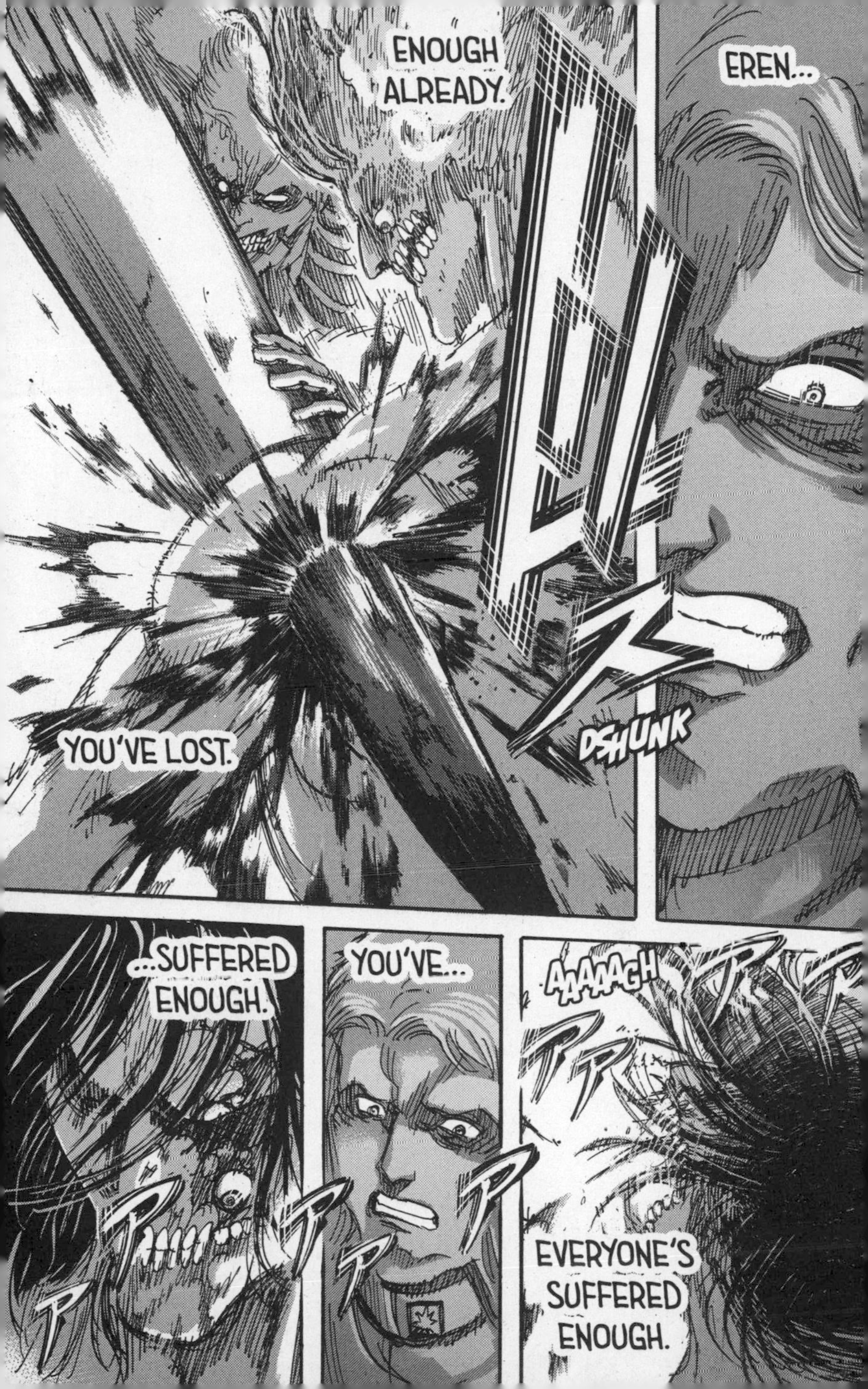
EREN...
ENOUGH ALREADY.
DSHUNK
YOU'VE LOST.
AAAAAGH
EVERYONE'S SUFFERED ENOUGH.
YOU'VE...
...SUFFERED ENOUGH.

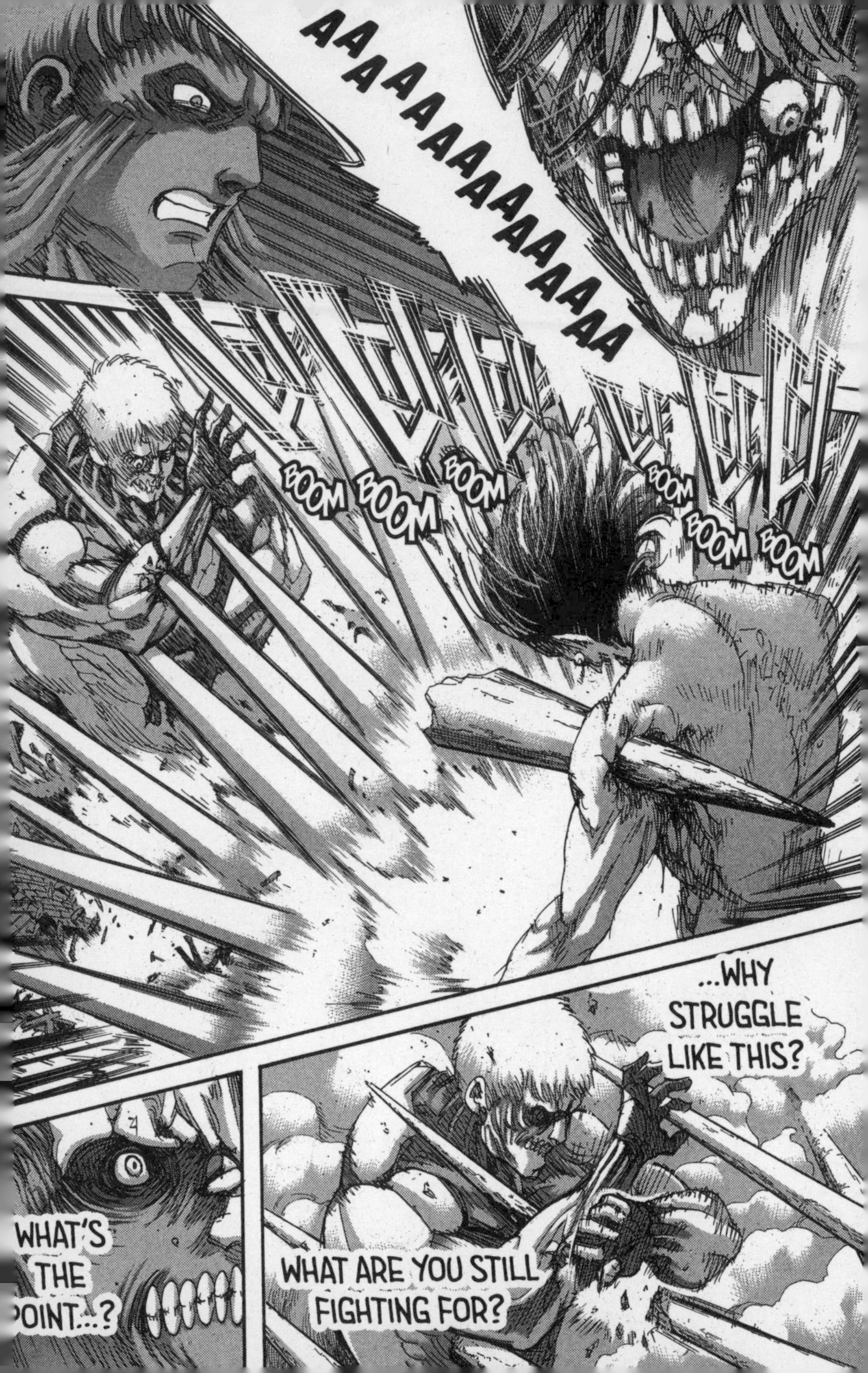
AAAAAAAAAAAAAAAA
BOOM BOOM BOOM
BOOM BOOM BOOM
...WHY STRUGGLE LIKE THIS?
WHAT ARE YOU STILL FIGHTING FOR?
WHAT'S THE POINT...?

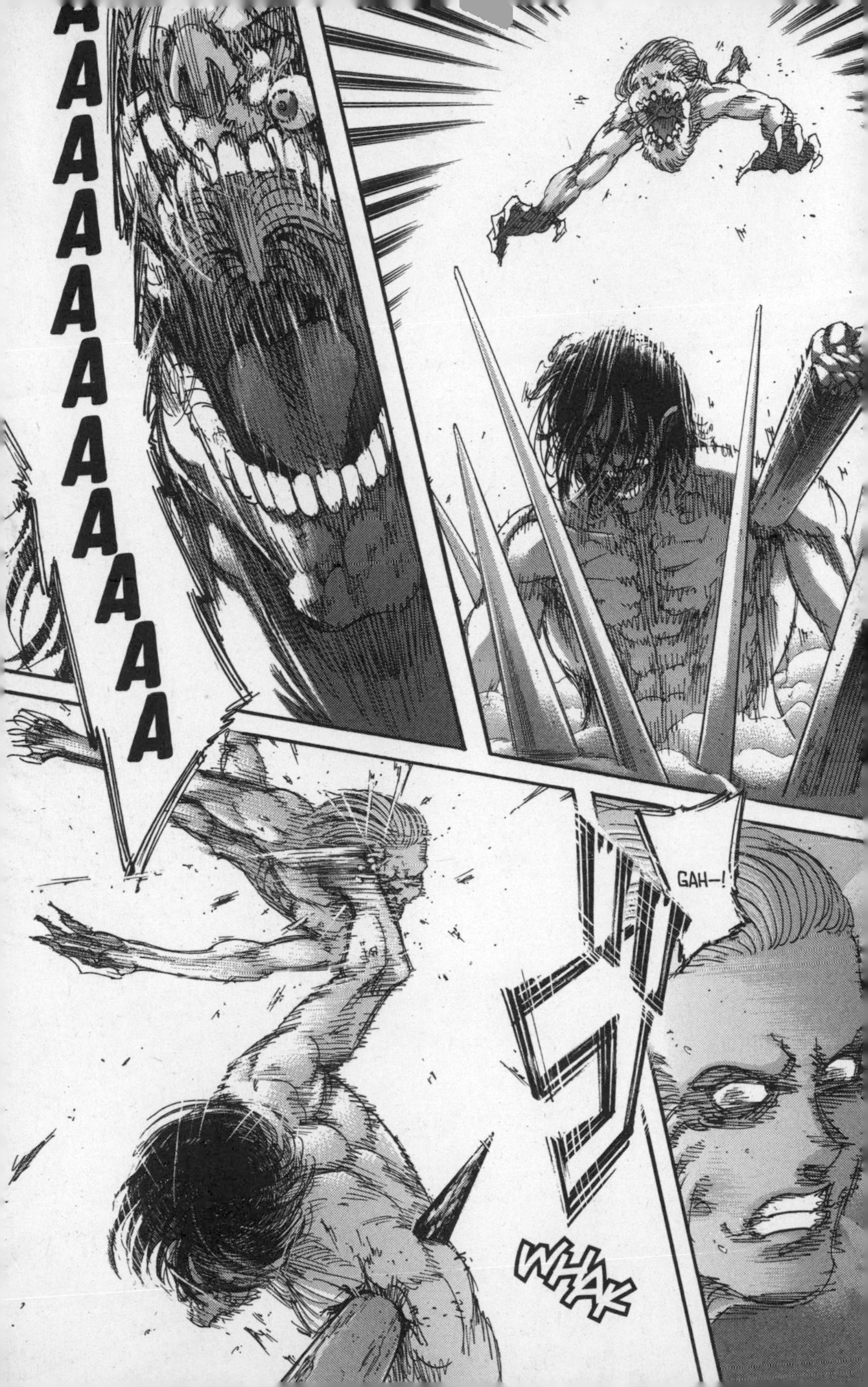
AAAAAAAAAAAA
GAH—!
WHAK

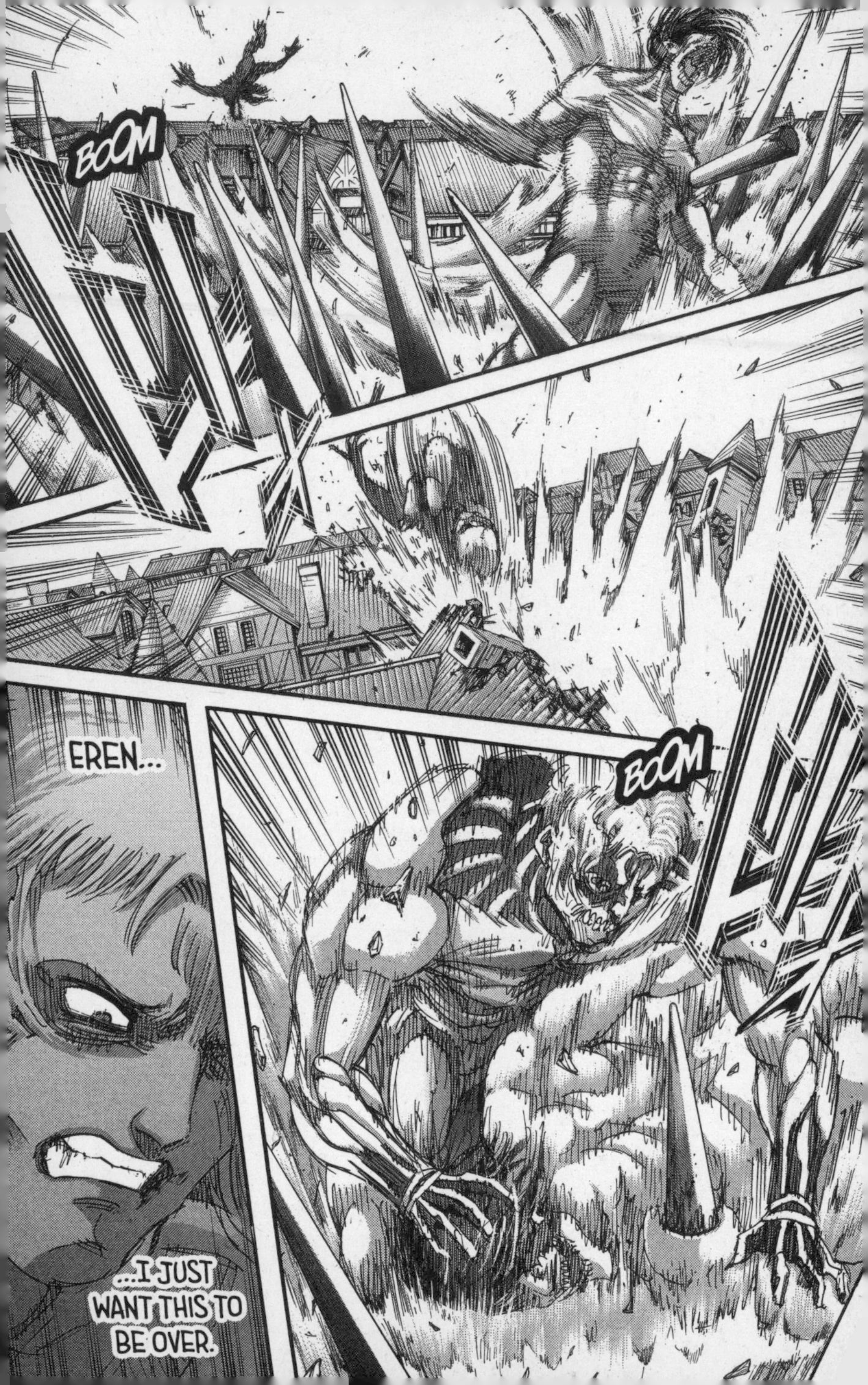
BOOM
BOOM
EREN...
...I JUST WANT THIS TO BE OVER.

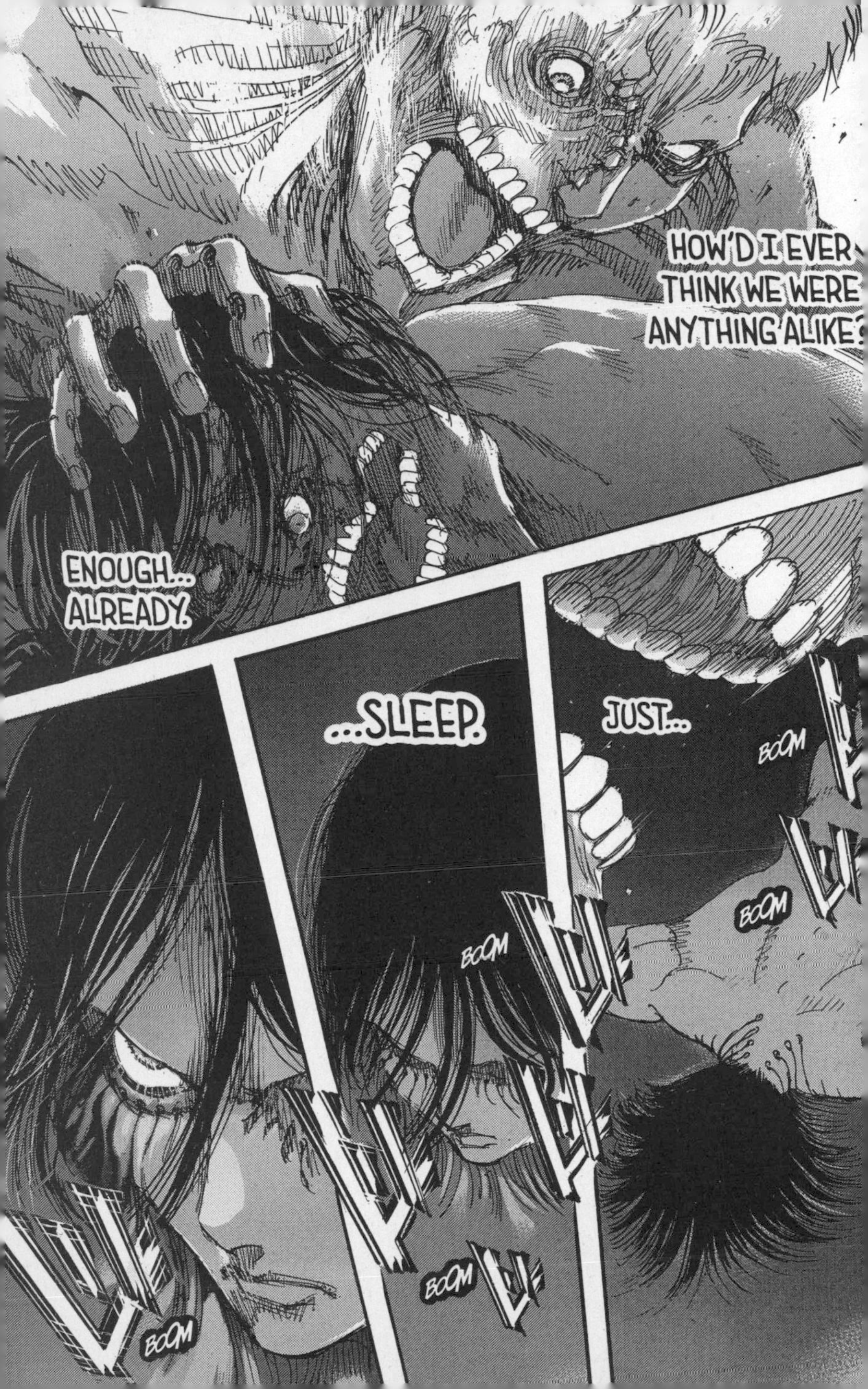

HOW'D I EVER THINK WE WERE ANYTHING ALIKE?
ENOUGH... ALREADY.
JUST...
BOOM
BOOM
...SLEEP.
BOOM
BOOM
BOOM

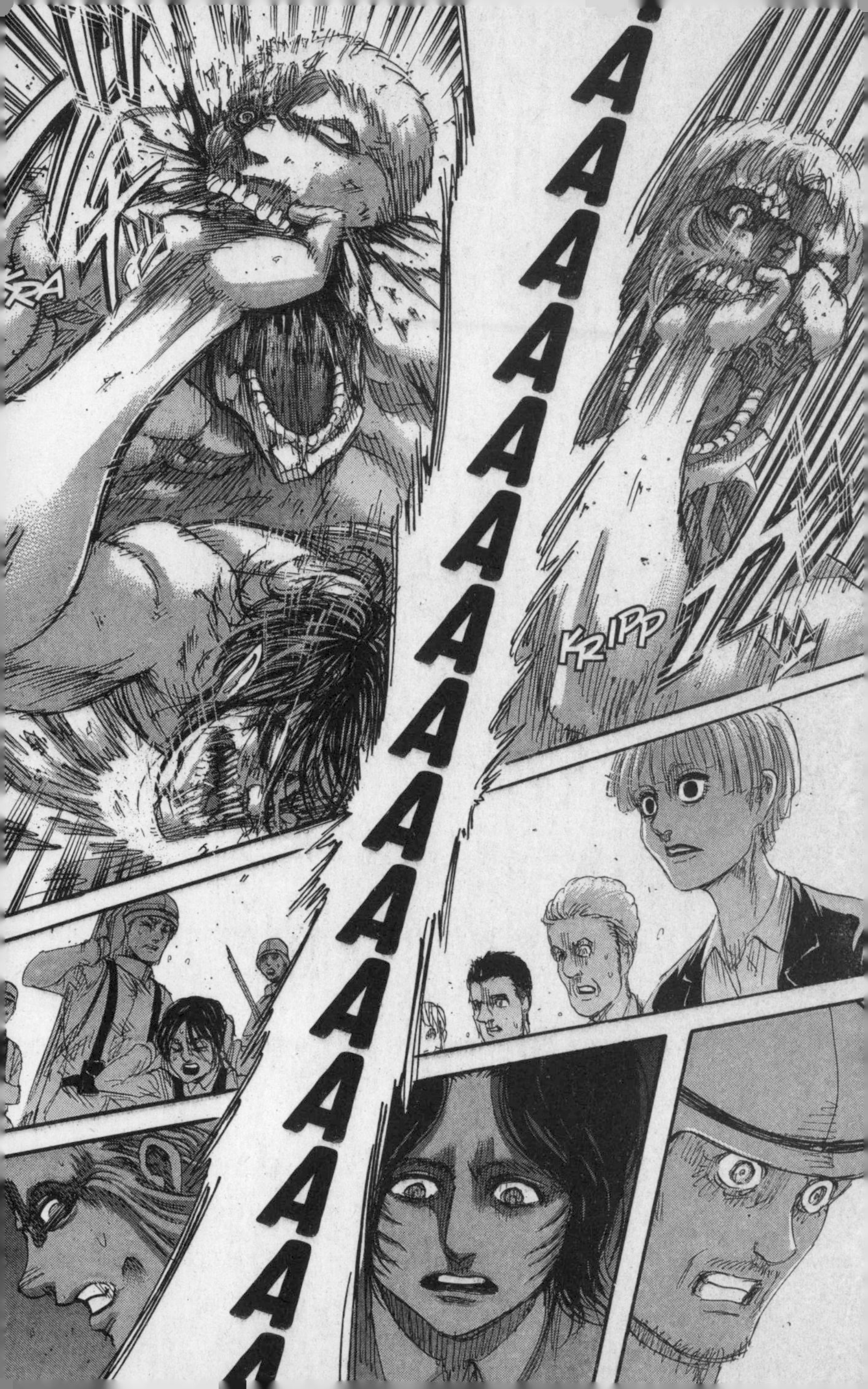
KRIPP
AAAAAAAAAAAAAAAAA
RA

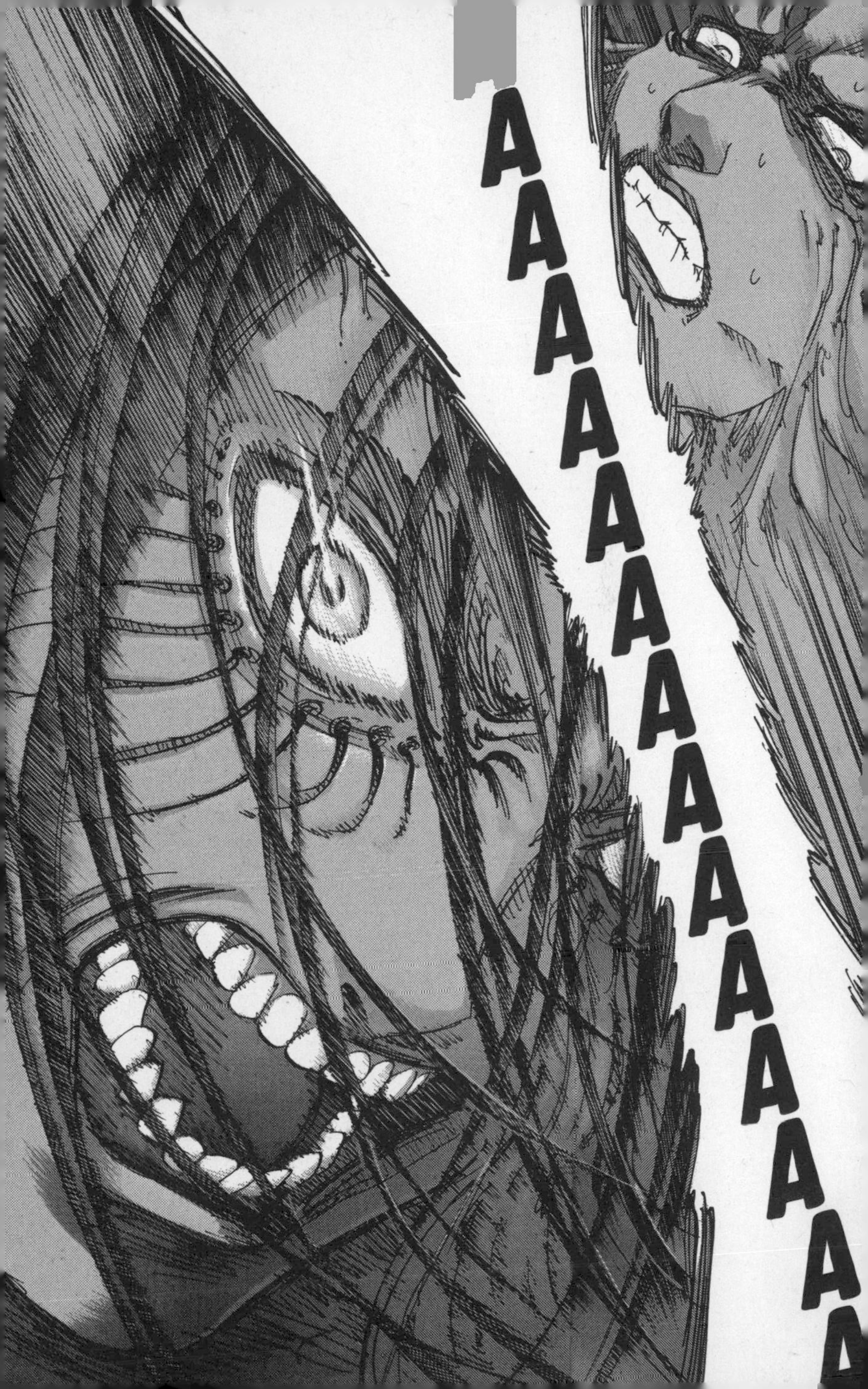
AAAAAAAAAAAAAA

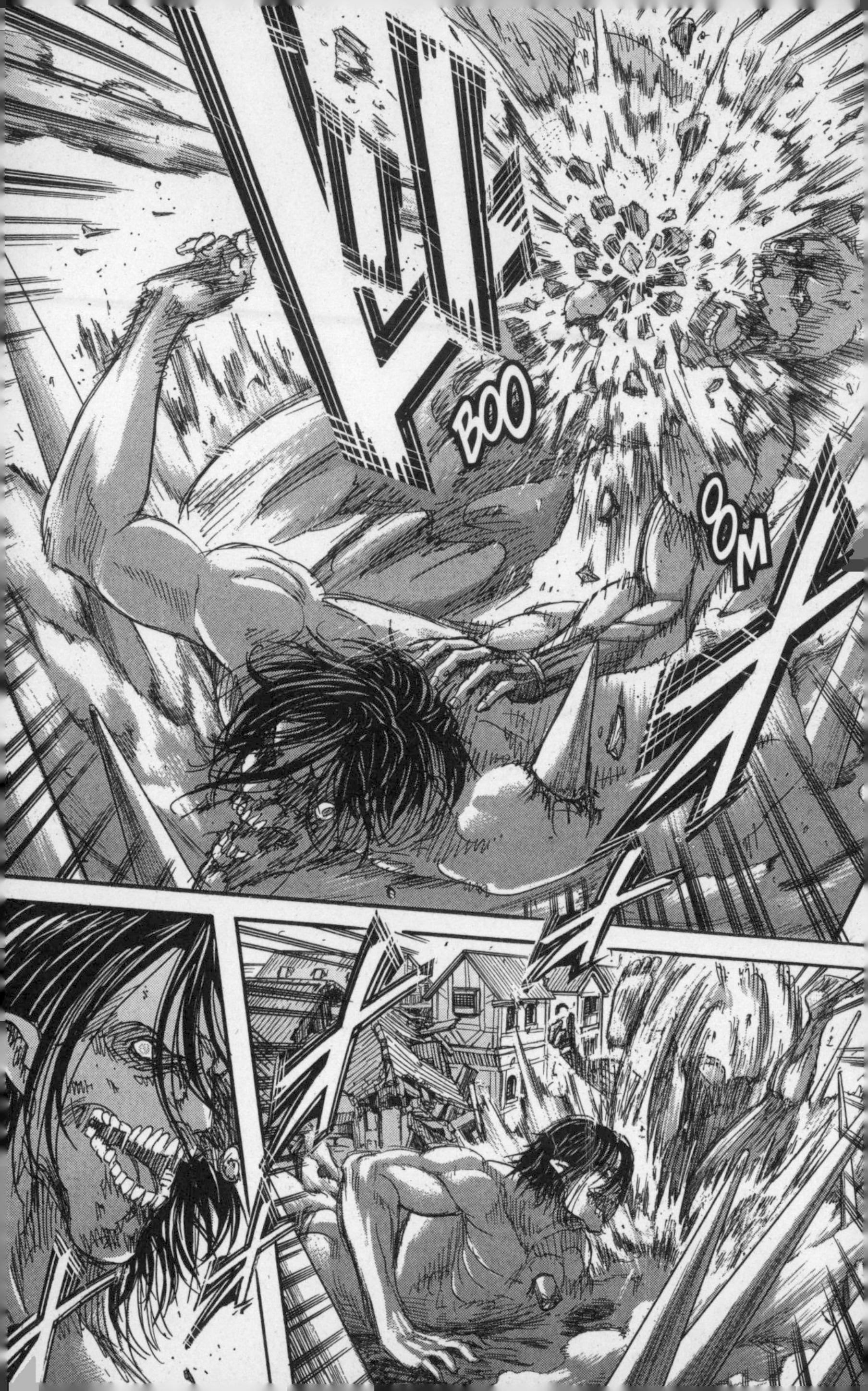
BOOOOM

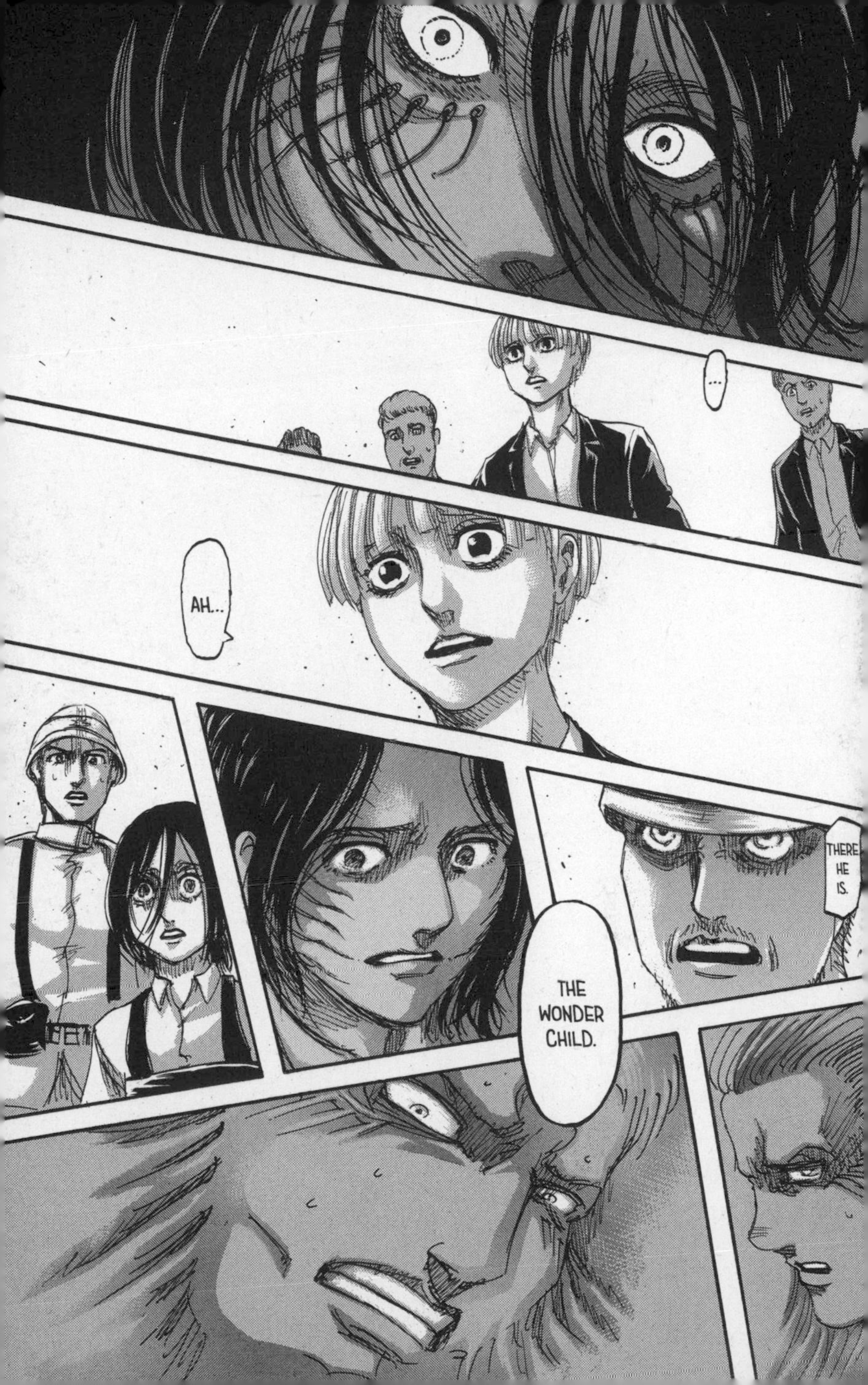
...
AH...
THERE HE IS.
THE WONDER CHILD.

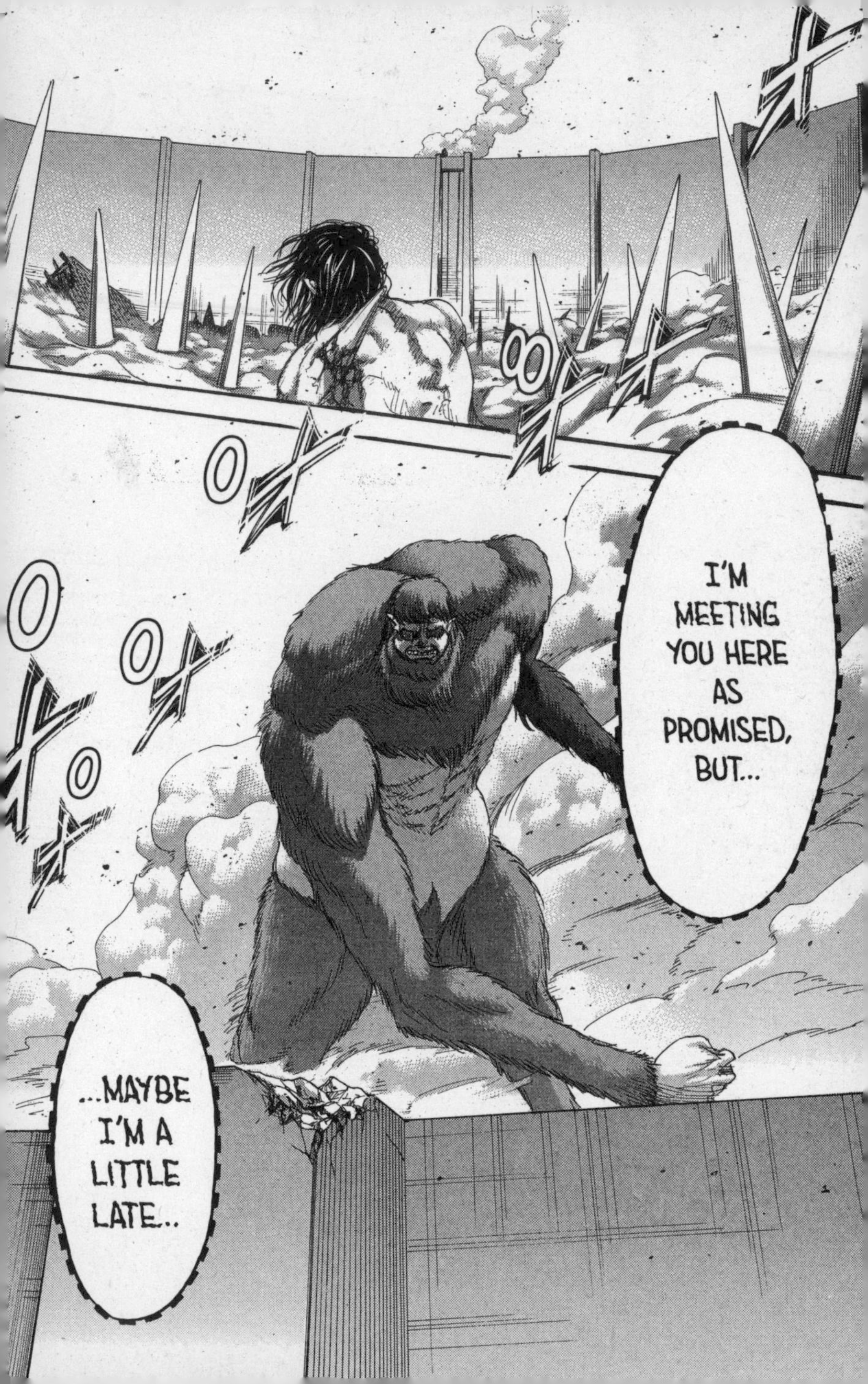
I'M MEETING YOU HERE AS PROMISED, BUT...
...MAYBE I'M A LITTLE LATE...

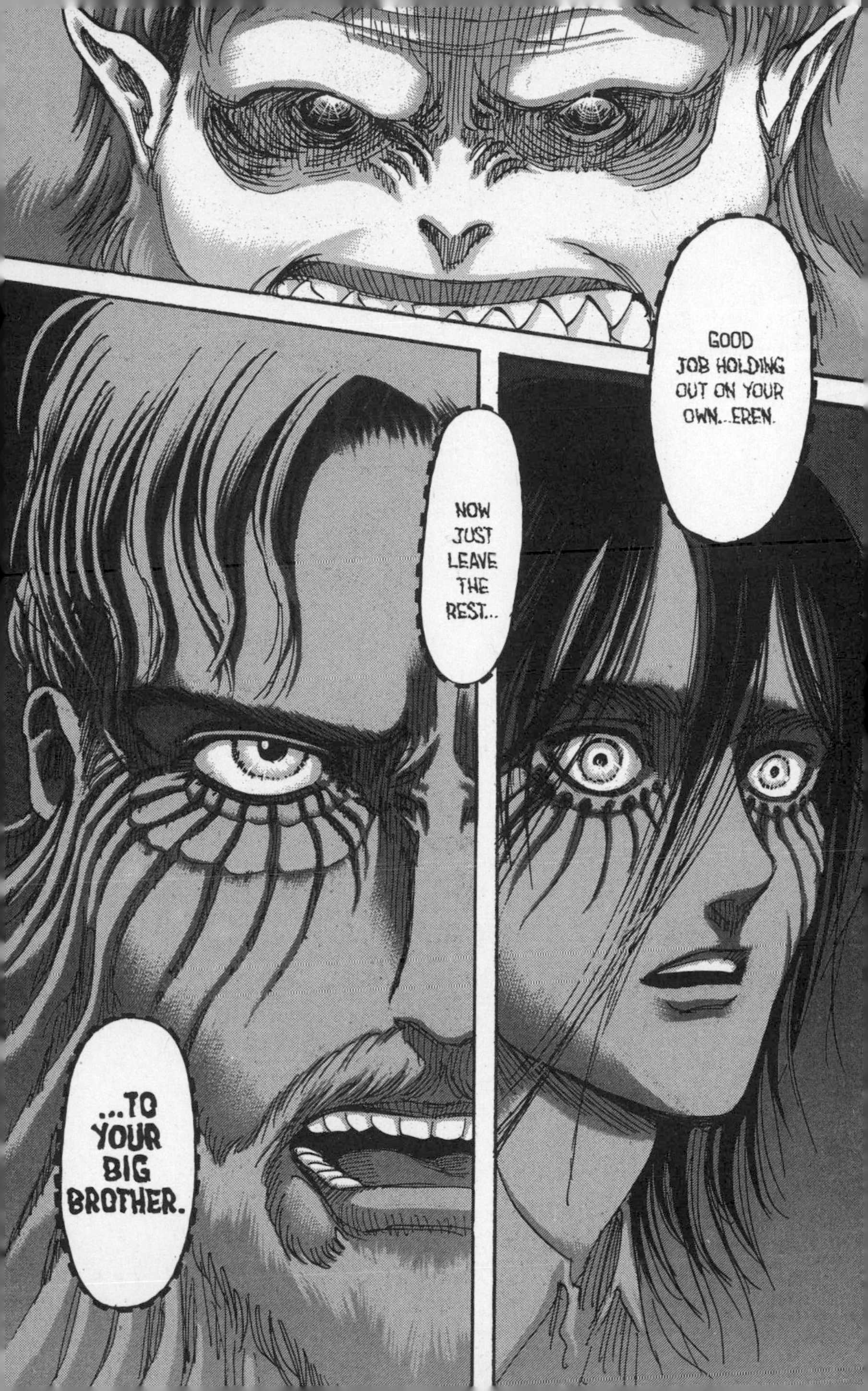
GOOD JOB HOLDING OUT ON YOUR OWN...EREN.
NOW JUST LEAVE THE REST...
...TO YOUR BIG BROTHER.

ATTACK on TITAN

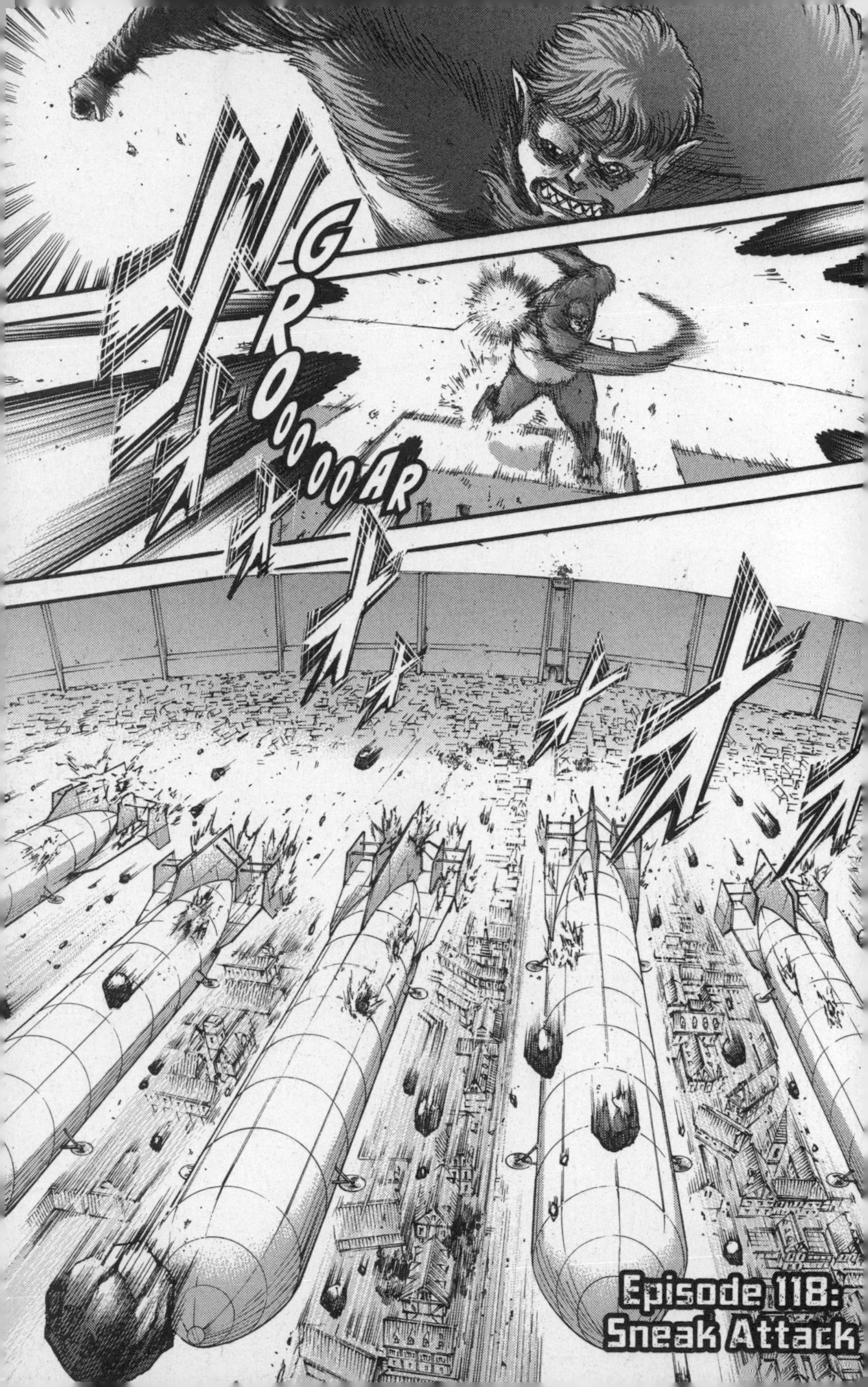
GROOOOOAR
Episode 118:
Sneak Attack

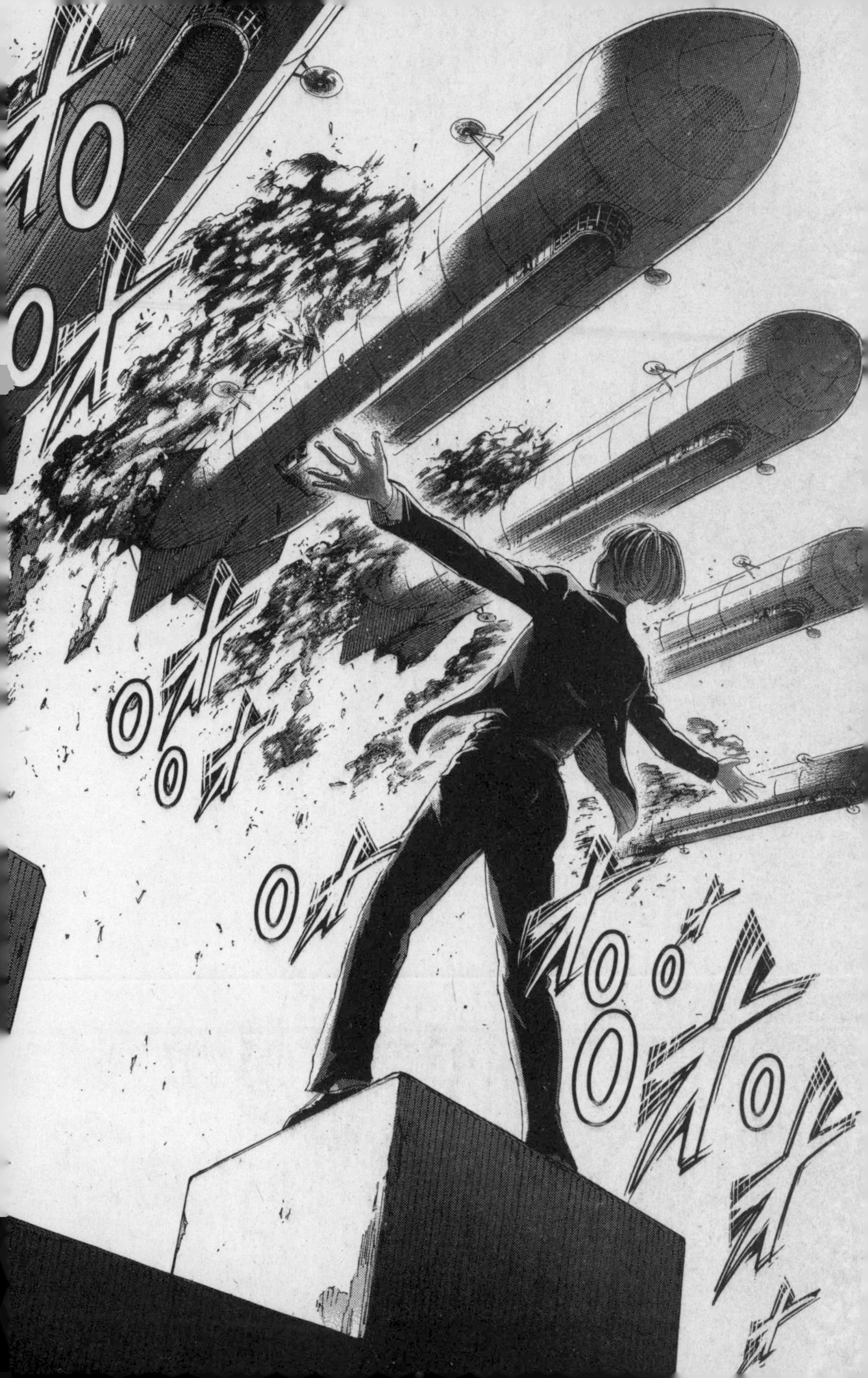

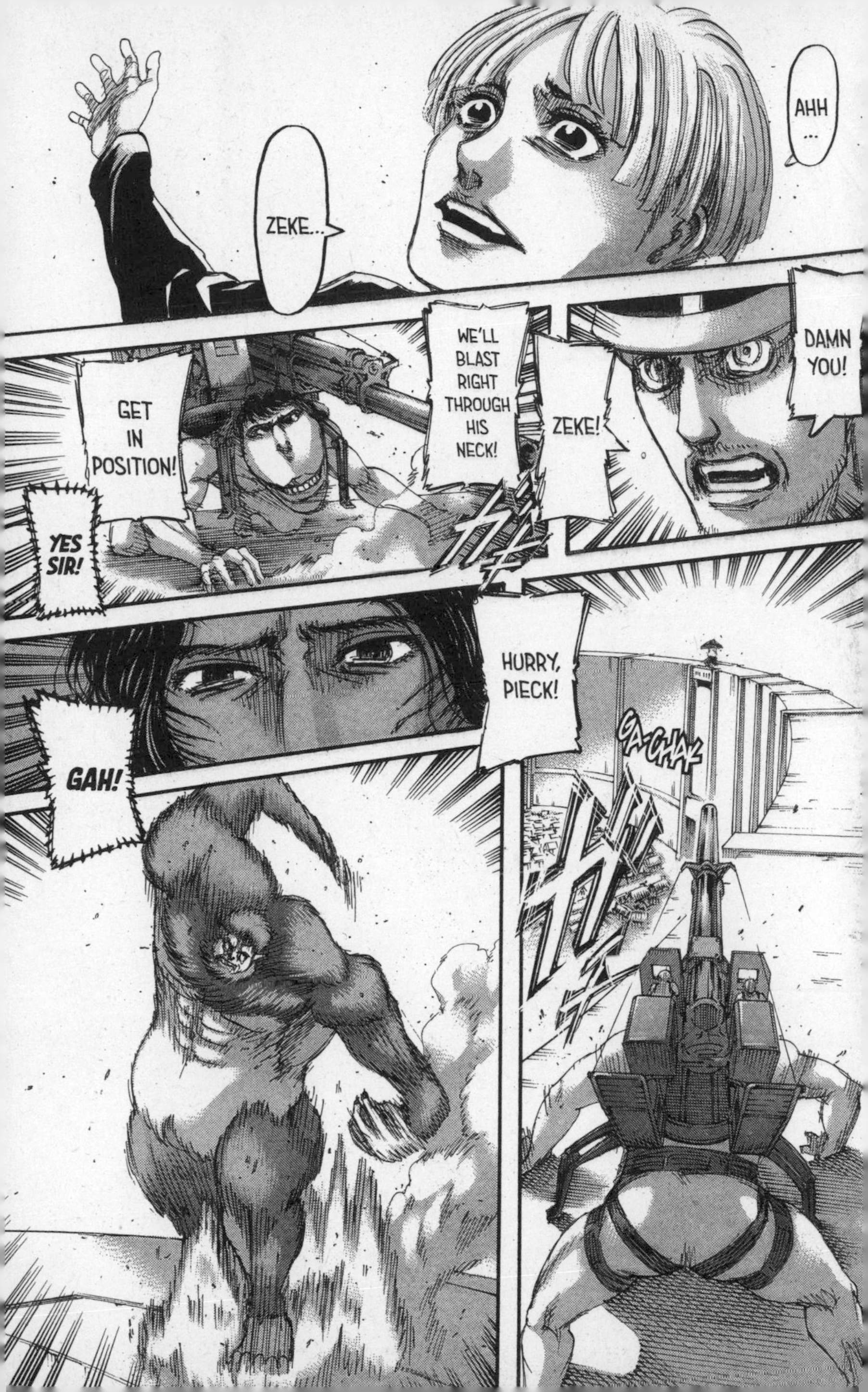
AHH ...
ZEKE...
DAMN YOU!
ZEKE!
WE'LL BLAST RIGHT THROUGH HIS NECK!
GET IN POSITION!
YES SIR!
HURRY, PIECK!
GA-CHAK
GAH!

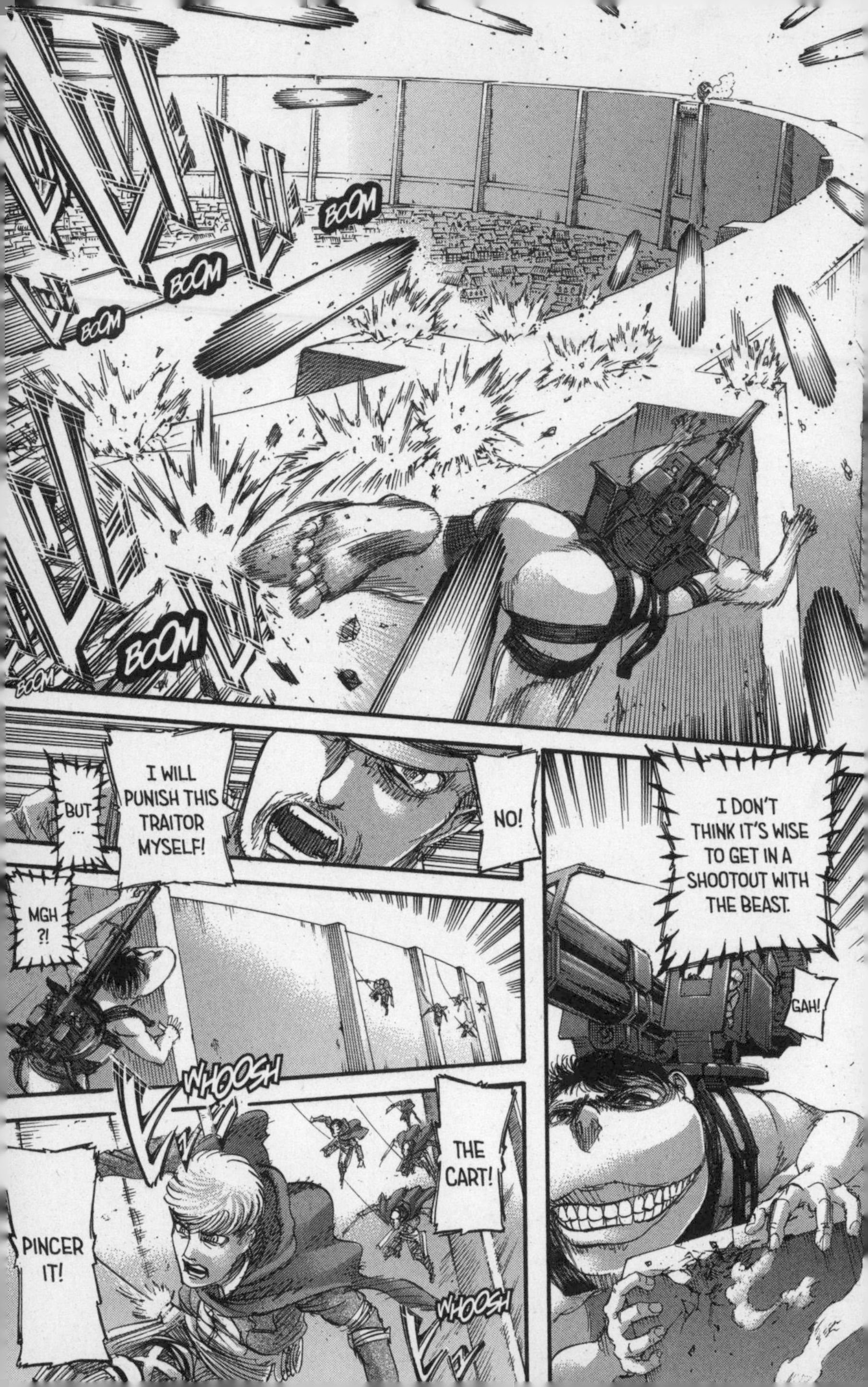
BOOM
BOOM
BOOM
BOOM
BOOM
I DON'T THINK IT'S WISE TO GET IN A SHOOTOUT WITH THE BEAST.
GAH!
NO!
I WILL PUNISH THIS TRAITOR MYSELF!
BUT ...
MGH ?!
WHOOSH
THE CART!
PINCER IT!
WHOOSH

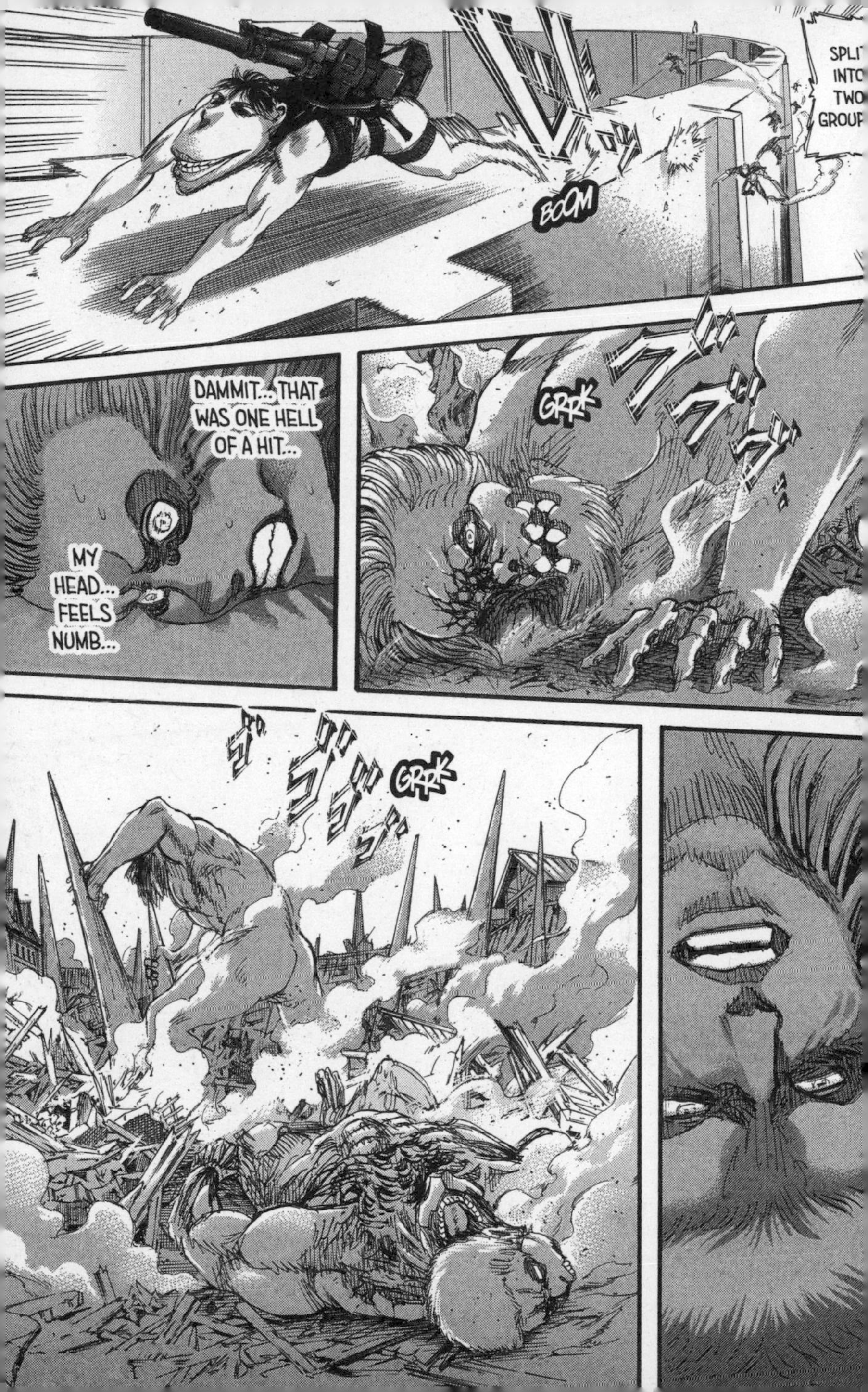
SPLIT INTO TWO GROUP
BOOM
GRRK
DAMMIT... THAT WAS ONE HELL OF A HIT...
MY HEAD... FEELS NUMB...
GRRK

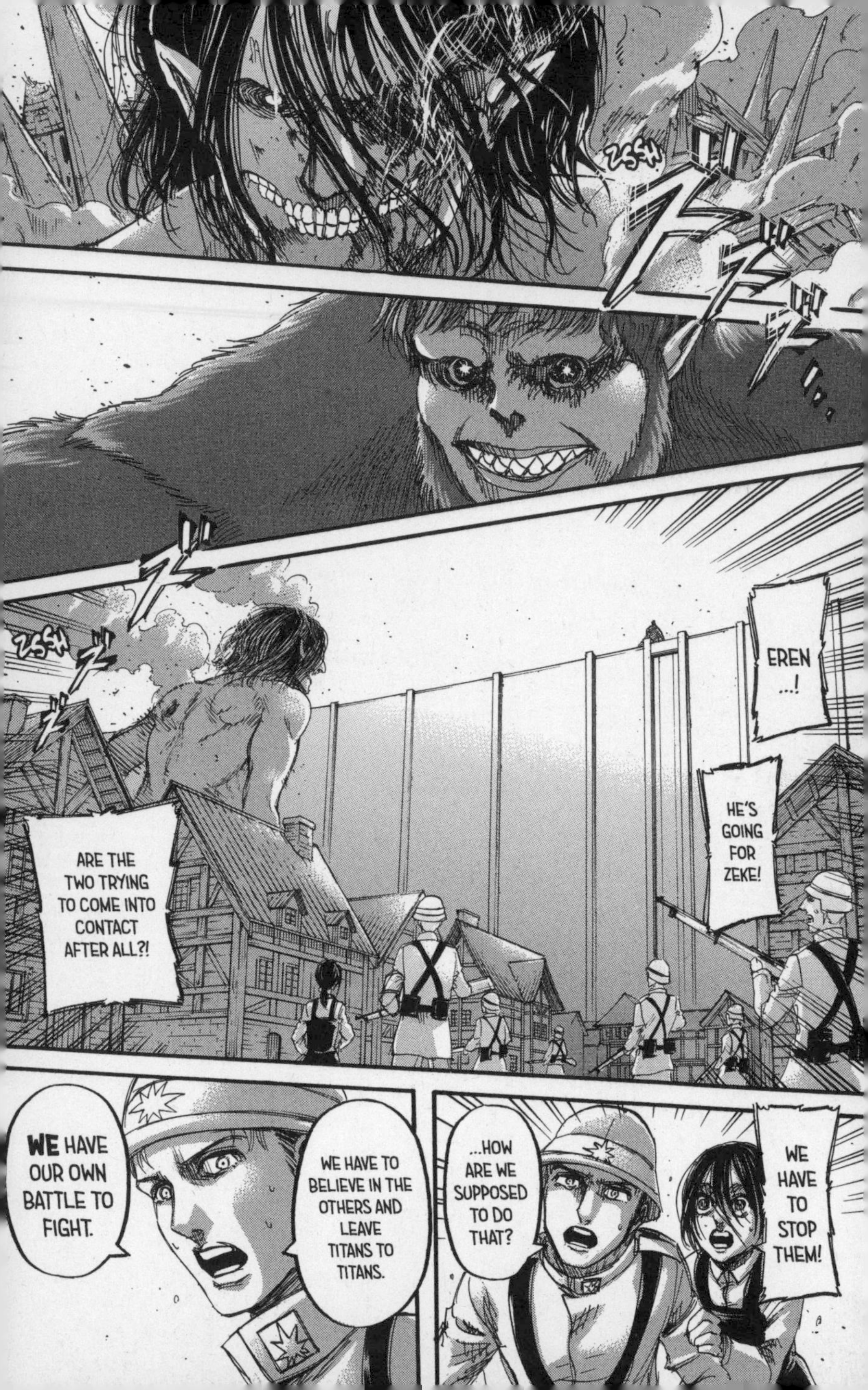
ZSSH
EREN ...!
HE'S GOING FOR ZEKE!
ARE THE TWO TRYING TO COME INTO CONTACT AFTER ALL?!
ZSSH
WE HAVE TO STOP THEM!
...HOW ARE WE SUPPOSED TO DO THAT?
WE HAVE TO BELIEVE IN THE OTHERS AND LEAVE TITANS TO TITANS.
WE HAVE OUR OWN BATTLE TO FIGHT.

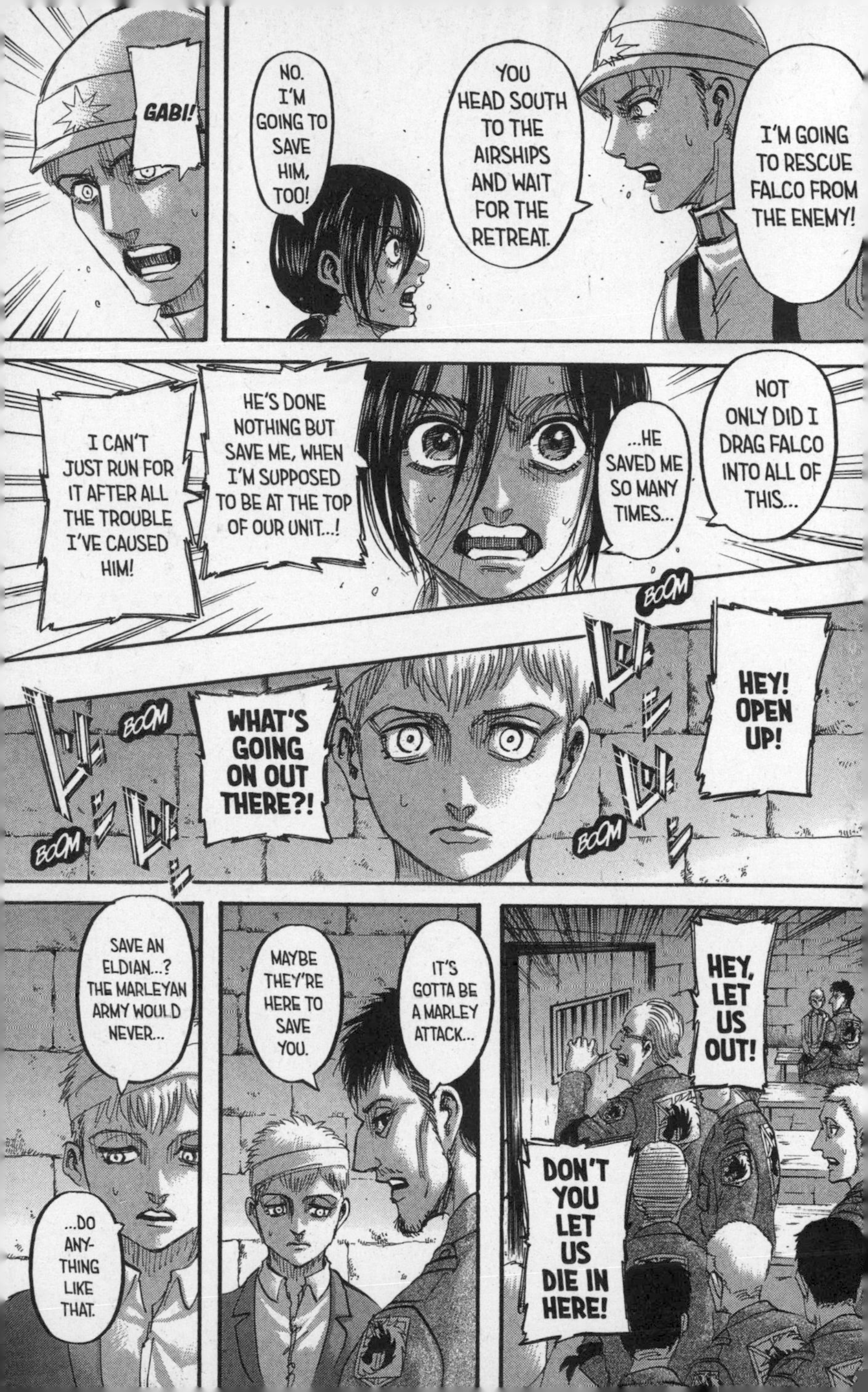
I'M GOING TO RESCUE FALCO FROM THE ENEMY!
YOU HEAD SOUTH TO THE AIRSHIPS AND WAIT FOR THE RETREAT.
NO. I'M GOING TO SAVE HIM, TOO!
GABI!
NOT ONLY DID I DRAG FALCO INTO ALL OF THIS...
...HE SAVED ME SO MANY TIMES...
HE'S DONE NOTHING BUT SAVE ME, WHEN I'M SUPPOSED TO BE AT THE TOP OF OUR UNIT...!
I CAN'T JUST RUN FOR IT AFTER ALL THE TROUBLE I'VE CAUSED HIM!
BOOM
HEY! OPEN UP!
BOOM
WHAT'S GOING ON OUT THERE?!
BOOM
BOOM
HEY, LET US OUT!
DON'T YOU LET US DIE IN HERE!
IT'S GOTTA BE A MARLEY ATTACK...
MAYBE THEY'RE HERE TO SAVE YOU.
SAVE AN ELDIAN...? THE MARLEYAN ARMY WOULD NEVER...
...DO ANY-THING LIKE THAT.

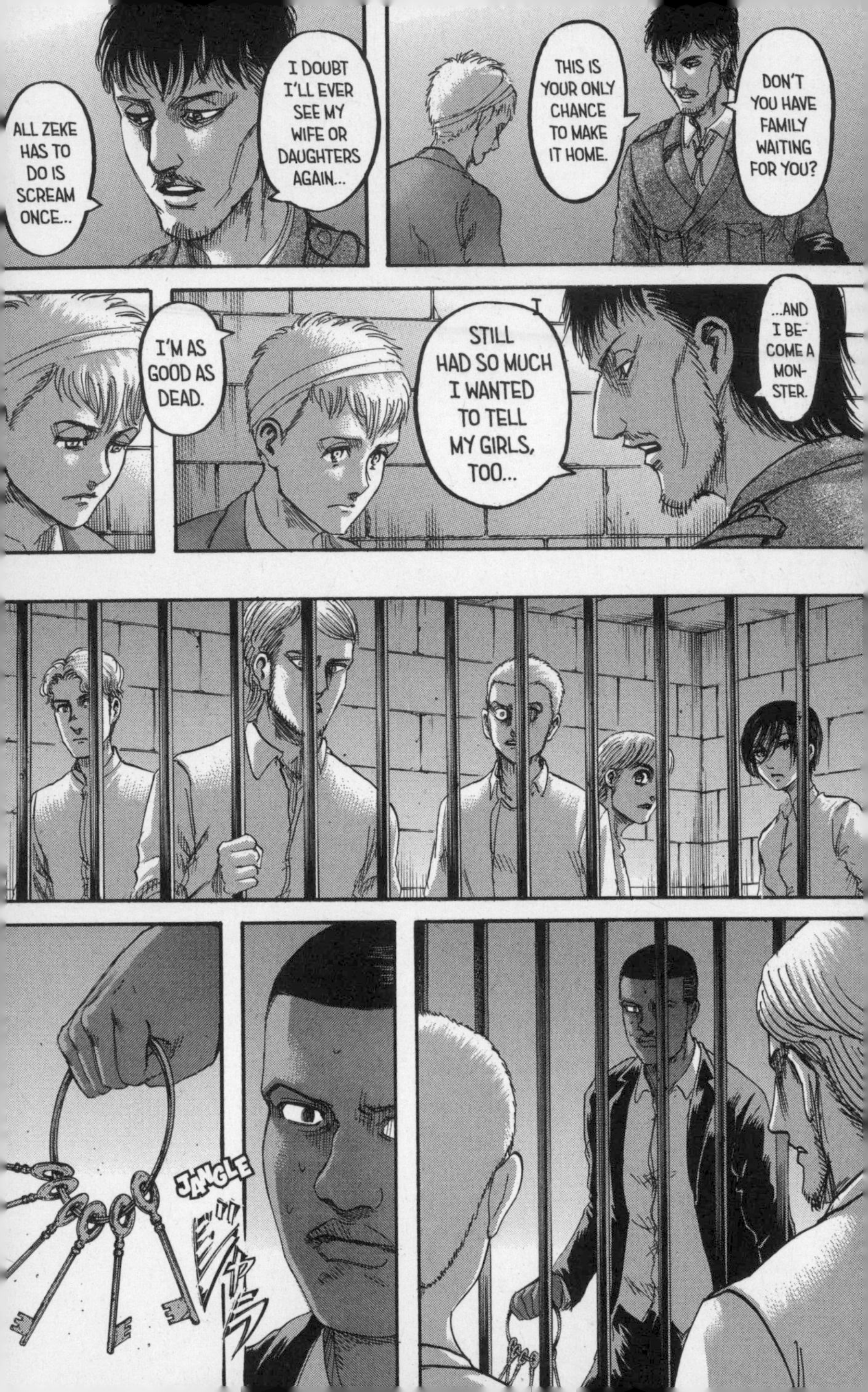
DON'T YOU HAVE FAMILY WAITING FOR YOU?
THIS IS YOUR ONLY CHANCE TO MAKE IT HOME.
I DOUBT I'LL EVER SEE MY WIFE OR DAUGHTERS AGAIN...
ALL ZEKE HAS TO DO IS SCREAM ONCE...
...AND I BE-COME A MON-STER.
STILL HAD SO MUCH I WANTED TO TELL MY GIRLS, TOO...
I'M AS GOOD AS DEAD.
JANGLE

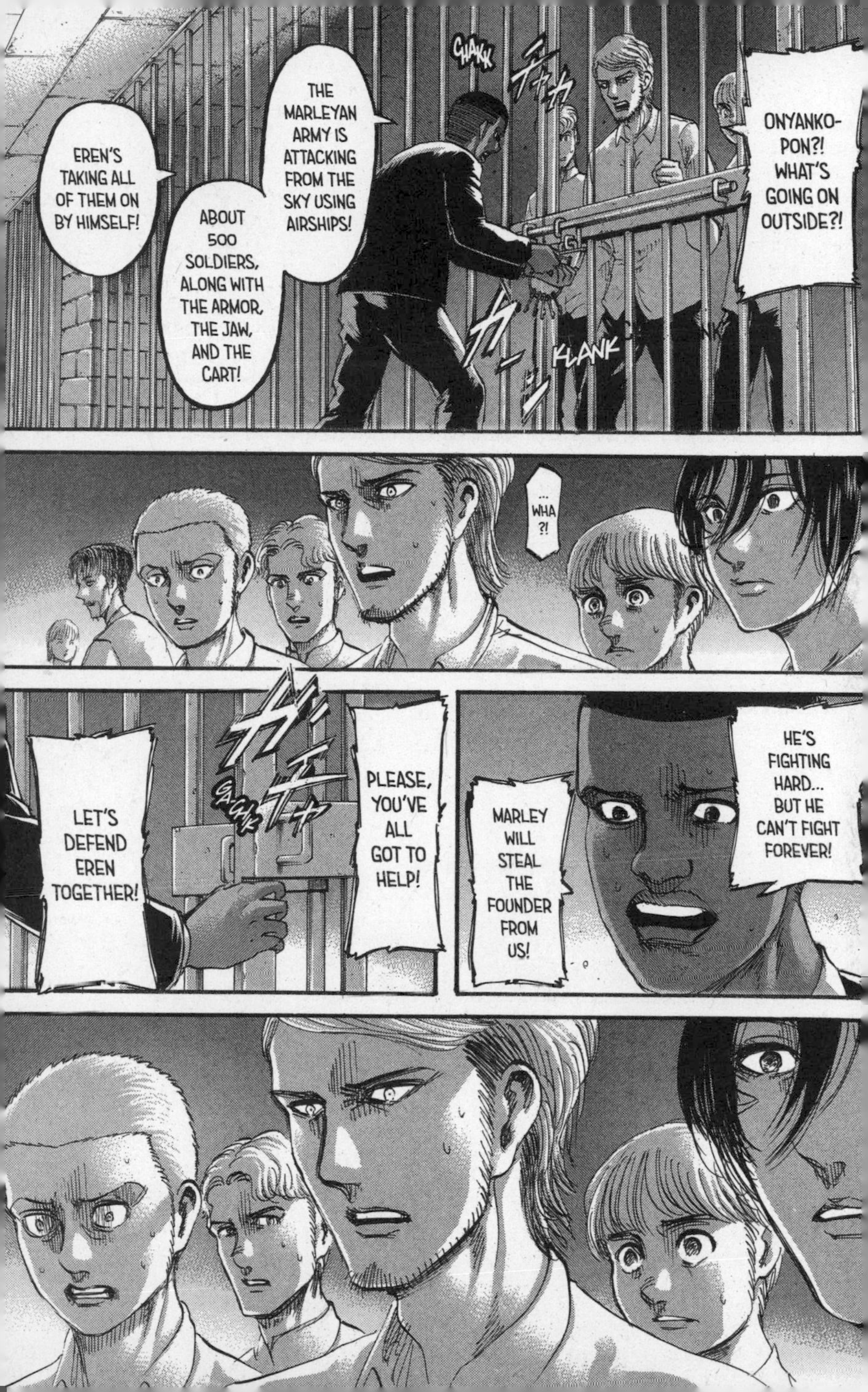
ONYANKO-PON?! WHAT'S GOING ON OUTSIDE?!
CHAKK
KLANK
THE MARLEYAN ARMY IS ATTACKING FROM THE SKY USING AIRSHIPS!
ABOUT 500 SOLDIERS, ALONG WITH THE ARMOR, THE JAW, AND THE CART!
EREN'S TAKING ALL OF THEM ON BY HIMSELF!
...WHA?!
HE'S FIGHTING HARD... BUT HE CAN'T FIGHT FOREVER!
MARLEY WILL STEAL THE FOUNDER FROM US!
GA-CHAK
PLEASE, YOU'VE ALL GOT TO HELP!
LET'S DEFEND EREN TOGETHER!

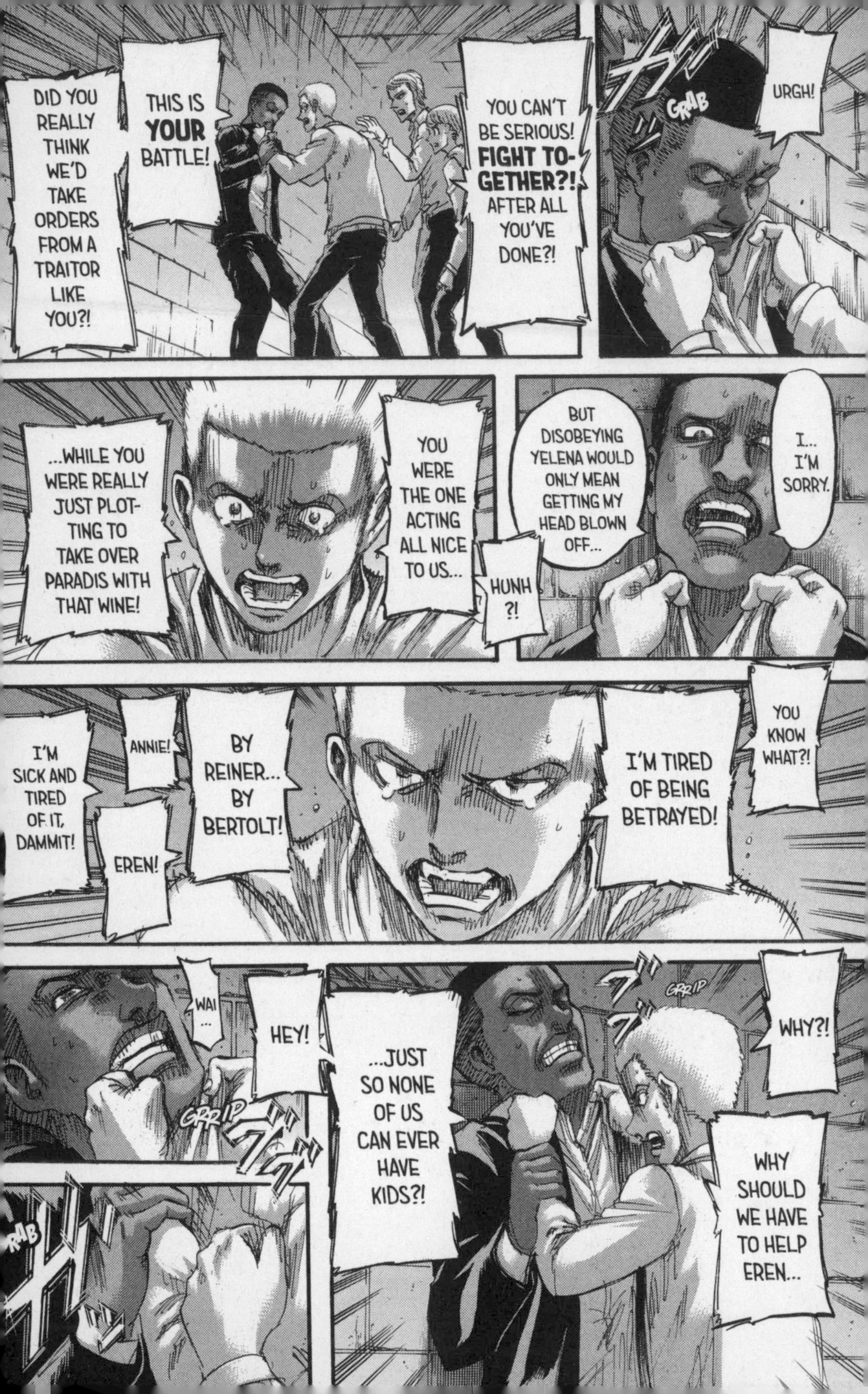
GRAB
URGH!
YOU CAN'T BE SERIOUS! **FIGHT TO-GETHER?!** AFTER ALL YOU'VE DONE?!
THIS IS **YOUR** BATTLE!
DID YOU REALLY THINK WE'D TAKE ORDERS FROM A TRAITOR LIKE YOU?!
I... I'M SORRY.
BUT DISOBEYING YELENA WOULD ONLY MEAN GETTING MY HEAD BLOWN OFF...
HUNH?!
YOU WERE THE ONE ACTING ALL NICE TO US...
...WHILE YOU WERE REALLY JUST PLOT-TING TO TAKE OVER PARADIS WITH THAT WINE!
YOU KNOW WHAT?!
I'M TIRED OF BEING BETRAYED!
BY REINER... BY BERTOLT!
ANNIE!
EREN!
I'M SICK AND TIRED OF IT, DAMMIT!
GRRIP
WHY?!
WHY SHOULD WE HAVE TO HELP EREN...
...JUST SO NONE OF US CAN EVER HAVE KIDS?!
HEY!
WAI...
GRRIP

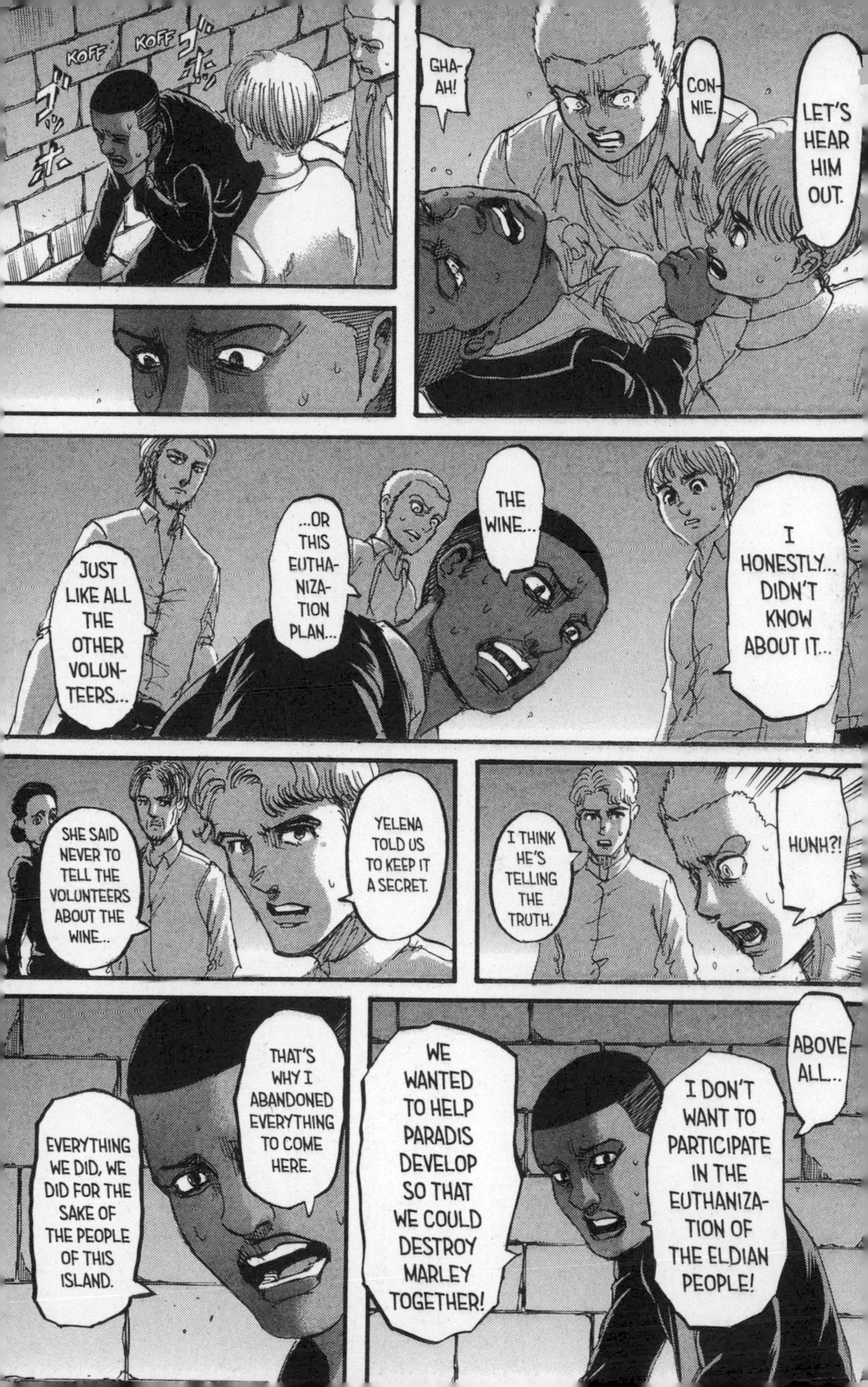
CON-NIE.
LET'S HEAR HIM OUT.
GHA-AH!
KOFF
KOFF
ゴホッ
ゴホッ
I HONESTLY... DIDN'T KNOW ABOUT IT...
THE WINE...
...OR THIS EUTHANIZATION PLAN...
JUST LIKE ALL THE OTHER VOLUNTEERS...
HUNH?!
I THINK HE'S TELLING THE TRUTH.
YELENA TOLD US TO KEEP IT A SECRET.
SHE SAID NEVER TO TELL THE VOLUNTEERS ABOUT THE WINE...
ABOVE ALL...
I DON'T WANT TO PARTICIPATE IN THE EUTHANIZATION OF THE ELDIAN PEOPLE!
WE WANTED TO HELP PARADIS DEVELOP SO THAT WE COULD DESTROY MARLEY TOGETHER!
THAT'S WHY I ABANDONED EVERYTHING TO COME HERE.
EVERYTHING WE DID, WE DID FOR THE SAKE OF THE PEOPLE OF THIS ISLAND.

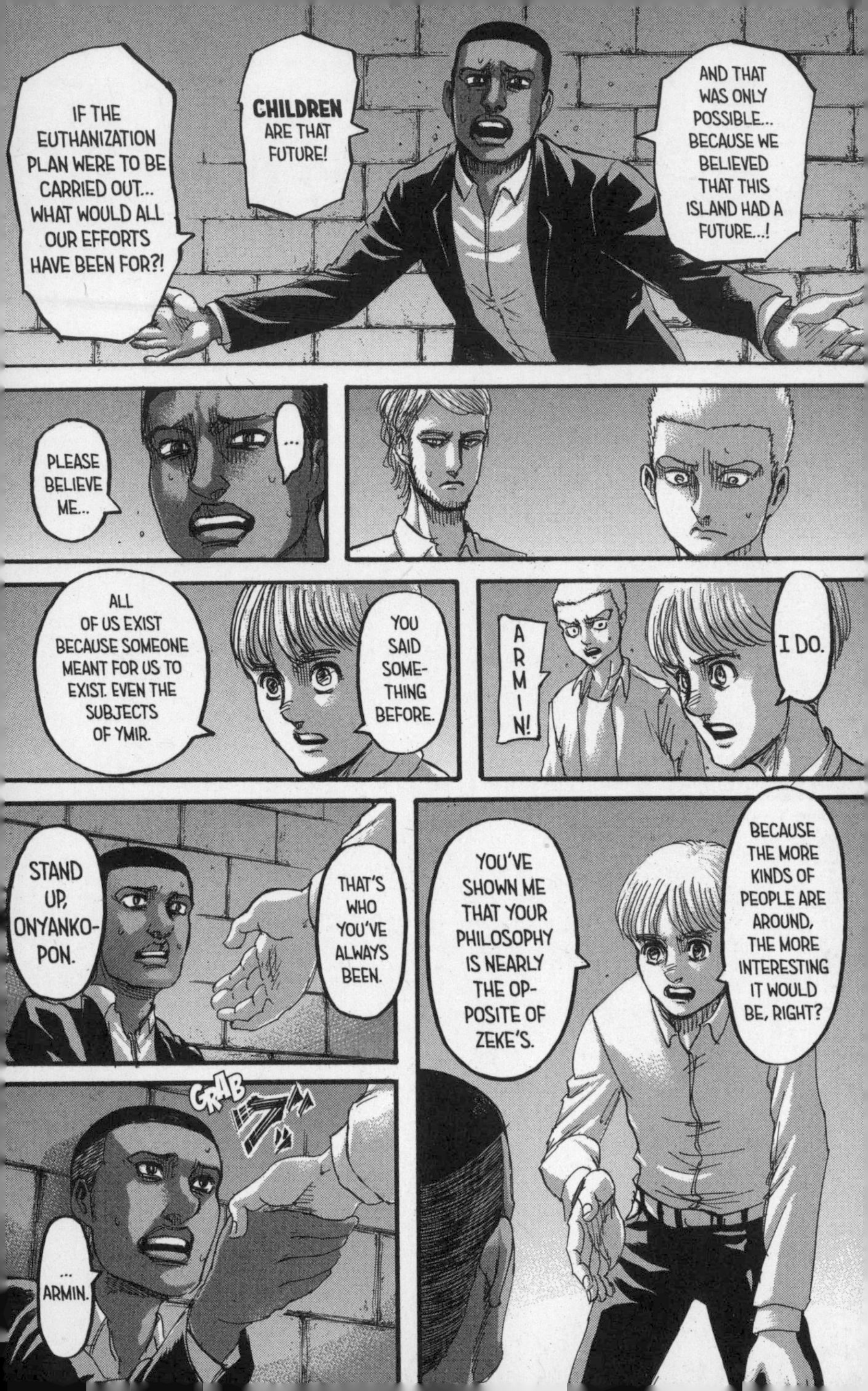
AND THAT WAS ONLY POSSIBLE... BECAUSE WE BELIEVED THAT THIS ISLAND HAD A FUTURE...!
CHILDREN ARE THAT FUTURE!
IF THE EUTHANIZATION PLAN WERE TO BE CARRIED OUT... WHAT WOULD ALL OUR EFFORTS HAVE BEEN FOR?!
...
PLEASE BELIEVE ME...
I DO.
ARMIN!
YOU SAID SOMETHING BEFORE.
ALL OF US EXIST BECAUSE SOMEONE MEANT FOR US TO EXIST. EVEN THE SUBJECTS OF YMIR.
BECAUSE THE MORE KINDS OF PEOPLE ARE AROUND, THE MORE INTERESTING IT WOULD BE, RIGHT?
YOU'VE SHOWN ME THAT YOUR PHILOSOPHY IS NEARLY THE OPPOSITE OF ZEKE'S.
THAT'S WHO YOU'VE ALWAYS BEEN.
STAND UP, ONYANKOPON.
GRAB
... ARMIN.

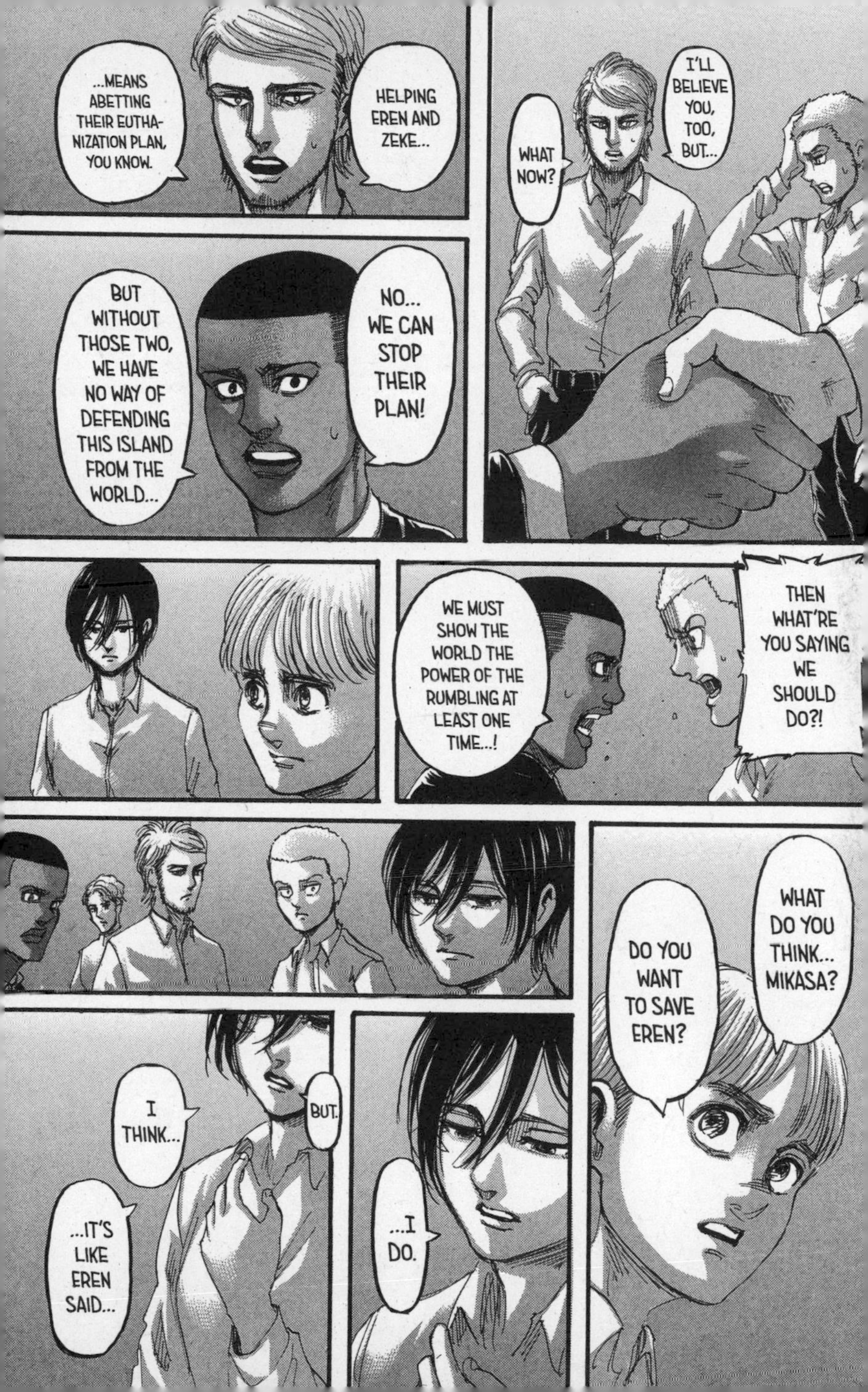
I'LL BELIEVE YOU, TOO, BUT...
WHAT NOW?
HELPING EREN AND ZEKE...
...MEANS ABETTING THEIR EUTHANIZATION PLAN, YOU KNOW.
NO... WE CAN STOP THEIR PLAN!
BUT WITHOUT THOSE TWO, WE HAVE NO WAY OF DEFENDING THIS ISLAND FROM THE WORLD...
THEN WHAT'RE YOU SAYING WE SHOULD DO?!
WE MUST SHOW THE WORLD THE POWER OF THE RUMBLING AT LEAST ONE TIME...!
WHAT DO YOU THINK... MIKASA?
DO YOU WANT TO SAVE EREN?
...I DO.
BUT.
I THINK...
...IT'S LIKE EREN SAID...

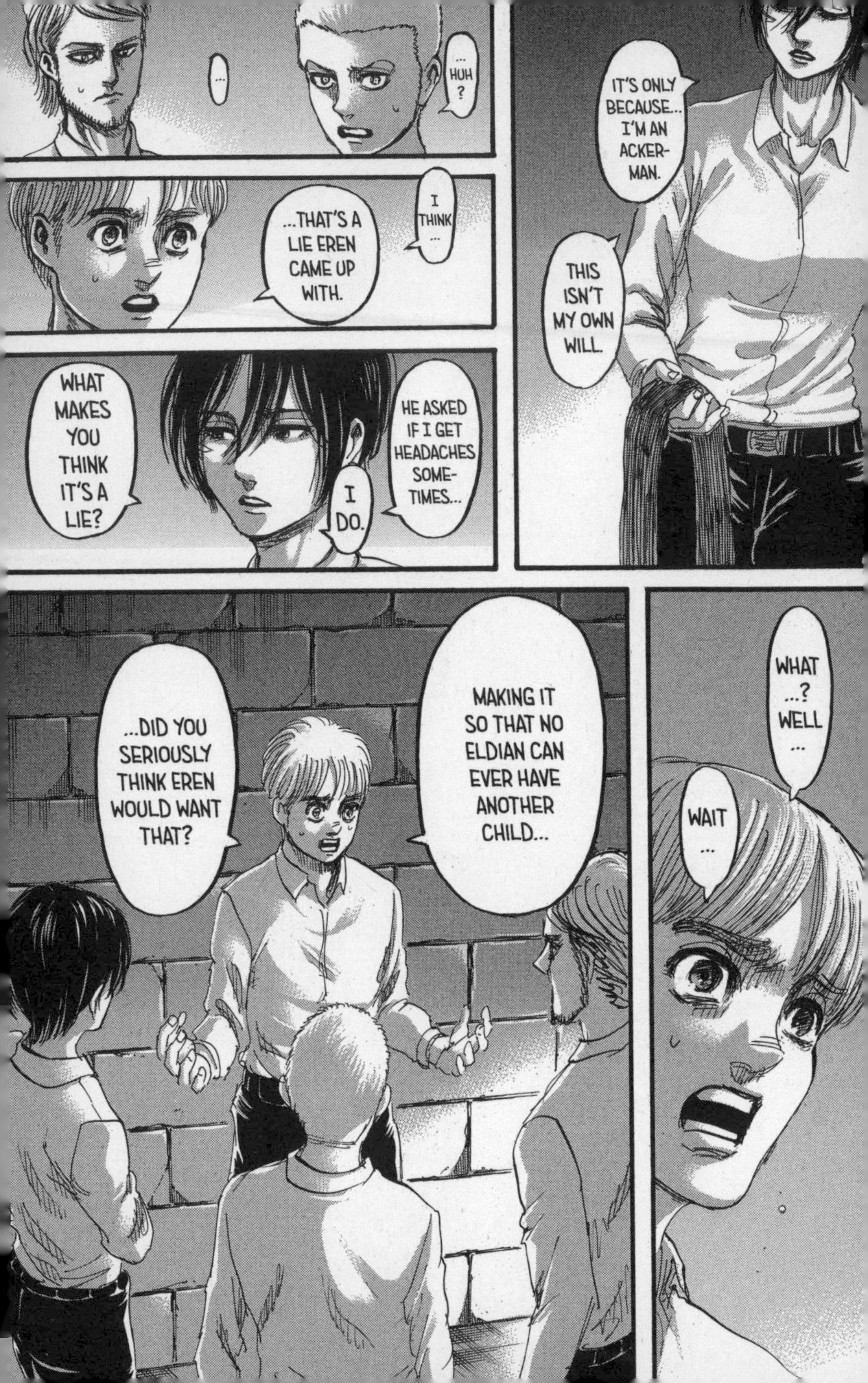
IT'S ONLY BECAUSE... I'M AN ACKERMAN.
THIS ISN'T MY OWN WILL.
...HUH?
...
I THINK...
...THAT'S A LIE EREN CAME UP WITH.
HE ASKED IF I GET HEADACHES SOMETIMES...
I DO.
WHAT MAKES YOU THINK IT'S A LIE?
WHAT...? WELL...
WAIT...
MAKING IT SO THAT NO ELDIAN CAN EVER HAVE ANOTHER CHILD...
...DID YOU SERIOUSLY THINK EREN WOULD WANT THAT?

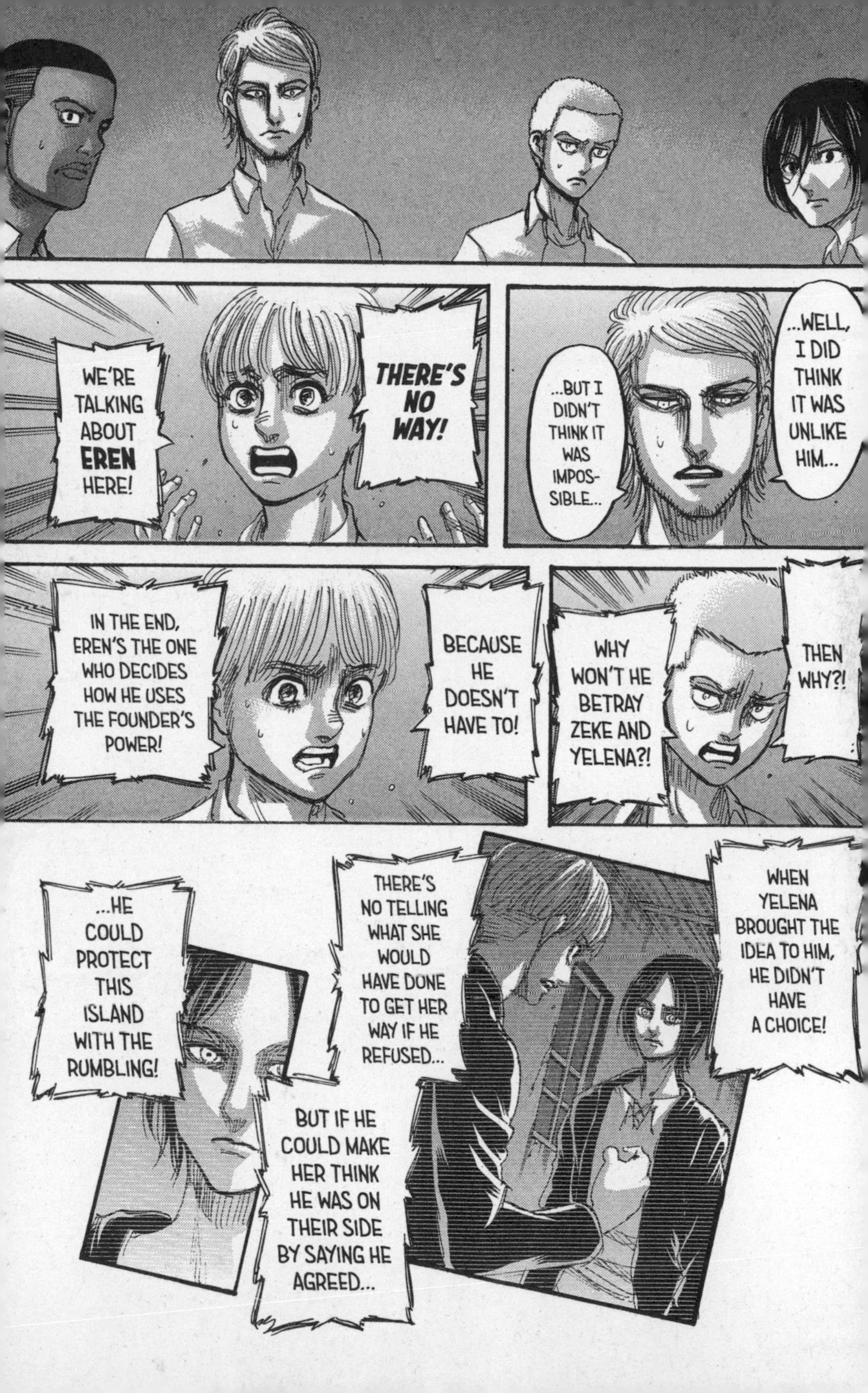
...WELL, I DID THINK IT WAS UNLIKE HIM...
...BUT I DIDN'T THINK IT WAS IMPOSSIBLE...
THERE'S NO WAY!
WE'RE TALKING ABOUT EREN HERE!
THEN WHY?!
WHY WON'T HE BETRAY ZEKE AND YELENA?!
BECAUSE HE DOESN'T HAVE TO!
IN THE END, EREN'S THE ONE WHO DECIDES HOW HE USES THE FOUNDER'S POWER!
WHEN YELENA BROUGHT THE IDEA TO HIM, HE DIDN'T HAVE A CHOICE!
THERE'S NO TELLING WHAT SHE WOULD HAVE DONE TO GET HER WAY IF HE REFUSED...
BUT IF HE COULD MAKE HER THINK HE WAS ON THEIR SIDE BY SAYING HE AGREED...
...HE COULD PROTECT THIS ISLAND WITH THE RUMBLING!

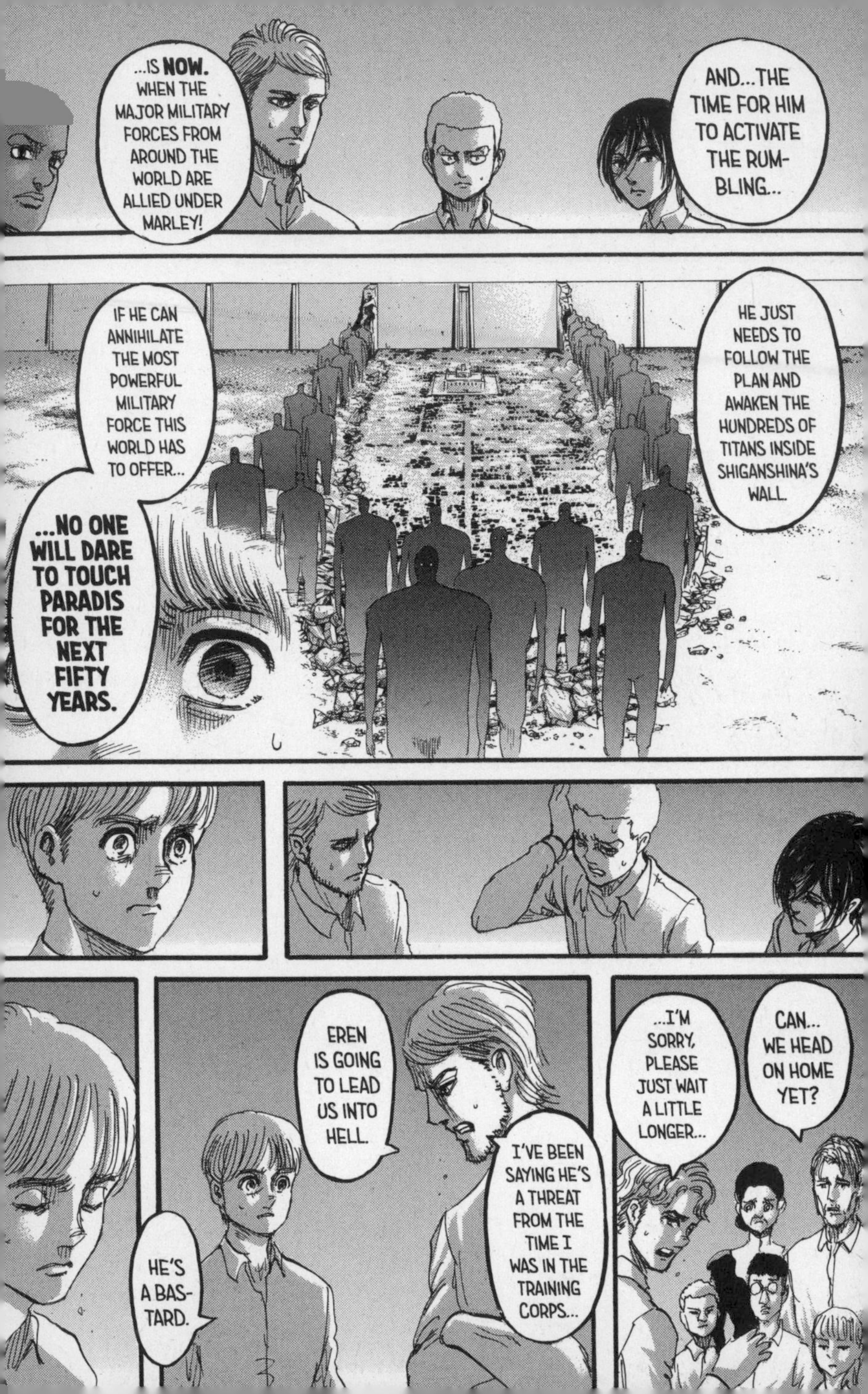
AND...THE TIME FOR HIM TO ACTIVATE THE RUM-BLING...
...IS **NOW.** WHEN THE MAJOR MILITARY FORCES FROM AROUND THE WORLD ARE ALLIED UNDER MARLEY!
HE JUST NEEDS TO FOLLOW THE PLAN AND AWAKEN THE HUNDREDS OF TITANS INSIDE SHIGANSHINA'S WALL.
IF HE CAN ANNIHILATE THE MOST POWERFUL MILITARY FORCE THIS WORLD HAS TO OFFER...
...NO ONE WILL DARE TO TOUCH PARADIS FOR THE NEXT FIFTY YEARS.
CAN... WE HEAD ON HOME YET?
...I'M SORRY, PLEASE JUST WAIT A LITTLE LONGER...
EREN IS GOING TO LEAD US INTO HELL.
I'VE BEEN SAYING HE'S A THREAT FROM THE TIME I WAS IN THE TRAINING CORPS...
HE'S A BAS-TARD.

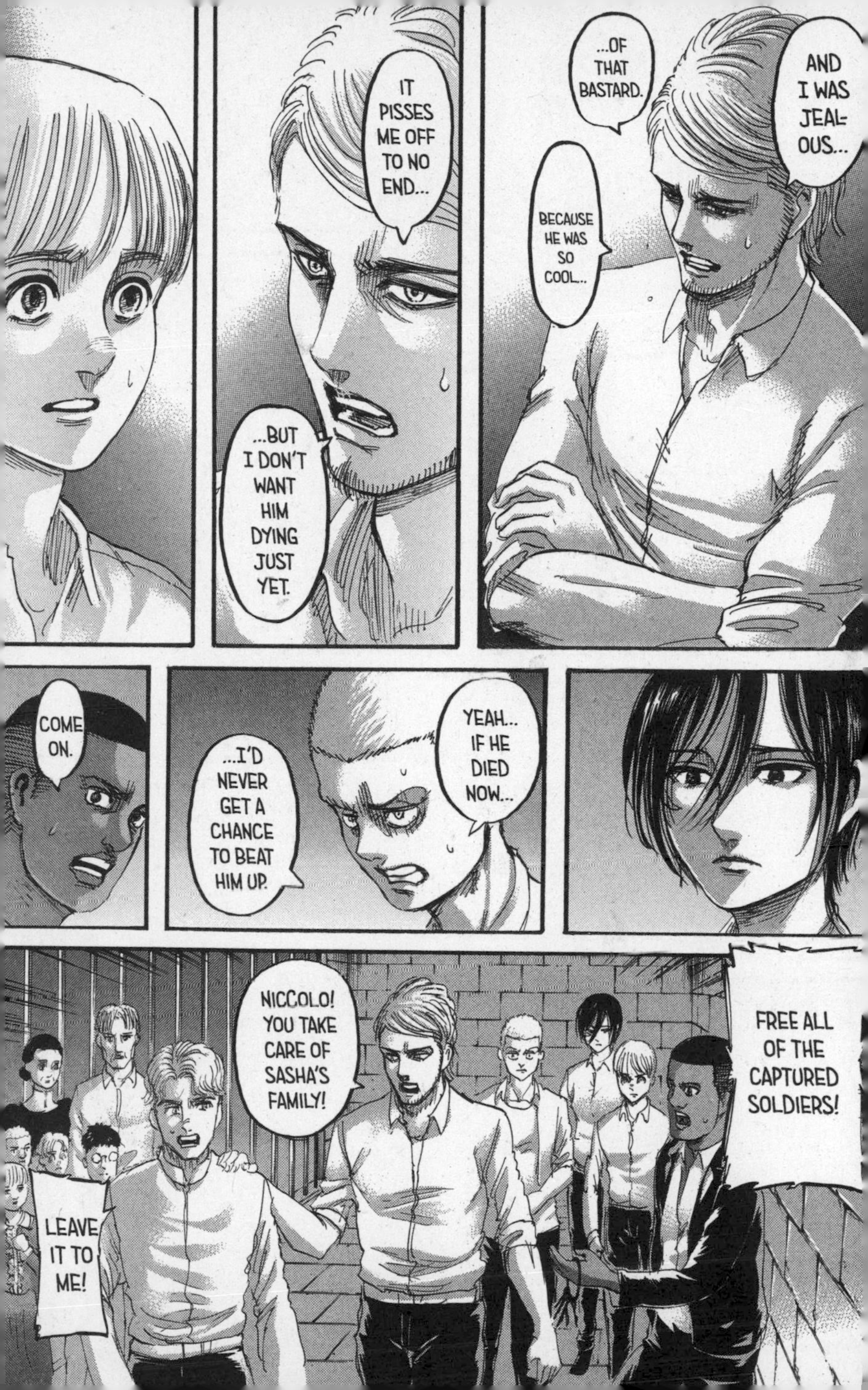
AND I WAS JEAL-OUS...
...OF THAT BASTARD.
BECAUSE HE WAS SO COOL..
IT PISSES ME OFF TO NO END...
...BUT I DON'T WANT HIM DYING JUST YET.
YEAH... IF HE DIED NOW...
...I'D NEVER GET A CHANCE TO BEAT HIM UP.
COME ON.
FREE ALL OF THE CAPTURED SOLDIERS!
NICCOLO! YOU TAKE CARE OF SASHA'S FAMILY!
LEAVE IT TO ME!

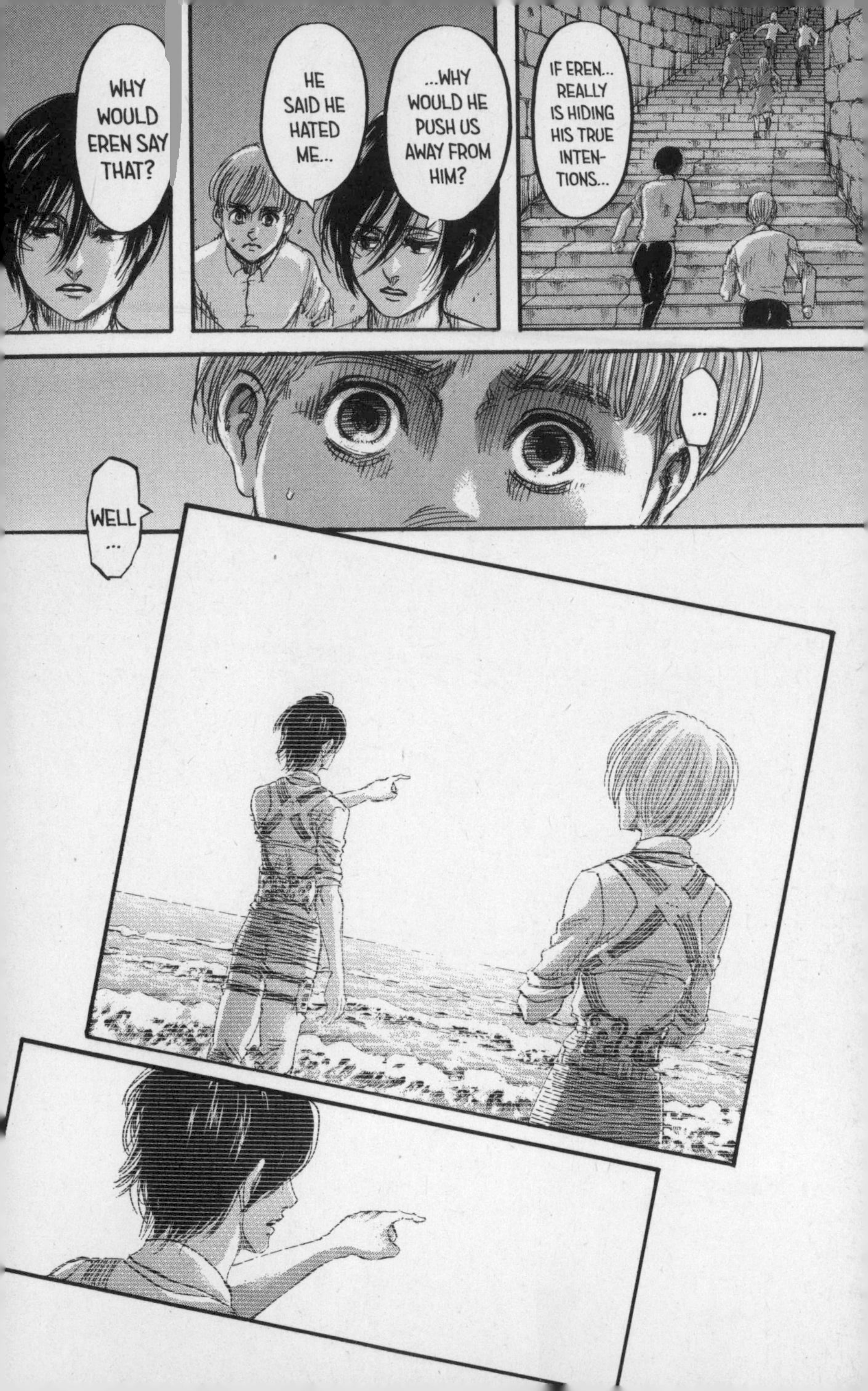
IF EREN... REALLY IS HIDING HIS TRUE INTEN- TIONS...
...WHY WOULD HE PUSH US AWAY FROM HIM?
HE SAID HE HATED ME...
WHY WOULD EREN SAY THAT?
...
WELL ...

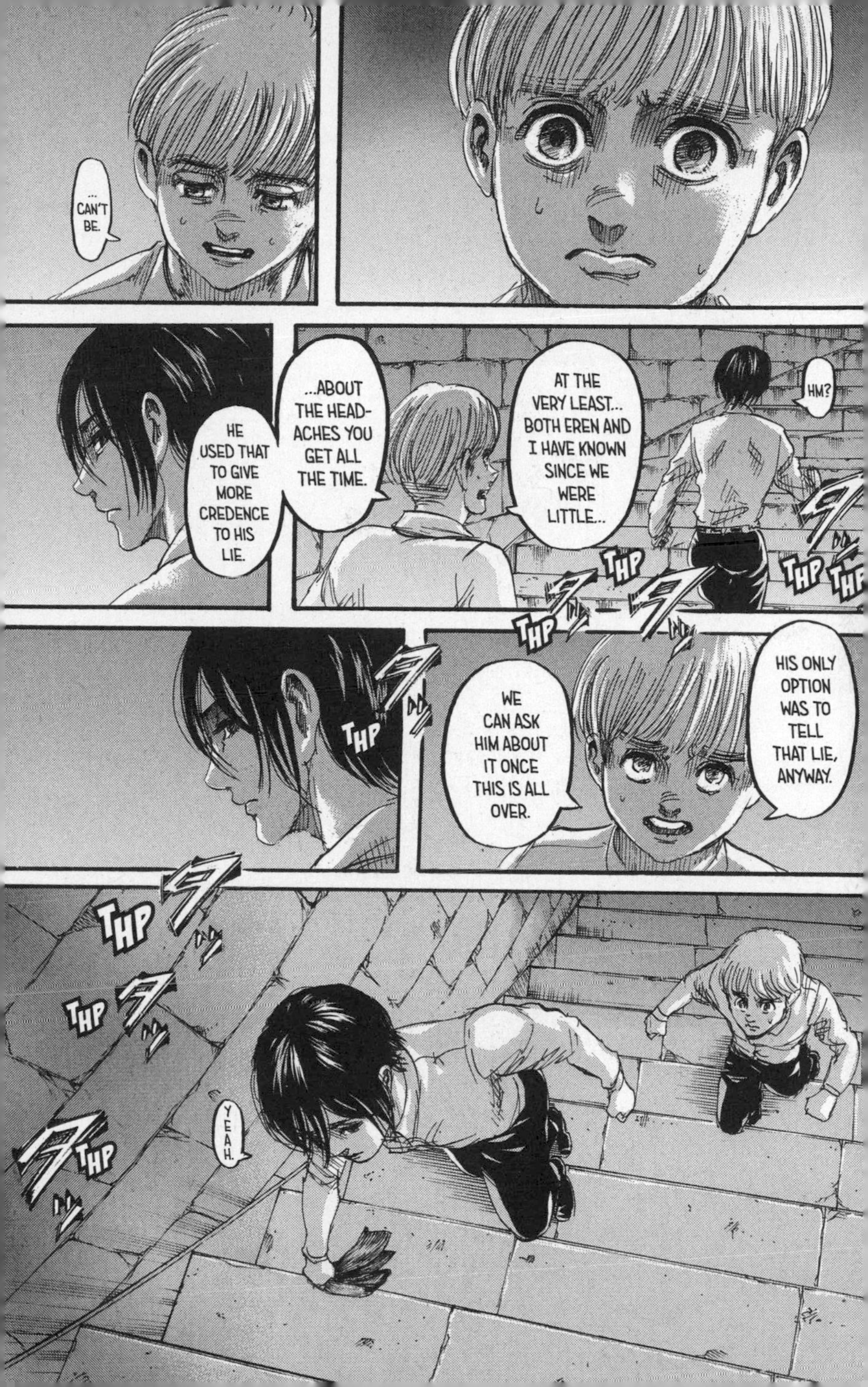
...CAN'T BE.
HM?
AT THE VERY LEAST... BOTH EREN AND I HAVE KNOWN SINCE WE WERE LITTLE...
...ABOUT THE HEAD-ACHES YOU GET ALL THE TIME.
THP THP
THP THP
HE USED THAT TO GIVE MORE CREDENCE TO HIS LIE.
HIS ONLY OPTION WAS TO TELL THAT LIE, ANYWAY.
WE CAN ASK HIM ABOUT IT ONCE THIS IS ALL OVER.
THP
THP
THP
YEAH.
THP

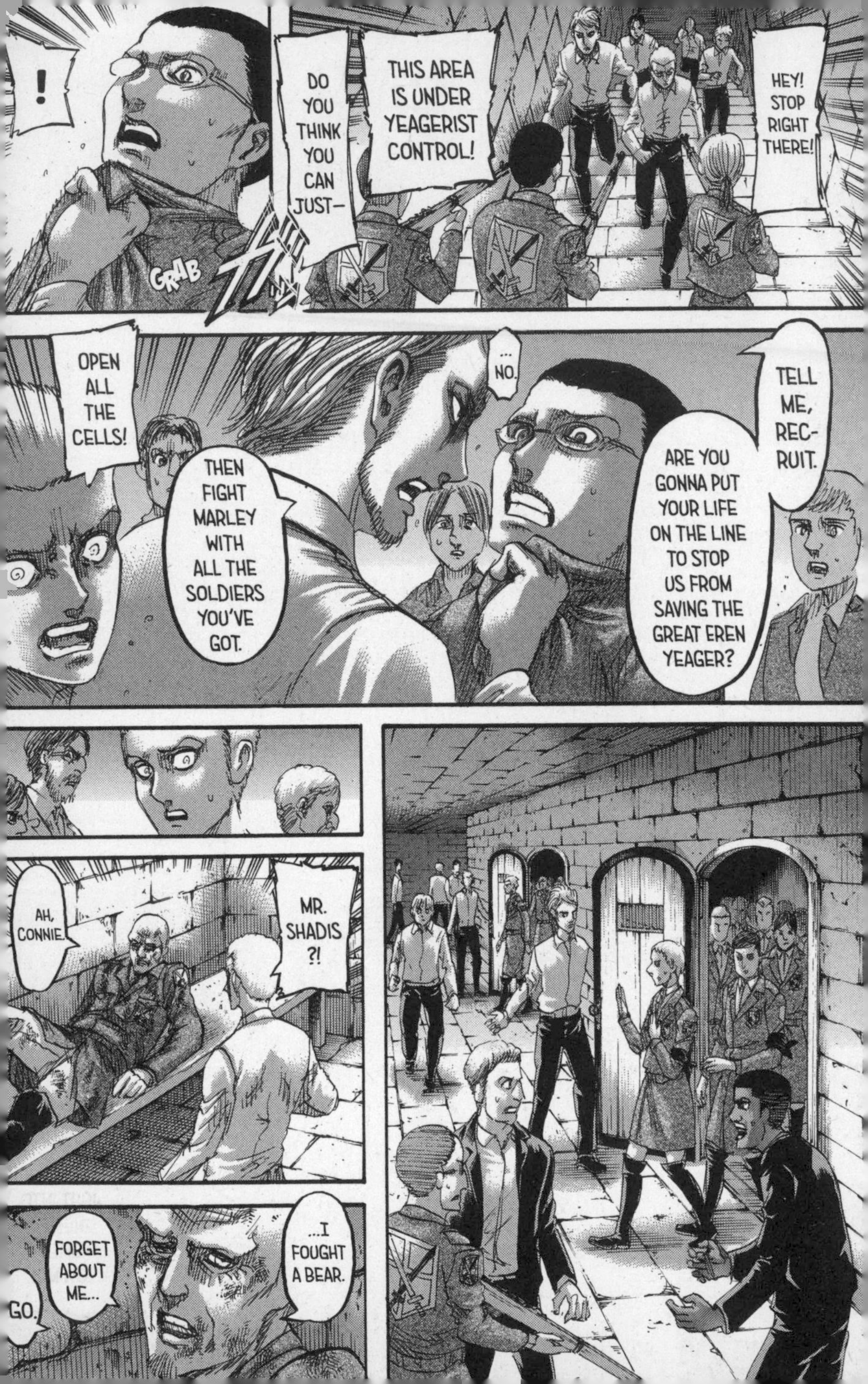
HEY! STOP RIGHT THERE!
THIS AREA IS UNDER YEAGERIST CONTROL!
DO YOU THINK YOU CAN JUST—
!
GRAB
TELL ME, RECRUIT.
ARE YOU GONNA PUT YOUR LIFE ON THE LINE TO STOP US FROM SAVING THE GREAT EREN YEAGER?
... NO.
THEN FIGHT MARLEY WITH ALL THE SOLDIERS YOU'VE GOT.
OPEN ALL THE CELLS!
MR. SHADIS ?!
AH, CONNIE.
...I FOUGHT A BEAR.
FORGET ABOUT ME...
GO.

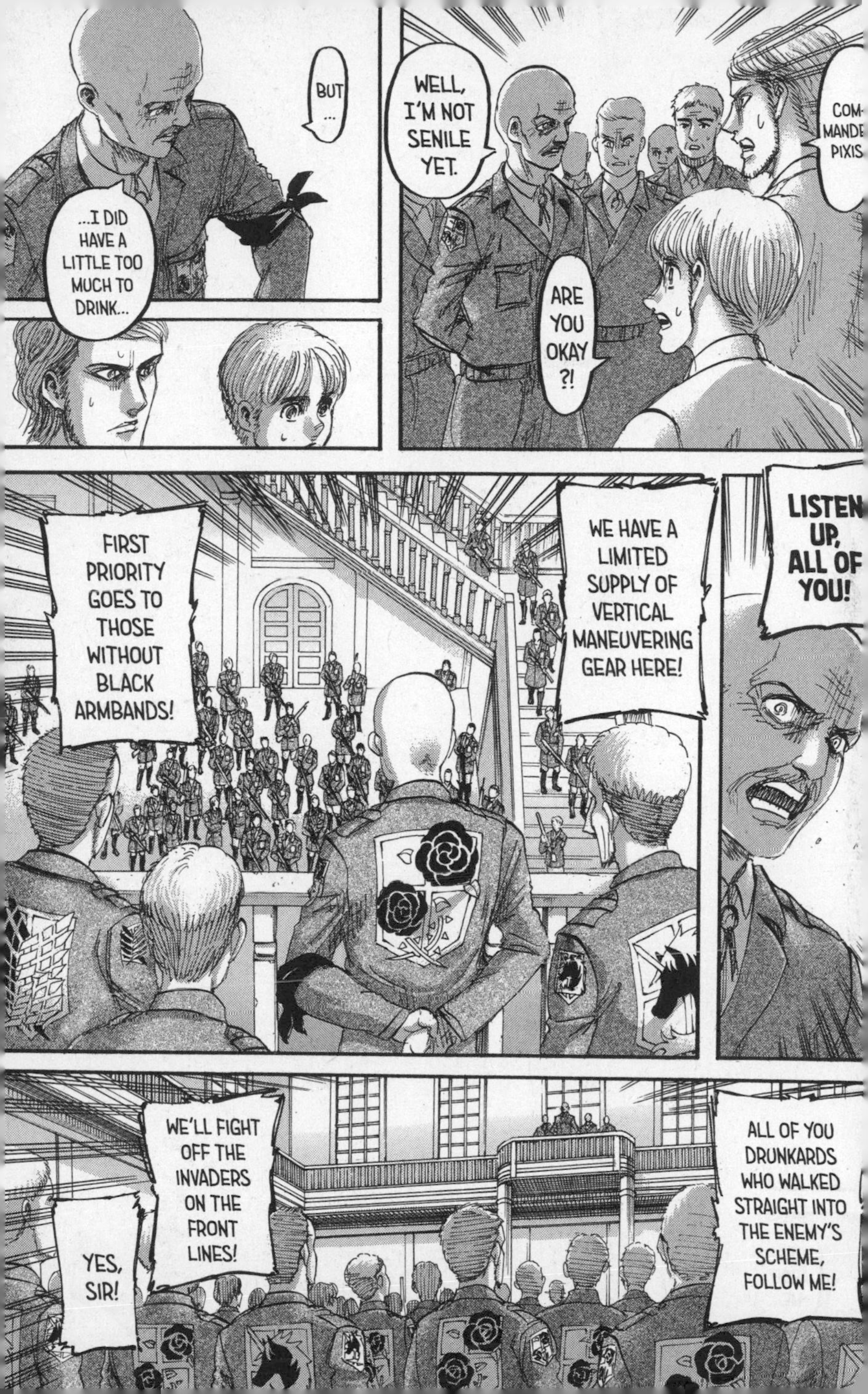
COM-
MANDE
PIXIS
ARE YOU OKAY ?!
WELL, I'M NOT SENILE YET.
BUT ...
...I DID HAVE A LITTLE TOO MUCH TO DRINK...
LISTEN UP, ALL OF YOU!
WE HAVE A LIMITED SUPPLY OF VERTICAL MANEUVERING GEAR HERE!
FIRST PRIORITY GOES TO THOSE WITHOUT BLACK ARMBANDS!
ALL OF YOU DRUNKARDS WHO WALKED STRAIGHT INTO THE ENEMY'S SCHEME, FOLLOW ME!
WE'LL FIGHT OFF THE INVADERS ON THE FRONT LINES!
YES, SIR!

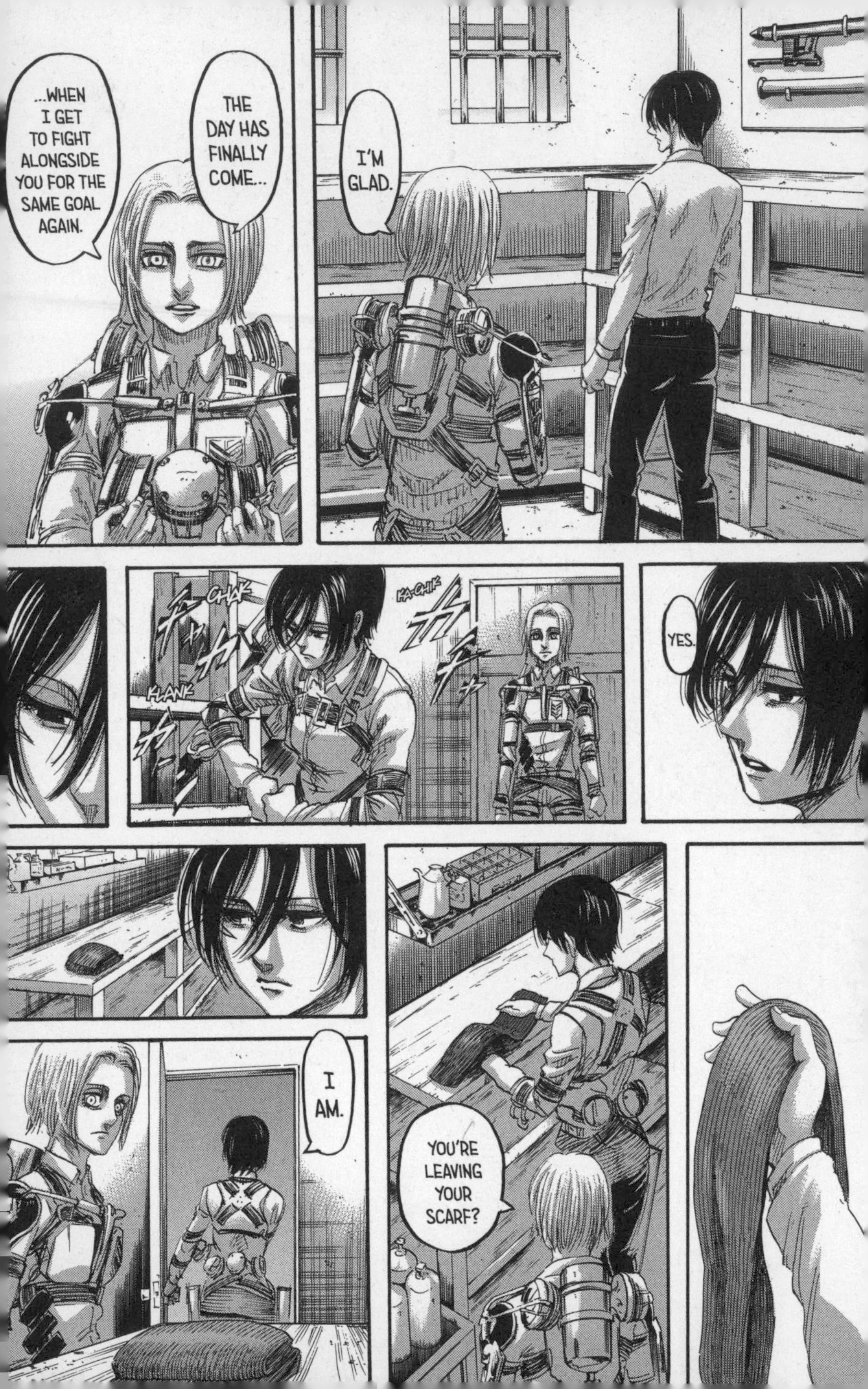
I'M GLAD.
THE DAY HAS FINALLY COME...
...WHEN I GET TO FIGHT ALONGSIDE YOU FOR THE SAME GOAL AGAIN.
YES.
KA-CHIK
CHAK
KLANK
YOU'RE LEAVING YOUR SCARF?
I AM.

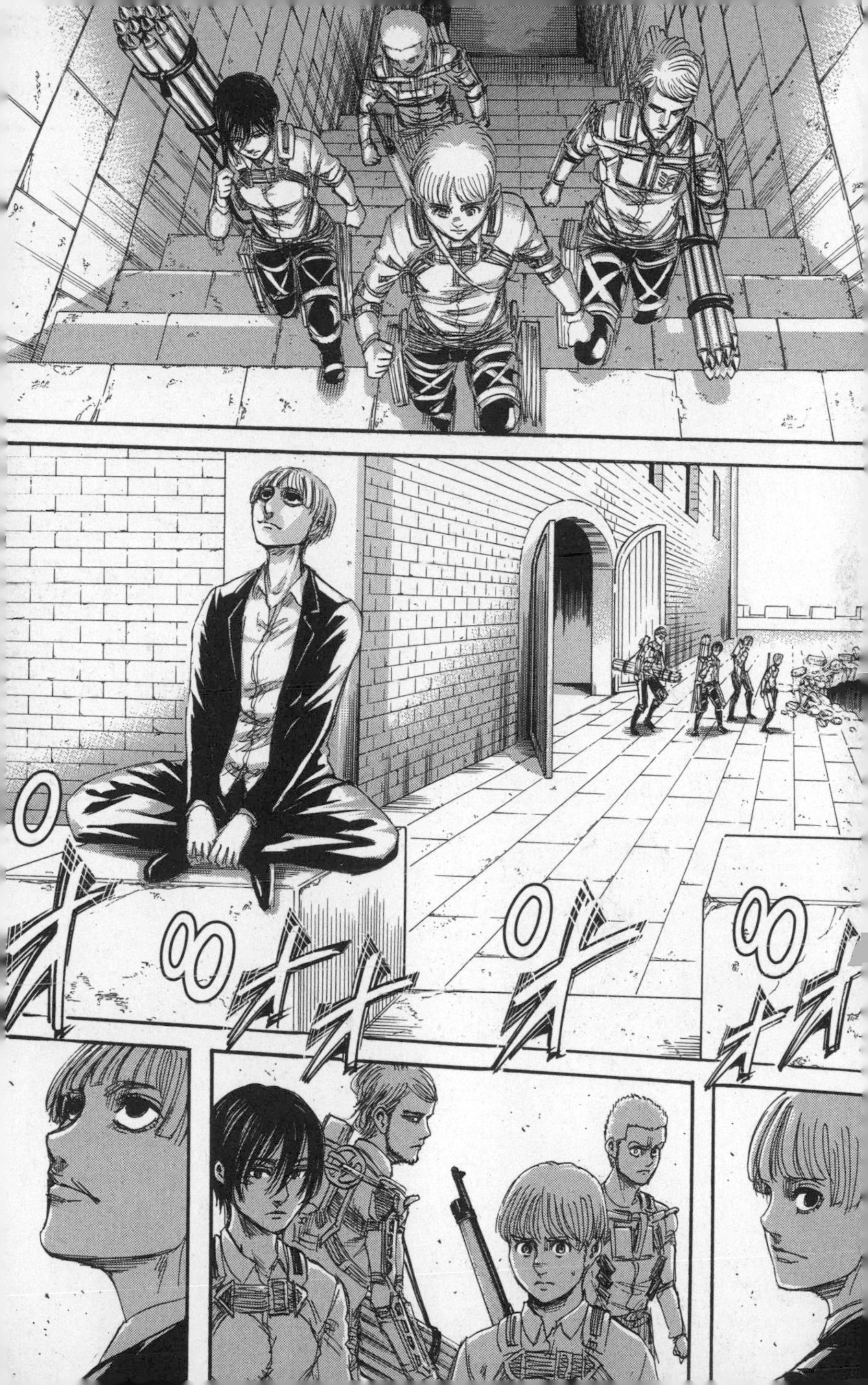

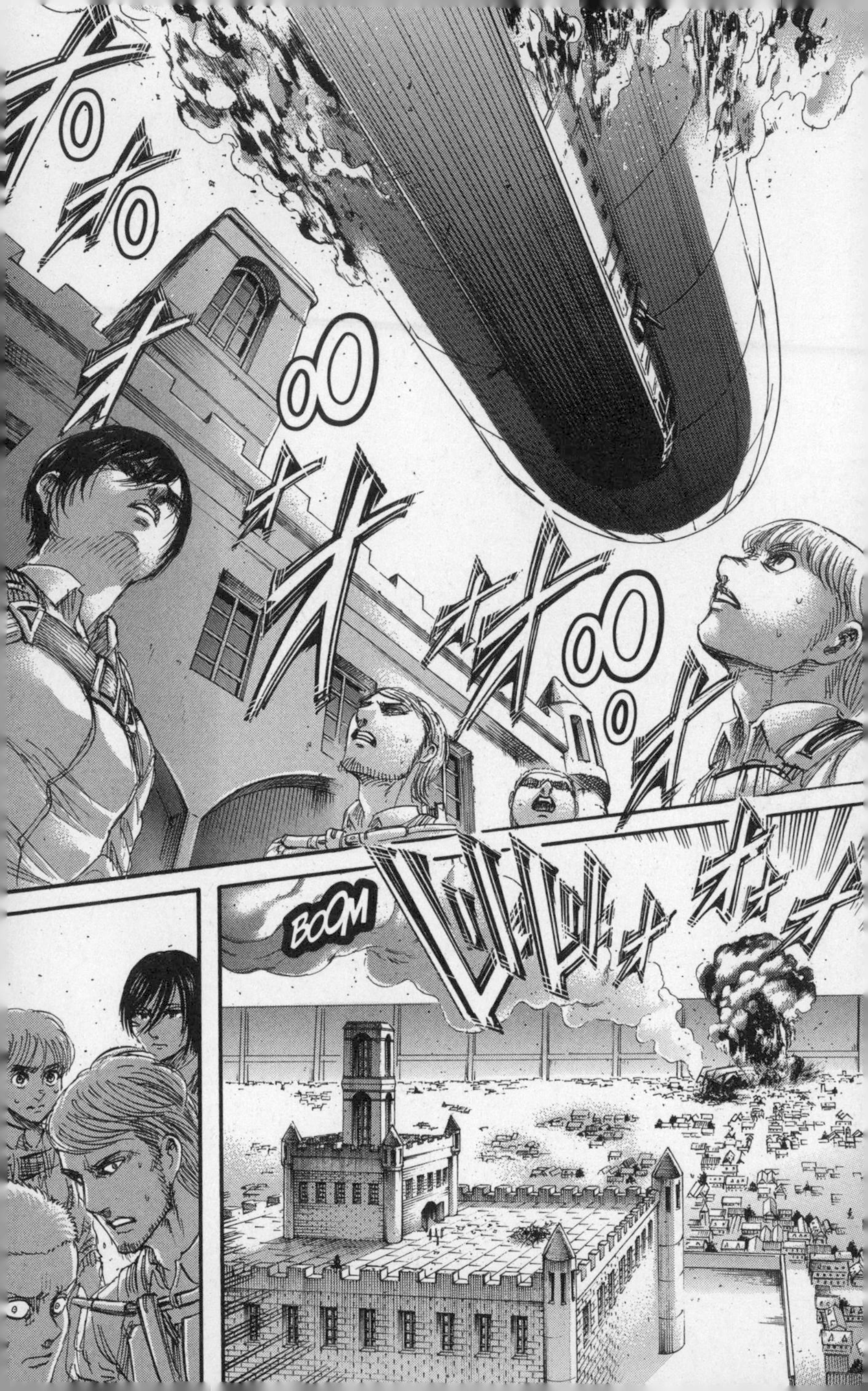
BOOM

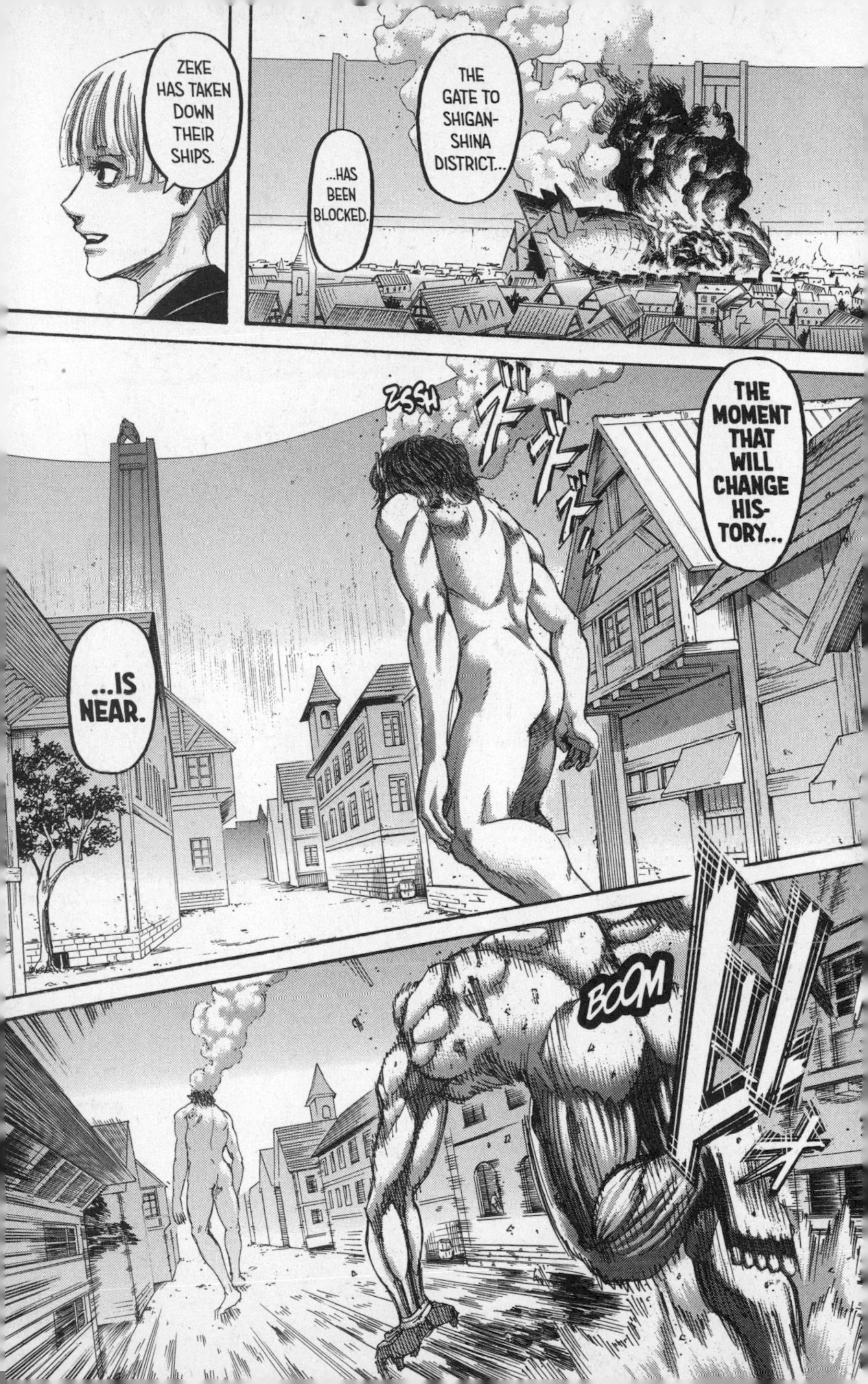
THE GATE TO SHIGAN-SHINA DISTRICT...
...HAS BEEN BLOCKED.
ZEKE HAS TAKEN DOWN THEIR SHIPS.
ZSSH
THE MOMENT THAT WILL CHANGE HIS-TORY...
...IS NEAR.
BOOM

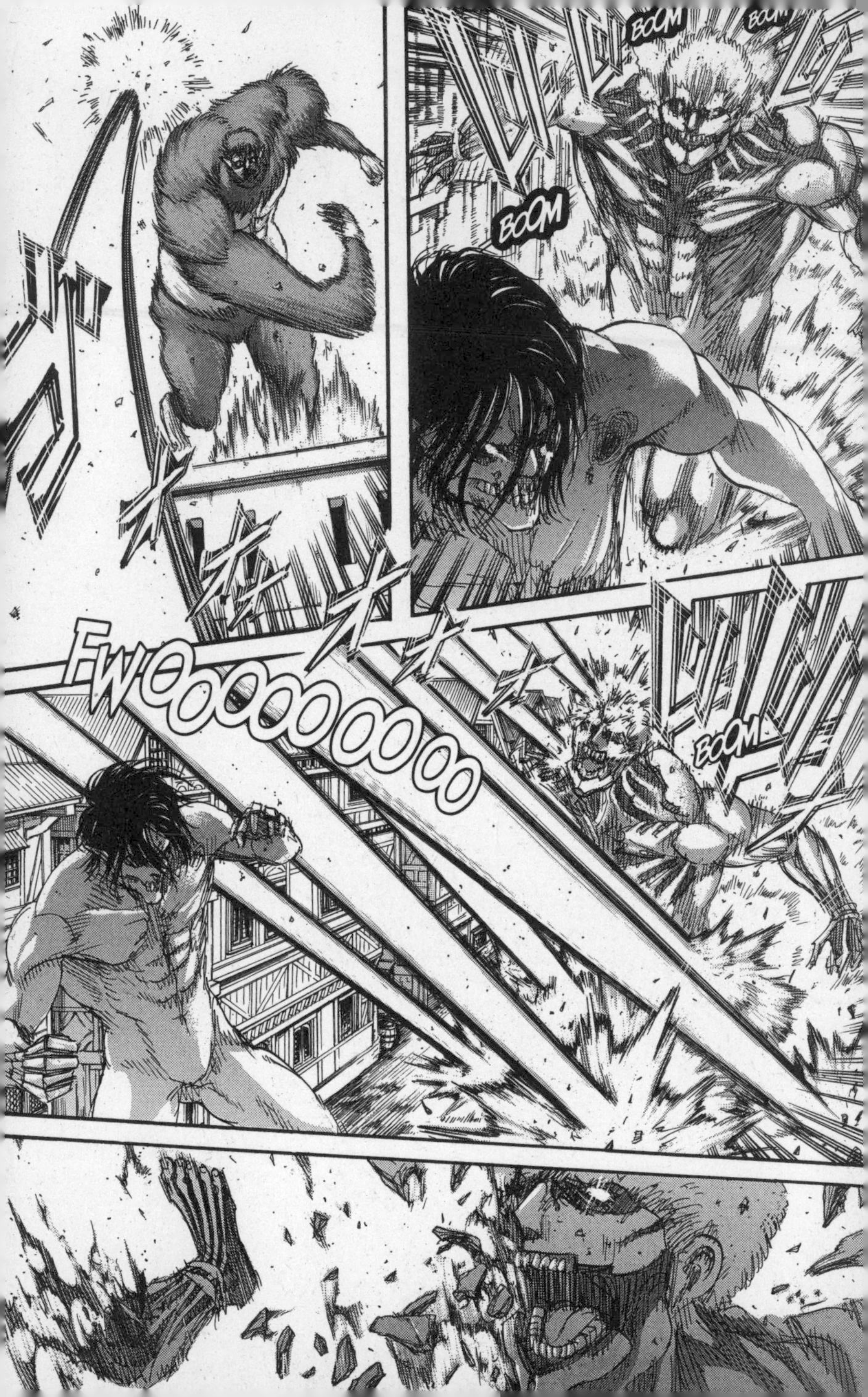

BOOM
BOOM
BOOM
FWOOOOOOOOOO
BOOM

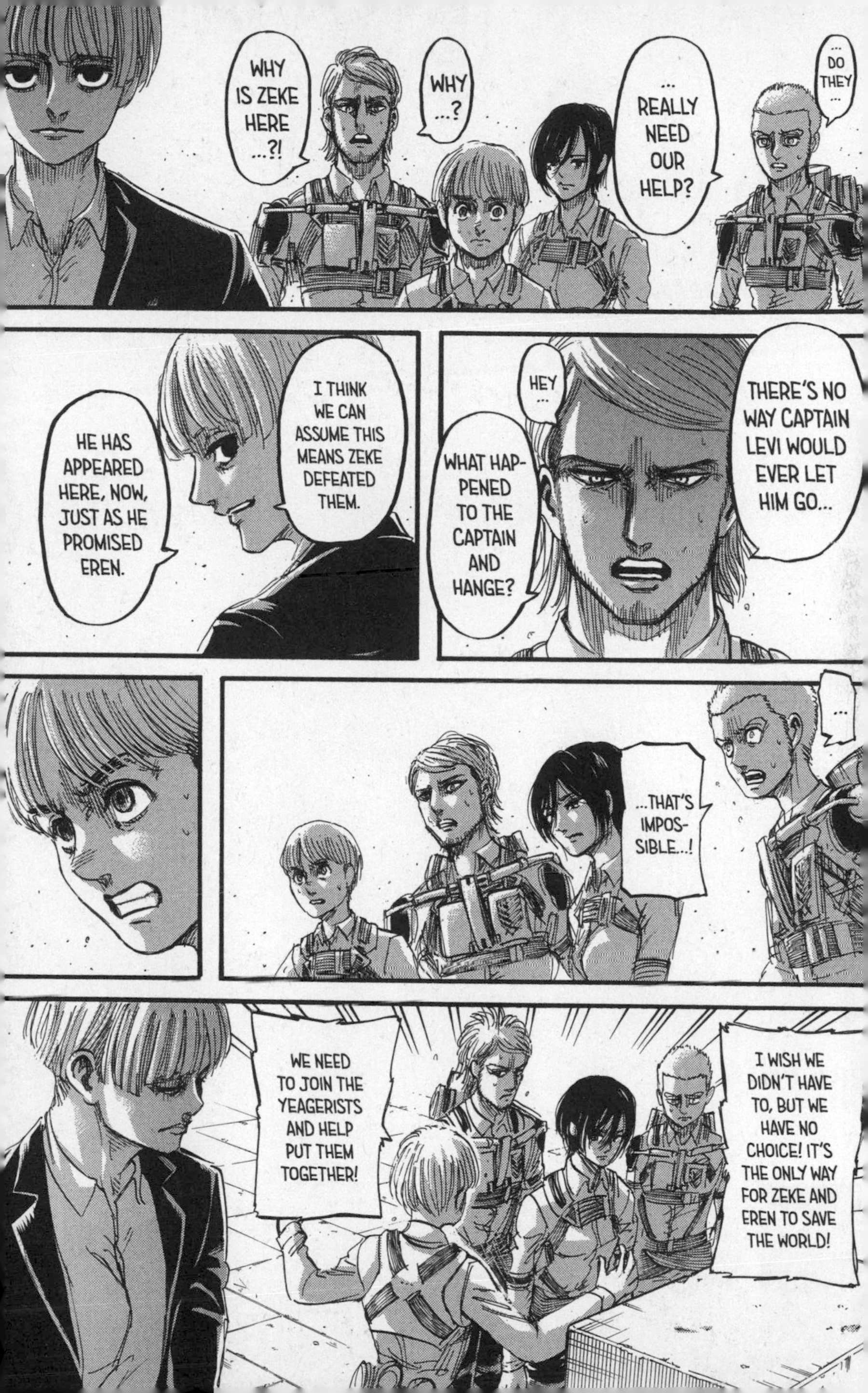
... DO THEY ...
... REALLY NEED OUR HELP?
WHY ...?
WHY IS ZEKE HERE ...?!
THERE'S NO WAY CAPTAIN LEVI WOULD EVER LET HIM GO...
HEY ...
WHAT HAPPENED TO THE CAPTAIN AND HANGE?
I THINK WE CAN ASSUME THIS MEANS ZEKE DEFEATED THEM.
HE HAS APPEARED HERE, NOW, JUST AS HE PROMISED EREN.
...
...THAT'S IMPOSSIBLE...!
I WISH WE DIDN'T HAVE TO, BUT WE HAVE NO CHOICE! IT'S THE ONLY WAY FOR ZEKE AND EREN TO SAVE THE WORLD!
WE NEED TO JOIN THE YEAGERISTS AND HELP PUT THEM TOGETHER!

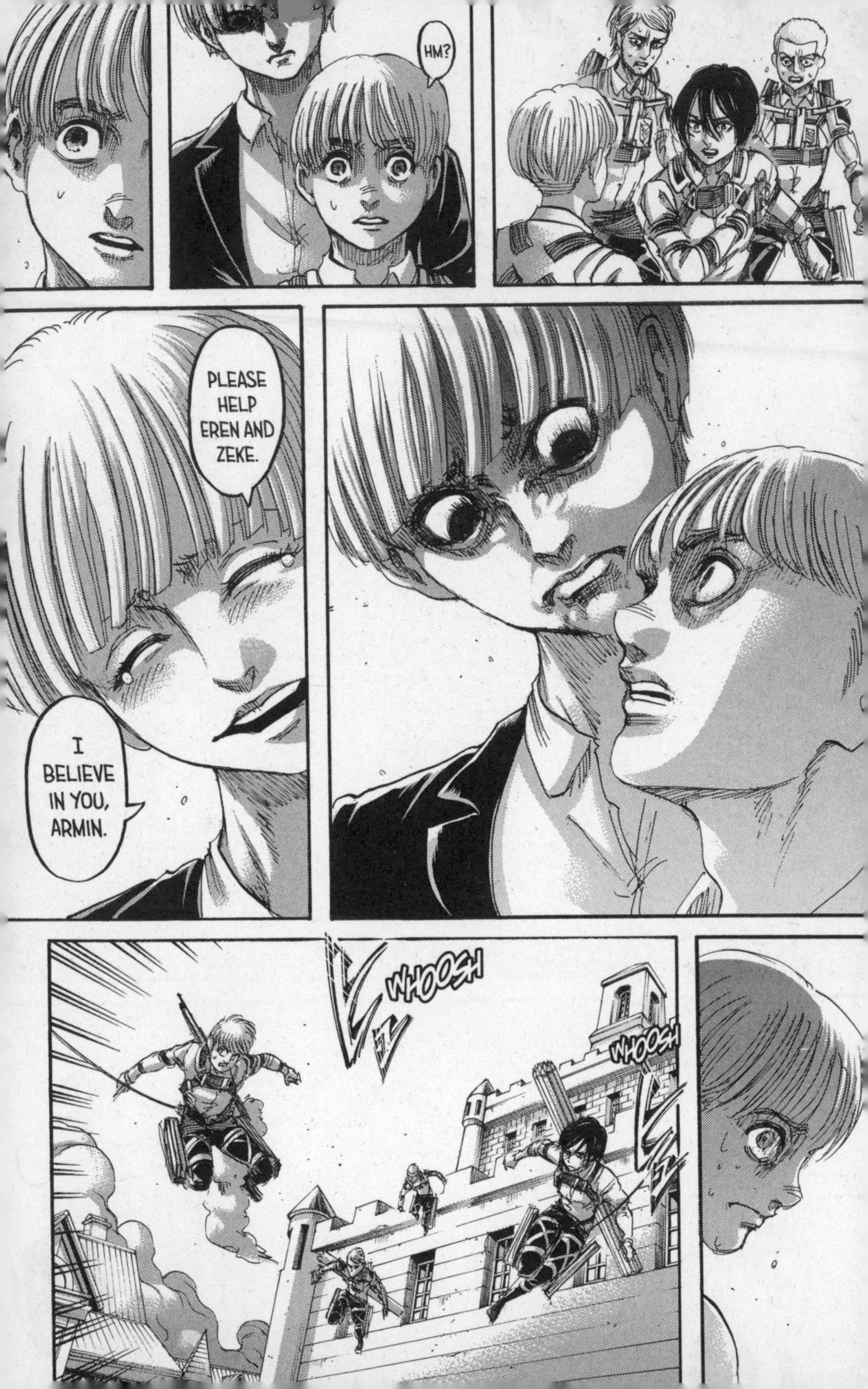
HM?
PLEASE HELP EREN AND ZEKE.
I BELIEVE IN YOU, ARMIN.
WHOOSH
WHOOSH

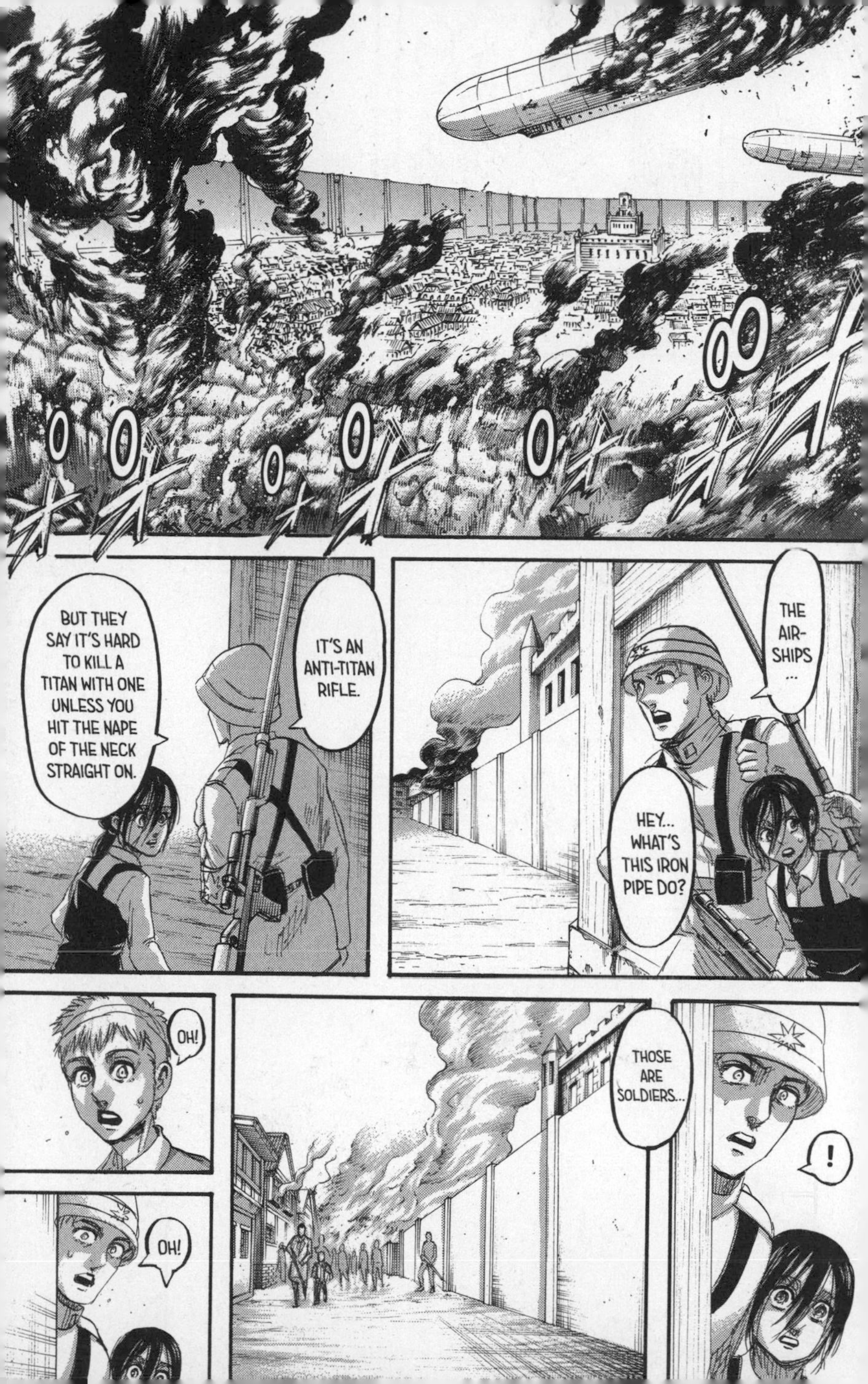
THE AIR-SHIPS ...
HEY... WHAT'S THIS IRON PIPE DO?
IT'S AN ANTI-TITAN RIFLE.
BUT THEY SAY IT'S HARD TO KILL A TITAN WITH ONE UNLESS YOU HIT THE NAPE OF THE NECK STRAIGHT ON.
!
THOSE ARE SOLDIERS...
OH!
OH!

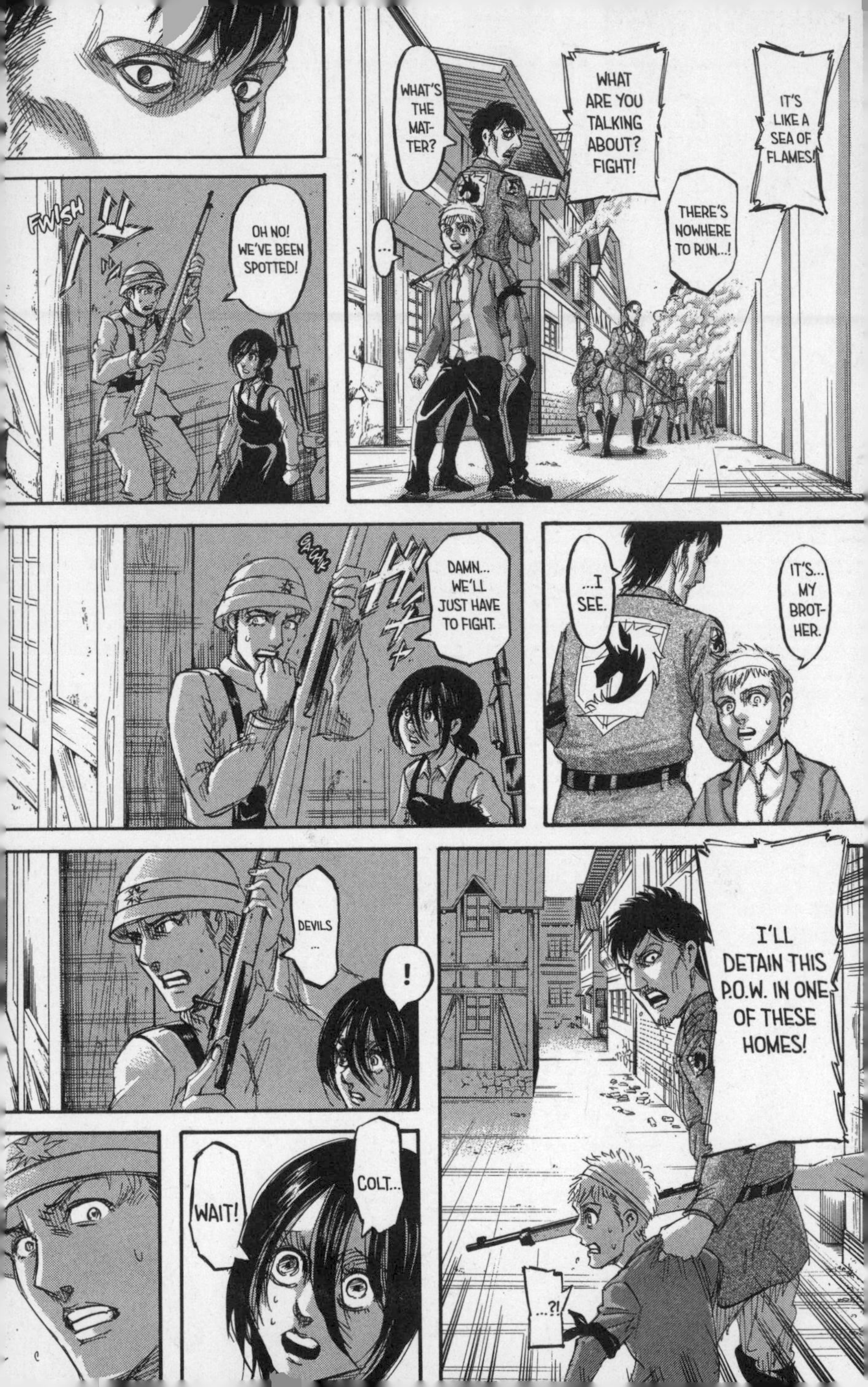
IT'S LIKE A SEA OF FLAMES!
WHAT ARE YOU TALKING ABOUT? FIGHT!
WHAT'S THE MATTER?
THERE'S NOWHERE TO RUN...!
...
FWISH
OH NO! WE'VE BEEN SPOTTED!
IT'S... MY BROTHER.
...I SEE.
DAMN... WE'LL JUST HAVE TO FIGHT.
I'LL DETAIN THIS P.O.W. IN ONE OF THESE HOMES!
...?!
DEVILS ...
!
COLT...
WAIT!

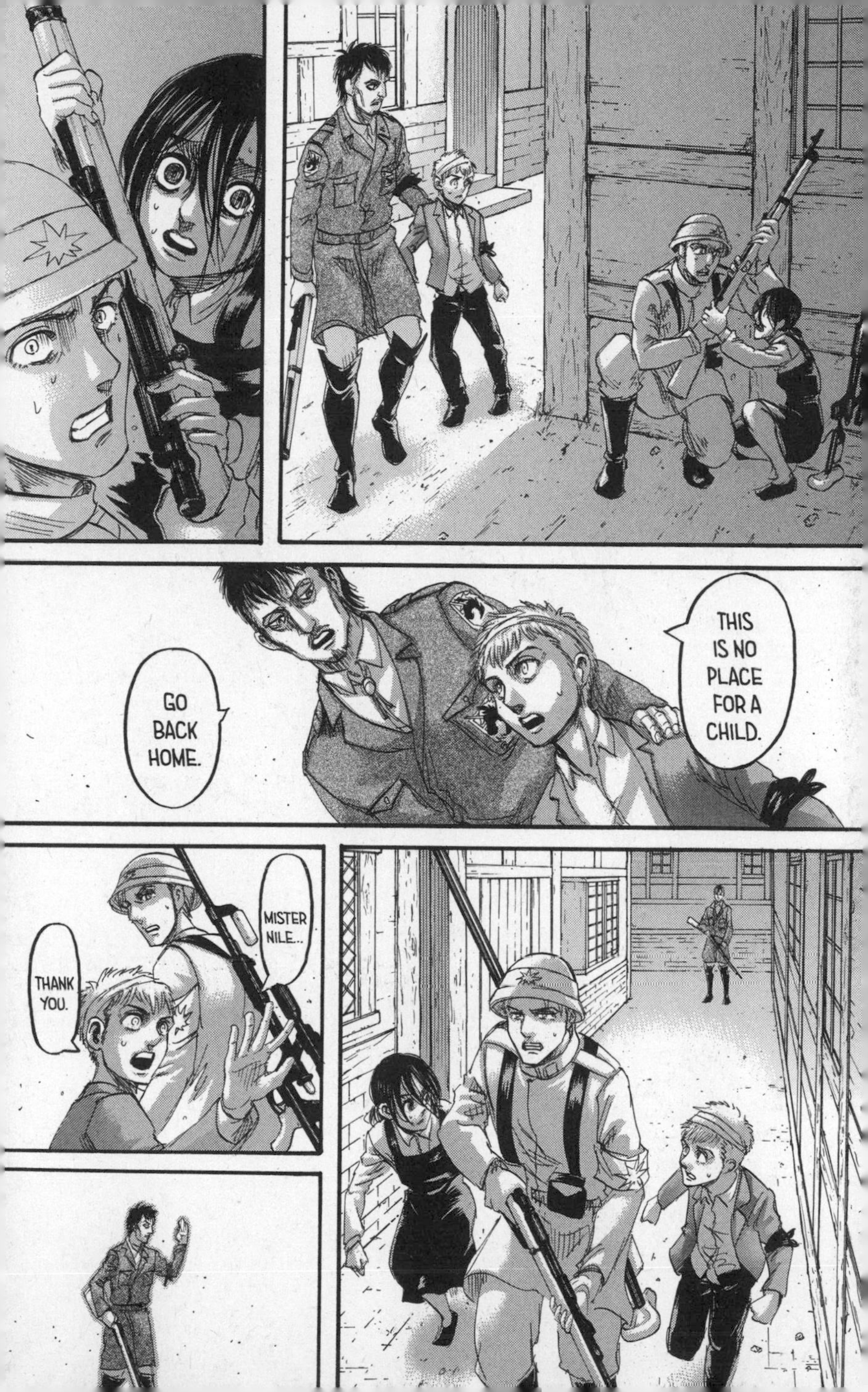
THIS IS NO PLACE FOR A CHILD.
GO BACK HOME.
MISTER NILE...
THANK YOU.

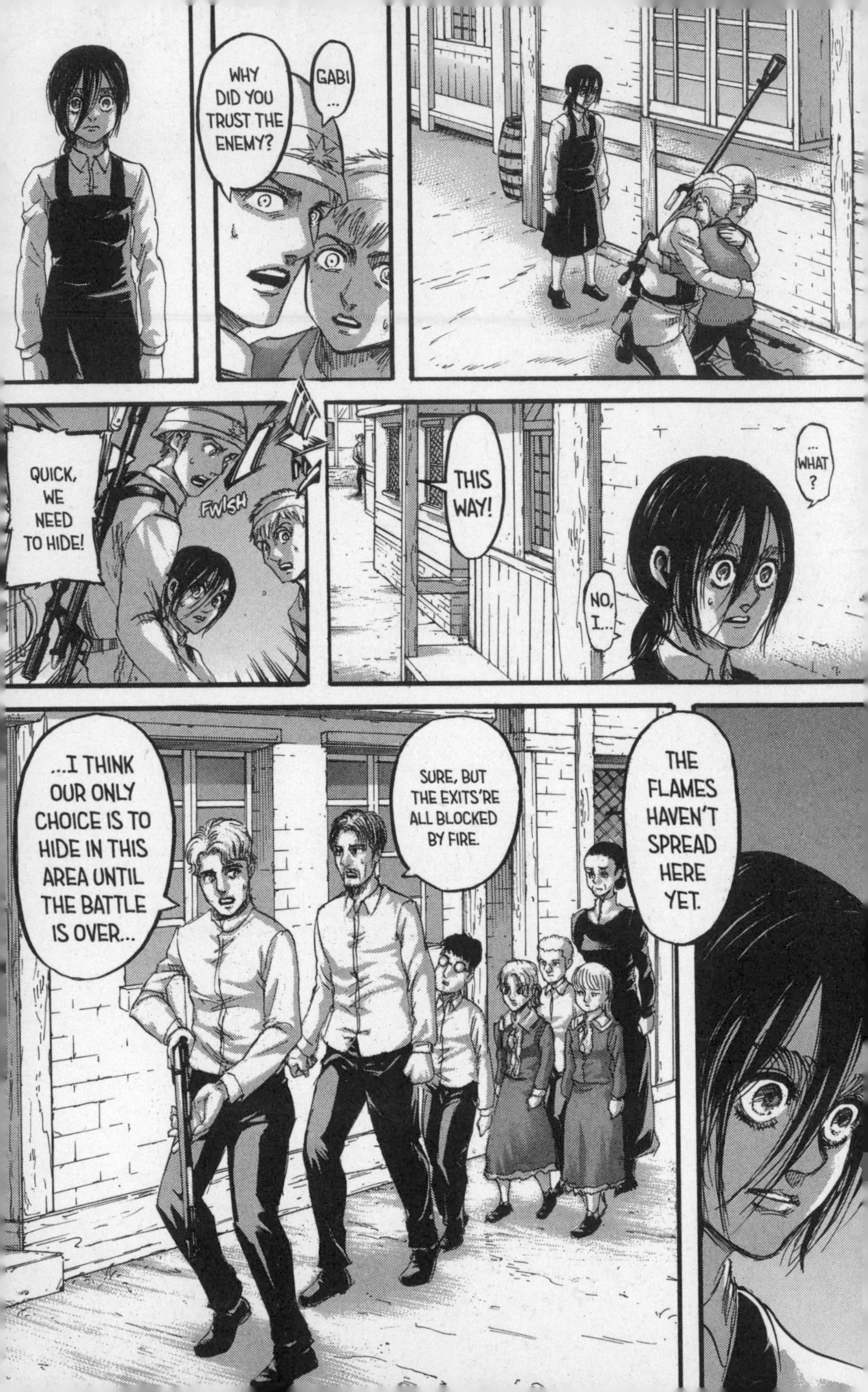
GABI ...
WHY DID YOU TRUST THE ENEMY?
... WHAT ?
THIS WAY!
NO, I...
QUICK, WE NEED TO HIDE!
FWISH
THE FLAMES HAVEN'T SPREAD HERE YET.
SURE, BUT THE EXITS'RE ALL BLOCKED BY FIRE.
...I THINK OUR ONLY CHOICE IS TO HIDE IN THIS AREA UNTIL THE BATTLE IS OVER...

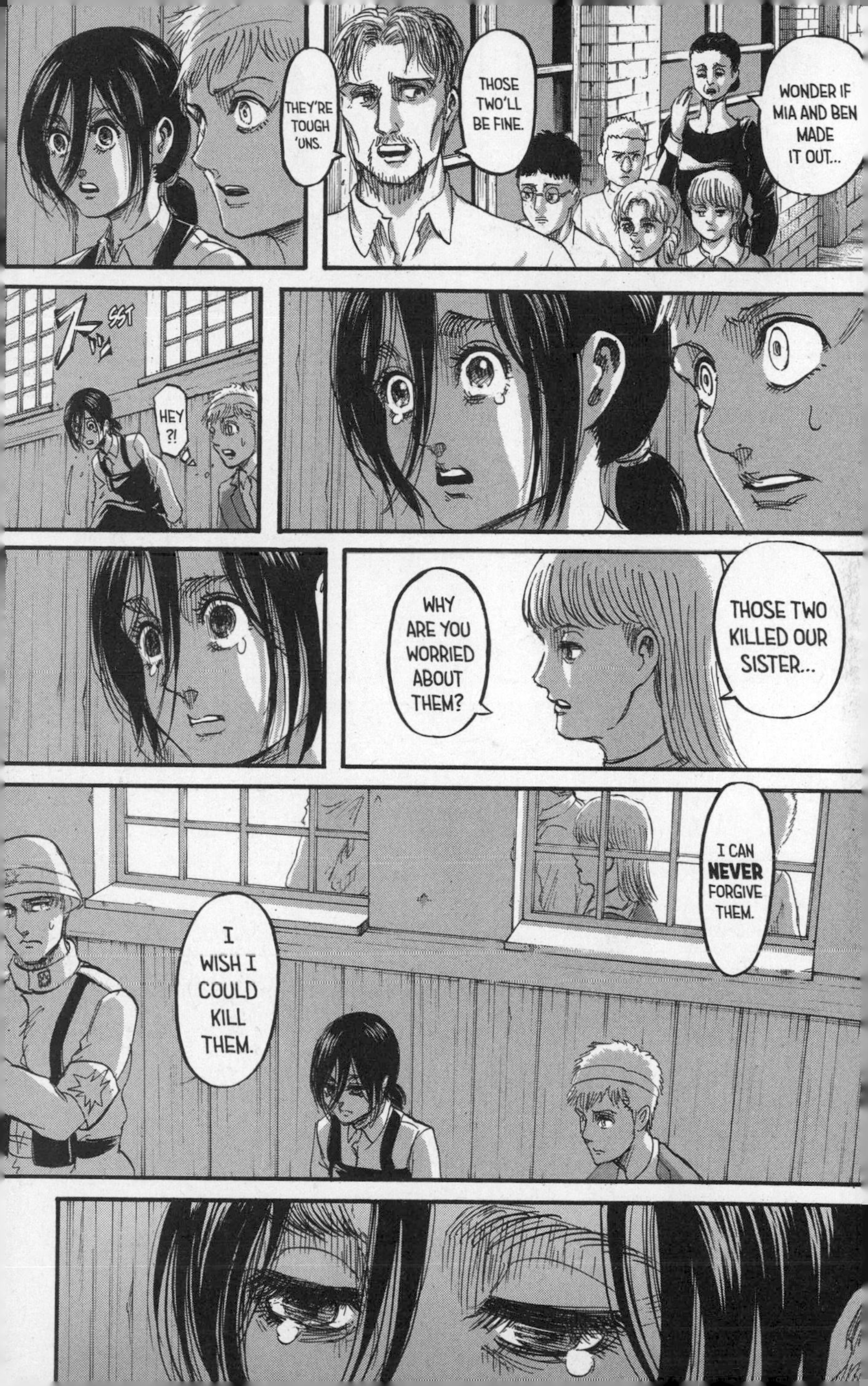
WONDER IF MIA AND BEN MADE IT OUT...
THOSE TWO'LL BE FINE.
THEY'RE TOUGH 'UNS.
SST
HEY ?!
THOSE TWO KILLED OUR SISTER...
WHY ARE YOU WORRIED ABOUT THEM?
I CAN **NEVER** FORGIVE THEM.
I WISH I COULD KILL THEM.

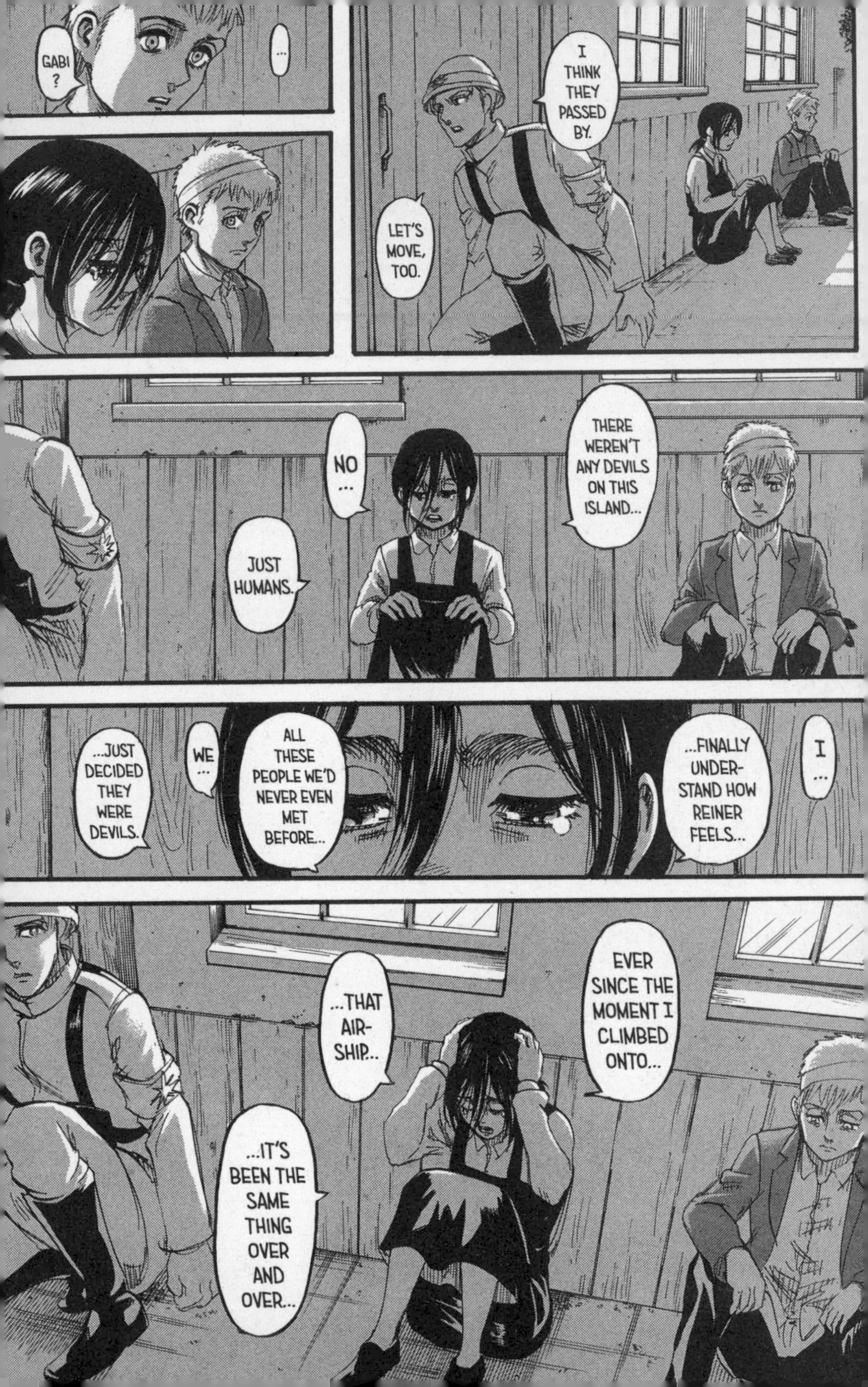
I THINK THEY PASSED BY.
LET'S MOVE, TOO.
...
GABI?
THERE WEREN'T ANY DEVILS ON THIS ISLAND...
NO ...
JUST HUMANS.
I ...
...FINALLY UNDER-STAND HOW REINER FEELS...
ALL THESE PEOPLE WE'D NEVER EVEN MET BEFORE...
WE ...
...JUST DECIDED THEY WERE DEVILS.
EVER SINCE THE MOMENT I CLIMBED ONTO...
...THAT AIR-SHIP...
...IT'S BEEN THE SAME THING OVER AND OVER...

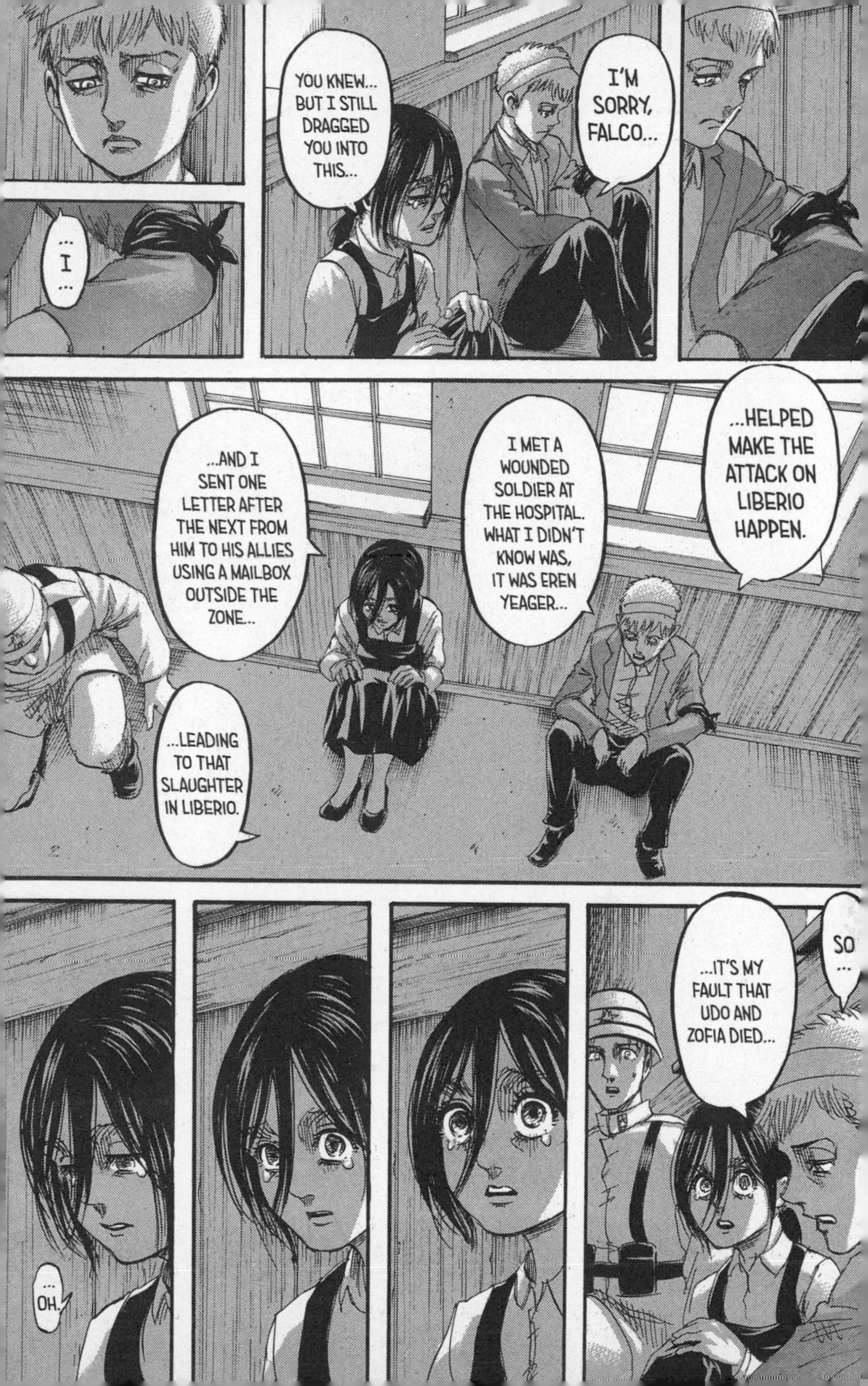
I'M SORRY, FALCO...
YOU KNEW... BUT I STILL DRAGGED YOU INTO THIS...
... I ...
...HELPED MAKE THE ATTACK ON LIBERIO HAPPEN.
I MET A WOUNDED SOLDIER AT THE HOSPITAL. WHAT I DIDN'T KNOW WAS, IT WAS EREN YEAGER...
...AND I SENT ONE LETTER AFTER THE NEXT FROM HIM TO HIS ALLIES USING A MAILBOX OUTSIDE THE ZONE...
...LEADING TO THAT SLAUGHTER IN LIBERIO.
SO ...
...IT'S MY FAULT THAT UDO AND ZOFIA DIED...
... OH.

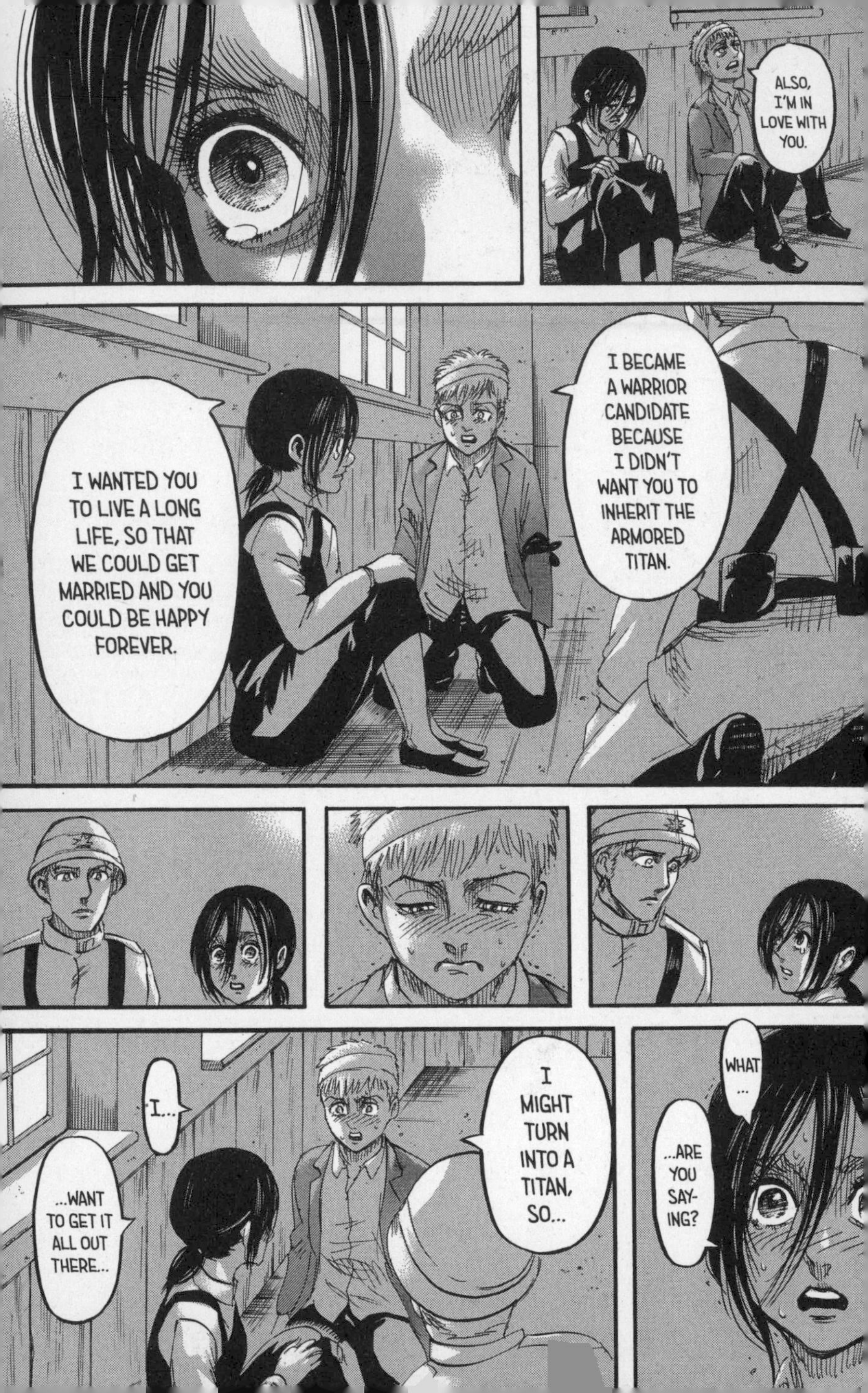
ALSO, I'M IN LOVE WITH YOU.
I BECAME A WARRIOR CANDIDATE BECAUSE I DIDN'T WANT YOU TO INHERIT THE ARMORED TITAN.
I WANTED YOU TO LIVE A LONG LIFE, SO THAT WE COULD GET MARRIED AND YOU COULD BE HAPPY FOREVER.
WHAT ...
...ARE YOU SAY-ING?
I MIGHT TURN INTO A TITAN, SO...
I...
...WANT TO GET IT ALL OUT THERE...

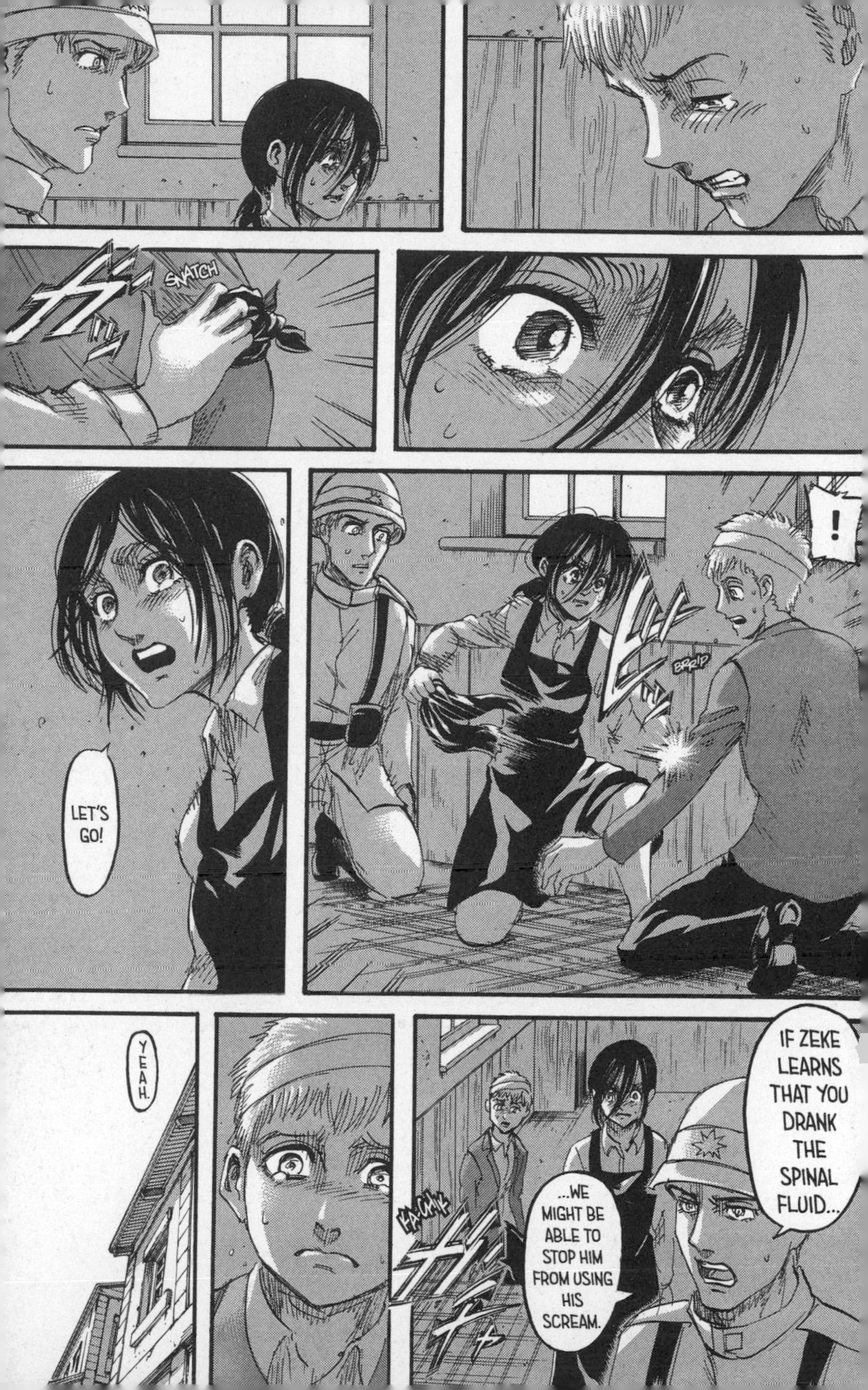
SNATCH
!
BRRIP
LET'S GO!
IF ZEKE LEARNS THAT YOU DRANK THE SPINAL FLUID...
...WE MIGHT BE ABLE TO STOP HIM FROM USING HIS SCREAM.
KA-CHAK
YEAH.

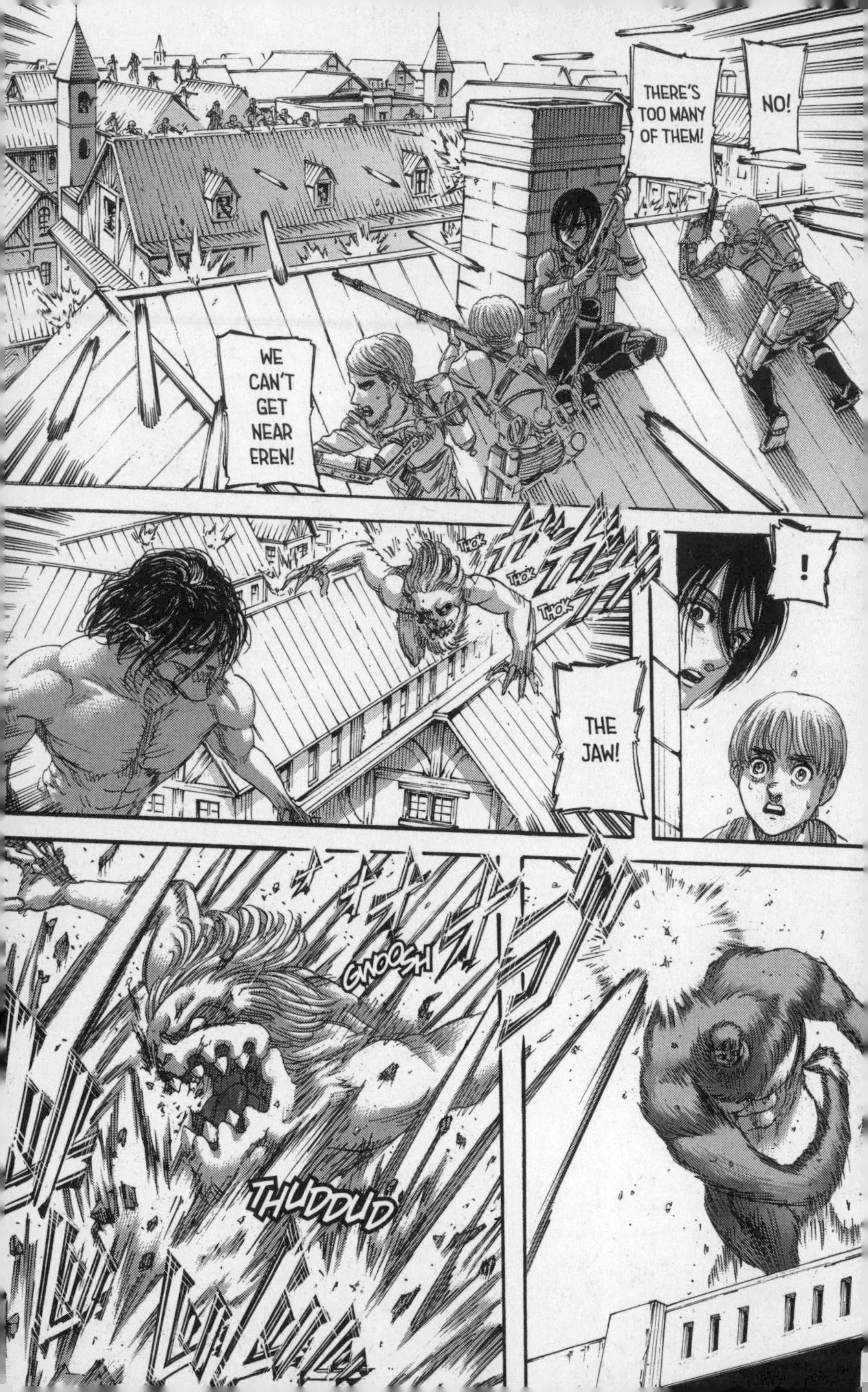
NO!
THERE'S TOO MANY OF THEM!
WE CAN'T GET NEAR EREN!
!
THE JAW!
THOK
THOK
THOK
GWOOSH
THUDDUD

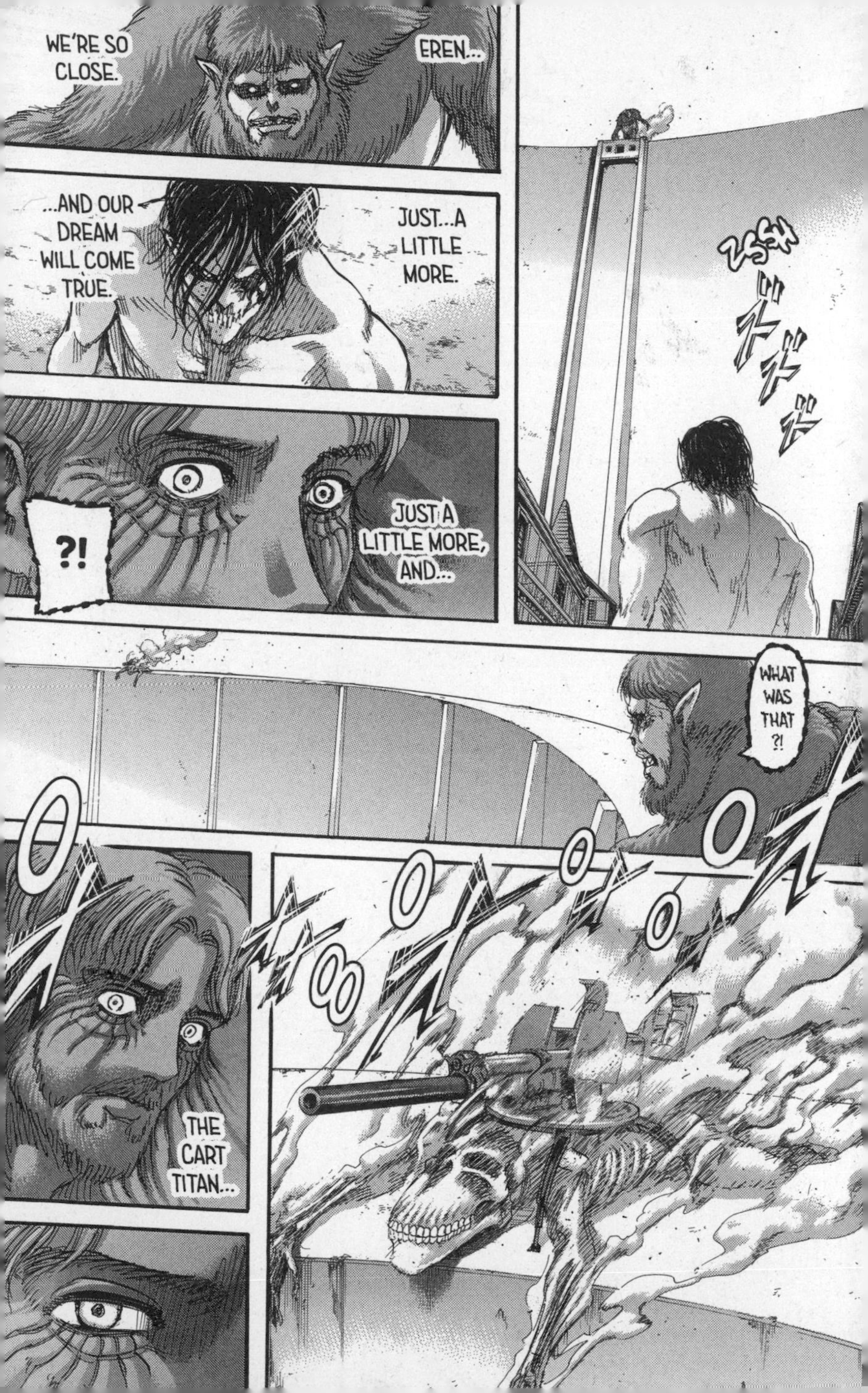
EREN...
WE'RE SO CLOSE.
JUST...A LITTLE MORE.
...AND OUR DREAM WILL COME TRUE.
JUST A LITTLE MORE, AND...
?!
WHAT WAS THAT ?!
THE CART TITAN...

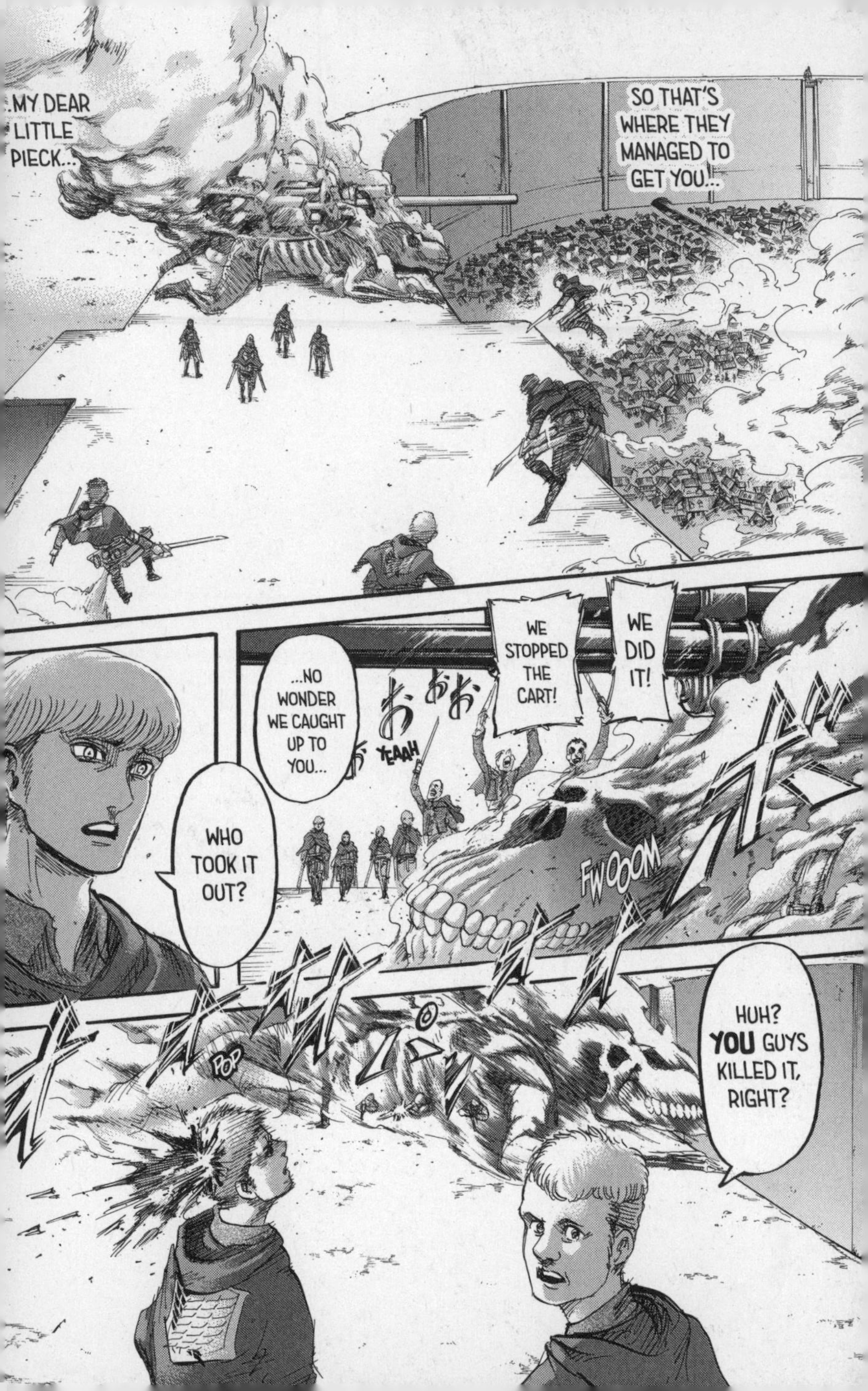
SO THAT'S WHERE THEY MANAGED TO GET YOU...
.MY DEAR LITTLE PIECK...
WE DID IT!
WE STOPPED THE CART!
おおお
...NO WONDER WE CAUGHT UP TO YOU...
YEAAH
FWOOOM
WHO TOOK IT OUT?
HUH? **YOU** GUYS KILLED IT, RIGHT?
POP

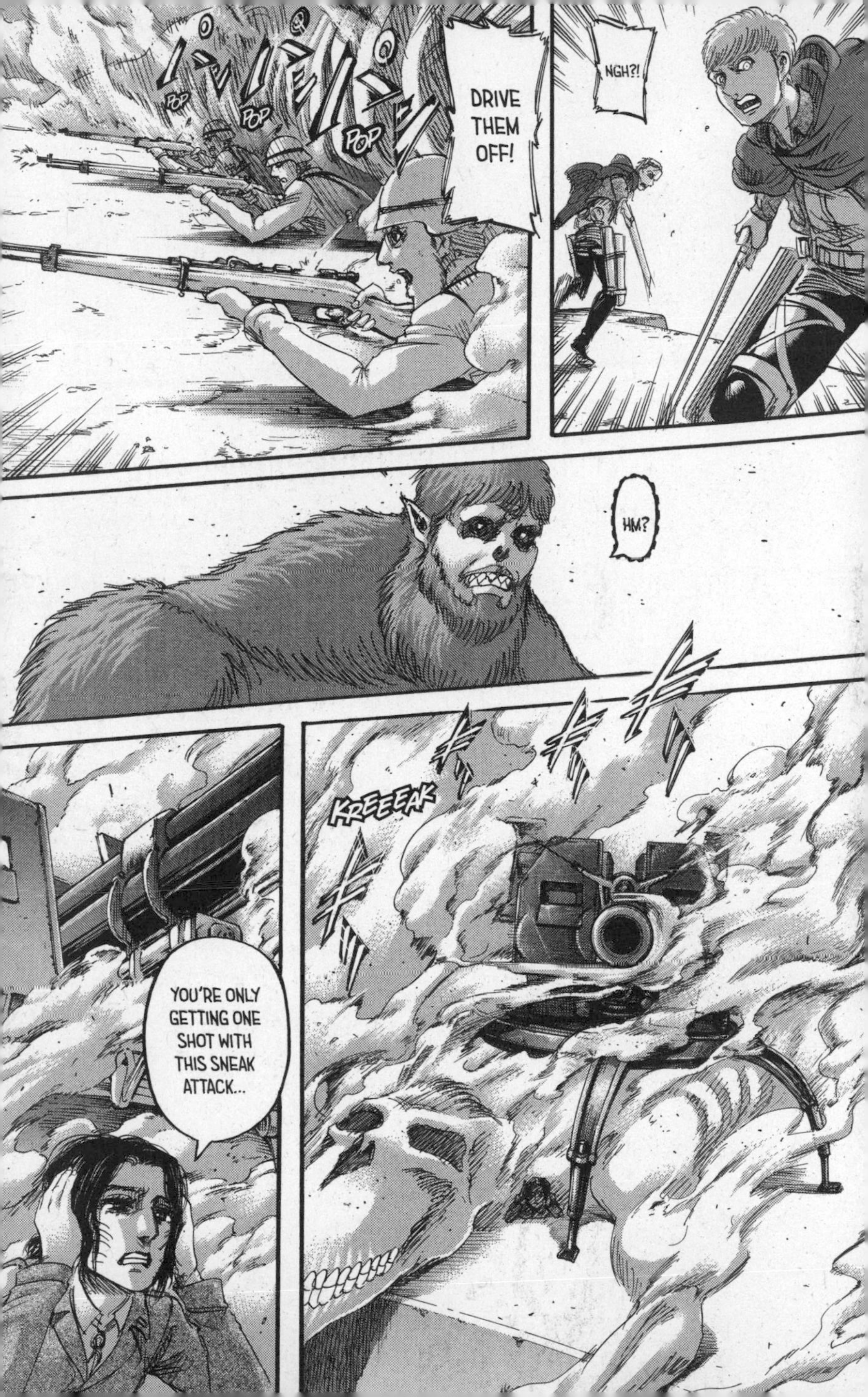
NGH?!
POP
POP
POP
DRIVE THEM OFF!
HM?
KREEEAK
YOU'RE ONLY GETTING ONE SHOT WITH THIS SNEAK ATTACK...

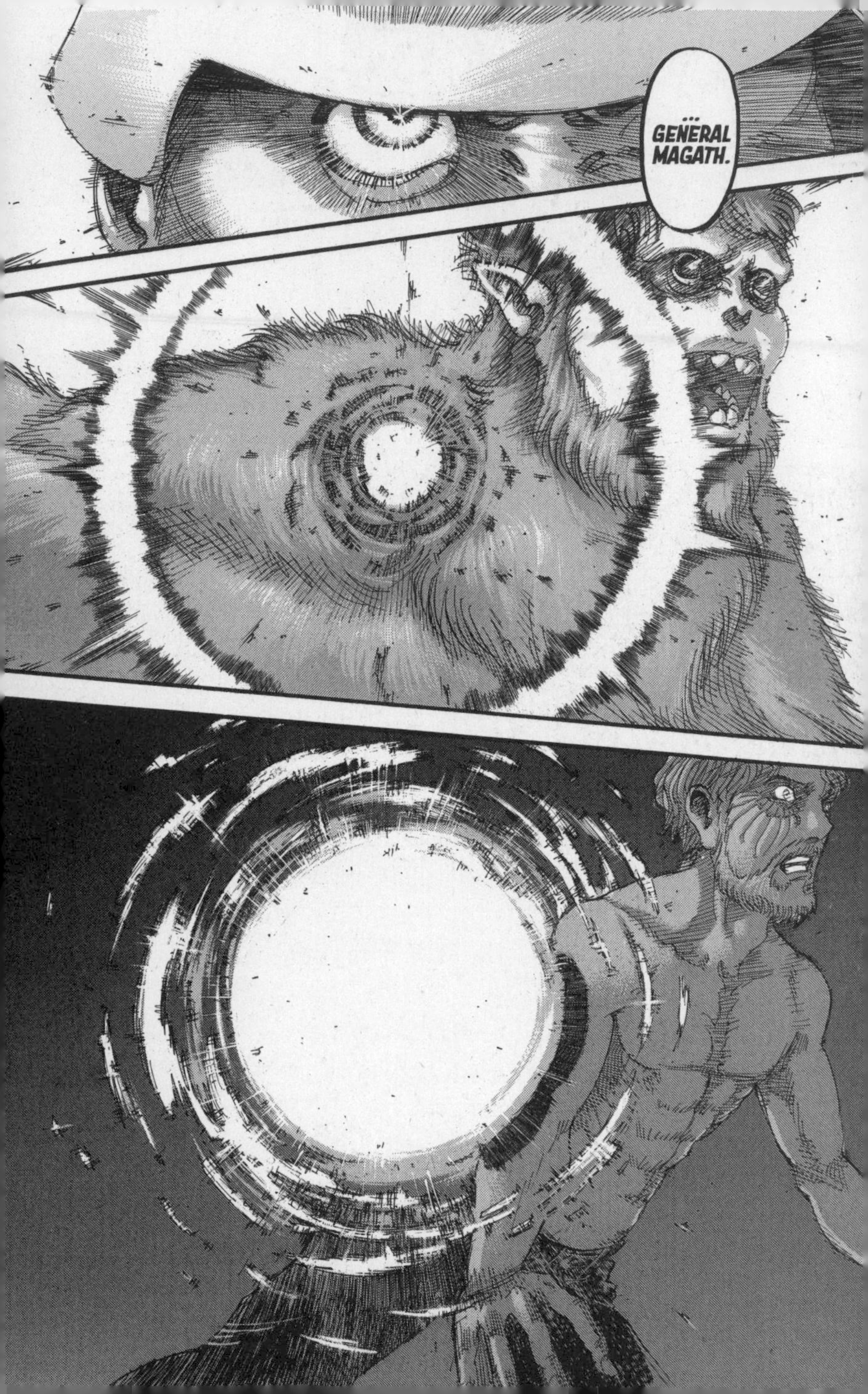
...GENERAL MAGATH.

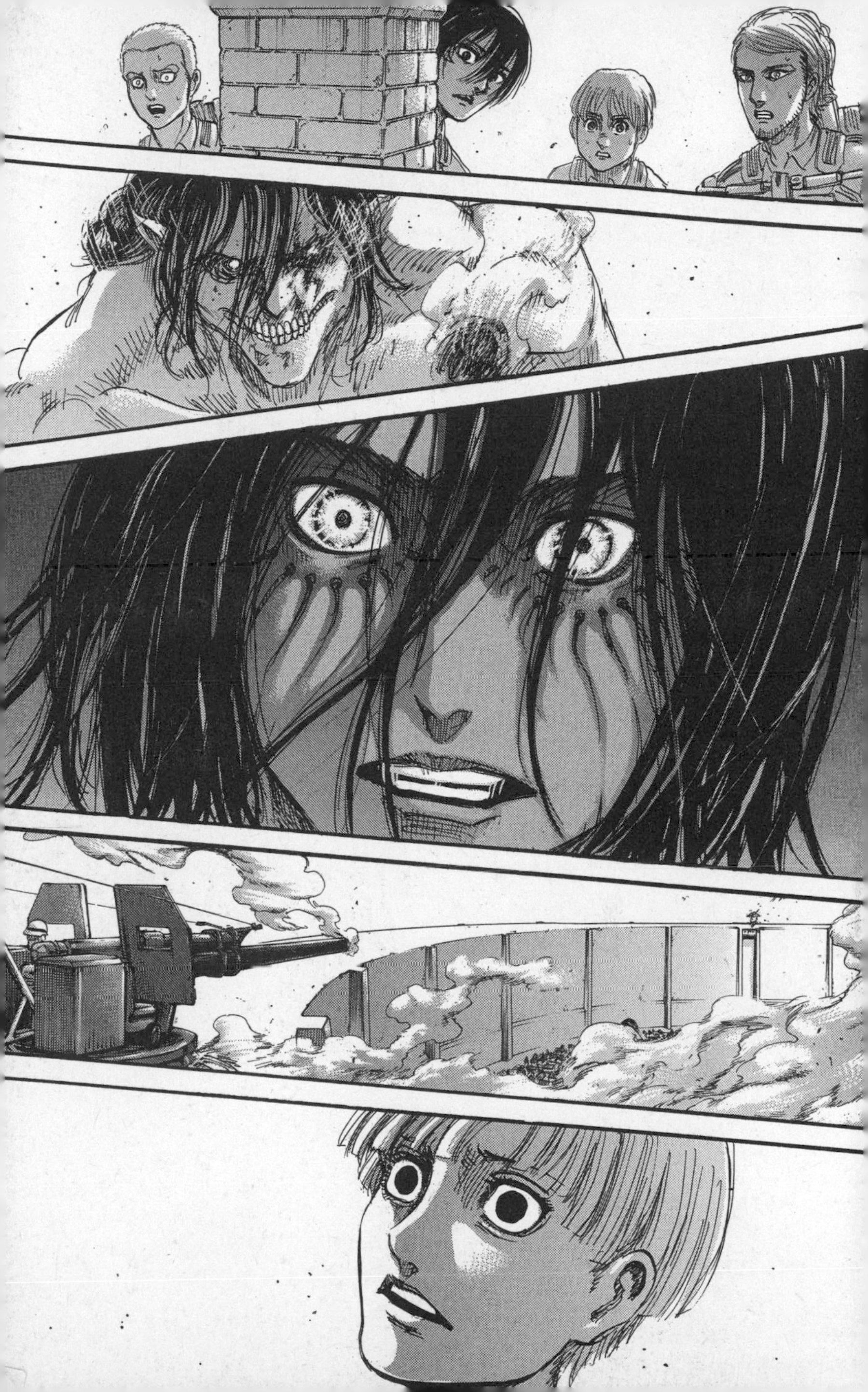

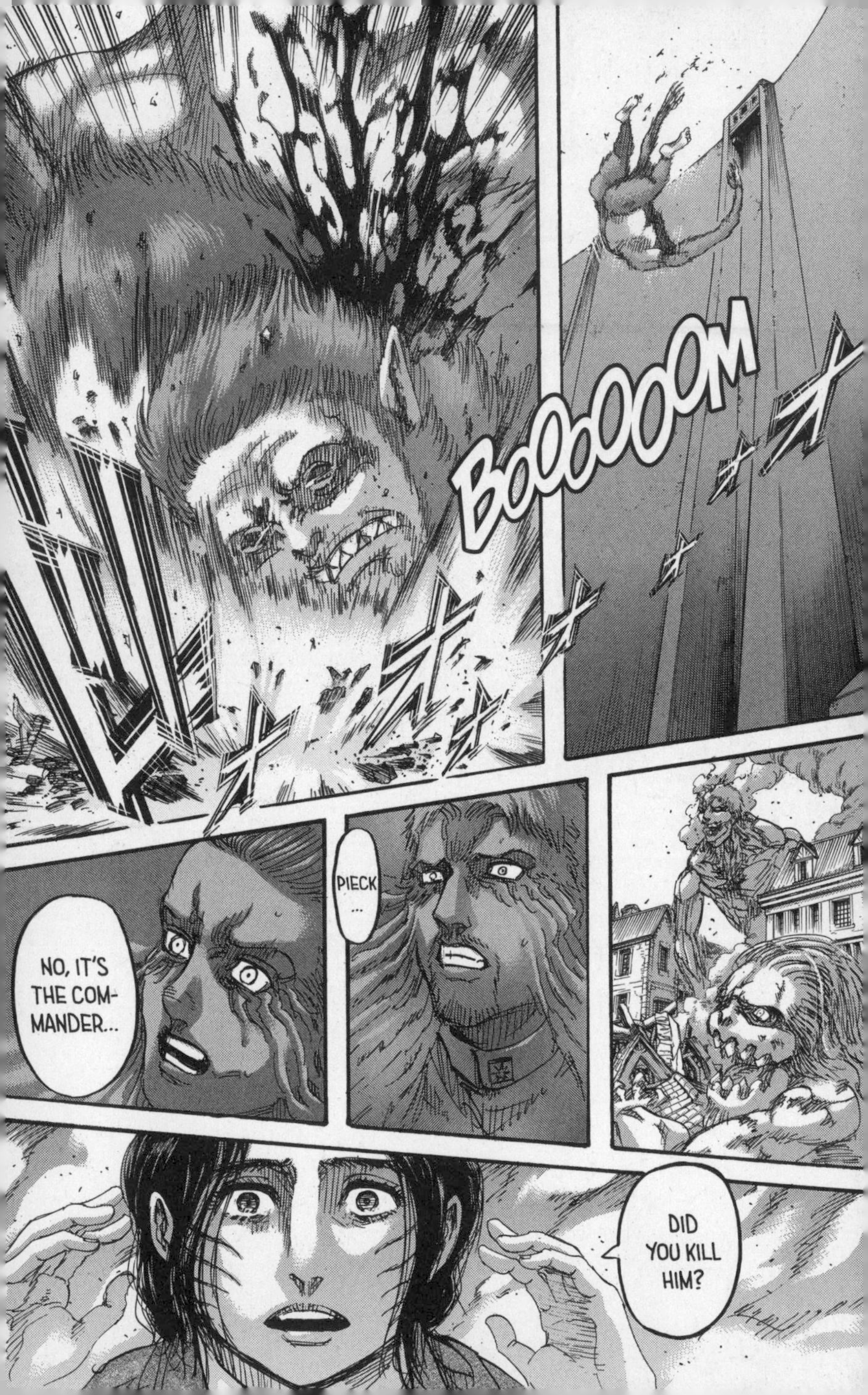
BOOOOOOM
PIECK...
NO, IT'S THE COMMANDER...
DID YOU KILL HIM?

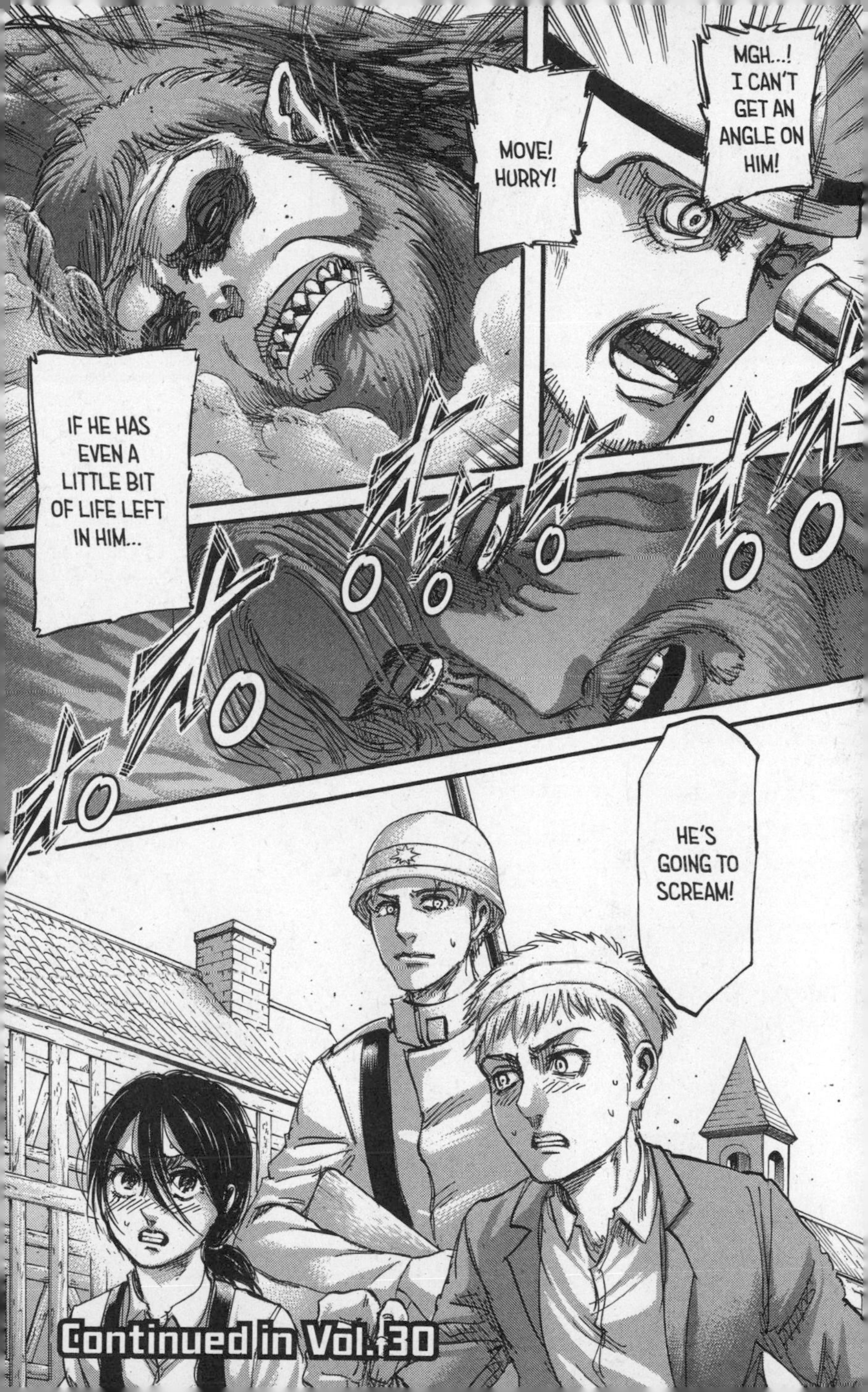
MGH...! I CAN'T GET AN ANGLE ON HIM!
MOVE! HURRY!
IF HE HAS EVEN A LITTLE BIT OF LIFE LEFT IN HIM...
HE'S GOING TO SCREAM!

Continued in Vol. 30

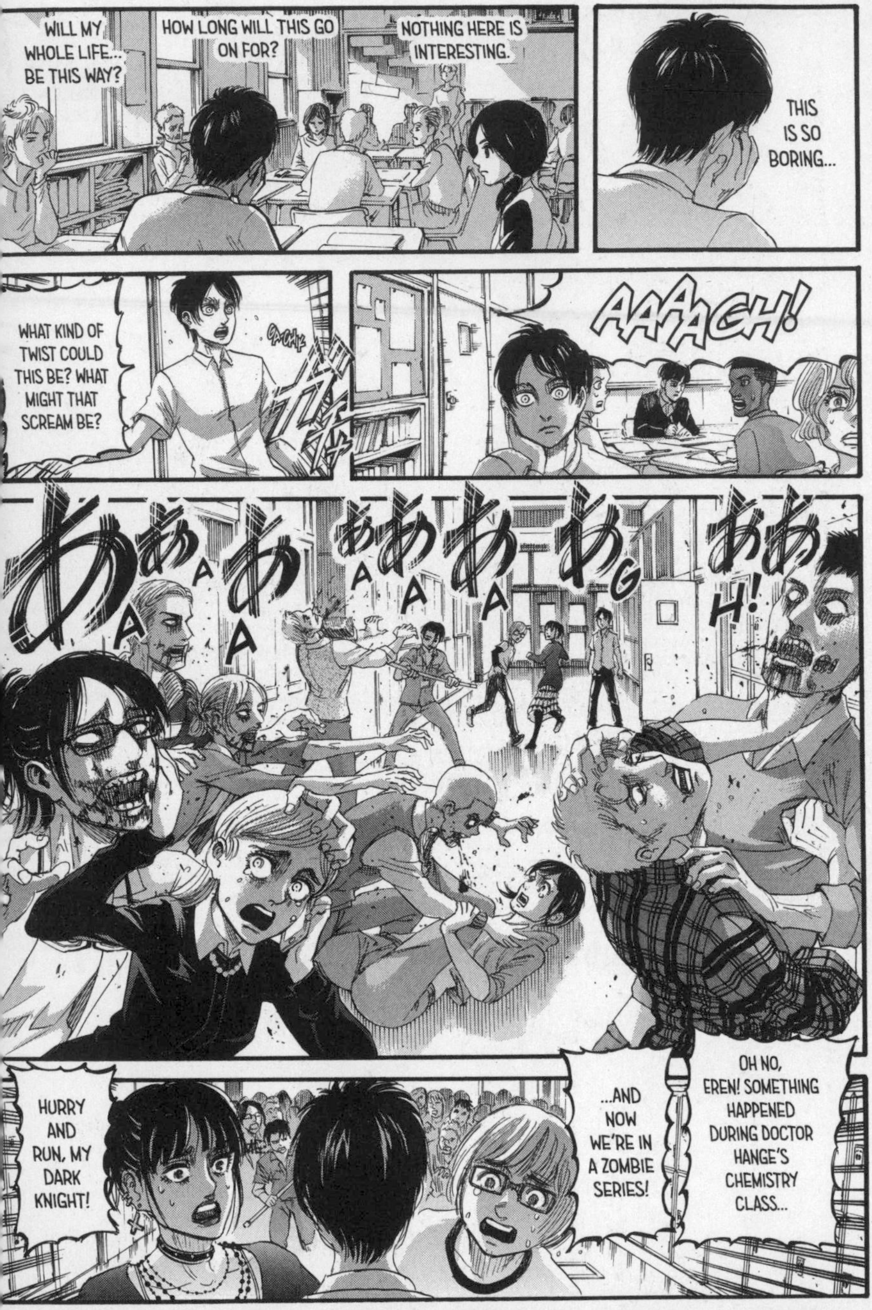
THIS IS SO BORING...
NOTHING HERE IS INTERESTING.
HOW LONG WILL THIS GO ON FOR?
WILL MY WHOLE LIFE... BE THIS WAY?
AAAACH!
GA-CHIK
WHAT KIND OF TWIST COULD THIS BE? WHAT MIGHT THAT SCREAM BE?
あああああああああ
AAAAAAGH!
OH NO, EREN! SOMETHING HAPPENED DURING DOCTOR HANGE'S CHEMISTRY CLASS...
...AND NOW WE'RE IN A ZOMBIE SERIES!
HURRY AND RUN, MY DARK KNIGHT!

COMING APRIL 2020!

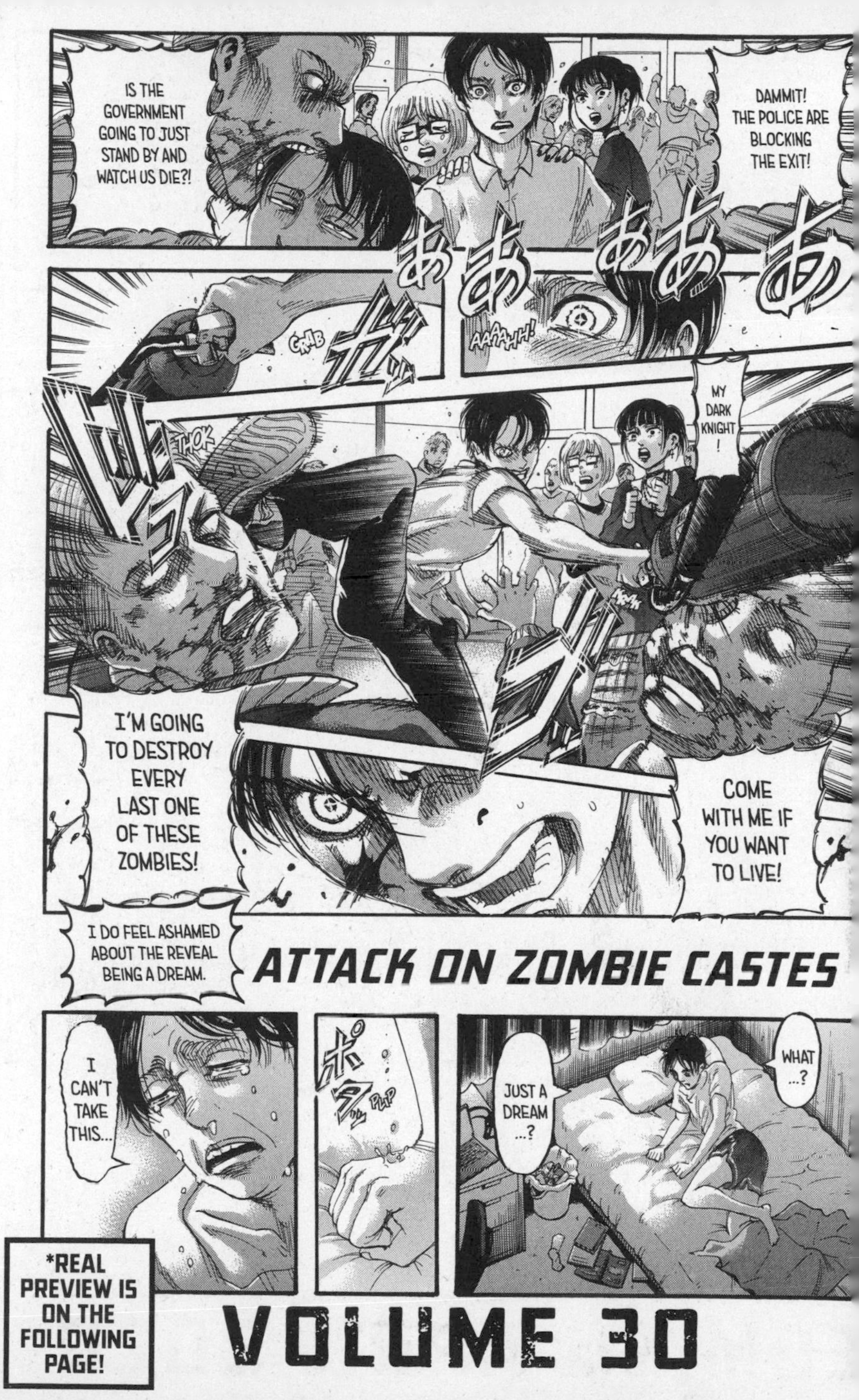
DAMMIT! THE POLICE ARE BLOCKING THE EXIT!
IS THE GOVERNMENT GOING TO JUST STAND BY AND WATCH US DIE?!
あああああ
AAAAHH!
GRAB
MY DARK KNIGHT !
KRAK
THOK
COME WITH ME IF YOU WANT TO LIVE!
I'M GOING TO DESTROY EVERY LAST ONE OF THESE ZOMBIES!
ATTACK ON ZOMBIE CASTES
I DO FEEL ASHAMED ABOUT THE REVEAL BEING A DREAM.
WHAT ...?
JUST A DREAM ...?
PLIP
I CAN'T TAKE THIS...
VOLUME 30
*REAL PREVIEW IS ON THE FOLLOWING PAGE!

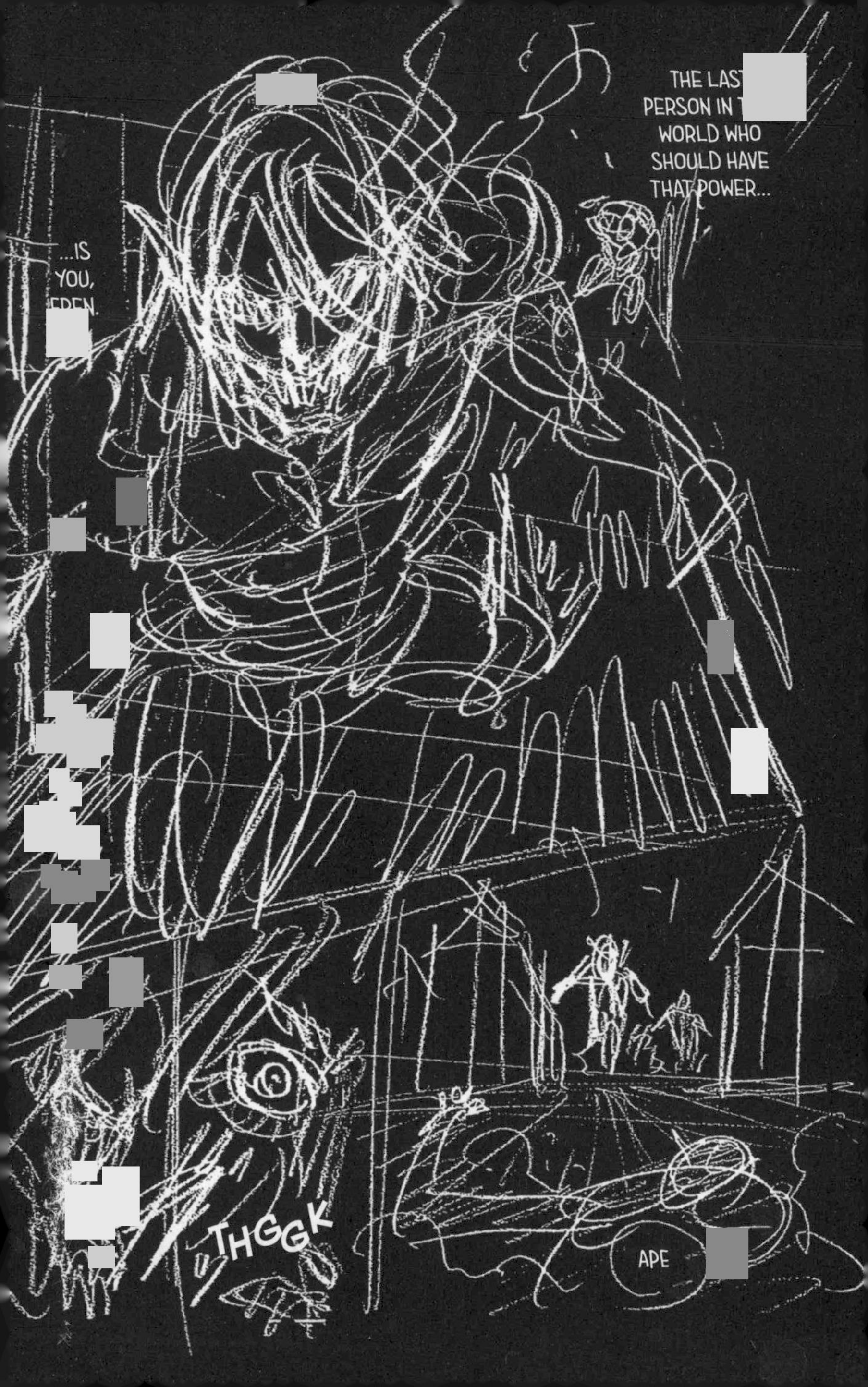
THE LAST PERSON IN T WORLD WHO SHOULD HAVE THAT POWER...
...IS YOU, EREN.
APE
THGGK

ONE MAN CAN
PROTECT THE
WORLD ALONE
FOR ONLY SO
LONG.

WHO WILL
REMAIN, AND
WHO WILL
PERISH...?

THE TIME
DRAWS NEAR.

A Kodansha Comics Trade Paperback Original
Attack on Titan 29 copyright © 2019 Hajime Isayama
English translation copyright © 2019 Hajime Isayama

Published in the United States by Kodansha Comics, an imprint of Kodansha USA Publishing, LLC, New York.

Publication rights for this English edition arranged through Kodansha Ltd., Tokyo.

First published in Japan in 2019 by Kodansha Ltd., Tokyo, as *Shingeki no kyojin*, volume 29.

ISBN 978-1-63236-828-7

Original cover design by Takashi Shimoyama (Red Rooster)

Printed in the United States of America.

www.kodanshacomics.com

9 8 7 6 5 4 3 2 1
Translation: Ko Ransom
Lettering: Dezi Sienty
Editing: Ben Applegate and Haruko Hashimoto
Kodansha Comics edition cover design by Phil Balsman

Publisher: Kiichiro Sugawara
Managing editor: Maya Rosewood
Vice president of marketing & publicity: Naho Yamada

Director of publishing services: Ben Applegate
Associate director of operations: Stephen Pakula
Publishing services managing editor: Noelle Webster
Assistant production manager: Emi Lotto